Lecture Notes in Computer Science 10240

Commenced Publication in 1973
Founding and Former Series Editors:
Gerhard Goos, Juris Hartmanis, and Jan van Leeuwen

More information about this series at http://www.springer.com/series/7407

Matthew J. Patitz · Mike Stannett (Eds.)

Unconventional Computation and Natural Computation

16th International Conference, UCNC 2017
Fayetteville, AR, USA, June 5–9, 2017
Proceedings

 Springer

Editors
Matthew J. Patitz
University of Arkansas
Fayetteville, AR
USA

Mike Stannett
University of Sheffield
Sheffield
UK

ISSN 0302-9743 ISSN 1611-3349 (electronic)
Lecture Notes in Computer Science
ISBN 978-3-319-58186-6 ISBN 978-3-319-58187-3 (eBook)
DOI 10.1007/978-3-319-58187-3

Library of Congress Control Number: 2017938636

LNCS Sublibrary: SL1 – Theoretical Computer Science and General Issues

Printed on acid-free paper

This Springer imprint is published by Springer Nature
The registered company is Springer International Publishing AG
The registered company address is: Gewerbestrasse 11, 6330 Cham, Switzerland

Preface

The 16th International Conference on Unconventional Computation and Natural Computation (UCNC 2017) was held June 5–9, 2017, on the campus of the University of Arkansas in Fayetteville, Arkansas, USA. The UCNC series of international conferences is genuinely interdisciplinary and it covers theory as well as experiments and applications. It is concerned with various proposals for computation that go beyond the Turing model, human-designed computation inspired by nature, and with the computational nature of processes taking place in nature. Typical, but not exclusive, topics are: hypercomputation; chaos and dynamical systems-based computing; granular, fuzzy, and rough computing; mechanical computing; cellular, evolutionary, molecular, neural, and quantum computing; membrane computing; amorphous computing, swarm intelligence; artificial immune systems; physics of computation; chemical computation; evolving hardware; the computational nature of self-assembly, developmental processes, bacterial communication, and brain processes.

More information about this conference series and its full history can be found on the following website: https://www.cs.auckland.ac.nz/research/groups/CDMTCS/conferences/uc/uc.html.

Submissions to UCNC 2017 comprised 21 full papers across a wide variety of topics, including (but not limited to) quantum computing, algorithmic self-assembly, and chemical reaction networks. Of these, 14 were accepted for presentation at the conference and publication in these proceedings. Beyond the contributed papers and associated talks, UCNC 2017 was greatly enhanced by the plenary talks and tutorials provided by several prestigious speakers. José Félix Costa from the University of Lisbon, Portugal, gave a plenary talk titled "The Power of Analogue-Digital Machines." Erik Demaine from the Massachusetts Institute of Technology, USA, presented his plenary talk "Computing with Glue, Balls, and Recycled Bits: New Physical Models of Computing." Masayuki Endo from Kyoto University, Japan, gave a plenary talk titled "High-speed AFM Imaging of Synthetic Nanomachines and Nanostructures." A tutorial titled "Ways to Compute in Euclidean Frameworks" was provided by Jérôme Durand-Lose from the Université d'Orléans, France, and Makoto Naruse from the National Institute of Information and Communications Technology, Japan, presented a tutorial titled "Decision Making by Photonics: Experiment and Category Theoretic Foundation."

Included during the conference were two workshops. The Workshop on Membrane Computing was organized by Matteo Cavaliere from the University of Edinburgh, UK, and Alfonso Rodriguez Paton from the Universidad Politecnica de Madrid, Spain. Invited speakers for that workshop were Alvaro Sanchez from Yale University, USA, and Sergey Verlan from the University Paris Est Créteil, France. The First International Workshop on Oritatami (Oritatami 2017) was organized by Shinnosuke Seki from the University of Electro-Communications, Japan, and the invited speakers for that workshop were Cody Geary from Caltech, USA, and Aarhus University, Denmark, and

Nicolas Schabanel from CNRS, University of Paris Diderot (IRIF), and ENS Lyon (IXXI), France.

UCNC 2017 brought together researchers from all over the world to share and discuss ideas on forms of computation inspired by natural systems and unconventional methods. Its success as the 16th conference in the series is owed to a great amount of help from many people and organizations. First and foremost, we would like to thank the Steering Committee co-chairs, Nataša Jonoska and Jarkko Kari, whose expert guidance and invaluable advice helped to shape all aspects of the conference. Next, a huge debt of gratitude is owed to the Program Committee members and external reviewers who carefully reviewed all submissions and provided important feedback to help decide which papers to accept. Beyond the technical details of assembling invited speakers and selecting contributed papers, the amount of work done to organize the venue, meals, excursion, and countless other details would have been completely overwhelming without the enthusiastic and tireless help of Cindy Pickney, as well as the other members of the Organizing Committee, Jamie Stafford, George Holmes, and Jason Crawley. There would have been no conference without their help. Important financial support was provided by the Department of Computer Science and Computer Engineering at the University of Arkansas, the College of Engineering at the University of Arkansas, and the National Science Foundation (which provided funding to support student travel to the conference). Finally, many thanks are owed to the LNCS team at Springer who helped with the publication of these proceedings.

June 2017

Matthew Patitz
Mike Stannett

Organization

UCNC 2017 was organized by the Department of Computer Science and Computer Engineering at the University of Arkansas.

Steering Committee

Thomas Back	Leiden University, The Netherlands
Cristian S. Calude	University of Auckland, New Zealand (Founding Chair)
Lov K. Grover	Bell Labs, USA
Nataša Jonoska	University of South Florida, USA (Co-chair)
Jarkko Kari	University of Turku, Finland (Co-chair)
Lila Kari	University of Waterloo, Canada
Seth Lloyd	Massachusetts Institute of Technology, USA
Giancarlo Mauri	Università degli Studi di Milano-Bicocca, Italy
Gheorghe Paun	Institute of Mathematics of the Romanian Academy, Romania
Grzegorz Rozenberg	Leiden University, The Netherlands (Emeritus Chair)
Arto Salomaa	University of Turku, Finland
Tommaso Toffoli	Boston University, USA
Carme Torras	Institute of Robotics and Industrial Informatics, Spain
Jan van Leeuwen	Utrecht University, The Netherlands

Program Committee

Andy Adamatzky	University of the West of England, UK
Martyn Amos	Manchester Metropolitan University, UK
Peter Banda	University of Luxembourg
Cristian Calude	University of Auckland, New Zealand
Matteo Cavaliere	University of Edinburgh, UK
Mark Daley	University of Western Ontario, Canada
Jérôme Durand-Lose	Université d'Orléans, France
Angel Goni-Moreno	Centre for Synthetic Biology and Bioexploitation, Newcastle University, UK
Jacob Hendricks	University of Wisconsin-River Falls, USA
Jarkko Kari	University of Turku, Finland
Lila Kari	University of Waterloo, Canada
Viv Kendon	Durham University, UK
Niall Murphy	University of Cambridge, UK
Makato Naruse	National Institute of Information and Communications Technology, Japan
Turlough Neary	University of Zurich/ETH Zurich, Switzerland

Pekka Orponen	Aalto University, Finland
Matt Patitz	University of Arkansas, USA (Co-chair)
Alfonso Rodriguez Patón	Universidad Politécnica de Madrid, Spain
Rebecca Schulman	Johns Hopkins University, USA
Mike Stannett	University of Sheffield, UK (Co-chair)
Susan Stepney	University of York, UK
Scott Summers	University of Wisconsin Oshkosh, USA
Sergey Verlan	University Paris Est Créteil, France
Damien Woods	Inria Paris, France

Organizing Committee

Matthew J. Patitz	University of Arkansas (Chair)
Cindy Pickney	University of Arkansas
Jamie Stafford	University of Arkansas
George Holmes	University of Arkansas
Jason Crawley	University of Arkansas

External Reviewers

Matthew Cook	Ethan Jackson
Mika Hirvensalo	Trent Rogers
James Hughes	Ilkka Törmä

Sponsoring Institutions

Department of Computer Science and Computer Engineering, University of Arkansas
College of Engineering, University of Arkansas
National Science Foundation

Invited Talks

The Power of Analogue-Digital Machines
(Extended Abstract)

José Félix Costa[1,2]

[1] Department of Mathematics, Instituto Superior Técnico,
Universidade de Lisboa, Lisboa, Portugal
fgc@math.tecnico.ulisboa.pt

[2] Centro de Filosofia das Ciências da Universidade de Lisboa, Lisboa, Portugal

Abstract. The ARNN (**A**nalogue **R**ecurrent **N**eural **N**et) abstract computer, extensively analysed in H.T. Siegelmann: Neural Networks and Analog Computation: Beyond the Turing Limit, Birkhäuser (1999), introduces an analogue-digital model of computation in discrete time. When the parameters of the system (so-called weights) are real-valued the computations cannot be specified by finite means: we have computation without a program. Several other models of analogue-digital computation were introduced around the same time to explore the power of reals added to digital computation. Under the polynomial time constraint, the ARNN efficiently performs not only all Turing machine efficient computations but also computes non-recursive functions such as (a unary encoding of) the halting problem (of Turing machines).

Computing with Glue, Balls, and Recycled Bits: New Physical Models of Computing

Erik D. Demaine

Computer Science and Artificial Intelligence Laboratory
Massachusetts Institute of Technology
32 Vassar St., Cambridge, MA 02139, USA
edemaine@mit.edu

Abstract. Real computers live in a physical world, which offers many different ways to compute other than standard CMOS chips. I'll talk about a few different models I've played with, which incorporate geometry and/or thermodynamics into the computational model.

1. **Glues:** We can build computers out of simple geometric nanoparticles (e.g. DNA) with somewhat selective glues that define how they stick together, or come apart. Our latest result is a way to build a universal replicator, like a photocopier for unknown nanostructures.

2. **Balls:** We can build computers out of obstacles and rolling balls that just respond to global signals like "roll all balls maximally to the right". The puzzle Tilt embodies this physics, which also have real-world applications in biomedicine.

3. **Recycled Bits:** We can build computers that recycle bits whenever possible instead of throwing them away a billion times a second. This requires developing a whole new suite of algorithms, but it can lead to several orders of magnitude improved energy efficiency, which ultimately may lead to a similar improvement in speed.

4. **In the Limit:** What happens when computation and memory are taken to their physical (geometric) limits? I think we should go back to studying algorithms for 1970s-era mesh computers.

Ways to Compute in Euclidean Frameworks

Jérôme Durand-Lose

Laboratoire d'Informatique Fondamentale d'Orléans,
Université d'Orléans, Orléans, France
jerome.durand-lose@univ-orleans.fr

Abstract. This tutorial presents what kind of computation can be carried out inside a Euclidean space with dedicated primitives—and discrete or hybrid (continuous evolution between discrete transitions) time scales. The presented models can perform Classical (Turing, discrete) computations as well as, for some, hyper and analog computations (thanks to the continuity of space). The first half of the tutorial presents three models of computation based on respectively: ruler and compass, local constraints and emergence of polyhedra and piece-wise constant derivative. The other half concentrates on signal machines: line segments are extended and replaced on meeting. These machines are capable hypercomputation and analog computation and to solve PSPACE-problem in "constant space and time" though partial fractal generation.

High-Speed AFM Imaging of Synthetic Nanomachines and Nanostructures

Masayuki Endo

Institute for Integrated Cell-Material Sciences and Department of Chemistry,
Graduate School of Science, Kyoto University,
Yoshida-ushinomiyacho, Sakyo-ku, Kyoto 606-8501, Japan
endo@kuchem.kyoto-u.ac.jp

Direct observation of molecular motions is one of the most fundamental issues for elucidating the physical properties of individual molecules and their reaction mechanisms. Atomic force microscopy (AFM) enables direct molecular imaging, especially for biomolecules in the physiological environment. We have developed AFM-based single-molecule observation systems for biomolecule imaging by employing DNA origami nanostructures and high-speed AFM. [1, 2] Using this system, we have characterized the DNA structural changes and enzyme reactions in the DNA nanostructures. We also employed photochemical reactions to construct the mobile nanosystems and devices controlled by hybridization and dehybridization of DNA strands by photo-irradiation. Using the photoresponsive systems, we directly observed the dynamic assembly and disassembly of hexagonal origami structures on a lipid bilayer during high-speed AFM scanning. [3] We further employed a lipid-bilayer to observe the dynamic 2D array formation from cross-shaped, triangular, and hexagonal origami monomers. [4] For control of a linear molecular movement, a pyrene-attached DNA motor and the track were assembled on the DNA origami tile. [5] We observed the photo-induced movement of the motor on the DNA origami surface as similar to an enzyme-induced DNA motor. In addition, we constructed a photo-controllable rotator system on the DNA origami tile, and the rotary movement of the photoresponsive DNA nanostructure was observed by switching UV/Vis irradiation. These chemically controlled DNA nanosystems are expected to be applied for construction of mobile nanostructures and nanodevices. Also the high-speed AFM observation supports the detailed analysis of the movements of the target molecules and the morphology changes of the nanostructures at nanoscale resolution.

References

1. Endo, M., Sugiyama, H.: Acc. Chem. **47**, 1645–1653 (2014)
2. Rajendran, A., Endo, M., Sugiyama, H.: Chem. **114**, 1493–1520 (2014)
3. Suzuki, Y., Endo, M., Yang, Y., Sugiyama, H.: J. Am. Chem. Soc. **136**, 1714–1717 (2014)
4. Suzuki, Y., Endo, M., Sugiyama, H.: Nature Commun. **6**, 8052 (2015)
5. Yang, Y., Goetzfried, M., Hidaka, K., You, M., Tan, W., Sugiyama, H., Endo, M.: Nano Lett. **15**, 6672–6676 (2015)

Decision Making by Photonics: Experiment and Category Theoretic Foundation

Makoto Naruse[1], Martin Berthel[2], Aurélien Drezet[3], Serge Huant[4],
Hirokazu Hori[5], and Song-Ju Kim[6]

[1] National Institute of Information
and Communications Technology, Tokyo, Japan
naruse@nict.go.jp
[2] University Grenoble Alpes, CNRS, Institute NEEL, Grenoble, France
martin.berthel@u-bordeaux.fr
[3] University Grenoble Alpes, CNRS, Institute NEEL, Grenoble, France
serge.huant@neel.cnrs.fr
[4] University Grenoble Alpes, CNRS, Institute NEEL, Grenoble, France
serge.huant@neel.cnrs.fr
[5] University of Yamanashi, Kofu, Japan
hirohori@yamanashi.ac.jp
[6] National Institute for Materials Science, Tsukuba, Japan
KIM.Songju@nims.go.jp

Decision making is a vital function in the age of artificial intelligence. Here we experimentally demonstrate that single photons can be used to make decisions in uncertain, dynamically changing environments and describe its category theoretic foundation. The specific decision making problem under study is the multi-armed bandit problem where a user tries to maximize the total reward from multiple slot machines. To find the machine with the highest reward probability, the user needs to explore. However, excessive exploration may result in frequent losses whereas insufficient exploration may lead to the user missing the best machine; there is a difficult trade-off called exploration-exploitation dilemma. We aim to physically resolve this problem by using the dual probabilistic and particle attributes of single photons. The propagation direction of a linearly polarized single photon that impinges on a polarization beam splitter changes probabilistically depending on the polarization. Meanwhile, an individual single photon was detected by either of the destination photodetectors. These quantum attributes of light were utilized in our optical system, which includes a nanodiamond as the single photon source and a polarization controller. Adequate and adaptive decision making for two-armed bandit problem was successfully solved [1]. Further, by introducing a hierarchical architecture, four-armed bandit has been solved leading to the scalability of photon decision making [2]. Further, we developed a category theory foundation for the single-photon-based decision making, including a quantitative analysis that agrees well with the experimental results [3]. Category theory is a branch of mathematics that formalizes mathematical structure into collections of objects and morphisms. One of the significant features of category theory is that objects and morphisms are determined by the role they play in a category via their relations to other objects and morphisms, i.e., by their position in a structure and not by what they are or what they are made. Such a nature of category theory is highly beneficial to reveal complex interdependencies of the entities in decision making in a most simplified manner, including the dynamically changing environment. In particular, the octahedral and braid structures of the triangulated categories provide a clear understanding and quantitative metrics of the underlying mechanisms for single-photon decision makers. This is the first demonstration of a category theory interpretation of decision making and it provides a solid understanding and a fundamental design for intelligence.

Acknowledgements. This work was supported in part by the Core-to-Core Program, A. Advanced Research Networks from the Japan Society for the Promotion of Science.

References

1. Naruse, M., Berthel, M., Drezet, A., Huant, S., Aono, M., Hori, H., Kim, S.-J.: Single-photon decision maker. Sci. Rep. **5**, 13253 (2015)
2. Naruse, M., Berthel, M., Drezet, A., Huant, S., Hori, H., Kim, S.-J.: Single photon in hierarchical architecture for physical decision making: photon intelligence. ACS Photonics, **3**, 2505–2514 (2016)
3. Naruse, M., Kim, S.-J., Aono, M., Berthel, M., Drezet, A., Huant, S., Hori, H.: Category theoretic foundation of single-photon-based decision making. arXiv:1602.08199

Contents

Invited Talks

The Power of Analogue-Digital Machines
(Extended Abstract)

José Félix Costa[1,2]([⊠])

[1] Department of Mathematics, Instituto Superior Técnico,
Universidade de Lisboa, Lisboa, Portugal
fgc@math.tecnico.ulisboa.pt
[2] Centro de Filosofia das Ciências da Universidade de Lisboa, Lisboa, Portugal

The ARNN abstract computer,[1] extensively analysed in [28], introduces an analogue-digital model of computation in discrete time. When the parameters of the system (so-called weights) are real-valued,[2] the computations cannot be specified by finite means: we have computation without a program. Several other models of analogue-digital computation were introduced around the same time to explore the power of reals added to digital computation (see [17,27,29]). Under the polynomial time constraint, the ARNN efficiently performs not only all Turing machine efficient computations,[3] but also computes non-recursive functions such as (a unary encoding of) the halting problem (of Turing machines). The reals[4] are introduced into the computation by means of measurements made either by a few neurons that read a weight byte by byte, or by means of a real-valued probability of transition. In the first case, the ARNN decides P/poly in polynomial time and, in the second case, the ARNN decides $BPP//\log\star$ in polynomial time. However, in these systems, measurements sound physically unrealistic since the function involved in computing the so-called activation of the neurons (the physical processors) is the well-behaved piecewise linear function, exhibiting sharp vertices. In an attempt to recover the classical analytic sigmoid activation function, in [25], the power of the deterministic ARNN in polynomial time drops to $P/\log\star$ as shown in [7,19].

Criticism was addressed towards the possibility of engineering such machines. In [20], Martin Davis pointed clearly that the only way a machine can go beyond the Turing limit is being provided with non-computable information and in [21] he says that, even if a machine could compute beyond the Turing limit, we would not be able to certify that fact (a phenomenon that can be well understood in [24], since only the computable character of a function can be verified — but not decided — in the limit). In [30], Younger et al. discuss the realization of $BPP//\log\star$ super-Turing machines with their electronic engineering project. In our paper, the general model is only intended to establish limits to abstract and ideal computing devices that, like the ARNN, have access to real numbers

---

[1] Analogue Recurrent Neural Net.
[2] Real weights are quite common in the neural net literature.
[3] A few rational weights being enough for the purpose.
[4] In fact, the truncated reals. The amount of precision depends on the size of the input.

© Springer International Publishing AG 2017
M.J. Patitz and M. Stannett (Eds.): UCNC 2017, LNCS 10240, pp. 3–7, 2017.
DOI: 10.1007/978-3-319-58187-3_1

by means of an ideal measurement in Classical Physics. It should be noted that measurements of physical quantities are also the subject of well-developed theory that started with Hempel and Carnap (see [18,22,23]). Their theory explains how numerical representations of qualitative attributes are possible and is laid out in the work of Krantz et al. [26].

In order to understand the computations of new paradigms of computing involving real numbers, it was proposed in [5,6] to replace the classical oracle to a Turing machine by an analogue device like those in the hybrid models of the sixties (see [16] for those analogue-digital models).

The oracles that we considered are physical processes that enable the Turing machine to measure quantities. As far as we have investigated (see [15]), measurements can be classified in one of the three types:[5] one-sided or threshold measurement, two-sided measurement and vanishing measurement. A one-sided experiment is an experiment that approximates the unknown value y just from one side, i.e. it approximates an unknown value y either with values z from above or with values z from below, checking either if $y < z$ or if $z < y$, but not both. A two-sided experiment[6] is an experiment that approximates the unknown value y from both sides, i.e. it approximates the unknown value y with values z from above and with values z from below, checking if $y < z$ and $z < y$. A vanishing experiment is an experiment that approximates the unknown value y measuring the number of ticks of a (Turing machine) clock.[7] This type of experimental classification is neither in Hempel's original work in [23], nor in the fully developed theory in [26].

For the previous types of oracle, the communication between the Turing machine and the oracle is ruled by one of the following protocols, inter alia (see [8] for the other protocols):

- Infinite precision: the oracle answers to the queried word with infinite precision;
- Arbitrary precision: the oracle answers to the queried word with probability of error that can be made as small as desired but is never 0;
- Fixed precision $\varepsilon > 0$: the oracle answers to the queried word with probability of error ε.

It was then realised that the interaction between the analogue part – experiment to conduct or value to be measured – and the digital part – the scientist or the computer – takes (physical) time that is at least exponential in the desired number of bits of precision (see [10–15]). (This physical time is intrinsic to physical law and does not represent the time needed for the activity of measurement itself.) Having discovered such a timing restriction (that in the ARNN model corresponds to the replacement of the piecewise linear or saturated sigmoid by the analytical sigmoid), we engaged in an investigation on experimental apparatuses

---

[5] This is still conjecture.
[6] ARNN computes with a two-sided experiment.
[7] A time constructible function.

in order to answer the question *What can one compute with the help of a measurement of a magnitude?* (see [1,4,8,13,15]). In [1,2,4,8,9] the upper bounds of analogue-digital computation in polynomial time under ideal conditions were placed in $BPP//\log\star$ in the case of both deterministic, and of probabilistic, computation. In fact, the power of measurements has been $BPP//\log\star$ persistently, across all limited precision protocols, while it drops from P/poly to $P/\log\star$ in the case of the deterministic measurement. We wondered whether the barrier $BPP//\log\star$ would persist in more general conditions. In [3], we show that under the most general (ideal) conditions the upper bounds of computational power of measurements of (deterministic) infinite, arbitrary and limited precisions are $BPP//\log\star$.

Among a number of theorems, we have shown that if these measurements are used as an oracle to a Turing machine, then, in polynomial time, we can compute the complexity classes listed in Table 1.

Table 1. The lower and upper bounds for the main complexity classes computed by the analogue-digital models characterised by either a non-analytic (C^0, but not C^2) or an analytic function (from C^2 to analytic). These results were presented in [5,6] for the first case and in [1,4,8] for the second case. Different classes such as $BPP//\log^2\star$ and $BPP//\log\star$ occur in further specialization of the protocols not considered in this extended abstract.

	Infinite	Unbounded	Fixed
Non-analytic analogue			
Lower bound	P/poly	P/poly	$BPP//\log\star$
Upper bound	P/poly	P/poly	$BPP//\log\star$
Analytic analogue			
Lower bound	$P/\log\star$	$BPP//\log\star$	$BPP//\log\star$
Upper bound	$P/\log\star$	$BPP//\log^2\star$ or $BPP//\log\star$	$BPP//\log^2\star$ or $BPP//\log\star$

Recently, we have moved towards understanding the computational limits of analogue-digital machines operating in bounded space. Some new research will be summarised.

References

1. Ambaram, T., Beggs, E., Costa, J.F., Poças, D., Tucker, J.V.: An analogue-digital model of computation: turing machines with physical oracles. In: Adamatzky, A. (ed.) Advances in Unconventional Computing. ECC, vol. 22, pp. 73–115. Springer, Cham (2017). doi:10.1007/978-3-319-33924-5_4
2. Beggs, E., Cortez, P., Costa, J.F., Tucker, J.V.: A hierarchy for $BPP//\log\star$ based on counting calls to an oracle. In: Adamatzky, A. (ed.) Emergent Computation. ECC, vol. 24, pp. 39–56. Springer, Cham (2017). doi:10.1007/978-3-319-46376-6_3

3. Beggs, E., Cortez, P., Costa, J.F., Tucker, J.V.: Classifying the computational power of stochastic physical oracles (2017, submitted)
4. Beggs, E., Costa, J.F., Poças, D., Tucker, J.V.: Oracles that measure thresholds: the Turing machine and the broken balance. J. Log. Comput. **23**(6), 1155–1181 (2013)
5. Beggs, E., Costa, J.F., Loff, B., Tucker, J.V.: Computational complexity with experiments as oracles. Proc. Roy. Soc. Ser. A (Math. Phys. Eng. Sci.) **464**(2098), 2777–2801 (2008)
6. Beggs, E., Costa, J.F., Loff, B., Tucker, J.V.: Computational complexity with experiments as oracles II. Upper bounds. Proc. Roy. Soc. Ser. A (Math. Phys. Eng. Sci.) **465**(2105), 1453–1465 (2009)
7. Beggs, E., Costa, J.F., Poças, D., Tucker, J.V.: A natural computation model of positive relativisation. Int. J. Unconv. Comput. **10**(1–2), 111–141 (2013)
8. Beggs, E., Costa, J.F., Poças, D., Tucker, J.V.: Computations with oracles that measure vanishing quantities. Math. Struct. Comput. Sci. (2017, to appear)
9. Beggs, E., Costa, J.F., Poças, D., Tucker, J.V.: An analogue-digital church-turing thesis. Int. J. Found. Comput. Sci. **25**(4), 373–389 (2014)
10. Beggs, E., Costa, J.F., Tucker, J.V.: Computational models of measurement and Hempel's axiomatization. In: Carsetti, A. (ed.) Causality, Meaningful Complexity and Embodied Cognition. (TDLA), vol. 46, pp. 155–184. Springer, Dordrecht (2010). doi:10.1007/978-90-481-3529-5_9
11. Beggs, E., Costa, J.F., Tucker, J.V.: Limits to measurement in experiments governed by algorithms. Math. Struct. Comput. Sci. **20**(06), 1019–1050 (2010)
12. Beggs, E., Costa, J.F., Tucker, J.V.: Physical oracles: the Turing machine and the Wheatstone bridge. Stud. Logica. **95**(1–2), 279–300 (2010)
13. Beggs, E., Costa, J.F., Tucker, J.V.: Axiomatising physical experiments as oracles to algorithms. Philos. Trans. Roy. Soc. Ser. A (Math. Phys. Eng. Sci.) **370**(12), 3359–3384 (2012)
14. Beggs, E., Costa, J.F., Tucker, J.V.: The impact of models of a physical oracle on computational power. Math. Struct. Comput. Sci. **22**(5), 853–879 (2012)
15. Beggs, E., Costa, J.F., Tucker, J.V.: Three forms of physical measurement and their computability. Rev. Symb. Log. **7**(4), 618–646 (2014)
16. Bekey, G.A., Karplus, W.J.: Hybrid Computation. Wiley, Hoboken (1968)
17. Bournez, O., Cosnard, M.: On the computational power of dynamical systems and hybrid systems. Theoret. Comput. Sci. **168**(2), 417–459 (1996)
18. Carnap, R.: Philosophical Foundations of Physics. Basic Books, New York City (1966)
19. Costa, J.F., Leong, R.: The ARNN model relativizes P == NP and P =/= NP. Theoret. Comput. Sci. **499**(1), 2–22 (2013)
20. Davis, M.: The myth of hypercomputation. In: Teuscher, C. (ed.) Alan Turing: The Life and Legacy of a Great Thinker, pp. 195–212. Springer, Heidelberg (2006). doi:10.1007/978-3-662-05642-4_8
21. Davis, M.: Why there is no such discipline as hypercomputation. Appl. Math. Comput. **178**(1), 4–7 (2006)
22. Geroch, R., Hartle, J.B.: Computability and physical theories. Found. Phys. **16**(6), 533–550 (1986)
23. Hempel, C.G.: Fundamentals of concept formation in empirical science. Int. Encycl. Unified Sci. **2**(7) (1952)
24. Kelly, K.T.: The Logic of Reliable Inquiry. Oxford University Press, Oxford (1996)
25. Kilian, J., Siegelmann, H.T.: The dynamic universality of sigmoidal neural networks. Inf. Comput. **128**(1), 48–56 (1996)

26. Krantz, D.H., Duncan Luce, R., Suppes, P., Tversky, A.: Foundations of Measurement, vol. I. Dover, Mineola (2007)
27. Moore, C.: Unpredictability and undecidability in dynamical systems. Phys. Rev. Lett. **64**(20), 2354–2357 (1990)
28. Siegelmann, H.T.: Neural Networks and Analog Computation: Beyond the Turing Limit. Birkhäuser, Basel (1999)
29. Woods, D., Naughton, T.J.: An optical model of computation. Theoret. Comput. Sci. **334**(2005), 227–258 (2004)
30. Younger, A.S., Redd, E., Siegelmann, H.: Development of physical super-turing analog hardware. In: Ibarra, O.H., Kari, L., Kopecki, S. (eds.) UCNC 2014. LNCS, vol. 8553, pp. 379–391. Springer, Cham (2014). doi:10.1007/978-3-319-08123-6_31

Ways to Compute in Euclidean Frameworks

Jérôme Durand-Lose[✉]

Laboratoire d'Informatique Fondamentale d'Orléans, Université d'Orléans,
Orléans, France
jerome.durand-lose@univ-orleans.fr

Abstract. This tutorial presents what kind of computation can be carried out inside a Euclidean space with dedicated primitives—and discrete
or hybrid (continuous evolution between discrete transitions) time scales.
The presented models can perform Classical (Turing, discrete) computations as well as, for some, hyper and analog computations (thanks
to the continuity of space). The first half of the tutorial presents three
models of computation based on respectively: ruler and compass, local
constraints and emergence of polyhedra and piece-wise constant derivative. The other half concentrates on signal machines: line segments are
extended and replaced on meeting. These machines are capable hypercomputation and analog computation and to solve PSPACE-problem in
"constant space and time" though partial fractal generation.

Keywords: Analog computation · Computability · Fractal computation · Fractal generation · Hybrid-computation · Hyper-computation ·
Mondrian Automata · Piece-wise constant derivative · Ruler and compass · Signal machine · Turing computation

1 Introduction

This tutorial provides some insight on the following question: *What can be done
with a Euclidean space with dedicated primitives and controls?* Space is not considered as the place to assemble gates and wires but as the substrate of computation itself. The general framework is not machines or automata but some
Euclidean space where information is displayed and evolved according to some
dynamics.

The approaches considered here are: constructions with ruler and compass,
polyhedra emerging from local constraints, extending a sequence of line segments
across polyhedral regions, extending line segments until they intersect, etc. In
each case, distance, carried information, available room, encounters/collisions,
etc., are elements where *spatial localization matters*.

Space is Euclidean, this means, on the one hand, that it is continuous and,
on the other hand, that the underlying geometry is the one of points, lines
and circles. This geometrical point of view is prevalent here as shown by the
illustrations. This general framework has limitations: no differential equation, no

M.J. Patitz and M. Stannett (Eds.): UCNC 2017, LNCS 10240, pp. 8–25, 2017.
DOI: 10.1007/978-3-319-58187-3_2

algebraic geometry, etc. Outside of instantaneous "border" crossing or apparatus operation, all is straightforward and absolutely plain. The models presented here belong to a more general framework: hybrid systems with continuous (related to the nature of space and possibly time) and discrete (phase transition, collision, etc.) traits.

Continuity opens the way to *Zenon effects*: an infinite number of discrete transitions during a finite (continuous) duration (in a finite space). Many models use this capability to *hyper-compute* (solving the Halting problem and even "less computable" problems, see Syropoulos (2010)).

Like Euclidean geometry, presented models are idealized: lines have zero width, positions are exact, etc. From the physics standpoint, they are more abstract than realistic: unbounded density of information, space is Euclidean at every scale, etc.

When Turing computability is addressed, *rational* versions of the models are used: all coordinates, speeds, etc., are rational numbers. On the one hand, this often allows exact manipulation on a computer and on the other hand, it prevents oracles to be encoded in the system as a real number [for example the solution to the Halting problem as Chaitin's omega number (Calude 2002, Chap. 7)].

Each presented model is described, main results and references are provided. Proofs are omitted as well as complex results. Clues are provided as long as they remain intelligible.

This tutorial has two parts. The first part presents three computing models. The first model, the *Geometric Computation Machines* of Huckenbeck (1989, 1991), uses an automaton to activate ruler and compass and generates points, lines and circles. The second one, the *Mondrian Automata* of Jacopini and Sontacchi (1990), starts from uniform local constraints (on open balls from $\mathbb{R}^n$) on space-time diagrams ensuring causality; from these emerge polyhedra at the usual scale. The third one, the *Piece-wise Constant Derivative* of Asarin and Maler (1995); Asarin et al. (1995), partitions space into polyhedral regions corresponding to constant speeds; the orbit starting from a single point can perform infinitely many region changes during a finite portion.

The second part concentrates on one model: the signal machines of Durand-Lose (2005, 2006). After the definition of the model, a simulation of a generic Turing machine is presented. Using the continuity of both space and time, it is possible to dynamically scale down the computation and accelerate to implement a form of the Black Hole model of computation (and to hyper-compute). Fractal generation scheme can be used in order to dispatch sub-computations and to achieve *fractal computation* (allowing, e.g., to solve quantified SAT in constant space and time). This part ends by showing that the model is capable of analog computation (computing over real numbers).

This survey of computing models involving space is not comprehensive. Some models like cellular automata or tile assembling systems have their own devoted conferences (or already had been the subject of a tutorial at UCNC) and have so much literature about that each would spread over a few books; it would be pointless to present them in a few pages. Models using higher level mathematics (differential equations, algebraic geometry, etc.) would not fit here and neither would algorithmic geometry. Many others (e.g. continuous counterparts of cellular automata like (Hagiya 2005; Takeuti 2005), use of optics to manipulate 2D-pictures (Naughton and Woods 2001; Woods and Naughton 2005)) are not addressed just because the purpose is to show the variety and specificity and not make an inventory.

This tutorial is based on the survey Durand-Lose (2016).

2 Three Models Operating on Euclidean Geometry

2.1 Ruler and Compass

This section is devoted to the work of Huckenbeck (1989, 1991) on *Geometric Computation Machines*. The primitives of these machines are the usual geometric operations that can be carried out with ruler and compass. The purpose is not to do algorithmic geometry (would it be discrete, symbolic or algebraic) but to construct in a two dimensional Euclidean space.

Each machine is an automaton (or program) equipped with a finite number of registers. There are three kinds of register: for points, for lines and for circles. The states of the automaton are used to represent both the program counter and to record the state of the computation (i.e. Unfinished, Finished and Error, the last two ones are final).

The available operations are:

- output a value (point, line or circle),
- put in a register the intersection of two lines,
- put in a register one of the intersections of a line and a circle (optionally different from some point),
- put in a register one of the intersections of two circles (optionally different from some point),
- put in a register the line going through two points,
- put in a register the circle whose center is given (as a point) as well as its radius (as the distance between two points),
- copy a register, and
- Finished.

Intersections do not necessarily exist and neither are unique. This means that the execution of the automaton is non deterministic. Whenever an instruction cannot be carried out, the branch (of the tree of all possible executions) ends with Error.

If the whole tree of possible executions is finite, has only Finished (i.e. no Error) leafs and all its branches generate the same output, then the computation succeeds and the output is the common output (it is generated by every branch). For example, the program of Fig. 1 computes the middle of a segment (whose extremities are A and B and are the only input). Please note that there are two possible executions (where are p_1 and p_2?), but their outputs are identical.

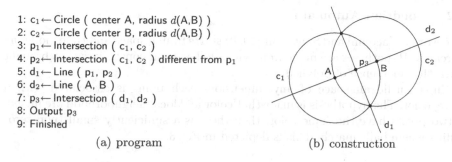

1: $c_1 \leftarrow$ Circle (center A, radius d(A,B))
2: $c_2 \leftarrow$ Circle (center B, radius d(A,B))
3: $p_1 \leftarrow$ Intersection (c_1, c_2)
4: $p_2 \leftarrow$ Intersection (c_1, c_2) different from p_1
5: $d_1 \leftarrow$ Line (p_1, p_2)
6: $d_2 \leftarrow$ Line (A, B)
7: $p_3 \leftarrow$ Intersection (d_1, d_2)
8: Output p_3
9: Finished

(a) program   (b) construction

Fig. 1. Constructing the middle of the segment AB.

With the given primitives, it is also possible to construct the perpendicular to a line passing through a point and then the parallel.

Conditional jump instructions are like "if $p_k \in E$ go to i: otherwise to j:" where p_k is a point-register and E is a predefined set used as an oracle.

A simple case is when E contains only the origin $(0,0)$ and points $(1,0)$ and $(0,1)$ are provided as constants. The functions (computable in bounded time) from an n-tuple of points to n-tuple of points are exactly the ones where the input is divided in finitely many pieces (defined as intersection of finitely many algebraic surfaces) where the coordinates of the output can be expressed with rational functions. This is related to the possibility to implement the following primitives: on the one hand, projections $(x, y) \rightarrow (x, 0)$, $(x, y) \rightarrow (y, 0)$ and reconstruction $(x, 0)\,(y, 0) \rightarrow (x, y)$ and, on the other hand, addition, multiplication and division on the x axis as on Fig. 2.

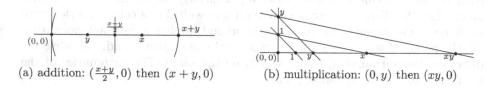

(a) addition: $(\frac{x+y}{2}, 0)$ then $(x + y, 0)$ (b) multiplication: $(0, y)$ then $(xy, 0)$

Fig. 2. Constructing from $(x, 0)$ and $(y, 0)$ with constants $(0, 0)$, $(1, 1)$ and $(0, 1)$.

This corresponds to the classical construction of numbers computable with rule and compass (Conway and Guy 1996, Chap. 7). These are also closed by square rooting. Here, the condition that each branch should generate the same output makes it impossible for root to appear (Huckenbeck 1991).

It should be noted that since the following operations can be performed: $(x, 0) \rightarrow (x + 1, 0)$, $(x, 0) \rightarrow (x - 1, 0)$, and test whether $(x, 0)$ is $(0, 0)$; an unbounded counter can be encoded with a point register. These machines can simulate any 2-counter automaton and are thus Turing-universal.

2.2   Mondrian Automata

The work of Jacopini and Sontacchi (1990) starts from a space and time modeling of reality. Hypotheses are made from which follow local constraints that brought forth the emergence of polyhedra.

In a Euclidean space of any dimension, each point is associated with a state/color. The hypothesis is made that color and local neighborhood are linked: if two points have the same color, then there is a sufficiently small (non-zero) radius where balls match. This is depicted in Fig. 3.

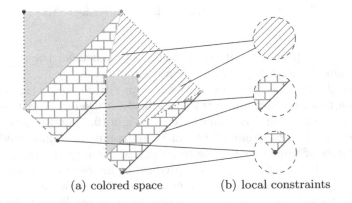

(a) colored space   (b) local constraints

Fig. 3. Mondrian space. (Color figure online)

As a consequence, if there is a ball of uniform color then any point of this color is only surrounded by this color. Topologically, this means that they form an open set. Similarly, if there is a curve (of zero width) of a color then the curve must be a line segment: identical neighborhood implies a constant derivative. All the points of this color must be on parallel line segments and, following any direction, the surrounding colors should be the same. The extremities of the segments should have different colors.

More generally, each color corresponds to polyhedral regions of equal and parallel dimension. When they are restricted to their dimensions, they are open and the frontiers of lesser dimensions should be colored differently. Whereas following any other direction, adjacent colors are always the same.

Another hypothesis is that there is a finite number of colors. Hence, having a common neighborhood (up to re-scaling) for each color defines all the constraints. They provide all the information on the dimensions and directions associated to each color as well as the color of the neighbors of higher dimensions.

Next step consists in adding one dimension for time and constraints for causality. This is defined by a speed of light, c and the condition that the color of a point is uniquely defined by what is inside the past cone (delimited by the speed of light). Figure 4(b) shows two portions of space at different dates where colors are displayed similarly. The two cones based on these portions and delimited by the speed of light are thus identical.

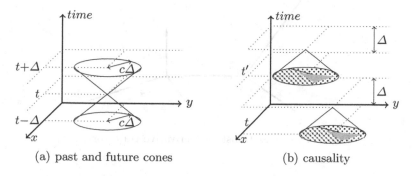

(a) past and future cones   (b) causality

Fig. 4. Cones and causality. (Color figure online)

Another argument from physical modelisation is that the system should be reversible at local scale. This implies that the same constraint is also applied with time running in the opposite direction. This corresponds to exchanging the cones (pointing to past and future) in Fig. 4(b).

Temporal constraints can also be read at the polyhedra scale. It is possible to think in terms of intersections and collisions (this kind of approach is developed in the signal machine section). At this level, simulating a Turing machine in dimension 2 (or 1 + 1 for time) would look like Fig. 8(b) except for reversibility. (Reversible signal machines can compute as proven in Durand-Lose (2012).)

2.3   Piece-Wise Constant Derivative

In this model introduced in Asarin and Maler (1995), space is partitioned into a finite number of polyhedral regions. On each region, a constant speed is defined. On Fig. 5, thick lines separate the regions and the arrows indicate the directions of speeds.

Starting from any point a trajectory is defined. When a region border is reached, movement just follows on the other side with the new speed. In Fig. 5, two trajectories are indicated. They both start on the left. The dashed trajectory changes direction twice and then goes away forever. The dotted one is wrapping itself infinitely around the intersection point of three regions.

This second trajectory is singular: it changes region infinitely often but nevertheless reaches its limit in finite time (as a convergent geometrical sum) and stops there. There are two distinct time scales: a continuous time one where the limit is reached in finite time and an infinite discrete time one (of region change events). This is a *Zeno* phenomenon/effect.

The rest of the section is restricted to rational initial points and vertices (of polyhedra). Those systems can compute considering that the input is the initial

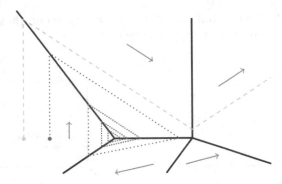

Fig. 5. Piece-wise Constant Derivative trajectories.

position (in a given zone) and that halt and result correspond to entering some other identified zone. In four dimensions, it is possible to encode the configuration of a Turing machine and operate it in the following way. The words over $\{a, b\}$ (left and right part of the tape) are encoded with the recursive function ψ defined by: $\psi(\varepsilon) = 1/4$, $\psi(a.w) = 1/3(1 + \psi(w))$, and $\psi(b.w) = 1/3(2 + \psi(w))$. Symbols can be accessed by the primitives in Fig. 6. (Scaling in Fig. 6(b) is done by changing the direction; proportions are preserved by Thales's theorem.) The tape needs two dimensions $((0, 1)^2)$. The state is encoded as the part in space the trajectory is in. The trajectory loops and that each loop corresponds to a transition of the Turing machine. Building and merging the "looping pipes" use the two extra dimensions.

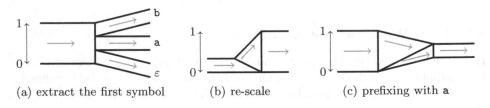

(a) extract the first symbol   (b) re-scale   (c) prefixing with a

Fig. 6. Primitives for manipulating sequences of symbols.

With a more involved proof, the Reachability problem—to decide whether a zone can be reached from a point—is thus undecidable in dimension 3 and above. Adding dimensions to the systems allows to add nested levels of Zeno effect and to climb hierarchies in the undecidable. With d dimensions, the level $d-2$ of the arithmetical hierarchy (viz. Σ_{d-2})[1] is decidable (Asarin and Maler 1995; Asarin et al. 1995). The model is even more powerful: Reachability is complete on levels of the hyper-arithmetic hierarchy[2] (Bournez 1997, 1999a,b).

---

[1] Σ_0 is the recursive sets, Σ_1 is recursively enumerable sets, e.g. the Halting problem.

[2] Extension of the arithmetical hierarchy to ordinal indices.

3   Signal Machines

This section is dedicated to *signal machines* (SM) (Durand-Lose 2005, 2006). This model was born as a continuous abstraction of Cellular Automata (CA) (Durand-Lose 2008). *Signals* allow to store and transmit information, to start a process, to synchronize, etc. They are the key tool in CA both for building CA and for understanding. CA dynamics are often detailed as signals interacting in collisions resulting in the generations of new signals.

CA-signals extend over one or more discrete cells whilst SM-signals are dimensionless points on a 1-dimensional Euclidean space. The main properties of CA are preserved: synchronicity (signals move at the same pace) and uniformity (the dynamics are always and everywhere the same: the speeds and interactions only rely on the nature of signals, like CA-patterns define the evolution of discrete signals). Signals have uniform movement and "draw" line segments on space-time diagrams. The nature of a signal is called a *meta-signal*.

A *Signal machine (SM)* is defined by a triplet (M, S, R) where M is a finite set of *meta-signals*, S is a function associating a *speed* to each meta-signal, and R is a set of collision rules. A *collision rule* associates to sets of at least two meta-signals of different speeds (*incoming*) a set of meta-signals of different speeds (*outgoing*). R is deterministic: a set appears at most once as the left (incoming) part of a rule.

In any configuration, there are finitely many signals and collisions. They are located in distinct places in space. Since a signal is completely defined by its associated meta-signal and a collision by a rule, a configuration is fully defined by associating to each point on the real axis a meta-signal, a rule or nothing.

As long as signals do not meet, each one moves uniformly; whereas as soon as two or more signals meet, a collision happens. Collisions provide a discrete time scale. Dynamics are defined using it: at any collision, incoming signals are instantly replaced by outgoing signals according to collision rules. In-between collisions, signals regularly propagate. This emphasizes the hybrid aspect of SM: continuous steps separated by discrete steps.

To find the location of a collision, a linear system of two equations in two variables has to be solved. Thus the location of any collision of signals whose speeds and initial locations are rational numbers, has to be rational. A signal machine is *rational* (ℚ-SM) if all speeds are rational numbers as well as any non-void positions in any initial configuration. In any generated space-time diagram, all collisions have rational locations and the positions of signals are rational at each collision time.

Example 1 (Finding the middle). It is possible to compute the middle of two signals, i.e. to position a signal exactly there. This is illustrated in Fig. 7 where a O signal is positioned exactly half-way between two W signals (bottom of Fig. 7(c)). The meta-signals and collision rules are defined in the left Fig. 7. On the right, is depicted a space-time diagram generated from a configuration with signals of meta-signals (left to right): Sub, Add, Add, W and W.

The process is started by the arrival of a Add signal on the left. When it encounters the left W, it is transformed into A and $\overrightarrow{R}$. The latter is three times faster than the former and bounces on the right W; it becomes then $\overleftarrow{R}$, still three times faster (but with opposite direction). It encounters A exactly halfway between the two W. The correct positioning of this collision can be proved by computing the locations of all the intermediate collisions.

Considering the rules in Fig. 7(b), finding the middle only uses the three first ones as can be read from the diagram. The fourth one allows to generate the middle between the left W and the first O on right of it. This is started by sending another Add from the left as illustrated in the middle in Fig. 7(c).

It is also possible to suppress the first O on the right of the left W. To achieve this, a Sub *order* is sent from the left. It becomes E when *passing* over W. Signal E collides and destroys the first O it encounters. This corresponds to the last two rules and the top of Fig. 7(c).

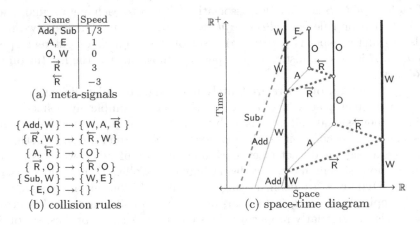

Name	Speed
Add, Sub	1/3
A, E	1
O, W	0
$\overrightarrow{R}$	3
$\overleftarrow{R}$	−3

(a) meta-signals

$\{\,\text{Add}, W\,\} \rightarrow \{\,W, A, \overrightarrow{R}\,\}$
$\{\,\overrightarrow{R}, W\,\} \rightarrow \{\,\overleftarrow{R}, W\,\}$
$\{\,A, \overleftarrow{R}\,\} \rightarrow \{\,O\,\}$
$\{\,\overrightarrow{R}, O\,\} \rightarrow \{\,\overrightarrow{R}, O\,\}$
$\{\,\text{Sub}, W\,\} \rightarrow \{\,W, E\,\}$
$\{\,E, O\,\} \rightarrow \{\,\}$

(b) collision rules

(c) space-time diagram

Fig. 7. Finding the middle and more.

Finding the middle is a key primitive for designing SM. For example, as shown above, it is possible to use it repeatedly to record any natural number in unary (with O's as in Fig. 7(c)) in a bounded space.

3.1   Turing Computability

Signal machines can simulate any Turing machine (TM) as shown in Fig. 8. The evolution of the TM in Fig. 8(a) can be seen in Fig. 8(b). Vertical (null speed) signals encode each cell of the tape. Zigzagging signals indicate the position of the head and record the state of the automaton. Another interest of SM is to provide graphical traces.

The enlargement of the tape is done with the middle construction, but backwards! It is also possible to set these speeds such that the distance is halved

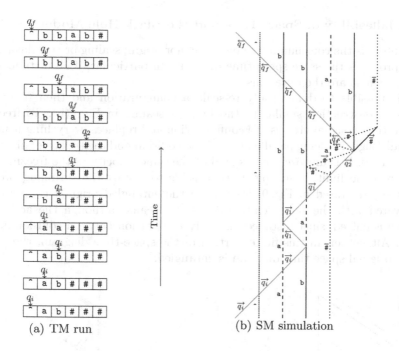

(a) TM run   (b) SM simulation

Fig. 8. Simulating a Turing machine with a signal machine.

each time. The width of the whole tape is then bounded independently from the number of cells.

This construction works on Q-SM that can be simulated exactly on any computer. Leaving open the definition of input, halt and output, Q-SM have exactly the same computing power as TM. This leads to the undecidability of many problems for Q-SM (expressible in classic context since everything is rational) like: decide whether the number of collisions is finite or decide whether a meta-signal appears or a collision rule is used.

Using various meta-signals similar to O in Fig. 7, it is possible to encode sequences of letters functioning as a stack. This can also be achieved by using positions to encode values (Durand-Lose 2006) (with irrational positions, it is even possible to encode infinite stacks). It is possible to simulate any TM with a constant number of signals and collisions involving only two signals resulting in exactly two signals (conservation of the number of signals), but moreover this remains true if rules should be injective: the rule is also defined by outgoing signals (reversibility) (Durand-Lose 2012). This simulation uses reversible universal TM (Bennett 1988; Lecerf 1963; Morita et al. 1989).

Signal machines can also be used to simulate the *Cyclic Tag Systems* introduced in Cook (2004). His work restarted the race to small universal machines, e.g. on TM (Woods and Neary 2009). The smallest Turing-universal SM known simulates any CTS and has 13 meta-signals and 21 collision rules (Durand-Lose 2011b).

3.2   Malleability of Space-Time and the Black Hole Model

The context is the continuum without scale nor origin; scaling or translating the initial produces the same space-time diagram. In particular, if all distances are halved, then so are the durations.

It is possible to dynamically re-scale a configuration and then to restart it with a construction similar to the PCD re-scaling in Fig. 6(b). To freeze a computation, a signal crosses the configuration and replaces everything it meets by parallel signals. Being parallel, there is no collision and the (relative) distances are preserved. It is unfrozen by a signal of the same velocity as the freezing one.

There is no limit to scaling. It is possible to restart the shrinking process forever as illustrated in Fig. 9. Each time the entangled original computation is activated with the same relative duration because although the activation duration is halved, since distances are halved, duration between collision is also halved. Altogether, in this finite portion of the space-time diagram, the whole infinite original space-time diagram is entangled.

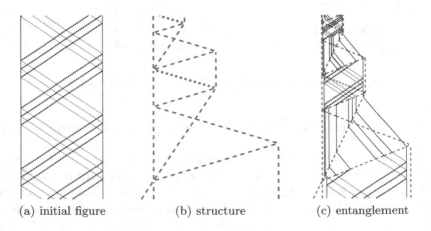

(a) initial figure   (b) structure   (c) entanglement

Fig. 9. Iterated shrinking.

With a bounded space simulation of a TM entangled, if the computation stops, then it is in bounded time. With minor modifications, it is possible to let some signal leave the iterated shrinking in such a case. Outside of the structure, this witness of the halt could be collected but this can only happen during a bounded delay. This bound on duration can be "implemented" in the space-time diagram by a collision with another signal. If the machine does not halt, then nothing is received before that collision, whilst in case of halting, the witness is collected before. Outside of the shrinking structure, the halt is decided. SM can hyper-compute by creating a local Zeno effect (Durand-Lose 2005, 2006).

The general principle behind this construction is to have two time-lines: one is infinitely accelerated and does the computation and possibly sends some signal while the other waits for it with some timeout. This corresponds to the so-called

Black Hole model of computation (Hogarth 2004; Andréka et al. 2009; Etesi and Németi 2002). The accumulation above the space-time diagram in Fig. 9(c) corresponds to the Black Hole.

3.3   Build and Use Fractals

Many fractals can be generated using SM in a straightforward way. For example, four meta-signals are enough to build the fractal accumulation in Fig. 10(a). The space-time diagram is undefined at this accumulation *singularity*. Recursively generating middles also generate a fractal as in Fig. 10(b). By considering left and right thirds instead of halves, a classical construction of the Cantor set is generated as in Fig. 10(c). By varying the speed and the proportion, it is possible to generate sets of any fractal dimension between 0 and 1 (Senot 2013, Chap. 5).

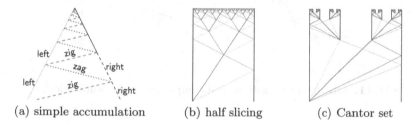

(a) simple accumulation   (b) half slicing   (c) Cantor set

Fig. 10. Fractals.

In Fig. 10(b) spaces are sliced in half at each step. This can be used to provide parallelism and deal with one sub-cases on each side. For boolean formulas, it is possible to recursively slice for each and every variable. All cases are thus generated. If the variables appear in some boolean formula whose satisfiability is to be checked, then one gets a scheme to solve the satisfaction of boolean formula (SAT). This scheme can also deal with quantified variables to solve the PSPACE-complete Quantify SAT (QSAT) (Sipser 1997, Sect. 8.3).

If a boolean formula contains 10 variables, then 10 levels of slicing are done. (What remains of the construction of the fractal in Fig. 10(b) is useless and dangerous since the diagram is not defined at the limit.) For example, in Fig. 11, the QSAT formula, $\exists x_1 \forall x_2 \forall x_3\ x_1 \wedge (\neg x_2 \vee x_3)$, is represented by a ray of signals encoding all its elements. Computation is organized following a complete binary tree (of depth 3). Evaluation is done on the leafs and results are aggregated on top of the space-time diagram.

A specific machine is generated for each formula. Using a more complex encoding, it is possible to use a unique machine for which the initial configuration totally encodes the formula (Duchier et al. 2012; Senot 2013, Chap. 8).

It is also possible to solve other problems on formulas: how many satisfying valuations (#SAT, #P-complete)? What is the "smallest" satisfying valuation? etc. One "just" has to change the way the variable-free formulas are evaluated

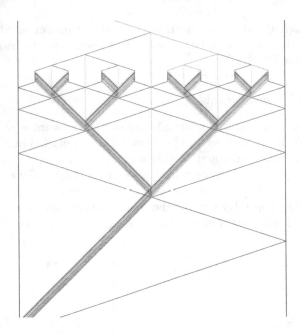

Fig. 11. Solving QSAT with fractal computation, the whole picture.

and the results are aggregated to generate an integer, a valuation, etc. This is a modular parametrization of the construction.

More levels of the fractal are generated as needed. It does not need more time or space. Altogether, there is a SM able to decide any instance of QSAT in constant space and time. Using a controlled and unfinished fractal construction to display parallel computations and then aggregate the result is called *fractal computation*.

Discrete complexity measures are defined by considering space-time diagrams as directed acyclic graphs. A *direct causal link* exists between two signals if the first ends in the collision where the second starts. A *causal link* is its transitive closure. *Time complexity* is then the size of the longest sequence of signals with direct causal link between each two consecutive signals (path in the DAG). *Space complexity* is the largest number of signals without any causal link. With these definitions, complexity is quadratic in time (cubic for the generic case) but exponential in space.

Figure 10(a) shows that it is possible to build a fractal with only four different speeds. With two speeds or less, the number of collisions is finite and bounded. With three speeds, the situation is two-fold: in a Q-SM, signals must travel on a regular mesh (without any accumulation). But accumlation might happen as soon as there is an irrational ratio between speeds or between initial positions. This can be understood by the presence of a mechanism computing the *gcd*, which only converges on rational (Becker et al. 2003).

What about the computing capability? In the rational case, the same mesh shows that usable memory is finite and bounded. Whereas in the other case, it is possible to simulate a TM using a fractal construction step to enlarge the tape (Durand-Lose 2013).

3.4 Analog Computation

This section deals with computation on real numbers. They are represented by the distance between two (parallel) signals of distinct meta-signals (base or value)—or one encoding zero (zero). Dividing by two corresponds to finding the middle. Multiplication by any constant can be done likewise. Adding two numbers can be done as in Fig. 12(a). The presence of a parallelogram proves the equality of the distances. Subtraction can be done similarly as depicted in Fig. 12(b) where the parallelogram is folded around the lower right value.

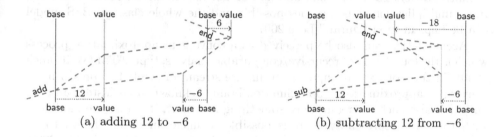

(a) adding 12 to −6   (b) subtracting 12 from −6

Fig. 12. Basic operations on reals.

Starting from a sequence of real values (like the sequence of cells of the tape of a TM), it is possible to multiply by constants and to add a value to another inside a window (bounded part of the sequence) and to move the window. These primitives could be triggered by some deterministic finite automata (or sequential program). The state of the automaton can be encoded in the meta-signals used to carry out the operations.

The automaton can be equipped with conditional transition: testing the sign of a value can be used to branch. The automaton can have an initial and final state (no more collisions then). Constants may be provided in the initial configuration.

Altogether, starting from a finite sequence of real numbers (infinity extendable on both side), it is possible to store in a cell the linear combination of values around it, branch according to sign and move inside the sequence. This corresponds to the BSS model (Blum et al. 1989, 1998) without inner multiplication. It is the linear version of it: lin-BSS (Bournez 1999b; Meer and Michaux 1997) with an unbounded number of registers.

Signal machines are capable of implementing lin-BSS. The converse is also true. The configuration of a SM can be represented by a sequence of blocks, each one encoding the meta-signal, the distance to next plus various temporary registers. The lin-BSS machine runs through the configuration and computes the minimal time to a collision. Since speeds are constant of the SM, they become constants of the lin-BSS machine, thus everything is linear.

Once this delay to the next collision time is known, the automaton runs through the configuration again. Distances are updated. When the distance is zero, then a collision happens. Involved signals are replaced according to rules (which are hard encoded into the automaton). If the number of signals is changed, all the values on the right are moved accordingly. When room is needed (or should be removed) shifting the values in the cells is done like for a TM.

BSS and Computable Analysis. Taking accumulations and infinitely many signals during finite duration into account allows to go further on.

For example, it is possible to extract an infinite sequence of 0 and 1 representing the binary encoding of a real number. This flow can be used to make a multiplication: each time half and add or not depending on the received bit. Inner multiplication thus becomes possible and the whole classical BSS model can be implemented (Durand-Lose 2007).

Accumulation can also be perceived as a convergent approximating process which is the foundation of recursive/computable analysis, type-2 TM (Weihrauch 2000). In this context, an input is an infinite stream of symbols representing a convergent approximation (approximation bound is known at each step) and the output is also such a stream (once something is output, it cannot be modified) with the same representation. It is possible to make an accumulation to be located according to a process generating such a stream (Durand-Lose 2009, 2011a) on a $\mathbb{Q}$-SM.

One last result about isolated accumulation on $\mathbb{Q}$-SM: not only they cannot happen everywhere (by a simple cardinality argument) but their possible locations are exactly characterized in (Durand-Lose 2011c). They can only happen at dates that correspond to *computably enumerable* (*c.e.*) real numbers (Calude 2002, Chap. 7), i.e. there is a TM that produces an increasing and convergent infinite sequence (there is no hypothesis on the quality of the approximation). The positions of isolated accumulations are exactly the differences of two such numbers. Position and date can be handled independently. This is proved by a two scales construction: an embedded TM is accelerated and stopped so that it provides the data on request in bounded time, the large scale directs the accumulation to the right spot according to the provided data.

4   Conclusion

Presented models operate inside continuous euclidean spaces. Their variety is huge as well as their computing capabilities. They bring forth a new kind of algorithmic where localization, distance, relative positions, etc., provide possibilities as well as constraints.

Unsurprisingly, the capability to compute in the Turing understanding is common. As soon as it is possible to take advantage of continuity of space and time, analog computation and hyper-computation arise too (thus transcending the Church-Turing thesis).

This remains true only in the ideal word of the model where there is no error, nor approximation, nor limit to sub-division or to density of information. This is a limit to the realism of the models. Other arguments are the unbounded quantity of information that can be stored and retrieved in a bounded space and the absence of Heisenberg's Uncertainty principle at any scale.

This leads to wonder what would be their discrete approximation. Discrete geometry and related issues are a totally different world. Nevertheless, for signal machines, the discrete counterpart exists (CA) and there are works on exact discretization: (Besson and Durand-Lose 2016).

References

Andréka, H., Németi, I., Németi, P.: General relativistic hypercomputing and foundation of mathematics. Nat. Comput. **8**(3), 499–516 (2009). doi:10.1007/s11047-009-9114-3

Asarin, E., Maler, O.: Achilles and the Tortoise climbing up the arithmetical hierarchy. In: Thiagarajan, P.S. (ed.) FSTTCS 1995. LNCS, vol. 1026, pp. 471–483. Springer, Heidelberg (1995). doi:10.1007/3-540-60692-0_68

Asarin, E., Maler, O., Pnueli, A.: Reachability analysis of dynamical systems having piecewise-constant derivatives. Theoret. Comput. Sci. **138**(1), 35–65 (1995). doi:10.1016/0304-3975(94)00228-B

Becker, F., Chapelle, M., Durand-Lose, J., Levorato, V., Senot, M.: Abstract geometrical computation 8: small machines, accumulations & rationality (2013, submitted). http://arxiv.org/abs/1307.6468

Bennett, C.H.: Notes on the history of reversible computation. IBM J. Res. Dev. **32**(1), 16–23 (1988)

Besson, T., Durand-Lose, J.: Exact discretization of 3-speed rational signal machines into cellular automata. In: Cook, M., Neary, T. (eds.) AUTOMATA 2016. LNCS, vol. 9664, pp. 63–76. Springer, Cham (2016). doi:10.1007/978-3-319-39300-1_6

Blum, L., Shub, M., Smale, S.: On a theory of computation and complexity over the real numbers: NP-completeness, recursive functions and universal machines. Bull. Am. Math. Soc. **21**(1), 1–46 (1989)

Blum, L., Cucker, F., Shub, M., Smale, S.: Complexity and Real Computation. Springer, New York (1998)

Bournez, O.: Some bounds on the computational power of piecewise constant derivative systems (extended abstract). In: Degano, P., Gorrieri, R., Marchetti-Spaccamela, A. (eds.) ICALP 1997. LNCS, vol. 1256, pp. 143–153. Springer, Heidelberg (1997). doi:10.1007/3-540-63165-8_172

Bournez, O.: Achilles and the Tortoise climbing up the hyper-arithmetical hierarchy. Theoret. Comput. Sci. **210**(1), 21–71 (1999a)

Bournez, O.: Some bounds on the computational power of piecewise constant derivative systems. Theory Comput. Syst. **32**(1), 35–67 (1999b)

Calude, C.S.: Information and Randomness: An Algorithmic Perspective. Texts in Theoretical Computer Science. An EATCS Series, 2nd edn. Springer, Heidelberg (2002). doi:10.1007/978-3-662-04978-5. ISBN 3540434666

Conway, J.H., Guy, R.L.: The Book of Numbers. Copernicus Series. Springer, Heidelberg (1996). ISBN 9780387979939

Cook, M.: Universality in elementary cellular automata. Complex Syst. **15**, 1–40 (2004)

Duchier, D., Durand-Lose, J., Senot, M.: Computing in the fractal cloud: modular generic solvers for SAT and Q-SAT variants. In: Agrawal, M., Cooper, S.B., Li, A. (eds.) TAMC 2012. LNCS, vol. 7287, pp. 435–447. Springer, Heidelberg (2012). doi:10.1007/978-3-642-29952-0_42. http://arxiv.org/abs/1105.3454

Durand-Lose, J.: Abstract geometrical computation for black hole computation. In: Margenstern, M. (ed.) MCU 2004. LNCS, vol. 3354, pp. 176–187. Springer, Heidelberg (2005). doi:10.1007/978-3-540-31834-7_14

Durand-Lose, J.: Abstract geometrical computation 1: embedding black hole computations with rational numbers. Fund. Inf. **74**(4), 491–510 (2006)

Durand-Lose, J.: Abstract geometrical computation and the linear blum, shub and smale model. In: Cooper, S.B., Löwe, B., Sorbi, A. (eds.) CiE 2007. LNCS, vol. 4497, pp. 238–247. Springer, Heidelberg (2007). doi:10.1007/978-3-540-73001-9_25

Durand-Lose, J.: The signal point of view: from cellular automata to signal machines. In: Durand, B. (ed.) Journees Automates cellulaires (JAC 2008), pp. 238–249 (2008)

Durand-Lose, J.: Abstract geometrical computation and computable analysis. In: Calude, C.S., Costa, J.F., Dershowitz, N., Freire, E., Rozenberg, G. (eds.) UC 2009. LNCS, vol. 5715, pp. 158–167. Springer, Heidelberg (2009). doi:10.1007/978-3-642-03745-0_20

Durand-Lose, J.: Abstract geometrical computation 5: embedding computable analysis. Nat. Comput. **10**(4), 1261–1273 (2011a). doi:10.1007/s11047-010-9229-6. Special issue on Unconv. Comp. 2009

Durand-Lose, J.: Abstract geometrical computation 4: small Turing universal signal machines. Theoret. Comput. Sci. **412**, 57–67 (2011b). doi:10.1016/.tcs.2010.07.013

Durand-Lose, J.: Geometrical accumulations and computably enumerable real numbers. In: Calude, C.S., Kari, J., Petre, I., Rozenberg, G. (eds.) UC 2011. LNCS, vol. 6714, pp. 101–112. Springer, Heidelberg (2011c). doi:10.1007/978-3-642-21341-0_15

Durand-Lose, J.: Abstract geometrical computation 6: a reversible, conservative and rational based model for black hole computation. Int. J. Unconv. Comput. **8**(1), 33–46 (2012)

Durand-Lose, J.: Irrationality is needed to compute with signal machines with only three speeds. In: Bonizzoni, P., Brattka, V., Löwe, B. (eds.) CiE 2013. LNCS, vol. 7921, pp. 108–119. Springer, Heidelberg (2013). doi:10.1007/978-3-642-39053-1_12. http://cie2013.disco.unimib.it/. Invited talk for special session Computation in nature

Durand-Lose, J.: Computing in perfect euclidean frameworks. In: Adamatzky, A. (ed.) Advances in Unconventional Computing. ECC, vol. 22, pp. 141–163. Springer, Cham (2017). doi:10.1007/978-3-319-33924-5_6

Etesi, G., Németi, I.: Non-turing computations via Malament-Hogarth space-times. Int. J. Theoret. Phys. **41**(2), 341–370 (2002). http://arxiv.org/abs/gr-qc/0104023

Hagiya, M.: Discrete state transition systems on continuous space-time: a theoretical model for amorphous computing. In: Calude, C.S., Dinneen, M.J., Păun, G., Pérez-Jímenez, M.J., Rozenberg, G. (eds.) UC 2005. LNCS, vol. 3699, pp. 117–129. Springer, Heidelberg (2005). doi:10.1007/11560319_12

Hogarth, M.L.: Deciding arithmetic using SAD computers. Br. J. Philos. Sci. **55**, 681–691 (2004)

Huckenbeck, U.: Euclidian geometry in terms of automata theory. Theoret. Comput. Sci. **68**(1), 71–87 (1989). doi:10.1016/0304-3975(89)90120-5

Huckenbeck, U.: A result about the power of geometric oracle machines. Theoret. Comput. Sci. **88**(2), 231–251 (1991). doi:10.1016/0304-3975(91)90375-C

Jacopini, G., Sontacchi, G.: Reversible parallel computation: an evolving space-model. Theoret. Comput. Sci. **73**(1), 1–46 (1990). doi:10.1016/0304-3975(90)90160-J

Lecerf, Y.: Machines de Turing réversibles. Récursive insolubilité en $n \in \mathbb{N}$ de l'équation $u = \theta^n u$, où θ est un isomorphisme de codes. Comptes rendus des séances de l'académie des sciences **257**, 2597–2600 (1963)

Meer, K., Michaux, C.: A survey on real structural complexity theory. Bull. Belg. Math. Soc. **4**, 113–148 (1997)

Morita, K., Shirasaki, A., Gono, Y.: A 1-tape 2-symbol reversible Turing machine. Trans. IEICE **E72**(3), 223–228 (1989)

Naughton, T.J., Woods, D.: On the computational power of a continuous-space optical model of computation. In: Margenstern, M., Rogozhin, Y. (eds.) MCU 2001. LNCS, vol. 2055, pp. 288–299. Springer, Heidelberg (2001). doi:10.1007/3-540-45132-3_20

Senot, M.: Modèle géométrique de calcul: fractales et barrières de complexité. Thèse de doctorat, Université d'Orléans, June 2013. https://tel.archives-ouvertes.fr/tel-00870600

Sipser, M.: Introduction to the Theory of Computation. PWS Publishing Co., Boston (1997). ISBN 0-534-944728-X

Syropoulos, A.: Hypercomputation. Springer, Heidelberg (2010)

Takeuti, I.: Transition systems over continuous time-space. Electron. Notes Theoret. Comput. Sci. **120**, 173–186 (2005). doi:10.1016/j.entcs.2004.06.043

Weihrauch, K.: Introduction to computable analysis. Texts in Theoretical Computer Science. Springer, Berlin (2000)

Woods, D., Naughton, T.J.: An optical model of computation. Theoret. Comput. Sci. **334**(1–3), 227–258 (2005). doi:10.1016/j.tcs.2004.07.001

Woods, D., Neary, T.: The complexity of small universal Turing machines: a survey. Theoret. Comput. Sci. **410**(4–5), 443–450 (2009). doi:10.1016/j.tcs.2008.09.051

Contributed Papers

Real-Time Computability of Real Numbers
by Chemical Reaction Networks

Xiang Huang[1], Titus H. Klinge[2], James I. Lathrop[1(✉)], Xiaoyuan Li[1],
and Jack H. Lutz[1]

[1] Department of Computer Science, Iowa State University, Ames, IA 50012, USA
{huangx,jil,forbesii,lutz}@iastate.edu
[2] Department of Computer Science, Grinnell College, Grinnell, IA 50112, USA
klingeti@grinnell.edu

Abstract. We explore the class of real numbers that are computed in
real time by deterministic chemical reaction networks that are *integral* in
the sense that all their reaction rate constants are positive integers. We
say that such a reaction network *computes* a real number α in *real time* if
it has a designated species X such that, when all species concentrations
are set to zero at time $t = 0$, the concentration $x(t)$ of X is within 2^{-t} of
the fractional part of α at all times $t \geq 1$, and the concentrations of all
other species are bounded. We show that every algebraic number is real
time computable by chemical reaction networks in this sense. We discuss
possible implications of this for the 1965 Hartmanis-Stearns conjecture,
which says that no irrational algebraic number is real time computable
by a Turing machine.

Keywords: Analog computation · Chemical reaction networks ·
Hartmanis-Stearns conjecture · Real-time computability

1 Introduction

Chemical reaction networks, originally conceived as descriptive mathematical
models of molecular interactions in well-mixed solutions, are also widely used
as prescriptive mathematical models for engineering molecular processes. In the
present century this prescriptive use of chemical reaction networks has been
automated by software compilers that translate chemical reaction networks into
complete specifications of DNA strand displacement systems that simulate them
[4,21]. Chemical reaction networks have thus become the programming language
of choice for many molecular programming applications.

There are several alternative semantics (operational meanings, also called
kinetics) for chemical reaction networks. The two oldest and most widely used
of these are *deterministic mass-action semantics* and *stochastic mass-action
semantics*. This paper concerns the former of these, so for the rest of this paper,

This research was supported in part by National Science Foundation Grants 1247051
and 1545028.

M.J. Patitz and M. Stannett (Eds.): UCNC 2017, LNCS 10240, pp. 29–40, 2017.
DOI: 10.1007/978-3-319-58187-3_3

a *chemical reaction network* (briefly, a *CRN* or a *deterministic CRN*) is a chemical reaction network with deterministic mass-action semantics. This model is precisely specified in Sect. 2 below. For this introduction, it suffices to say that such a CRN is an ordered pair $N = (S, R)$, where S is a finite set of *species* (abstract molecule types), and R is a finite set of *reactions*, each of which has some form like:

$$X + Z \xrightarrow{k} 2Y + Z,$$

where $X, Y, Z \in S$ are species and $k \in [0, \infty)$ is a *rate constant*. A *state* x of N specifies the real-valued *concentration* $x(Y) \in [0, \infty)$ of each species Y. Given an initial state $x(0)$ at time $t = 0$, deterministic mass action semantics specify the (continuous) evolution of the state $x(t)$ over time.

Even prior to the implementation of chemical reaction networks as a programming language it was clear that they constitute a model of computation. In the case of deterministic CRNs, Stansifer has reportedly proven [5] that this model is Turing universal, i.e., that every algorithm can be simulated by a deterministic CRN. (Note: The title of [17] seems to make this assertion, but the paper only exhibits a way to use deterministic CRNs to simulate finite Boolean circuits.)

Deterministic chemical reaction networks are an analog model of computation, both in the intuitive sense that their states are vectors of real-valued concentrations that vary continuously over real-valued times and in the technical sense that they are a special case of Shannon's *general purpose analog computer* (*GPAC*) [20], as explained in Sect. 5 below.

This paper studies the ability of deterministic CRNs to rapidly compute real numbers in the following analog sense. We say that a deterministic CRN *computes* a real number α *in real time* if it has a designated species X such that the following three things hold. (See Sect. 3 for more details.) First, the CRN's reaction rate constants are positive integers, and it is initialized with all concentrations set to zero at time $t = 0$. This implies that the CRN is, like any reasonable model of computation, finitely specifiable. It also implies that only countably many real numbers are real time CRN-computable. Second, there is some fixed bound on all the CRN's concentrations. Under deterministic mass-action semantics, this implies that all the reaction rates of the CRN are bounded, whence time is a meaningful resource. Third, the concentration $x(t)$ of the designated species $X(t)$ is within 2^{-t} of the fractional part $\{\alpha\} = \alpha - \lfloor \alpha \rfloor$ of α – i.e., within t bits of accuracy of $\{\alpha\}$ – at all times $t \geq 1$. We say that the real number α is *real time computable by chemical reaction networks* (briefly, *real time CRN-computable*) if there is a CRN that computes α in this sense. Elementary properties of real-time CRN computability are developed in Sect. 3.

Our main theorem says that every algebraic number (i.e., every real solution of a polynomial with integer coefficients) is real time CRN-computable. This result is proven in Sect. 4. We conjecture, but have not proven at the time of this writing, that some transcendental (i.e., non-algebraic) real numbers are also real time CRN-computable.

Our main theorem is a counterpoint – but not a disproof – of the 52-year-old, open Hartmanis-Stearns conjecture that no algebraic irrational is real time computable by a Turing machine [12]. Section 5 discusses this contrast in some detail and poses two questions whose answers would shed further light on the computational complexities of algebraic irrationals.

2   Chemical Reaction Networks

A *species* is an abstract type of molecule. Capital Roman characters such as X, Y, and Z are commonly used to distinguish different species, but we also use decorations such as X_0, $\widehat{Y}$, and $\overline{Z}$ to distinguish them.

A *reaction* over a finite set S of species is a tuple $\rho = (\boldsymbol{r}, \boldsymbol{p}, k) \in \mathbb{N}^S \times \mathbb{N}^S \times (0, \infty)$ and its components are called the *reactant vector*, the *product vector*, and the *rate constant*, respectively. (Here $\mathbb{N}^S$ denotes the set of all functions mapping S into $\mathbb{N}$.) To avoid excessive use of subscripts, for a reaction ρ we use $\boldsymbol{r}(\rho)$, $\boldsymbol{p}(\rho)$, and $k(\rho)$ to access the individual components of ρ. A species $Y \in S$ is called a *reactant* if $\boldsymbol{r}(Y) > 0$, called a *product* if $\boldsymbol{p}(Y) > 0$, and called a *catalyst* if $\boldsymbol{r}(Y) = \boldsymbol{p}(Y) > 0$. The *net effect* of reaction $\rho = (\boldsymbol{r}, \boldsymbol{p}, k)$ is the vector $\Delta\rho \in \mathbb{N}^S$ defined by

$$\Delta\rho(Y) = \boldsymbol{p}(Y) - \boldsymbol{r}(Y)$$

for each $Y \in S$.

A *chemical reaction network* (*CRN*) is an ordered pair $N = (S, R)$ where S is a finite set of species and R is a finite set of reactions over S. Although this completes the definition of the *syntax* of a CRN, we have yet to define the *semantics* used in this paper.

Under *deterministic mass action semantics*, the *state* of a CRN $N = (S, R)$ at time t is a real-valued vector $\boldsymbol{x}(t) \in [0, \infty)^S$, and for $Y \in S$, we call $\boldsymbol{x}(t)(Y)$ the *concentration* of Y in $\boldsymbol{x}(t)$. We also write $y(t) = \boldsymbol{x}(t)(Y)$ to denote the concentration of species Y at time t.

The *rate* of a reaction ρ at time t is defined as

$$\text{rate}_\rho(t) = k(\rho) \cdot \prod_{Y \in S} y(t)^{\boldsymbol{r}(\rho)(Y)}. \tag{2.1}$$

This conforms to the so-called law of mass action which states that the rate of a reaction is proportional to the concentration of its reactants.

The *total rate of change* of a species $Y \in S$ depends on the rates of all reactions in the CRN and the magnitude of their net effect on Y. Therefore the concentration $y(t)$ conforms to the ordinary differential equation (ODE)

$$\frac{dy}{dt} = \sum_{\rho \in R} \Delta\rho(Y) \cdot \text{rate}_\rho(t) \tag{2.2}$$

If we let $\mathcal{E}_Y$ be the ODE above for each $Y \in S$, then the *mass action system* of the CRN is the coupled system

$$(\mathcal{E}_Y \mid Y \in S). \tag{2.3}$$

Given an initial state $x_0 \in [0, \infty)^S$, the behavior of the CRN is defined as the solution to the initial value problem (IVP) of the mass action system (2.3) along with the initial condition

$$y(0) = x_0(Y)$$

for each $Y \in S$.

3 Real-Time CRN Computability

We say that a real number α is *real time computable by chemical reaction networks* (briefly, *real time CRN-computable*), and we write $\alpha \in \mathbb{R}_{RTCRN}$, if there exist a chemical reaction network $N = (S, R)$ and a species $X \in S$ with the following three properties:

1. (integrality). The CRN N is *integral* in the sense that:

$$k(\rho) \in \mathbb{Z}^+ \tag{3.1}$$

   for all $\rho \in R$.
2. (boundedness). There is a constant $\beta > 0$ such that, if N is initialized with $y(0) = 0$ for all $Y \in S$, then, for all $Y \in S$ and $t \in [0, \infty)$,

$$y(t) \leq \beta. \tag{3.2}$$

3. (real-time convergence). If N is initialized with $y(0) = 0$ for all $Y \in S$, then for all $t \in [1, \infty)$,

$$|x(t) - \{\alpha\}| \leq 2^{-t} \tag{3.3}$$

   where $\{\alpha\} = \alpha - \lfloor \alpha \rfloor$ is the *fractional part* of α.

The integrality condition (3.1) prevents the CRN N from "cheating" by having information about α explicitly encoded into its rate constants. To see that this is necessary to avoid nontriviality, note that, for any $\alpha \in (0, 1)$, if the simple CRN:

$$\emptyset \xrightarrow{\alpha} X,$$
$$X \xrightarrow{1} \emptyset$$

is initialized with $x(0) = 0$, then

$$x(t) = \alpha(1 - e^{-t})$$

for all $t \in [0, \infty)$.

The boundedness condition (3.2) imposes a "speed limit" on the CRN N. This prevents N from acting as a "Zeno machine" (machine that does infinite work in finite time) in the sense of Weyl [26]. More precisely, condition (3.2) ensures that the reaction rates (2.1) of N are all bounded. This implies that the arc length of the curve traced by the state $x(s)$ of N for $0 \leq s \leq t$ is $\theta(t)$, i.e., bounded above and below by positive constant multiples of t. Pouly [1,19] has convincingly argued (in a more general setting) that this arc length, which we call the *reaction clock time*, is the correct measure of the time that a CRN spends computing during the interval $[0, t]$. Viewed in this light, condition (3.2) ensures that t is, up to constant multiples, an accurate measure of the reaction clock time of N during the interval $[0, t]$.

The real-time convergence condition (3.3) requires the CRN N to compute $\{\alpha\}$ to within t bits of accuracy by each time $t \geq 1$. Note that this is an *analog* approximation of $\{\alpha\}$. The CRN N is not required to explicitly produce symbols in any sort of digital representation of $\{\alpha\}$.

For the rest of this paper, unless otherwise noted, all CRNs $N = (S, R)$ are assumed to be initialized with $y(0) = 0$ for all $Y \in S$.

To save space in our first lemma, we define the predicate

$$\Phi_{\tau,\gamma}(\alpha) \equiv \text{there exist a CRN } N = (S, R) \text{ and a species } X \in S$$
$$\text{satisfying (3.1) and (3.2) such that, for all } t \in [\tau, \infty),$$
$$|x(t) - \{\alpha\}| \leq e^{-\gamma t}$$

for each $\tau, \gamma \in (0, \infty)$ and $\alpha \in \mathbb{R}$. Note that $\Phi_{1, \ln 2}(\alpha)$ is the assertion that $\alpha \in \mathbb{R}_{RTCRN}$. The following convenient lemma says that the definition of $\mathbb{R}_{RTCRN}$ is robust with respect to linear changes in condition (3.2).

Lemma 3.1. *For each $\alpha \in \mathbb{R}$ the following conditions are equivalent.*

1. $\alpha \in \mathbb{R}_{RTCRN}$.
2. There exists $\tau, \gamma \in (0, \infty)$ such that $\Phi_{\tau,\gamma}(\alpha)$ holds.
3. For every $\tau, \gamma \in (0, \infty)$, $\Phi_{\tau,\gamma}(\alpha)$ holds.

Proof. Let $\alpha \in \mathbb{R}$. It is clear that $(3) \Rightarrow (1) \Rightarrow (2)$, so it suffices to prove that $(2) \Rightarrow (3)$. For this, let N, X, τ, and γ testify that (2) holds, i.e., let N and X testify that $\Phi_{\tau,\gamma}(\alpha)$ holds. To prove (3), let $\widehat{\tau}, \widehat{\gamma} \in (0, \infty)$. It suffices to show that $\Phi_{\widehat{\tau}, \widehat{\gamma}}(\alpha)$ holds. Let

$$a = \max\left\{\left\lceil \frac{\tau}{\widehat{\tau}} \right\rceil, \left\lceil \frac{\widehat{\gamma}}{\gamma} \right\rceil\right\},$$

and let $\widehat{N} = (S, \widehat{R})$, where

$$\widehat{R} = \{(r, p, ak) \mid (r, p, k) \in R\}.$$

That is, $\widehat{N}$ is exactly like N, except that each rate constant of N has been multiplied by the positive integer a. Then $\widehat{N}$ is an integral CRN that is a "sped up version" of N in the sense that, for all $y \in S$ and $t \in [0, \infty)$,

$$y_{\widehat{N}}(t) = y_N(at), \tag{3.4}$$

where y_N and $y_{\widehat{N}}$ are the values of y in N and $\widehat{N}$, respectively. This immediately implies that $\widehat{N}$ satisfies (3.2). Now let $t \in [\widehat{\tau}, \infty)$. Then $at \in [\tau, \infty)$, so our assumption $\Phi_{\tau,\gamma}(\alpha)$ tells us that

$$|x_{\widehat{N}}(t) - \{\alpha\}| = |x_N(at) - \{\alpha\}|$$
$$\leq e^{-\gamma at}$$
$$\leq e^{-\widehat{\gamma}t},$$

affirming $\Phi_{\widehat{\tau},\widehat{\gamma}}(\alpha)$. $\qquad\square$

The following lemma is a warm-up for our examination of $\mathbb{R}_{RTCRN}$

Lemma 3.2. $\mathbb{Q} \subsetneqq \mathbb{R}_{RTCRN}$

Proof. If $\alpha \in \mathbb{Z}$, then the CRN

$$X \xrightarrow{1} \emptyset$$

satisfies

$$|x(t) - \{\alpha\}| = x(t) = e^{-t} \leq 2^{-t},$$

so $\alpha \in \mathbb{R}_{RTCRN}$. If $\alpha \in \mathbb{Q} \setminus \mathbb{Z}$, then we can write $\{\alpha\} = \frac{a}{b}$, where $a, b \in \mathbb{Z}^+$. Then the integral CRN

$$\emptyset \xrightarrow{a} X$$
$$X \xrightarrow{b} \emptyset$$

satisfies

$$x(t) = \frac{a}{b}(1 - e^{-bt}),$$

so $\alpha \in \mathbb{R}_{RTCRN}$ by Lemma 3.1. This shows that $\mathbb{Q} \subseteq \mathbb{R}_{RTCRN}$.

To see that $\mathbb{Q} \neq \mathbb{R}_{RTCRN}$, it suffices to show that $\frac{1}{\sqrt{2}} \in \mathbb{R}_{RTCRN}$. Since the integral CRN

$$\emptyset \xrightarrow{1} X$$
$$2X \xrightarrow{2} X$$

satisfies

$$x(t) = \frac{1}{\sqrt{2}}\left(\frac{1 - e^{-2\sqrt{2}t}}{1 + e^{-2\sqrt{2}t}}\right),$$

we have that

$$\left|x(t) - \frac{1}{\sqrt{2}}\right| = \frac{1}{\sqrt{2}}\left(\frac{e^{-2\sqrt{2}t}}{1 + e^{-2\sqrt{2}t}}\right)$$
$$\leq \frac{1}{\sqrt{2}}e^{-2\sqrt{2}t} < e^{-2\sqrt{2}t},$$

so $\frac{1}{\sqrt{2}} \in \mathbb{R}_{RTCRN}$ by Lemma 3.1. $\qquad\square$

Computable real numbers were introduced by Turing [23,24] and have been extensively investigated [14,25].

A real number α is *computable*, and we write $\alpha \in \mathbb{R}_{comp}$, if there is a computable function $\widehat{\alpha} : \mathbb{N} \to \mathbb{Q}$ such that, for all $r \in \mathbb{N}$

$$|\widehat{\alpha}(r) - \alpha| \le 2^{-r}.$$

Lemma 3.3. $\mathbb{R}_{RTCRN} \subsetneq \mathbb{R}_{comp}$

Proof. Let $\alpha \in \mathbb{R}_{RTCRN}$, and let $N = (S, R)$ and $X \in S$ testify to this fact. Let $Y_1, \ldots, Y_n$ be the distinct species in S. Then the ODEs (2.2) can be written in the form

$$y_1' = f_1(y_1, \ldots, y_n),$$
$$\vdots \tag{3.5}$$
$$y_n' = f_n(y_1, \ldots, y_n),$$

where $f_1, \ldots, f_n$ are polynomials with integer coefficients. By the boundedness condition (3.2) and Theorem 16 of [8], the solution $\boldsymbol{y} : [0, \infty) \to [0, \infty)^n$ of (3.5) is polynomial time computable. It follows by the real-time convergence condition (3.3) that α is computable in polynomial time in the sense of Ko [14]. Hence, $\alpha \in \mathbb{R}_{comp}$.

It is well known [14] that not every computable real is computable in polynomial time, so the preceding paragraph proves the lemma. $\qquad\square$

4   Algebraic Numbers Are Real Time CRN Computable

This section is devoted to proving the following result, which is our main theorem.

Theorem 4.1. *Every algebraic number is an element of* $\mathbb{R}_{RTCRN}$.

Our proof of Theorem 4.1 uses the stability theory of ordinary differential equations. We review the elements of this theory that we need here, referring the reader to standard textbooks (e.g., [13,22]) for more thorough treatments.

We first note that the ordinary differential equations (2.2) of a CRN $N = (S, R)$ are *autonomous*, meaning that they only depend on the time t via the species concentrations $y(t)$. Hence, if we let $Y_1, \ldots, Y_n$ be the distinct species in S, then the ODEs (2.2) can be written as

$$y_1' = f_1(y_1, \ldots, y_n),$$
$$\vdots \tag{4.1}$$
$$y_n' = f_n(y_1, \ldots, y_n),$$

where $f_1, \ldots, f_n : \mathbb{R}^n \to \mathbb{R}$ are polynomials. If we let $\boldsymbol{f}_N : \mathbb{R}^n \to \mathbb{R}^n$ be the function whose components are $f_1, \ldots, f_n$, then (4.1) can be written in the vector form

$$\boldsymbol{x}' = \boldsymbol{f}_N(\boldsymbol{x}). \tag{4.2}$$

The *Jacobian matrix* of the CRN N is the Jacobian matrix of $\boldsymbol{f}_N$, i.e., the $n \times n$ matrix

$$J_N = \begin{pmatrix} \frac{\partial f_1}{\partial y_1} & \cdots & \frac{\partial f_1}{\partial y_n} \\ \vdots & \ddots & \vdots \\ \frac{\partial f_n}{\partial y_1} & \cdots & \frac{\partial f_n}{\partial y_n} \end{pmatrix}.$$

More precisely, the *Jacobian matrix* of N *in a state* $\boldsymbol{x} \in [0, \infty)^S$ is the matrix $J_N(\boldsymbol{x})$ in which each of the partial derivatives in J_N is evaluated at the point $\boldsymbol{x}$. The *eigenvalues* of the CRN N *in a state* $\boldsymbol{x} \in [0, \infty)^S$ are the eigenvalues of the matrix $J_N(\boldsymbol{x})$, i.e., the numbers $\lambda \in \mathbb{C}$ for which there exists $\boldsymbol{y} \in \mathbb{R}^n$ such that $J_N(\boldsymbol{x})(\boldsymbol{y}) = \lambda \boldsymbol{y}$.

A *fixed point* of the CRN N is a state $\boldsymbol{z} \in [0, \infty)^S$ such that $\boldsymbol{f}_N(\boldsymbol{z}) = 0$. A fixed point $\boldsymbol{z}$ of N is *exponentially stable* if there exist $\alpha, \delta, C \in (0, \infty)$ such that, for all $\boldsymbol{x}_0 \in [0, \infty)^S$ with $|\boldsymbol{x}_0 - \boldsymbol{z}| \leq \delta$, if N is initialized with $\boldsymbol{x}(0) = \boldsymbol{x}_0$, then, for all $t \in [0, \infty)$,

$$|\boldsymbol{x}(t) - \boldsymbol{z}| \leq Ce^{-\alpha t} |\boldsymbol{x}(0) - \boldsymbol{z}|. \tag{4.3}$$

The well known *exponential stability theorem*, specialized to CRNs, says that a fixed point $\boldsymbol{z}$ of N is exponentially stable if all its eigenvalues have negative real parts [13,22].

In this paper we define a real number $\alpha \in \mathbb{R}$ to be *negative eigenvalue computable by chemical reaction networks* (briefly, *negative eigenvalue CRN-computable*), and we write $\alpha \in \mathbb{R}_{NECRN}$, if there exist a CRN $N = (S, R)$, a species $X \in S$, and a state $\boldsymbol{z} \in [0, \infty)^S$ with $\boldsymbol{z}(X) = \alpha$ such that the following conditions hold.

1. (integrality). The CRN N is integral as in (3.1).
2. (boundedness). Concentrations are bounded as in (3.2).
3. (fixed point). $\boldsymbol{z}$ is a fixed point of N.
4. (negative eigenvalues). All the eigenvalues of N in the state $\boldsymbol{z}$ have negative real parts.
5. (basin of attraction). If α, δ, and C are the constants testifying that $\boldsymbol{z}$ is exponentially stable, then the zero-vector $\boldsymbol{0} \in [0, \infty)^S$ defined by $\boldsymbol{0}(Y) = 0$ for all $Y \in S$ satisfies $|\boldsymbol{0} - \boldsymbol{z}| \leq \delta$.

Our interest in the class $\mathbb{R}_{NECRN}$ is that the following three lemmas suffice to prove Theorem 4.1.

Lemma 4.2. $\mathbb{R}_{NECRN}$ *is a countable subfield of* $\mathbb{R}$.

Lemma 4.3. $\mathbb{R}_{NECRN} \subseteq \mathbb{R}_{RTCRN}$.

Proof. Let $\alpha \in \mathbb{R}_{NECRN}$. We show in the full version of this paper that $\alpha - \lfloor \alpha \rfloor$ is also in $\mathbb{R}_{NECRN}$. Without loss of generality, we assume that $\alpha \in (0, 1)$. Hence we have $\alpha = \{\alpha\}$ in the following proof.

By the definition of $\mathbb{R}_{NECRN}$, there is a CRN $N = (S, R)$, a species $X \in S$, and a state $\boldsymbol{z} \in [0, \infty)^S$ with $\boldsymbol{z}(X) = \alpha$ such that $\boldsymbol{0}$ falls in the basin of attraction of $\boldsymbol{z}$. Therefore $\lim_{t \to \infty} \boldsymbol{x}(t) = \boldsymbol{z}$.

Since $J_N(z)$ has eigenvalues with negative real parts, then z is exponentially stable, i.e. there exist $\alpha, \delta, C \in (0, \infty)$ such that for all $\mathbf{x}_0 \in [0, \infty)^S$ with $|\mathbf{x}_0 - z| \leq \delta$, if N is initialized with $\mathbf{x}(0) = \mathbf{x}_0$, then for all $t \in [0, \infty)$, $|\mathbf{x}(t) - z| \leq Ce^{-\alpha t}|\mathbf{x}_0 - z|$.

Consider the CRN N initialized so that $\boldsymbol{x}(0) = \mathbf{0}$. Since $\lim_{t \to \infty} \boldsymbol{x}(t) = z$, we let τ_0 be the point such that $|\boldsymbol{x}(\tau_0) - z| \leq \delta$, then by exponential stability of z, we have $|\boldsymbol{x}(t) - z| \leq Ce^{-\alpha(t - \tau_0)}|\mathbf{x}_0 - z|$ for all $t \geq \tau_0$.

Pick a number γ such that,

$$Ce^{\alpha \tau_0}|\mathbf{x}_0 - z| \leq e^{\gamma \tau_0}$$

and let $a = \left\lceil \frac{2\gamma}{\alpha} \right\rceil$, construct a "sped up version" of N, $\widehat{N}$, as in Lemma 3.1, by multiplying each rate constant of N by the positive integer a. Now let $\tau = \frac{\tau_0}{a}$. Then for all $t \geq \tau$, i.e., $at \geq \tau_0$, we have

$$
\begin{aligned}
|\boldsymbol{x}_{\widehat{N}}(X)(t) - \alpha| &\leq |\mathbf{x}_{\widehat{N}}(t) - z| \\
&= |\boldsymbol{x}(at) - z| \\
&\leq Ce^{-\alpha(at - \tau_0)}|\mathbf{x}_0 - z|, \text{ since } at \geq \tau_0 \\
&\leq e^{\gamma \tau_0}e^{-a\alpha t} \\
&\leq e^{\gamma \tau_0}e^{-2\gamma t} \\
&\leq e^{-\gamma t}
\end{aligned}
$$

Hence $\Phi_{\tau, \gamma}(\alpha)$ holds, and by Lemma 3.1, $\alpha \in \mathbb{R}_{RTCRN}$. $\square$

Lemma 4.4. *Every algebraic number is an element of* $\mathbb{R}_{NECRN}$.

5   Discussion

We have shown that every algebraic number is real time computable by deterministic chemical reaction networks. What does this say about the complexity of algebraic irrationals on other models of computation?

The first thing to understand here is that deterministic chemical reaction networks are, in a very precise sense, a model of analog computation. In 1941, Shannon [20] introduced the *general-purpose analog computer (GPAC)*. A GPAC is a mathematical abstraction of the *differential analyzer*, an early analog computer that Bush [3] had constructed at MIT, and which Shannon had operated as a graduate research assistant. The GPAC model has been corrected and otherwise modified a number of times over the years [7,9,15,18]. Its present form can be characterized in terms of circuits, but it is more simply characterized as a system

$$\boldsymbol{y}'(t) = \boldsymbol{p}(t, y), \tag{5.1}$$

of ordinary differential equations, where $\boldsymbol{p}$ is a vector of polynomials. A deterministic CRN is thus a special type of GPAC of the form

$$\boldsymbol{y}'(t) = \boldsymbol{p}(y), \tag{5.2}$$

where each component p_i of p has the "kinetic" form $p_i(y) = q_i(y) - y_i r_i(y)$, with q_i and r_i having nonnegative coefficients [11]. Our CRNs in this paper have the added constraints that all the coefficients in these polynomials are integers, and all concentrations are initialized to zero. Our main theorem thus implies that all algebraic numbers are real time computable by GPACs that have only finite information coded into their parameters and initializations.

We now turn from analog computation to discrete computation. A famous conjecture of Hartmanis and Stearns [12] says that no irrational algebraic number is real time computable by a Turing machine. This conjecture has been open for over 50 years. Fischer et al. [6] proved that real-time computability on a Turing machine is equivalent to linear-time computability on a Turing machine. Hence the Hartmanis-Stearns conjecture is equivalent to the statement that no irrational algebraic number is linear-time computable by a Turing machine. As observed by Gurevich and Shelah [10], linear time is a very model-dependent notion. Hence, as stated, the Hartmanis-Stearns conjecture is a very specific conjecture about linear-time computation on Turing machines.

Our main theorem does not disprove the Hartmanis-Stearns conjecture (nor was it intended to), but conceptually locating the gap between our main theorem and a disproof of the Hartmanis-Stearns conjecture would shed light on the computational complexities of algebraic irrationals. This raises the following questions.

Question 1. Can CRNs in our model (or GPACs with only finite information encoded into their parameters and initializations) produce in linear time the individual digits of each real number that is real time CRN-computable? If so, our main theorem implies that the Hartmanis-Stearns conjecture fails for analog computation. If not, the Hartmanis-Stearns conjecture holds for analog computation and is essentially about producing the individual digits as opposed to the analog convergence that we have used here.

Question 2. Is there a reasonable discrete model of computation on which some algebraic irrational can be computed in linear time? If so, then the Hartmanis-Stearns conjecture is either false or model-dependent. If not, then the Hartmanis-Stearns conjecture is true in a strong, model-independent way, at least for discrete computation. (Note that "reasonable" here excludes models that perform numerical operations faster than we know how to do them, because Brent [2] has shown how to compute $\sqrt{2}$ in linear time if integer multiplication can be done in linear time. See also [16].)

References

1. Bournez, O., Graça, D.S., Pouly, A.: Polynomial time corresponds to solutions of polynomial ordinary differential equations of polynomial length: the general purpose analog computer and computable analysis are two efficiently equivalent models of computations. In: Proceedings of the 43rd International Colloquium on Automata, Languages, and Programming, Leibniz International Proceedings in Informatics, vol. 55, pp. 109:1–109:15. Schloss Dagstuhl-Leibniz-Zentrum fuer Informatik (2016)

2. Brent, R.P.: Fast multiple-precision evaluation of elementary functions. J. ACM (JACM) **23**(2), 242–251 (1976)
3. Bush, V.: The differential analyzer. A new machine for solving differential equations. J. Frankl. Inst. **212**(4), 447–488 (1931)
4. Chen, Y.-J., Dalchau, N., Srinivas, N., Phillips, A., Cardelli, L., Soloveichik, D., Seelig, G.: Programmable chemical controllers made from DNA. Nat. Nanotechnol. **8**(10), 755–762 (2013)
5. Cook, M., Soloveichik, D., Winfree, E., Bruck, J.: Programmability of chemical reaction networks. In: Condon, A., Harel, D., Kok, J.N., Salomaa, A., Winfree, E. (eds.) Algorithmic Bioprocesses. Natural Computing Series, pp. 543–584. Springer, Heidelberg (2009)
6. Fischer, P.C., Meyer, A.R., Rosenberg, A.L.: Time-restricted sequence generation. J. Comput. Syst. Sci. **4**(1), 50–73 (1970)
7. Graça, D.S., Costa, J.F.: Analog computers and recursive functions over the reals. J. Complex. **19**(5), 644–664 (2003)
8. Graça, D.S., Pouly, A.: Computational complexity of solving polynomial differential equations over unbounded domains. Theoret. Comput. Sci. **626**(2), 67–82 (2016)
9. Graça, D.S.: Some recent developments on Shannon's general purpose analog computer. Math. Logic Q. **50**(4–5), 473–485 (2004)
10. Gurevich, Y., Shelah, S.: Nearly linear time. In: Meyer, A.R., Taitslin, M.A. (eds.) Logic at Botik 1989. LNCS, vol. 363, pp. 108–118. Springer, Heidelberg (1989). doi:10.1007/3-540-51237-3_10
11. Hárs, V., Tóth, J.: On the inverse problem of reaction kinetics. Qual. Theory Differ. Equ. **30**, 363–379 (1981)
12. Hartmanis, J., Stearns, R.E.: On the computational complexity of algorithms. Trans. Am. Math. Soc. **117**, 285–306 (1965)
13. Hirsch, M.W., Smale, S., Devaney, R.L.: Differential Equations, Dynamical Systems, and an Introduction to Chaos. Academic Press, Cambridge (2012)
14. Ko, K.-I.: Complexity Theory of Real Functions. Birkhäuser, Basel (1991)
15. Lipshitz, L., Rubel, L.A.: A differentially algebraic replacement theorem, and analog computability. Proc. Am. Math. Soc. **99**(2), 367–372 (1987)
16. Lipton, R.J.: Why the Hartmanis-Stearns conjecture is still open (2012). Blog post. https://rjlipton.wordpress.com/2012/06/15/why-the-hartmanis-stearns-conjecture-is-still-open/. Accessed 3 Feb 2017
17. Magnasco, M.O.: Chemical kinetics is Turing universal. Phys. Rev. Lett. **78**(6), 1190–1193 (1997)
18. Pour-el, B.M.: Abstract computability and its relations to the general purpose analog computer. Trans. Am. Math. Soc. **199**, 1–28 (1974)
19. Pouly, A.: Continuous models of computation: from computability to complexity. Ph.D. thesis, École Polytechnique et Universidad do Algarve (2015)
20. Shannon, C.E.: Mathematical theory of the differential analyzer. Stud. Appl. Math. **20**(1–4), 337–354 (1941)
21. Soloveichik, D., Seelig, G., Winfree, E.: DNA as a universal substrate for chemical kinetics. Proc. Nat. Acad. Sci. **107**(12), 5393–5398 (2010)
22. Teschl, G.: Ordinary Differential Equations and Dynamical Systems. Graduate Studies in Mathematics, vol. 140. American Mathematical Society, Providence (2012)
23. Turing, A.M.: On computable numbers, with an application to the Entscheidungsproblem. Proc. Lond. Math. Soc. **42**(1), 230–265 (1936)

24. Turing, A.M.: On computable numbers, with an application to the Entscheidungsproblem. A correction. Proc. Lond. Math. Soc. **43**(2), 544–546 (1937)
25. Weihrauch, K.: Computable Analysis: An Introduction. Springer, Heidelberg (2000)
26. Weyl, H.: Philosophie der Mathematik und Naturwissenschaft: Nach der 2. Walter de Gruyter GmbH & Co KG (1927). Philosophy of Mathematics and Natural Science, Princeton University Press; with a new introduction by Frank Wilczek (2009)

Towards Temporal Logic Computation Using DNA Strand Displacement Reactions

Matthew R. Lakin[1,2,3(✉)] and Darko Stefanovic[2,3]

[1] Department of Chemical and Biological Engineering, University of New Mexico,
Albuquerque, NM, USA
[2] Department of Computer Science, University of New Mexico,
Albuquerque, NM, USA
{mlakin,darko}@cs.unm.edu
[3] Center for Biomedical Engineering, University of New Mexico,
Albuquerque, NM, USA

Abstract. Time-varying signals are ubiquitous throughout science, and studying the high-level temporal structure of such processes is of significant practical importance. In this context, techniques from computer science such as temporal logic are a powerful tool. Temporal logic allows one to describe temporal properties of time-varying processes, e.g., the order in which particular events occur. In this paper, we show that DNA strand displacement reaction networks can be used to implement computations that check certain temporal relationships within time-varying input signals. A key aspect of this work is the development of DNA circuits that incorporate a primitive memory, so that their behavior is influenced not just by the current observed chemical environment, but also by environments observed in the past. We formalize our circuit designs in the DSD programming language and use simulation results to confirm that they function as intended. This work opens up the possibility of developing DNA circuits capable of long-term monitoring of processes such as cellular function, and points to possible designs of future DNA circuits that can decide more sophisticated temporal logics.

1 Introduction

Dynamic processes that produce time-varying signals are found throughout nature. In molecular biology, for example, changes in levels of protein expression over time are a cornerstone of cellular regulatory systems. In this context, a molecular computing system able to analyze both the current state of the protein expression levels as well as the "historical record" of previously observed protein expression levels would be able to make sophisticated decisions about the cell state by observing protein expression over an extended period of time.

A fundamental goal of research into molecular computing and synthetic biology is to *produce* time-varying signals, an early example being the "repressilator" oscillatory network produced by a ring of three mutually inhibiting transcription factors [1]. However, there has been relatively little work on using molecular computers or engineered bacteria to *analyze* time-varying signals. This is because

© Springer International Publishing AG 2017
M.J. Patitz and M. Stannett (Eds.): UCNC 2017, LNCS 10240, pp. 41–55, 2017.
DOI: 10.1007/978-3-319-58187-3_4

published research on molecular circuit designs has focused in large part on analyzing the input signals present in the chemical environment *at a particular point in time*. Examples include previously published DNA circuits that implement digital logic circuits [2], analog neural networks [3], and population protocols for approximate majority voting [4]. The most notable examples of synthetic biomolecular circuits designed for processing temporal signals are designs for DNA strand displacement circuits to carry out discrete-time signal processing tasks using a combination of "fast" and "slow" reactions [5], and prior experimental work on using recombinase enzymes to integrate expressed single-stranded DNA into the genomes of engineered bacteria, as a record of events experienced in the past [6]. More tangentially related to the current topic are studies of learning and adaptation in engineered biochemical circuits [7,8] and abstract chemical reaction networks [9–11], including DNA strand displacement learning circuits [9,12] designed using buffered strand displacement gates [13]. The concept of memory in DNA reaction networks has also been explored indirectly via a postulated DNA implementation of a "reservoir computing" system [14], as well as by proposals for chemical memories implemented using bistable switches [15] and delay lines [16].

In this paper we broaden the focus of research in molecular circuit design to produce systems that can analyze the current chemical environment not just in isolation, but rather in the context of previous states of the chemical environment observed by the system. We will present designs for DNA strand displacement circuits that can analyze the temporal structure of time-varying input signals modeled as a sequence of additions of input strands that are subsequently degraded. (This could be realized in an experimental system by using RNA inputs and RNAse-containing media [17].) The structures of our networks will be designed such that the reactions triggered by the additions of the input strands at different points in time activate strand displacement gates whose outputs act as a "memory", so that the state of the network effectively stores information about its past experience. By cascading multiple such gates together, we will design systems in which the cascade only executes to completion (and thus produces an output signal) if the input signals are presented in an order that satisfies the temporal relationships that are encoded in the network structure, and we will verify correct operation of our circuit designs using computational simulations of an ordinary differential equation (ODE) model of the circuit kinetics. This work therefore demonstrates a path toward molecular computing systems that can analyze non-trivial temporal properties of time-varying signals, with potential applications in the analysis of biochemical systems and in the diagnosis and treatment of disease.

The remainder of this paper is structured as follows. We introduce a basic logic of temporal relationships for sequential signals in Sect. 2 and present designs for DNA strand displacement circuits that test whether a sequential presentation of input signals satisfies a particular formula in Sect. 3. We present results from simulations of example circuits in Sect. 4 and conclude with a discussion in Sect. 5.

2   A Logic of Temporal Relationships for Sequential Signals

In this section we present a logic for expressing simple temporal relationships within sequential input sequences. We begin by specifying the well-formed formulae φ of our logic, which are as follows:

$$\varphi ::= A \sqsubset B \sqsubset \cdots \sqsubset Z$$
$$\mid \varphi_1 \wedge \varphi_2$$
$$\mid \varphi_1 \vee \varphi_2$$

The formula $A \sqsubset B$ should be read as "A before B", and its intended meaning is that an occurrence of input A is observed in the sequence of input signals before an occurrence of B is observed.

Let σ range over finite input sequences $[A_1 \cdots A_n]$. These finite input sequences will serve as models for our formulae. We now define satisfaction of a formula by an input sequence, written $\sigma \vDash \varphi$, by recursion on the structure of formulae, as follows:

$$\sigma \vDash A \sqsubset B \sqsubset \cdots \sqsubset Z \iff \exists \sigma_0, \sigma_1, \ldots, \sigma_n.\ \sigma = [\sigma_0 A \sigma_1 B \sigma_2 \cdots \sigma_{n-1} Z \sigma_n]$$
$$\sigma \vDash \varphi_1 \wedge \varphi_2 \iff \sigma \vDash \varphi_1 \wedge \sigma \vDash \varphi_2$$
$$\sigma \vDash \varphi_1 \vee \varphi_2 \iff \sigma \vDash \varphi_1 \vee \sigma \vDash \varphi_2$$

The semantics of conjunction and disjunction formulae are standard. A BEFORE formula $A \sqsubset B \sqsubset \cdots \sqsubset Z$ is satisfied by an input sequence σ if there exist subsequences $\sigma_0, \sigma_1, \ldots, \sigma_n$ such that the input sequence σ can be expressed as the concatenation $[\sigma_0 A \sigma_1 B \sigma_2 \cdots \sigma_{n-1} Z \sigma_n]$. In other words, we require that there exist occurrences of $A, B, \ldots, Z$ that appear in the input sequence in the correct order. Since we do not place any restrictions on the number of times a particular input may appear in the sequence, there may be multiple different decompositions of this form, but we do not distinguish this in the semantics.

For example, consider the formula $\varphi = (A \sqsubset B) \wedge (A \sqsubset C)$. The following both hold:

$$[ABC] \vDash (A \sqsubset B) \wedge (A \sqsubset C)$$
$$[ACB] \vDash (A \sqsubset B) \wedge (A \sqsubset C),$$

but, on the other hand,

$$[CAB] \nvDash (A \sqsubset B) \wedge (A \sqsubset C)$$

because A does not occur before C in the input sequence $[CAB]$.

In the following section, we will define a translation of these formulae into chemical reaction networks realized using DNA strand displacement reactions. Viewed through the prism of the definitions presented above, the DNA reaction networks that we define will each embody a formula φ, and we will challenge the network by a sequence of input additions that correspond to a particular input sequence σ. Then, the goal for our network will be to respond (by producing a "high" concentration of an output species) iff the input sequence satisfies the implemented formulae, i.e., iff $\sigma \vDash \varphi$ holds.

We note that, if all signals mentioned in the subformula are unique, we can define the $A \sqsubseteq B \sqsubseteq \cdots \sqsubseteq Z$ construct in terms of the two-input case, as follows:

$$A_1 \sqsubseteq A_2 \sqsubseteq \cdots \sqsubseteq A_n = \bigwedge_{i \in \{1,...,n\}} \bigwedge_{j \in \{i+1,...,n\}} (A_i \sqsubseteq A_j)$$

However, for the purposes of producing a DNA implementation it is simpler and far more compact to implement the extended version using a single gate cascade than it is to add a large number of additional AND gates. In defining this expansion, we consider two formulae φ_1 and φ_2 to be equivalent iff they are satisfied by the same set of input sequences, i.e., iff $\{\sigma \mid \sigma \vDash \varphi_1\} = \{\sigma \mid \sigma \vDash \varphi_2\}$.

3   DNA Circuits for Analyzing Temporal Relationships

In this section we present our designs for DNA circuits that carry out temporal analysis tasks. Our chemical framework of choice is DNA strand displacement [18]. Strand displacement is a scheme for implementing reaction networks in DNA in which "signals" are represented by single strands of DNA in solution that interact with structures known as "gates" that consume certain input strands from solution and release output strands, with different sequences, back into solution. These interactions take place via a two-step process: the incoming strand first binds reversibly to the gate via a short complementary domain known as a "toehold", which positions the incoming strand to initiate the process of "branch migration", whereby it competes with the neighboring incumbent strand to bind to the gate. When the branch migration process completes, the end result is that the input strand is bound to the gate and the incumbent strand is released into solution. By designing structures so that multiple strand displacement reactions proceed in a pre-defined sequence, possibly with the assistance of other "fuel" molecules in solution, strand displacement gates can implement a range of computational tasks. Here we focus in particular on two-domain DNA strand displacement [19], a simplified form of strand displacement that has proven itself amenable to experimental implementation [4].

We will model our systems using the DSD programming language, which provides a text-based syntax for representing strand displacement gate structures and processes that represent the combination of multiple different gates and strands in a dilute, well-mixed solution. The semantics of the DSD language specifies a formally-defined translation of those structural models into a kinetic model, by enumerating all possible interactions between the DNA components that could possibly occur within the system. For reasons of brevity, we do not provide a full exposition of the DSD language here, rather, we refer the reader to previous work that formally defines the syntax and semantics of the DSD language [13].

In the DSD syntax, each two-domain signal A in our circuits will be represented by a DSD module $\texttt{Signal}(A)$ that just consists of a single two-domain DNA strand $<ta\hat{}\ a>$. Furthermore, we will model the input signals that appear in temporal formulae as degrading over time (with standard exponential decay kinetics) when they are free in solution. This approximates a real-world temporal analysis scenario where the DNA circuit is monitoring the occurrence of environmental markers that may also be consumed by other downstream chemical reactions that are taking place simultaneously.

We will implement our DNA reaction networks using three different kinds of strand displacement gates: "catalyst" reaction gates that implement abstract reactions of the form $C + X \rightarrow C + Z$, "AND" logic gates that compute the logical conjunction of two inputs, and "OR" logic gates that compute the logical disjunction of two inputs. Reaction schemes for each of these gate types are presented in Fig. 1.[1] The basic pattern is that the input strands bind to an input-accepting gate in a pre-programmed order, and with the help of a fuel strand enable the release of an intermediate strand that initiates a similar cascade of reactions on an output-releasing gate, which requires additional fuel strands to be present and which releases the output strands from the gate into solution. The function implemented by each gate is dependent on the patterns of input and output signals, so, for example, the "AND" gate has two input strands that must both be consumed in order to enable the release of a single output strand.

We can now define translation of the language of formulae from Sect. 2 into DNA strand displacement systems. For a formula φ, the translation $[\![\varphi]\!]$ returns a DSD process P (which is just a collection of parallel DSD species) and an output species Z. The output species is the one whose concentration will indicate the output of the computation: if it goes high then the input signal sequence *satisfies* the formula encoded in the network, and if it stays low then the input signal sequence *does not satisfy* the formula encoded in the network.

The definition of the translation is presented in Fig. 2. The key case is the one for the formulae with actual temporal meaning, that is, the formulae of the form $A \sqsubset B \sqsubset \cdots \sqsubset Y$. Temporal formulae such as this are encoded using a cascade of strand displacement catalyst gates, catalyzed by the input signals $A, B, \ldots, Y$. These reactions catalyze conversion of a "substrate" species X_1 to X_2, then to X_3, and so on, until the final catalyst gate produces the overall output species Z. (The DSD process produced by this case of the translation also includes the initial substrate species X_1.) Crucially, the input signals $A, B, \ldots, Y$ catalyze this cascade of reactions *in the same order as they appear in the temporal formula*, ordered from earliest to latest. This means that, if the input signals are actually observed in this order, then these catalyst reactions will all be activated in turn, leading to the eventual release of the output species. However, if one or more of the input signals is never observed, or is observed out of the required sequence, then one or more of the catalyst reactions will not be

---

[1] See the Supporting Information (available from the first author's web page) for full DSD code listings for each system simulated in this paper, including full definitions of the modules.

(a) `CatalystGate`(C,X,Z) implements $C + X \rightarrow C + Z$

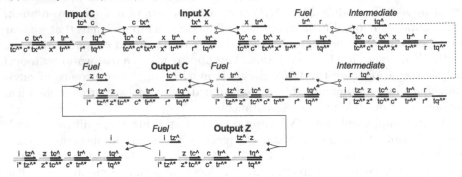

(b) `AndGate`(X,Y,Z) implements $Z = X \wedge Y$

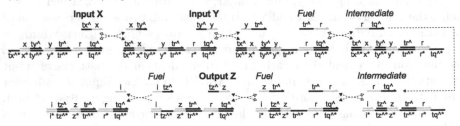

(c) `OrGate`(X,Y,Z) implements $Z = X \vee Y$

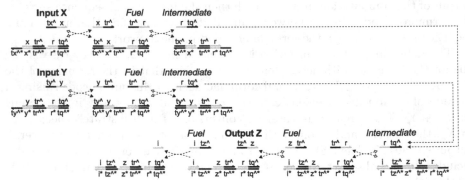

Fig. 1. Strand displacement reactions that implement (a) the abstract catalytic reaction $C + X \rightarrow C + Z$, (b) the "AND" logic gate $Z = X \wedge Y$, and (c) the "OR" logic gate $Z = X \vee Y$.

activated, and thus the output species will not be produced at the end of the cascade. Hence, presence or absence of the output species corresponds to whether the input signals were observed in the correct temporal ordering, and hence to satisfaction of the temporal formula. The key to our circuit design is that the

$$[\![A \sqsubseteq B \sqsubseteq \cdots \sqsubseteq Y]\!] = (P, Z)$$

where $P = \texttt{Signal}(X_1)$
$\mid \texttt{CatalystGate}(A, X_1, X_2)$ $\# A + X_1 \to A + X_2$
$\mid \texttt{CatalystGate}(B, X_2, X_3)$ $\# B + X_2 \to B + X_3$
$\mid \cdots$ $\# \cdots$
$\mid \texttt{CatalystGate}(Y, X_n, Z)$ $\# Y + X_n \to Y + Z$
and $X_1, X_2, \ldots, X_n, Z$ are fresh species

$$[\![\varphi_1 \wedge \varphi_2]\!] = (P, Z)$$

where $P = P_1 \mid P_2 \mid \texttt{AndGate}(X_1, X_2, Z)$ $\# Z = X_1 \wedge X_2$
and $[\![\varphi_1]\!] = (P_1, X_1)$
and $[\![\varphi_2]\!] = (P_2, X_2)$
and Z is a fresh species

$$[\![\varphi_1 \vee \varphi_2]\!] = (P, Z)$$

where $P = P_1 \mid P_2 \mid \texttt{OrGate}(X_1, X_2, Z)$ $\# Z = X_1 \vee X_2$
and $[\![\varphi_1]\!] = (P_1, X_1)$
and $[\![\varphi_2]\!] = (P_2, X_2)$
and Z is a fresh species

Fig. 2. Definition of the translation $[\![\varphi]\!]$ of formulae φ into a DSD process P and an output species Z. The "comments" on the right-hand side provide informal descriptions of the meaning of the DSD modules, for clarity. We note that, in the first case of the translation, the execution time is proportional to the number of compared signals.

conversion of the substrate species, catalyzed by the input signals, serves as a "memory" that records the past experience of the networks interactions with the observed input species. This ensures that each input signal will be (almost) entirely removed from the system before the next input signal is presented, which prevents unwanted circuit responses being generated by overlapping input signals.

The remaining two cases of the definition of the translation, for "AND" and "OR" formulae, are comparatively straightforward. In each of these cases, the processes and output species for the two subformulae are defined recursively, and these processes are then returned in parallel with a new logic gate whose input species are the output species from the translations of the two subformulae and whose output species is a freshly generated signal.

4   Simulation Results

DNA strand displacement reaction networks that carry out temporal analysis tasks were compiled and simulated using Visual DSD [20], using the "Infinite" semantics. In particular, we used the "beta" version of DSD [21] that supports scheduled additions of inputs via mixing events as well as the inclusion of user-defined reactions.

Briefly, the simulation conditions were as follows: we use a 1000 nM initial concentration of strand displacement gates and fuel strands, with the exception of the output part of the "OR" gates, of which we use 10 nM (so that the output signal strength of the "OR" gate is the same whether one or two positive input signals is present). The input signal sequence was implemented by adding a

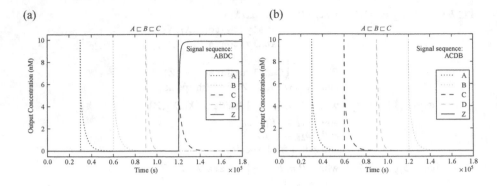

Fig. 3. Concentration time courses of selected species for the formula $A \sqsubset B \sqsubset C$, for input signal sequences (a) $[ABDC]$ and (b) $[ACDB]$.

10 nM concentration of each input signal in a pre-programmed order, with a wait time between addition of input signals of 30000 s. The degradation rate of those input signals is $0.0005\,\mathrm{s}^{-1}$, that is, for each input signal A a unimolecular degradation reaction $A \to \varnothing$ with rate constant $k=0.0005\,\mathrm{s}^{-1}$ was explicitly added to the model. We kept this rate constant between simulations for consistency, however, our circuits could be adapted to different degradation rates by modifying the rates of the other DNA reactions, e.g., by lengthening toehold domains or by increasing fuel concentrations. Additionally, for each input-consuming gate, a 10 nM concentration of the strand that is displaced by the binding of the first input was also included, to provide a degree of "backpressure" that presents inputs from being sequestered by binding to the gates, which allows them to be released back into solution so that they can be degraded. This is crucial to prevent unwanted circuit responses triggered by input signals left over from earlier stages of the simulation.[2]

Figure 3 shows time courses of the concentrations of the input signals (A, B, C, and D) and the output species (Z) for two different input signal sequences, $[ABDC]$ and $[ACDB]$, when added to a network that tests satisfaction of the formula $A \sqsubset B \sqsubset C$. Hence, we expect that the response (i.e., the final concentration of the output species Z) should be high for the input sequence $[ABDC]$ (since A appears before B and B appears before C in $[ABDC]$) but should be low for the input sequence $[ACDB]$ (since B does not appear before C in $[ACDB]$). Indeed, the plots from Fig. 3 confirm this, as the final concentration of Z is high in part (a) but low in part (b). Thus, in this case the circuit construction for testing satisfaction of temporal formulae functioned as intended.

We further investigated the correctness of our circuit designs for all possible permutations of the input signals A, B, C, and D, for three different formulae that collectively employ all three kinds of formula: $A \sqsubset B \sqsubset C$, $(A \sqsubset B) \wedge$

---

[2] See the Supporting Information (available from the first author's web page) for full DSD code listings for each system simulated in this paper, including full definitions of the modules.

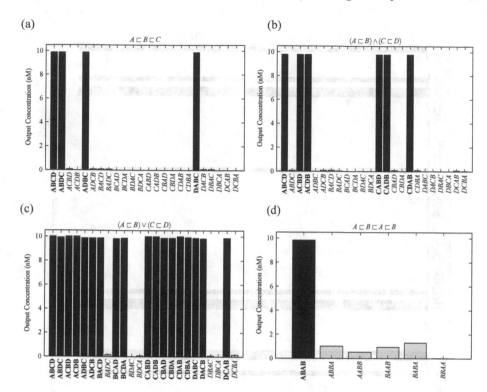

Fig. 4. Final concentrations of the output species for formulae (a) $A \sqsubseteq B \sqsubseteq C$, (b) $(A \sqsubseteq B) \wedge (C \sqsubseteq D)$, (c) $(A \sqsubseteq B) \vee (C \sqsubseteq D)$, and (d) $A \sqsubseteq B \sqsubseteq A \sqsubseteq B$. In parts (a)–(c), the bars represent the output for all possible permutations of the input signals A, B, C, and D, and in part (d) the bars represent the output for all possible permutations of the input signals A, A, B, and B. Black bars (with boldface labels) represent those simulations where the formula is satisfied by the corresponding input signal sequence, and light grey bars (with italic labels) represent those simulations where it is *not* satisfied.

$(C \sqsubseteq D)$, and $(A \sqsubseteq B) \vee (C \sqsubseteq D)$. The final concentrations of the output species in each case are presented in Fig. 4(a)–(c), where the black bars are those where the output of the circuit is expected to be high, and the light grey bars are those where the output of the circuit is expected to be low. For clarity, the labels of those bars were typeset in boldface and italics, respectively. These results show that, in all cases, the circuit designs were able to correctly compute whether the corresponding formula was satisfied by the particular sequence of input signals, with a high ratio of signal to leakage (unwanted circuit activation). This indicates that our compilation from formulae into DNA circuits is functioning correctly.

Since our definitions do not require that the inputs in the input sequence are unique, we also used our circuits to test satisfaction of the temporal formula $A \sqsubseteq B \sqsubseteq A \sqsubseteq B$, which is satisfied by any input sequence in which A appears followed by B, followed again by A and then B. Figure 4(d) shows the final concentration

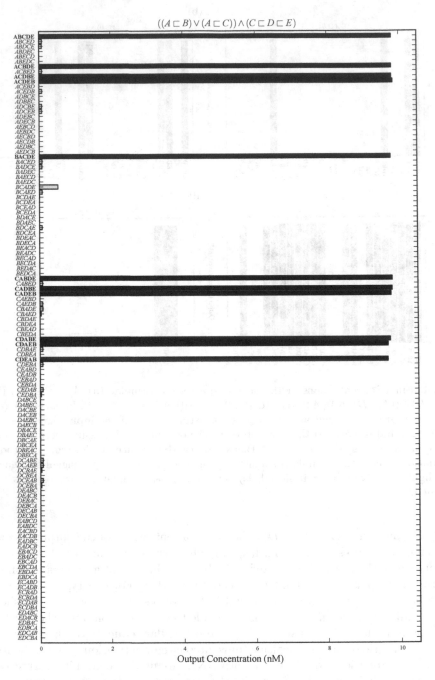

Fig. 5. Final concentrations of the output species for the formula $((A \sqsubseteq B) \vee (A \sqsubseteq C))$ $\wedge (C \sqsubseteq D \sqsubseteq E)$. The bars represent the output for all possible permutations of the input signals A, B, C, D, and E. Formatting of bars and labels is as explained in Fig. 4.

Table 1. Circuit sizes for circuits simulated in Figs. 4 and 5, expressed in terms of the number of species. The number of species in each case was calculated by considering all logic gates and fuel strands that must be present initially, as well as all signals that are either present initially or introduced during the course of the experiment.

Formula	Signals	Gate structures	Fuel strands	Total
$A \sqsubset B \sqsubset C$	5	6	15	26
$(A \sqsubset B) \wedge (C \sqsubset D)$	6	10	24	40
$(A \sqsubset B) \vee (C \sqsubset D)$	6	11	25	42
$A \sqsubset B \sqsubset A \sqsubset B$	3	8	20	31
$((A \sqsubset B) \vee (A \sqsubset C)) \wedge (C \sqsubset D \sqsubset E)$	8	19	44	71

of the output species from this circuit, when tested with all possible input signal sequences that contain two occurrences of A and two occurrences of B. As the figure shows, the circuit only returned a high response for the input sequence $[ABAB]$, as expected. Thus, our DNA circuits could be used as a crude means of detecting switching, or oscillatory, input signals.

Finally, we tested a larger example formula $(((A \sqsubset B) \vee (A \sqsubset C)) \wedge (C \sqsubset D \sqsubset E))$ that includes all three formula types in a single circuit, with a total of five input signals (A, B, C, D, and E). This gave a total of 120 distinct input sequences, and the final concentration of the output species for each of these is presented in Fig. 5. Again, we see that the circuit responded correctly, with a high output concentration whenever the input signal sequence satisfied the encoded formula, and a low output concentration whenever it did not. This demonstrates that our approach can be scaled to larger circuits that implement larger formulae. This scalability is further demonstrated by Table 1, which presents the circuit sizes for all five example circuits from Figs. 4 and 5. The largest of these circuits, the one from Fig. 5, has a number of initial species roughly comparable to the largest strand displacement system implemented experimentally [2], which contained 74 initial DNA species, excluding inputs.

5   Discussion

To summarize, we have shown that our simple logic of temporal relationships, which allows properties concerning the relative temporal occurrence of signals in a linear input sequence to be expressed, can be compiled systematically into DNA strand displacement reaction networks such that the output networks encode the semantics of the corresponding formulae. Then, when those networks are presented with a linear temporal sequence of input signals, each network produces a high concentration of its output species if the input signal sequence *satisfies* the encoded formula, and produces little or no output species if the input signal sequence *does not satisfy* the encoded formula. For simplicity, in our simulations we assumed that those input signals undergo exponential decay when free in solution. Our simulation results indicate that our circuit designs and compilation process function correctly for a range of input signals and different temporal formulae, and that our design approach can be scaled to larger formulae (subject to the usual limitations imposed by the DNA sequence space).

In practice, degrading inputs could be implemented by using RNA input strands (and RNA outputs from the catalyst gates) with nuclease-containing media [17] so that single-stranded RNA in solution is degraded. An alternative approach could be to include additional DNA circuit components that act as a sink for the input strands. We used two-domain strand displacement catalyst gates as the basis for our designs because of their highly modular and composable nature. However, an alternative framework could be the strand displacement catalyst system developed by Zhang et al. [22]. A practical advantage of this system is that it would require fewer strands for an experimental implementation. Furthermore, that catalyst design actually recycles the original input strand back into solution, as opposed to our design based on two-domain strand displacement in which a distinct copy of the input strand is released back into solution. Thus, this approach might be more easily integrated with the RNA-based approach to implementing degradable inputs, as discussed above.

Another alternative circuit design might employ fork gates instead of catalyst gates, which would mean that the input signals, once used by a gate to modify the populations of substrate species, would not be released back into solution at all. This could be a simpler solution for the purposes of building an experimental system but would mean that the circuit would have a significant impact on the system that it was measuring—a key rationale for using catalytic reactions is that the recycled input strands could continue to undergo reactions elsewhere in the system, thereby allowing our circuits to be used for real-time monitoring of biochemical systems, such as cellular regulatory networks, without significantly perturbing the system under observation. An additional advantage of using simpler strand displacement gates to implement temporal sensing is that most designs for multi-input strand displacement logic gates impose an implicit ordering on the binding of multiple inputs to the logic gate [23], thereby providing another alternative mechanism for the experimental implementation of temporal sensing.

The logic that we defined in Sect. 2 does not include negation, which is in keeping with previous work that used dual rail expansions to eliminate negation from DNA logic circuits [2]. In our logic, however, such expansions are more challenging. It is tempting to think that we can achieve a similar effect by using de Morgan's laws to push negations through conjunctions and disjunctions, and by expanding BEFORE formulae when the negations reach them, e.g.:

$$\neg(A_1 \sqsubset A_2 \sqsubset \cdots \sqsubset A_n) = \bigvee_{i \in \{1,\ldots,n\}} \bigvee_{j \in \{i+1,\ldots,n\}} (A_j \sqsubset A_i)$$

$$\neg(\varphi_1 \wedge \varphi_2) = (\neg\varphi_1) \vee (\neg\varphi_2)$$

$$\neg(\varphi_1 \vee \varphi_2) = (\neg\varphi_1) \wedge (\neg\varphi_2)$$

However, even for simple examples such as $\neg(A \sqsubset B)$, which expands to $B \sqsubset A$, this expansion misbehaves when one or both of the mentioned input signals are absent, e.g., $[AC] \not\vDash A \sqsubset B$ and $[AC] \not\vDash B \sqsubset A$. More disturbingly, $\neg(A \sqsubset A)$ expands to $A \sqsubset A$. Clearly more work on the semantics of negation in logics such as this is required. Indeed, one can think of our logic as a quantifier-free, negation-free subset of first order logic where the temporal ordering between signals could be implemented as a ternary predicate over a signal sequence and the two signals in question, and in this view the implementation of negation is less problematic but would still require our DNA circuits to be able to detect the *absence* of a particular signal from the input sequence.

To simplify the presentation, in this paper we assumed that the times in which the different inputs are present in the system do not overlap. However, in practical applications the signals that we might want to analyze are unlikely to be so clear-cut and regimented. An obvious first step would be to relax the requirement that all inputs are non-overlapping, so there could be two or more input signals present in solution simultaneously. In this case, the $A \sqsubset B$ formula could be generalized to an $A \sqsubseteq B$ formula, which would be satisfied if A occurs before, or at the same time as, B, and the implementation would need to be generalized accordingly, e.g., by using cooperative hybridization to detect the simultaneous presence of input signals [24].

Another important generalization would be to handle input concentration profiles that change continuously over time, rather than being added at discrete points as in this paper. In this context, our circuits would likely need to discretize the incoming signals in terms of their concentration, as well as in time. For the former, prior work on digital and analog DNA circuits implemented using "seesaw gates" [2,3] employed a thresholding mechanism, which could be used to discretize concentrations of the signals in the input time course. To discretize signals in time, Jiang et al. [5] use both synchronous (via an oscillatory chemical "clock") and asynchronous (self-timed) approaches.

Finally, the logic that we implemented in this paper is relatively straightforward, as it just allows statements about the order in which different input signals were observed in the linear input sequence. However, there are many more temporal logics in practical and industrial use, such as computation tree logic (CTL), linear temporal logic (LTL), and interval temporal logic (ITL). These discrete-time logics deal with branching time, infinite linear time, and finite linear time, respectively, and include more powerful logical primitives such as checking whether a proposition is globally true, or eventually true, or true until some other proposition becomes true. In the case of CTL, there are also logical primitives to deal with whether these properties hold along all branching paths in time, or just some. Clearly, these are much more powerful logics than that which we defined in this paper. A fruitful direction for future research would be to investigate designs for DNA-based circuits that can decide satisfaction of these more powerful logics, or to recognize strings drawn from regular languages (in which case, the DNA network would encode a regular expression). These recognition tasks are non-trivial because solving them would require far more information about the past states observed by the network to be stored, such as the length of time that has passed since a given signal was observed. Tackling this problem in an efficient and scalable manner would require us to be able to use the same input signal irrespective of its position in the temporal ordering, and we note that previous work on chemical memories [15,16] provides a possible solution to these challenges associated with reusing inputs and deciding more sophisticated temporal logics.

Acknowledgments. This material is based upon work supported by the National Science Foundation under grants 1525553, 1518861, and 1318833.

References

1. Elowitz, M.B., Leibler, S.: A synthetic oscillatory network of transcriptional regulators. Nature **403**, 335–338 (2000)
2. Qian, L., Winfree, E.: Scaling up digital circuit computation with DNA strand displacement cascades. Science **332**, 1196–1201 (2011)
3. Qian, L., Winfree, E., Bruck, J.: Neural network computation with DNA strand displacement cascades. Nature **475**, 368–372 (2011)
4. Chen, Y.-J., Dalchau, N., Srinivas, N., Phillips, A., Cardelli, L., Soloveichik, D., Seelig, G.: Programmable chemical controllers made from DNA. Nat. Nanotechnol. **8**, 755–762 (2013)
5. Jiang, H., Salehi, S.A., Riedel, M.D., Parhi, K.K.: Discrete-time signal processing with DNA. ACS Synth. Biol. **2**(5), 245–254 (2013)
6. Farzadfard, F., Lu, T.K.: Genomically encoded analog memory with precise in vivo DNA writing in living cell populations. Science **346**(6211), 1256272 (2014)
7. Fernando, C.T., Liekens, A.M.K., Bingle, L.E.H., Beck, C., Lenser, T., Stekel, D.J., Rowe, J.E.: Molecular circuits for associative learning in single-celled organisms. J. Royal Soc. Interface **6**, 463–469 (2009)
8. McGregor, S., Vases, V., Husbands, P., Fernando, C.: Evolution of associative learning in chemical networks. PLoS Comput. Biol. **8**(11), e1002739 (2012)
9. Lakin, M.R., Minnich, A., Lane, T., Stefanovic, D.: Design of a biochemical circuit motif for learning linear functions. J. Royal Soc. Interface **11**(101), 20140902 (2014)
10. Banda, P., Teuscher, C., Lakin, M.R.: Online learning in a chemical perceptron. Artif. Life **19**(2), 195–219 (2013)
11. Banda, P., Teuscher, C., Stefanovic, D.: Training an asymmetric signal perceptron through reinforcement in an artificial chemistry. J. Royal Soc. Interface **11**, 20131100 (2014)
12. Lakin, M.R., Stefanovic, D.: Supervised learning in adaptive DNA strand displacement networks. ACS Synth. Biol. **5**(8), 885–897 (2016)
13. Lakin, M.R., Youssef, S., Cardelli, L., Phillips, A.: Abstractions for DNA circuit design. J. Royal Soc. Interface **9**(68), 470–486 (2012)
14. Goudarzi, A., Lakin, M.R., Stefanovic, D.: DNA reservoir computing: a novel molecular computing approach. In: Soloveichik, D., Yurke, B. (eds.) DNA 2013. LNCS, vol. 8141, pp. 76–89. Springer, Cham (2013). doi:10.1007/978-3-319-01928-4_6
15. Padirac, A., Fujii, T., Rondelez, Y.: Bottom-up construction of in vitro switchable memories. Proc. Natl. Acad. Sci. USA **109**(47), E3212–E3220 (2012)

16. Moles, J., Banda, P., Teuscher, C.: Delay line as a chemical reaction network. Parallel Process. Lett. **21**(1), 1540002 (2015)
17. O'Steen, M.R., Cornett, E.M., Kolpashchikov, D.M.: Nuclease-containing media for resettable operation of DNA logic gates. Chem. Commun. **51**, 1429–1431 (2015)
18. Zhang, D.Y., Seelig, G.: Dynamic DNA nanotechnology using strand-displacement reactions. Nat. Chem. **3**(2), 103–113 (2011)
19. Cardelli, L.: Two-domain DNA strand displacement. Math. Struct. Comput. Sci. **23**, 247–271 (2013)
20. Lakin, M.R., Youssef, S., Polo, F., Emmott, S., Phillips, A.: Visual DSD: a design and analysis tool for DNA strand displacement systems. Bioinformatics **27**(22), 3211–3213 (2011)
21. Yordanov, B., Kim, J., Petersen, R.L., Shudy, A., Kulkarni, V.V., Phillips, A.: Computational design of nucleic acid feedback control circuits. ACS Synth. Biol. **3**(8), 600–616 (2014)
22. Zhang, D.Y., Turberfield, A.J., Yurke, B., Winfree, E.: Engineering entropy-driven reactions and networks catalyzed by DNA. Science **318**, 1121–1125 (2007)
23. Soloveichik, D., Seelig, G., Winfree, E.: DNA as a universal substrate for chemical kinetics. Proc. Natl. Acad. Sci. USA **107**(12), 5393–5398 (2010)
24. Zhang, D.Y.: Cooperative hybridization of oligonucleotides. J. Am. Chem. Soc. **133**, 1077–1086 (2011)

Quantum-Dot Cellular Automata: A Clocked Architecture for High-Speed, Energy-Efficient Molecular Computing

Enrique P. Blair$^{(\boxtimes)}$

Baylor University, Waco, TX 76798, USA
Enrique_Blair@baylor.edu
http://web.ecs.baylor.edu/faculty/blair

Abstract. Quantum-dot cellular automata (QCA) is a non-transistor-based, classical computing paradigm. QCA devices may be implemented using mixed-valence molecules, and logic circuits are formed by laying out ordered arrays of QCA molecules on a substrate. Molecules are locally coupled via the Coulomb field. The molecular circuits can be clocked using an applied perpendicular electric field. A fully-quantum model of field-driven electron transfer (ET) is used to determine the ET rate for specific QCA candidate molecules. The diferrocenyl acetylene (DFA) molecule is taken as an example QCA molecule, and this model indicates DFA may support classical computation at speeds well beyond the GHz range.

Keywords: Molecular classical computing · High-speed computing · Beyond-CMOS computing · Energy-efficient computing

1 Introduction

Strong motivation now exists for alternatives to complementary metal-oxide semiconductor (CMOS) transistor-based computing. The scaling of CMOS devices to the very limits of scaling has resulted in device operation plagued by vast power dissipation [7]. Thus, modern CMOS-based computing devices use tremendous amounts of energy. Furthermore, it is estimated that by 2030, transistor-based information and communication technology will consume 30–50% of global power output and contribute up to 23% of global greenhouse gas emissions [1].

One general-purpose computing paradigm designed to circumvent such problems is quantum-dot cellular automata (QCA^1) [15,19]. QCA has a molecular

---

^{1} It is important to provide some disambiguation. In this context, "QCA" refers to "quantum-dot cellular automata," a paradigm for general-purpose *classical* computing proposed by Lent, Tougaw, Porod, and Bernstein [19]. Here, classical bits are manipulated by exploiting quantum phenomena: quantum tunneling, and the quantization of charge. "QCA" also stands for "quantum cellular automata," a model for universal *quantum* computing. Since this abbreviation has served extensively in the distinct bodies of literature, we seek to avoid further other confusion by providing this note here, and by continuing to use "QCA" to refer in this context only to the classical computing paradigm.

© Springer International Publishing AG 2017
M.J. Patitz and M. Stannett (Eds.): UCNC 2017, LNCS 10240, pp. 56–68, 2017.
DOI: 10.1007/978-3-319-58187-3_5

implementation, which supports ultra-high device densities and operating speeds, as well as low levels of power dissipation.

Here, an overview of the QCA paradigm is given. The discussion begins with a review of QCA with a focus on the molecular implementation of QCA devices. An architecture for logic based on electric-field-clocked molecular QCA is outlined. Then, a model of electric-field-driven electron transfer is described. This model is applied specifically to diferrocenyl acetylene (DFA) molecules, and electron transfer rates are calculated. The results suggest that if implemented using DFA-like molecules, molecular QCA can support very high operating speeds. These results are based on quantum mechanical theory and are part of a larger effort to realize molecular QCA computing devices.

2 Overview of QCA

The elementary computational device in QCA is the cell, a system having some mobile charge and several charge localization centers known as quantum dots. A schematic of a six-dot cell with two mobile electrons is shown in Fig. 1(a). Here, two degenerate, information-bearing, active states are labeled "0" and "1". The "Null" state bears no information, but enables clocking. Coulomb repulsion drives the alignment of active states for cells in juxtaposition, as in the row of cells in upper left of Fig. 1(b). This Coulomb coupling enables general-purpose computing using arrays of QCA cells. Figure 1(b) shows a logically complete set of devices: a QCA inverter circuit (lower left), and a three-input majority gate, which can function as a two-input, programmable AND/OR gate [19,27].

2.1 Implementing QCA

QCA has various implementations. Devices have been built and tested using metallic dots [22,26]. Also, cells have been constructed from semiconductor dots [8,13] and atomic dots [10]. Additionally, QCA may be implemented using mixed-valence compounds [15,17,20]. Here, individual molecules function as cells, with redox centers providing dots. This molecular implementation, like the atomic-scale implementation, supports room-temperature operation at switching speeds well beyond the GHz range. Other features of this implementation are synthetically uniform devices and ultra-high device densities in the molecular limit. Figure 2 shows ball-and-stick models of molecules studied as QCA candidates. An uncolocked diferrocenyl acetylene (DFA) molecule has two Fe centers, each providing a quantum dot. Designed specifically as a molecular QCA candidate, the zwitterionic nido carborane ($Fc^+FcC_2B_9^-$) is a self-doping molecule with three redox centers, and which supports electric-field clocking [6].

$Fc^+FcC_2B_9^-$ is a net neutral molecule with a hole as the mobile charge. Its dots are assigned labels in Fig. 3(a), and the three localized electronic states are shown in Fig. 3(b). When the hole occupies either of the active dots (0 or 1),

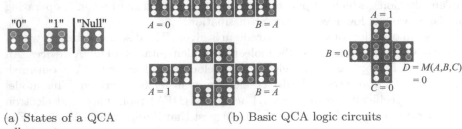

(a) States of a QCA
cell.

(b) Basic QCA logic circuits

Fig. 1. Constructing logic from QCA cells. (a) The localized states of a six-dot QCA cell. White discs represent quantum dots, and two red discs represent two mobile electrons. The smaller size of middle dots—called "null" dots—indicates that they lie on the substrate, whereas the corner dots—called "active" dots—are elevated above the substrate. (b) A set of QCA devices. Binary wires are implemented using a row of cells (upper left); diagonal intercellular coupling leads to bit inversion (lower left); and, a majority gate is the natural three-input (A, B, and C), single-output (D) logic gate in QCA. One input may be treated as a control bit, allowing the majority gate to function as a programmable, 2-input AND/OR gate. The majority gate and the inverter constitute a logically complete set.

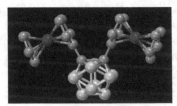

(a) Diferrocenyl acetylene (DFA).

(b) Zwitterionic nido carborane ($Fc^+FcC_2B_9{}^-$).

Fig. 2. Some molecules studied for QCA applications. (a) Diferrocenyl acetylene (DFA) provides a double-dot molecule. A pair of DFA molecules could be grouped to form a four-dot cell without null dots. (b) The $Fc^+FcC_2B_9{}^-$ molecule was designed and synthesized to function as clockable QCA half-cell. A pair of these molecules can function as a six-dot cell [see Fig. 1(a)].

the cell takes an active state, and a fixed neutralizing charge of one electron is uncovered on the null dot. When the cell is in the "Null" state, |Null⟩, the mobile charge covers the fixed neutralizing charge [6].

2.2 Clocked Molecular QCA Devices

Molecular QCA may be clocked using an externally-applied electric field [11]. Consider a pair of three-dot molecules like $Fc^+FcC_2B_9{}^-$ paired to function as a six-dot cell, as in of Fig. 1(a). Figure 4(a) shows such a system with the cell adsorbed onto the substrate such that the active dots are elevated above the null

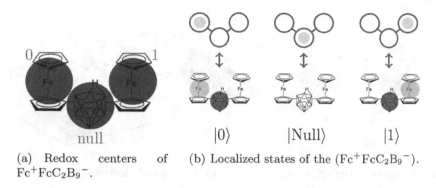

(a) Redox centers of $Fc^+FcC_2B_9^-$.

(b) Localized states of the $(Fc^+FcC_2B_9^-)$.

Fig. 3. Zwitterionic nido carborane $(Fc^+FcC_2B_9^-)$ provides a clockable three-dot cell. (a) $Fc^+FcC_2B_9^-$ has three redox centers, which function as dots: one dot on each of the two ferrocene groups, and one dot on the central carborane cage. (b) The localized states of a mobile hole define the states $|0\rangle$, $|Null\rangle$, and $|1\rangle$. In the active states, $|0\rangle$ or $|1\rangle$, the mobile hole (translucent green spot) occupies dot 0 or 1, leaving the carborane cage negatively ionized (red spot). In the null state, the mobile hole resides on the carborane cage, resulting in a molecule with zero dipole moment. The schematic picture above each state depicts only the dots (circles) and the mobile hole (solid green disc). Lines indicate tunneling paths. (Color figure online)

dots. Here, mobile electrons are assumed. A charged conductor buried beneath the device layer may be used to establish the applied clocking electric field. An electric field with a negative $\hat{z}$-component E_z will drive the cell to the active state preferred by interactions with neighboring cells. For $E_z > 0$, however, the mobile electrons will be attracted to the null dots, driving the cell to the null state regardless of neighbor interactions.

QCA circuits may be clocked using an array of wires, as in Fig. 4(b). Here, independently charged conductors establish an electric field with an inhomogeneous $\hat{z}$ component at the device layer on the substrate. Domains of this field with $E_z < 0$ will activate cells, whereas cells will be driven to the null state in regions where $E_z > 0$ [3].

Time-varying clocking excitations result in moving active domains. Consider the plan view of clocking wires shown in Fig. 5(a). The upper part of this subfigure shows one period of one particular phase of a four-phase clock. When the four-phase clocking excitation is applied to this array of wires, the electric field is established with active domains that propagate to the right.

The motion of active domains across the QCA plane drives the flow of data and calculations through QCA circuits. Figure 5(b) shows a shift register at work. Since bit packets exist only within active domains, the translation of an active domain across the device layer also moves the bit packet(s) contained within it. Thus, the active domain propagates rightward, driving the bit through the shift register. Calculations take place in the circuitry at the leading edge of the active domain, and erasures occur at the trailing edge.

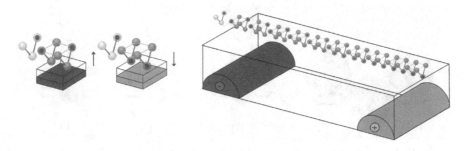

(a) A single clocked QCA cell.   (b) An array of clocked QCA cells.

Fig. 4. An externally-applied electric field is used to clock molecular QCA cells. (a) Two three-dot molecules are paired to form cells with six dots (dots are blue spheres). A single cell with two mobile electrons (red discs) is clocked to an active state by applying a negative charge to a buried conductor (red slab below the six-dot cell). The resulting electric field repels the electrons to the active dots, and the cell's state is determined by neighbor interactions. On the other hand, if the polarity of the conductor charge is reversed (indicated by the green color of the slab below the six-dot cell), the electric field reverses polarity, attracting the electrons to the null dots. The cell is clocked to the null state regardless of neighboring molecular states. (b) Two buried, independently-charged wires (red for negative and green for positive voltage) create an inhomogeneous electric field at the surface of the substrate. This field activates cells in certain regions called active domains, where the field's vertical ($\hat{z}$-component) is negative ($E_z < 0$). In null domains, $E_z > 0$, and cells are driven to the null state. (Color figure online)

More complex logic circuits are possible. Figure 6 shows the operation of a majority gate and a permuter circuit. Additionally, more complex clocking schemes can support memories and feedback loops [3,16]. Finally, an estimated upper limit of power dissipation in the clocking wires indicates that such dissipation will be quite manageable, even up to clocking speeds of 100 GHz [4].

2.3   Challenges in Molecular QCA: Circuit Layout and Bit Readout

Tasks taken for granted in CMOS technologies can become more challenging in molecular QCA because of the nanometer scale of the devices. We briefly discuss the challenges posed by the layout of molecules and the readout of QCA bits on individual molecules.

The layout of QCA cells on the substrate is important: a two-dimensional cellular lattice cannot provide adequate functionality for general-purpose computing. Photolithography is suitable for fabricating metal-dot and semiconductor-dot QCA arrays, but the layout of molecular QCA cells requires a different approach.

One interesting layout concept relies on self-assembly and involves the use of rafts or tiles formed using DNA [25] or PNA, as depicted in Fig. 7. These rigid structures will provide tiny molecular circuit boards for cells. Placement

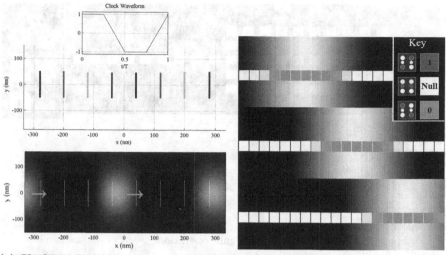

(a) Clocking wires create a time-dependent clocking field.   (b) A field-clocked shift register.

Fig. 5. A time-varying clocking electric field drives a bit packet through a shift register. (a) A layout of wires (middle) is charged using a four-phase clocking voltage. Here, the conductors are color-coded, indicating a separate phase of a four-phase clock. A single phase of this T-periodic clock is shown (top). The $\hat{z}$-component of the electric field, E_z (pointing out of the page), is plotted in the grayscale background of the bottom panel, with the position of wires marked using white lines. White regions of the field are active domains, and black regions are null domains. The phase sequence of the clock drives active domains rightward. (b) A "0" bit packet propagates rightward within an active domain along a row of cells, resulting in shift-register action. The state of the cell is encoded on its face color. Bit packets reside inside active domains, and thus are driven through registers or other circuitry by the motion of the active domains. Three panels show three successive snapshots in time.

and adhesion on the boards can be achieved by building into the DNA structure preferred attachment sites [see Fig. 7(a)]. The QCA cells, in turn, must have as part of their design an appendage to conjugate with an attachment site. The DNA structures may be programmed to link with one another, forming larger composite structures which can adhere to a substrate [see Fig. 7(b)] appropriately patterned through photolithography. The DNA tiles, then, are an intermediate layer between the QCA devices and the substrate. Seeman crystals [28] and DNA origami [24] can provide useful techniques for realizing tiles. While DNA tiles will have numerous stray charges likely disruptive to QCA operation, PNA structures are charge-neutral and may address the problem of stray charge on the tiles [18].

Another important task in QCA is that of reading the state of a nanometer-scale QCA cell. Single-electron transistors (SETs) provide one potential solution

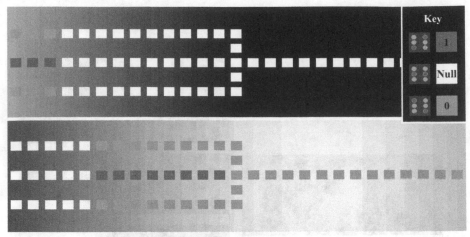

(a) Majority gate operation.

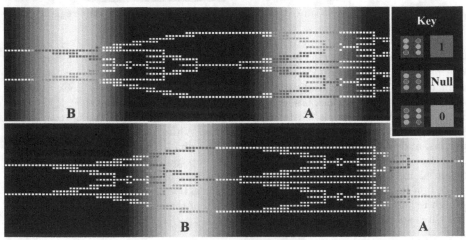

(b) Permuter operation.

Fig. 6. Time snapshots show the clocking field (grayscale background) driving data through circuits (colored foreground squares). (a) The majority gate processes three input bits. The clock shifts three bit packets $(0, 1, 0)$ into the device cell from the left. The result is a zero bit. (b) The clock pipelines data and calculations through a QCA permuter circuit. Two distinct active domains, labeled "A" and "B" drive two calculations through the circuit. The top panel shows that in domain A, a two-bit word entered the circuit as $a_{\text{top}}a_{\text{bottom}} = 01$ from the left (top panel), followed by $b_{\text{top}}b_{\text{bottom}} = 10$ in active domain B. At some time later, the bottom panel shows the word in domain A exiting, permuted to $a_{\text{top}}a_{\text{bottom}} = 10$. The word $b_{\text{top}}b_{\text{bottom}}$ will follow, being permuted to $b_{\text{top}}b_{\text{bottom}} = 01$ by the time domain B exits the circuit. Fixed cells are used to program majority gates as AND or OR gates. (Color figure online)

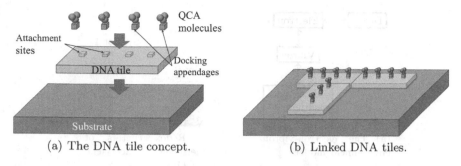

(a) The DNA tile concept.   (b) Linked DNA tiles.

Fig. 7. The use of DNA tiles in the layout of QCA circuits. (a) A DNA tile structure (yellow slab) provides a molecular circuit board for QCA cells. A particular QCA molecule (three clustered blue spheres) is designed with a docking appendage. Cells of this type conjugate with the DNA tile at built-in attachment sites. (b) DNA tiles can be programmed to link with other tiles and adhere to a substrate (gray slab). This will enable the assembly of large-scale molecular QCA circuits. (Color figure online)

[23]. SETs are exquisitely sensitive electrometers, having an unequivocal response to sub-nanometer displacements of single electrons [14].

3   Modeling Electron Transfer Rates in Molecular QCA

Modeling electron transfer in molecular QCA is of particular interest in QCA design. QCA device switching occurs through ET, and driven ET rates are directly related to maximum device operating speed, a key figure of merit for any computational hardware. Molecular QCA likely will support operation at speeds well beyond the GHz-range speeds seen in modern classical computing.

A fully-quantum model of field-driven, intramolecular ET was developed, in which a field-driven ET event is coupled to molecular vibrations [2]. The molecular vibrations, then, are damped by the thermal environment at temperature T—in this case, the substrate. This model is shown schematically in Fig. 8(a).

The model is described here briefly, in the context of a DFA molecule. In this model, the system energetics are captured in the Hamiltonian $\hat{H}(t)$, given by

$$\hat{H}(t) = -\gamma\hat{\sigma}_x + \frac{\Delta(t)}{2}\hat{\sigma}_z + \frac{g_{ev}}{2}\hat{\sigma}_z\hat{Q} + \frac{\hat{P}_Q^2}{2m} + \frac{m\omega_{\text{vib}}^2\hat{Q}^2}{2}. \tag{1}$$

Here, the first two terms describe the energetics of the two-state electronic system: γ is the hopping energy between the two dots [see Fig. 8(b)], and $\Delta(t)$ is the bias between the states $|1\rangle$ and $|0\rangle$ [see Fig. 8(c)] due to the electrostatic field from neighboring molecules. The operators $\hat{\sigma}_x$ and $\hat{\sigma}_z$ are two of the three Pauli operators. The nuclear displacements are captured in a single vibrational coordinate Q, which is modeled as a quantum harmonic oscillator with effective mass m and angular oscillation frequency ω_{vib}. The oscillator, the excitations of which

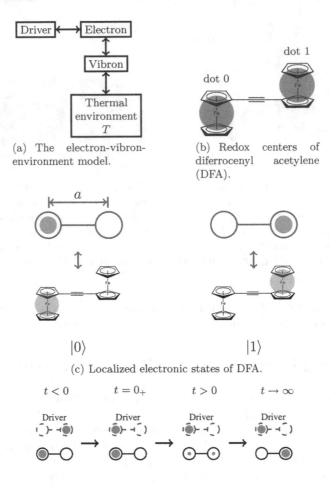

(a) The electron-vibron-environment model.

(b) Redox centers of diferrocenyl acetylene (DFA).

(c) Localized electronic states of DFA.

(d) A driven ET event in a two-dot QCA cell.

Fig. 8. A model of electric-field-driven ET in a target molecule. (a) A schematic block diagram of the quantum system. The electron and vibron comprise the model target system described by $\hat{\rho}(t)$. The charge configuration of the driver establishes a potential, which may transfer energy to or from the electron+vibron system, and the electron+vibron system may transfer energy to the environment at temperature T. (b) DFA has one redox center per ferrocene group, providing a total of two quantum dots. Dots are treated as points separated by distance a. (c) The localized states of a mobile electron (translucent red disc) define the states $|0\rangle$ and $|1\rangle$. The schematic picture above each state depicts the dots (blue circles) and the mobile electron (solid red disc). Lines indicate tunneling paths. (d) A set of four snapshots illustrate the driven ET process: (i) for $t < 0$ the driver configuration, along with a confining potential (not pictured) confine the target electron to the left dot; (ii) at $t = 0$, the confining potential is abruptly lifted, and the driver configuration is abruptly switched, establishing a Δ that drives ET to the right dot; (iii) at some time $0 < t \leq \infty$, the ET is in progress via quantum-mechanical, interdot tunneling; and, (iv) after sufficient time ($t \to \infty$), the electron has transferred to the right dot. (Color figure online)

are called "vibrons," has position and momentum operators $\hat{Q}$ and $\hat{P}_Q$, respectively, which may be expressed in terms of vibronic creation and annihilation operators, $\hat{a}_Q^\dagger$ and $\hat{a}_Q$, respectively:

$$\hat{Q} = \sqrt{\frac{\hbar}{2m\omega_{\text{vib}}}} \left(\hat{a}_Q^\dagger + \hat{a}_Q \right) \quad \text{and} \quad \hat{P}_Q = i\sqrt{\frac{m\omega_{\text{vib}}\hbar}{2}} \left(\hat{a}_Q^\dagger - \hat{a}_Q \right). \tag{2}$$

The energetics of the vibronic system alone are captured in the last two terms of $\hat{H}(t)$. The middle term in $\hat{H}(t)$ describes the electron-vibron coupling. This depends on the coupling constant $g_{ev} = \sqrt{2m\omega_{\text{vib}}\lambda}$, where λ is the reorganization energy of the molecule [2,12]. Molecular parameters such as γ, λ, m, and ω_{vib} may be obtained through quantum chemistry calculations or experiment. Here, the model parameters used are characteristic of DFA: $a = 0.67$ nm, $\gamma = 50$ meV, $m = 5.6$ amu, $\lambda = 440$ meV, and $f_{\text{vib}} = \omega_{\text{vib}}/2\pi = 298$ cm^{-1}. Of course, the model can be applied to other molecules as well, if the appropriate characteristic molecular parameters are provided.

To model environmental damping on this system, we assume that the environment is Markovian or memoryless. In this limit, model dynamics are described by the Lindblad equation [9,21]:

$$\frac{d}{dt}\hat{\rho} = -\frac{i}{\hbar}\left[\hat{H}, \hat{\rho}\right] + \mathfrak{D}, \quad \text{with} \quad \mathfrak{D} = \sum_{j=1}^{s} \hat{L}_j \hat{\rho} \hat{L}_j^\dagger - \frac{1}{2}\left\{ \hat{L}_j^\dagger \hat{L}_j, \hat{\rho} \right\}. \tag{3}$$

Here, the density operator $\hat{\rho}(t)$ describes the state of the electron+vibron system. Equivalent to the Schrödinger equation, the first term of (3) describes unitary evolution of the quantum mechanical system. The summation $\mathfrak{D}$, referred to as the Lindbladian term or the dissipator, describes the non-unitary and irreversible time evolution, including quantum decoherence and dissipative effects. Here, $[\hat{A}, \hat{B}]$ and $\{\hat{A}, \hat{B}\}$ are the commutator and the anticommutator, respectively, of operators $\hat{A}$ and $\hat{B}$; and, the operators $\{\hat{L}_j\}$ are Lindblad operators [5]. A particular model of environmental effects requires a specific choice of operators $\{\hat{L}_j\}$, and for this model, two operators were used:

$$\hat{L}_1 = \sqrt{\frac{1}{T_1}} \hat{a}_Q \quad \text{and} \quad \hat{L}_2 = \exp\left(-\frac{\hbar\omega}{2k_B T}\right) \sqrt{\frac{1}{T_1}} \hat{a}_Q^\dagger. \tag{4}$$

Here, T is the environmental temperature, k_B is Boltzmann's constant, and T_1 is the environmental energy relaxation time, which measures the strength of the vibron-environment interaction. This combination of $\hat{L}_1$ and $\hat{L}_2$ models a system that achieves a Boltzmann distribution in the steady state. Model dynamics are obtained by numerically solving Eq. (3).

A driven ET event is depicted schematically in Fig. 8(d). A neighboring driver cell and a confining potential are established to strongly favor electron occupation on the left dot of the target molecule for $t < 0$. Then, at $t = 0$, the confining potential is lifted, and the neighboring molecule is abruptly switched, driving rightward ET in the target molecule. From the solution $\hat{\rho}(t)$, we calculate t_{ET}, the time required for the electron to tunnel to the right dot, and the ET rate $k = 1/t_{ET}$. Figure 9 shows calculations of k using this model. This data indicates that DFA-based QCA cells could support THz-scale ET rates.

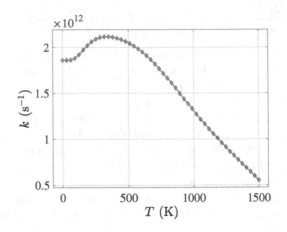

Fig. 9. The DFA molecule supports ET rates k of the order of 10^{12} transfers per second over the terrestrial range of temperatures. Calculations were done with parameters characteristic of DFA: interdot distance $a = 0.67$ nm, $\gamma = 50$ meV, $\lambda = 440$ meV, $m = 5.6$ amu, and $f_{\mathrm{vib}} = 298$ cm^{-1}.

4   Conclusion

QCA is a paradigm for computing with a molecular implementation that promises high device densities, room temperature operation, low power dissipation, and high operating speeds. While results for the DFA molecule indicate that THz-scale operation is possible, other molecules may support even higher speeds. The results presented here are theoretical in nature and are part of a larger, transdisciplinary effort to realize molecular QCA.

Modeling the performance of candidate QCA molecules is important because synthesizing and testing molecules is a time-consuming, labor-intensive project that at present, may take several person-years. This model, along with models of other relevant phenomena in QCA, can shed light on desirable molecular properties and provide a clear objective for molecular designers. Additionally, such models can close a theoretical design feedback loop that allows a candidate QCA molecule to be characterized using quantum chemistry calculations, to be evaluated for performance, and redesigned as necessary *before* undertaking the costly process of determining a synthesis route. These theoretical models can yield tremendous savings in time and effort in molecular design and synthesis, and can contribute directly to the realization of high-performance, energy-efficient, general-purpose computing devices based on molecular QCA.

References

1. Andrae, A., Edler, T.: On global electricity usage of communication technology: Trends to 2030. Challenges **6**, 117–157 (2015)
2. Blair, E., Corcelli, S., Lent, C.: Electric-field-driven electron-transfer in mixed-valence molecules. J. Chem. Phys. **145**, 014307 (2016)
3. Blair, E., Lent, C.: An architecture for molecular computing using quantum-dot cellular automata. In: IEEE Conference on Nanotechnology, vol. 1, pp. 402–405. IEEE (2003)
4. Blair, E., Yost, E., Lent, C.: Power dissipation in clocking wires for clocked molecular quantum-dot cellular automata. J. Comput. Electron. **9**(1), 49–55 (2010)
5. Breuer, H.P., Petruccione, F.: The Theory of Open Quantum Systems. Oxford Scholarship Online (2010)
6. Christie, J., Forrest, R., Corcelli, S., Wasio, N., Quardokus, R., Brown, R., Kandel, S., Lu, Y., Lent, C., Henderson, K.: Synthesis of a neutral mixed-valence diferrocenyl carborane for molecular quantum-dot cellular automata applications. Angew. Chem. **127**, 15668–15671 (2015)
7. Frank, D.: Power-constrained CMOS scaling limits. IBM J. Res. Dev. **46**(2/3), 235–244 (2002)
8. Gardelis, S., Smith, C., Cooper, J., Ritchie, D., Linfield, E., Jin, Y.: Evidence for transfer of polarization in a quantum dot cellular automata cell consisting of semiconductor quantum dots. Phys. Rev. B **67**(3), 033302 (2003)
9. Gorini, V., Kossakowski, A., Sudarshan, E.: Completely positive dynamical semigroups of n-level systems. J. Math. Phys. **17**(5), 821–825 (1976)
10. Haider, M.B., Pitters, J.L., DiLabio, G.A., Livadaru, L., Mutus, J.Y., Wolkow, R.A.: Controlled coupling and occupation of silicon atomic quantum dots at room temperature. Phys. Rev. Lett. **102**, 046805 (2009)
11. Hennessy, K., Lent, C.S.: Clocking of molecular quantum-dot cellular automata. J. Vac. Sci. Technol. B **19**(5), 1752–1755 (2001)
12. Holstein, T.: Studies of polar on motion part I. The molecular-crystal model. Ann. Phys. New York **8**, 325–342 (1959)
13. Imre, A., Csaba, G., Ji, L., Orlov, A., Bernstein, G.H., Porod, W.: Majority logic gate for magnetic quantum-dot cellular automata. Science **311**(5758), 205–208 (2006)
14. Karbasian, G., Orlov, A., Mukasyan, A., Snider, G.: Single-electron transistors featuring silicon nitride tunnel barriers prepared by atomic layer deposition. In: 2016 Joint International EUROSOI Workshop and International Conference on Ultimate Integration on Silicon (EUROSOI-ULIS 2016). IEEE, January 2016
15. Lent, C.S.: Molecular electronics - bypassing the transistor paradigm. Science **288**, 1597–1599 (2000)
16. Lent, C., Henderson, K., Kandel, S., Corcelli, S., Snider, G., Orlov, A., Kogge, P., Niemier, M., Brown, R., Christie, J., Wasio, N., Quardokus, R., Forrest, R., Peterson, J., Silski, A., Turner, D., Blair, E., Lu, Y.: Molecular cellular networks: a non von Neumann architecture for molecular electronics. In: 2016 IEEE International Conference on Rebooting Computing (ICRC), pp. 1–7. IEEE, October 2016
17. Lent, C., Isaksen, B., Lieberman, M.: Molecular quantum-dot cellular automata. J. Am. Chem. Soc. **125**, 1056–1063 (2003)
18. Lent, C.S., Snider, G.L.: The development of quantum-dot cellular automata. In: Anderson, N.G., Bhanja, S. (eds.) Field-Coupled Nanocomputing. LNCS, vol. 8280, pp. 3–20. Springer, Heidelberg (2014). doi:10.1007/978-3-662-43722-3_1

19. Lent, C., Tougaw, P., Porod, W., Bernstein, G.: Quantum cellular automata. Nanotechnology **4**, 49 (1993)
20. Lieberman, M., Chellamma, S., Varughese, B., Wang, Y., Lent, C., Bernstein, G., Snider, G., Peiris, F.: Quantum-dot cellular automata at a molecular scale. Ann. N.Y. Acad. Sci. **960**, 225–239 (2002)
21. Lindblad, G.: On the generators of quantum dynamical semigroups. Commun. Math. Phys. **48**, 119–130 (1967)
22. Orlov, A.O., Amlani, I., Bernstein, G.H., Lent, C.S., Snider, G.L.: Realization of a functional cell for quantum-dot cellular automata. Science **277**(5328), 928–930 (1997)
23. Prager, A., George, H., Orlov, A., Snider, G.: Experimental demonstration of hybrid CMOS-single electron transistor circuits. J. Vac. Sci. Tenchnol. B **29**(4), 041004 (2011)
24. Rothemund, P.: Folding DNA to create nanoscale shapes and patterns. Nature **440**, 297–302 (2006)
25. Sarveswaran, K., Huber, P., Lieberman, M., Russo, C., Lent, C.: Nanometer scale rafts built from DNA tiles. In: IEEE-NANO, Third IEEE Conference on Nanotechnology, vol. 1, pp. 402–405. IEEE (2003)
26. Snider, G.L., Orlov, A.O., Amlani, I., Bernstein, G.H., Lent, C.S., Merz, J.L., Porod, W.: Quantum-dot cellular automata: line and majority logic gate. Jpn. J. Appl. Phys. **38**(12B), 7227–7229 (1999)
27. Tougaw, P., Lent, C.: Logical devices implemented using quantum cellular automata. J. Appl. Phys. **75**(3), 1818–1825 (1994)
28. Winfree, E., Liu, F., Wenzler, L., Seeman, N.: Design and self-assembly of two-dimensional DNA crystals. Nature **394**, 539–544 (1998)

Platform Color Designs for Interactive Molecular Arrangements

Jasper Braun, Daniel Cruz$^{(\boxtimes)}$, and Nataša Jonoska

Department of Mathematics and Statistics, University of South Florida,
Tampa, FL, USA
dcruz@mail.usf.edu

Abstract. It has been shown that alternating attachments of two types (species) of floating molecular (DNA based) tiles on a predesigned array that consists of communicating neighboring DNA tiles complementary to the floating tiles can dynamically simulate some types of cellular automata (CA). We show that the model can simulate any elementary one dimensional CA confirming the universal computational power of the model. We address the question of which design of the platform array provides communication across the whole plane. We show that for square tiles only the checkerboard arrangement of the two species can provide communication between any two tiles of the plane. On the other hand, there are an uncountable number of arrangements of two colors of hexagonal tiles on the plane which provide communication between any two tiles.

1 Introduction

Experimental DNA self-assembly has demonstrated molecular information processing mainly through assemblies of structures as results of computations [17,20], or structures that represent computations (e.g. logic circuits [13], space-time representations of cellular automata [18], binary counters [5], etc.). In all those cases, the cooperation between the building blocks is guided by the sticky ends, and once a molecule assumes its location within a larger structure, it has no further computational interaction with its environment. Recent developments have shown arrays made by DNA origami tiles [12], incorporating signaling strands within DNA origami [6] and controlled step-by-step tile assembly through signal activated sticky ends [14]. These results have motivated several recent works which, at least theoretically, describe models, where through constant interaction with the environment, computations dynamically change the structures. Many of these works show simulations of cellular automata using a variety of models such as reaction network based simulations of (asynchronous) cellular automata [8,11,19], models based on signal passing tile assemblies [10] and a recent model relying on continuous changes of molecular arrangements on a 2D array through a global control of the environment [9]. The proposed system in [9] consists of a 2D DNA origami array (platform) made of two types (species) of tiles ('black' and 'white') that serve as a transmission storage (equipped with

© Springer International Publishing AG 2017
M.J. Patitz and M. Stannett (Eds.): UCNC 2017, LNCS 10240, pp. 69–81, 2017.
DOI: 10.1007/978-3-319-58187-3_6

"communication" strands) and two types (species) of free floating tiles able to attach to their respective counterparts on the platform. Only one species of floating tiles is attached to the platform at a time. In an alternate manner, at each cycle, one of the platform colors receives corresponding floating tiles and computes the identity of the floating tiles of the next cycle for the other color. Thus, the floating tiles communicate by transmitting signals through the platform to their oppositely colored neighbors. The exchange of the tile types on the array is assumed to be achieved through a global environmental control, for example with tiles equipped with differently shaped gold particles [4,7], or newly designed chemistry [1,21]. This global control has the potential to provide a "clock" in the system allowing synchronous exchange of the arrangements between the two species of tiles.

In this paper, we address two questions arising from the model description in [9]: (a) what is the computational power of the system and (b) which color designs of the platform allow communication across the whole plane? To no surprise, we observe that the checkerboard coloring of the platform allows simulation of any elementary cellular automaton in Sect. 2. This is achieved through a dynamic simulation without storing or recording the history of the computation and follows an approach similar to the simulation in [10]. The 2D cellular automaton simulation proposed in [9] has a lag; two steps of floating tile arrangements correspond to a single configuration of the automaton being simulated. In contrast, the simulation in Sect. 2 is such that each automaton configuration corresponds to a single arrangement of tiles over one of the colors in the platform. In the remaining sections, we study coloring designs of the platform which allow communication between the floating tiles. We show that communication between any two tiles on a colored platform through signals sent from a tile to oppositely colored neighboring tiles is possible only on a checkerboard coloring of the platform. Further, we observe that a platform made by other types of tiles (such as hexagonal tiles) may have uncountably many colorings that provide communication between any two tiles across the plane.

1.1 Preliminaries

In this paper, $G = (V, E)$ is always an undirected, simple graph with a finite or infinite set of vertices V. The number of edges in the shortest simple path from u to v is denoted $dist(u, v)$. Vertices represent tiles on the plane (platform), and the edges correspond to the connections between the tiles. When thinking of a platform, G is also planar. However, our observations in Sect. 4 hold in general and the planarity of G is not assumed. In the case of the square tiling of the plane, we take G to be the integer lattice with vertices $\mathbb{Z}^2$ and edges $\{u, v\}$ if and only if $||u - v|| = 1$. Let C be a finite set; a mapping $\varphi : V \to C$ is *a coloring of G by C*. A coloring φ is *binary* if $|C| = 2$. As per the experimental implementation suggested in [9], the platform is partitioned into two types of tiles which can be distinguished by associating two colors. Therefore, in this paper all colorings are binary and we set $C = \{0, 1\}$. We refer to color 1 as 'black', and to color 0 as 'white'. A *checkerboard* coloring of $\mathbb{Z}^2$ is uniquely determined by the color of the

parity of $x + y$ for $u = (x, y) \in \mathbb{Z}^2$, that is for a fixed i, (x, y) is colored i if and only if $x + y$ is even. There are two checkerboard colorings of $\mathbb{Z}^2$, depending on whether $i = 0$ or $i = 1$. We define checkerboard colorings of arbitrary graphs in Sect. 4.

Because communication across the tiles is performed only between oppositely colored tiles, we consider paths in the graph where successive vertices are oppositely colored. A path $p = v_0, \ldots, v_n$ in G is φ-*alternating* if for any two consecutive vertices v_{i-1}, v_i in p, $\varphi(v_i) = 1 - \varphi(v_{i-1})$. We say that $u, v \in V$ *communicate under* φ if there is a φ-alternating path from u to v. Let $C_v^\varphi = (V_v, E_v)$ denote the subgraph of G induced by v and the set of vertices which communicate with v under φ. We call C_v^φ the *communicating graph of v under* φ. We abuse the notation and drop the superscript φ when the coloring is clear from the context. A colored graph is called φ-*connected* if any two vertices in the graph are connected by a φ-alternating path. This implies that in a φ-connected graph G, the communicating graph C_v^φ coincides with G for every v. A coloring φ is said to be *communicating* if for every vertex v the graph C_v^φ contains vertices other than v.

2 Simulation

In this section, we recall the computing model introduced in [9] and show how this model simulates the dynamics of any elementary cellular automaton. The model is defined over the graph $\mathbb{Z}^2$. Let $\varphi : \mathbb{Z}^2 \to \{0, 1\}$ be a binary communicating coloring of $\mathbb{Z}^2$. We set $B = \varphi^{-1}(1)$ to be the set of black vertices and $W = \varphi^{-1}(0)$ to be the set of white vertices.

We define $N = \{(1, 0), (0, 1), (-1, 0), (0, -1)\}$, and for $v \in \mathbb{Z}^2$, $N_v = v + N = \{v + u \mid u \in N\}$ is the neighborhood of v in $\mathbb{Z}^2$. Let Σ be a finite set, and take $\epsilon \notin \Sigma$. We denote $\hat{\Sigma} = \Sigma \cup \{\epsilon\}$. A map $a : N \to \hat{\Sigma}$ is represented with a 4-tuple (a_1, a_2, a_3, a_4) where $a_1 = a(1, 0), a_2 = a(0, 1), a_3 = a(-1, 0)$, and $a_4 = a(0, -1)$.

Definition 1. *A system of interactive molecular arrangement over $\mathbb{Z}^2$ (SIMA) is a four-tuple $\mathcal{S} = (\varphi, \Sigma, \phi_B, \phi_W)$ where φ is a binary communicating coloring of $\mathbb{Z}^2$, Σ is a finite set of states and $\phi_B, \phi_W : \hat{\Sigma}^N \to \Sigma$ are local functions.*

Definition 2. *Let $\mathcal{S} = (\varphi, \Sigma, \phi_B, \phi_W)$ be a SIMA with $\epsilon \notin \Sigma$. An arrangement is a mapping $\sigma_C : \mathbb{Z}^2 \to \hat{\Sigma}$, where $C \in \{B, W\}$, defined by*

$$\sigma_C(v) = \begin{cases} s \in \Sigma & \text{if } v \in C \\ \epsilon & \text{otherwise} \end{cases}$$

Since ϵ is not an element of Σ, we use it as a 'place holder', and we refer to it as the 'empty state'. So, an arrangement is an assignment of states in $\mathbb{Z}^2$ such that vertices of one of the colors are assigned states from Σ and vertices of the opposite color are assigned the empty state.

Definition 3. *For a given SIMA* $\mathcal{S} = (\varphi, \Sigma, \phi_B, \phi_W)$ *and a seed arrangement* σ_B^0, *a computation of* $\mathcal{S}$ *is a sequence of arrangements* $\sigma_B^0, \sigma_W^0, \sigma_B^1, \ldots, \sigma_W^{n-1}, \sigma_B^n,$ $\sigma_W^n, \sigma_B^{n+1}, \ldots$ *such that*

$$\sigma_W^n(v) = \begin{cases} \phi_W(\sigma_B^n|_{N_v}) & \text{if } v \in W \\ \epsilon & \text{otherwise} \end{cases} \text{ for } n \geq 0$$

$$\sigma_B^n(v) = \begin{cases} \phi_B(\sigma_W^{n-1}|_{N_v}) & \text{if } v \in B \\ \epsilon & \text{otherwise} \end{cases} \text{ for } n \geq 1$$

In the sequence of arrangements forming a computation, the state at each point $v \in \mathbb{Z}^2$ of an arrangement is obtained by applying the corresponding local function to the neighborhood N_v under the preceding arrangement.

Recall that a one-dimensional cellular automaton (CA) is a three-tuple $\mathcal{C} = (A, N, \ell)$ where A is a finite set of states, N is a finite subset of $\mathbb{Z}$, and $\ell : A^N \to A$ is the local function. For a configuration $\alpha : \mathbb{Z} \to A$ of $\mathcal{C}$ and $v \in \mathbb{Z}$, denote $\alpha_v = \alpha(v)$. Given $\Gamma = \{\alpha \mid \alpha : \mathbb{Z} \to A\}$ of $\mathcal{C}$, the associated *global function* is the function $G_\ell : \Gamma \to \Gamma$ defined with $(G_\ell(\alpha))_v = \ell(\alpha_{v+N})$ where $v + N = \{v + j \mid j \in N\}$ for $v \in \mathbb{Z}$. A one-dimensional CA where $N = \{-1, 0, 1\}$ is said to have a *radius 1* neighborhood. An *elementary CA* is a CA $\mathcal{C} = (A, N, \ell)$ with $A = \{0, 1\}$ and a radius 1 neighborhood.

Definition 4. *Let* $\mathcal{C} = (A, d, N, \ell)$ *be a CA and* $\mathcal{S} = (\varphi, \Sigma, \phi_B, \phi_W)$ *be a SIMA. An arrangement* σ_C, *where* $C \in \{B, W\}$, *encodes a configuration* $\alpha : \mathbb{Z}^d \to A$ *in* $D \subseteq C$ *if*

(i) there exists $\Sigma_A \subseteq \Sigma$ *with* $\sigma_C(D) \subseteq \Sigma_A$ *and a bijection* $\theta : A \to \Sigma_A$,
(ii) there exists a bijection $\psi : D \to \mathbb{Z}^d$ *such that* $\sigma_C|_D = \theta \circ \alpha \circ \psi$.

Informally, an arrangement σ_C encodes a configuration α in $D \subseteq C$ if the domain and the image of α can be embedded in the domain and the image of $\sigma_C|_D$, respectively. That is, $\sigma_C|_D$ represents an equivalent arrangement of states over D as α does over $\mathbb{Z}^d$.

Definition 5. *A SIMA* $\mathcal{S} = (\varphi, \Sigma, \phi_B, \phi_W)$ *simulates a cellular automaton* $\mathcal{C} = (A, d, N, \ell)$ *if there exists* $D \subseteq \mathbb{Z}^2$ *such that for any configuration* $\alpha : \mathbb{Z}^d \to A$ *of* $\mathcal{C}$, *there is a seed arrangement* σ_B^0 *that encodes* α *in* $D \cap B$, *and a computation* $\sigma_B^0, \sigma_W^0, \sigma_B^1, \sigma_W^1, \ldots$ *of* $\mathcal{S}$ *such that there exists an increasing sequence* $\{m_i\}_{i=0}^\infty \subset \mathbb{Z}$ *satisfying for any* $n \geq 0$, *either* $\sigma_B^{m_n}$ *encodes* $G_\ell^n(\alpha)$ *in* $D \cap B$ *or* $\sigma_W^{m_n}$ *encodes* $G_\ell^n(\alpha)$ *in* $D \cap W$.

We say that SIMA $\mathcal{S}$ simulates the cellular automaton $\mathcal{C}$ *uniformly* if the increasing sequence $\{m_0, m_1, m_2, \ldots\} \subset \mathbb{Z}$ is an arithmetic sequence, and it simulates *strictly* $\mathcal{C}$ if $m_{i+1} = m_0 + \lfloor \frac{i}{2} \rfloor$.

Lemma 1. *For any CA* $\mathcal{C}$ *with a radius 1 neighborhood, there exists a SIMA* $\mathcal{S}$ *which simulates* $\mathcal{C}$ *strictly.*

Proof. Let $\mathcal{C}$ be a CA with a radius 1 neighborhood, a set of states A, and a local function ℓ, and let φ be a checkerboard coloring of $\mathbb{Z}^2$ with $\varphi(0,0) = 0$. Hence φ is communicating. Let $\Sigma = A \cup \{L, R, \delta\}$, where L represents the "left border," R represents the "right border," and δ is reserved for the cases not related to the simulation. For $C \in \{B, W\}$, define ϕ_C as follows

$$\phi_C(a_1, a_2, a_3, a_4) = \begin{cases} b & \text{if } a_1, a_2, a_4 \in A, a_3 = L, \text{ and } \ell(a_4, a_1, a_2) = b \\ b & \text{if } a_2, a_3, a_4 \in A, a_1 = R, \text{ and } \ell(a_4, a_3, a_2) = b \\ L & \text{if } a_2, a_4 = L, a_3 = \delta, \text{ and } a_1 \in A \\ R & \text{if } a_2, a_4 = R, a_1 = \delta, \text{ and } a_3 \in A \\ \delta & \text{otherwise} \end{cases}$$

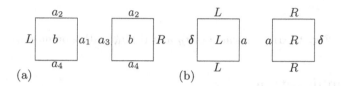

(a)   (b)

Fig. 1. The function ϕ_C. (a) $b = \ell(a_4, a_1, a_2)$ when there is a border L on the left and $b = \ell(a_4, a_3, a_2)$ when there is a border R on the right; (b) left and right border tiles that are not part of the encoding of a configuration of $\mathcal{C}$.

The first two cases of the definition of ϕ_C are shown in Fig. 1(a) and the second two in Fig. 1(b). Let $D = \{(x, y) \in \mathbb{Z}^2 \mid x = 0, 1\}$, and let α be a configuration of the cellular automaton $\mathcal{C}$. The configuration α is encoded with the arrangement $\sigma_B^0 : \mathbb{Z}^2 \to \hat{\Sigma}$ by setting the black vertices in D with $\sigma_B^0(x, y) = \alpha_y$ (recall $(x, y) \in B$ iff $x + y$ is odd). The black vertices with x-coordinate -1 are associated the left border L and the black vertices with x-coordinate 2 are associated with the right border R. All other black vertices are mapped to δ. A segment of the configuration σ_B^0 is presented in Fig. 2(a).

For $\psi_B : D \cap B \to \mathbb{Z}$ with $\psi_B(x, y) = y$, we have $\sigma_B^0|_{D \cap B} = \alpha \circ \psi_B$, and hence σ_B^0 encodes α in $D \cap B$. Observe that σ_W^0 encodes $G_\ell(\alpha)$ in $D \cap W$ (see Fig. 2(b)). Inductively, one obtains that $\sigma_B^{n/2}$ encodes $G_\ell^n(\alpha)$ in $D \cap B$ for n even and $\sigma_B^{\lfloor n/2 \rfloor}$ encodes $G_\ell^n(\alpha)$ in $D \cap W$ for n odd which concludes the proof. ∎

Observe that Lemma 1 reaffirms the result in [8] that there exists a SIMA which is Turing complete. Indeed, there exists a SIMA which simulates elementary CA Rule 110 by the lemma, and it is known that Rule 110 is Turing complete [3,16]. Although a SIMA can simulate a two-dimensional CA [9], the characterization of those two-dimensional CA which can be simulated by SIMAs is unknown, to the best of our knowledge.

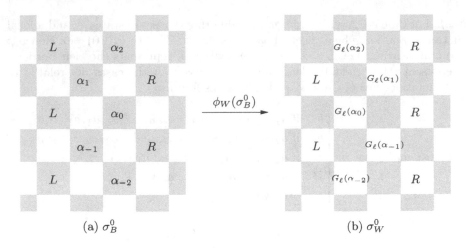

(a) σ_B^0 (b) σ_W^0

Fig. 2. Arrangements (a) σ_B^0 and (b) σ_W^0 with ϵ ommited.

3   Communication

Recall that a simple bi-infinite path in an infinite graph G is an injective map $p : \mathbb{Z} \to V$ such that $\{p(i), p(i+1)\} \in E$ for all $i \in \mathbb{Z}$. Given a binary coloring φ, a simple bi-infinite path is called φ-*alternating* if $\varphi(p(i)) = 1 - \varphi(p(i+1))$ for all $i \in \mathbb{Z}$. For a bi-infinite path p, we define the set of vertices visited by p to be $V_p = \{p(i) \mid i \in \mathbb{Z}\}$. A simple bi-infinite path p does not visit a vertex twice, so the set V_p is infinite. We say that w is in the intersection of two bi-infinite paths p and q if $w \in V_p \cap V_q$.

Definition 6. *Let φ be a binary coloring of an infinite graph G. Let $v \in V$, and let d be the maximum number of φ-alternating simple bi-infinite paths whose pairwise intersection is just $\{v\}$. If $d \geq 1$, then φ provides communication in d directions at v. We say that φ provides communication in d directions on G if there exists $v \in V$ where φ provides communication in d directions at v. If for all $v \in V, \varphi$ provides communication in d directions at v, then we say that φ is d-directional.*

We say that φ *provides finite communication at* $v \in V$ if C_v^φ is finite. If φ provides finite communication at every vertex in G, then we say that G has *finite communication under* φ. Of course, communication at every vertex is finite if G is finite. When $v \in V$ has finite communication under a binary coloring φ of G, there exist no φ-alternating simple bi-infinite paths which contain v. The requirement that d-directional communication in Definition 6 be established by φ-alternating simple bi-infinite paths distinguishes d-directional communication from finite communication.

Following the definition in [15], a binary coloring φ on $G = (V, E)$ is *1-perfect* or *isotropic* if the number of vertices adjacent to $v \in V$ with color $j \in \{0, 1\}$ only depends on the color of v. In this case, we may represent φ with a 2×2

coloring matrix $\{a_{i,j}\}_{i,j=0}^{1}$ which indicates that a vertex with color i has $a_{i,j}$ adjacent vertices of color j. For the rest of the section, we consider the integer lattice $(\mathbb{Z}^2, E)$ where $\{u, v\} \in E \Leftrightarrow ||u - v|| = 1$.

Proposition 1 (Theorem 8 of [2]). *Any communicating 1-perfect coloring of $\mathbb{Z}^2$ has a coloring matrix which is equivalent to one of the matrices $M_1 - M_9$. Matrices M_4 and M_8 correspond to uncountably many 1-perfect colorings, M_7 corresponds to two colorings, and all other matrices correspond to a unique (up to isomorphism) 1-perfect coloring.*

$$M_1 = \begin{pmatrix} 0 & 4 \\ 1 & 3 \end{pmatrix} \quad M_2 = \begin{pmatrix} 0 & 4 \\ 2 & 2 \end{pmatrix} \quad M_3 = \begin{pmatrix} 0 & 4 \\ 4 & 0 \end{pmatrix}$$

$$M_4 = \begin{pmatrix} 1 & 3 \\ 1 & 3 \end{pmatrix} \quad M_5 = \begin{pmatrix} 1 & 3 \\ 2 & 2 \end{pmatrix} \quad M_6 = \begin{pmatrix} 1 & 3 \\ 3 & 1 \end{pmatrix}$$

$$M_7 = \begin{pmatrix} 2 & 2 \\ 1 & 3 \end{pmatrix} \quad M_8 = \begin{pmatrix} 2 & 2 \\ 2 & 2 \end{pmatrix} \quad M_9 = \begin{pmatrix} 3 & 1 \\ 1 & 3 \end{pmatrix}$$

Observe that any binary coloring φ of $\mathbb{Z}^2$ provides communication in at most 2 directions at a vertex. Indeed, each vertex in $\mathbb{Z}^2$ has a degree of four, so at most two φ-alternating simple bi-infinite paths can have an intersection which is just v. We observe the following corollaries to Proposition 1.

Corollary 1. *A 1-perfect coloring φ of $\mathbb{Z}^2$ with a coloring matrix equivalent to one of the matrices $M_1, M_4, M_7,$ or M_9 provides finite communication in $\mathbb{Z}^2$.*

Proof. Let φ be such a coloring of $\mathbb{Z}^2$, and let $v \in \mathbb{Z}^2$. Without loss of generality, assume that φ has a coloring matrix equal to one of the matrices $M_1, M_4, M_7,$ or M_9. Figure 3 depicts the communicating graph C_v^φ for the corresponding coloring. For all matrices, the subgraph C_v contains five to two vertices, respectively. ∎

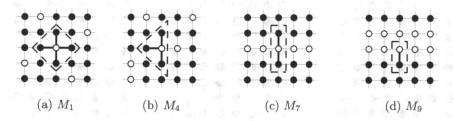

(a) M_1	(b) M_4	(c) M_7	(d) M_9

Fig. 3. For $v \in \mathbb{Z}^2, C_v$ is depicted within dashed lines above the associated coloring matrix (a) M_1, (b) M_4, (c) M_7, or (d) M_9. Note that if $\varphi(v) = 1, v$ may be taken as any one of the black vertices in the depictions of C_v above. The 1-perfect coloring shown in (c) is one of the infinitely many 1-perfect colorings whose coloring matrix is equivalent to M_7; however, the subgraph C_v for $v \in \mathbb{Z}^2$ is the same for all such 1-perfect colorings.

Note that if a vertex has exactly two oppositely colored neighbors under φ, then a φ-alternating simple bi-finite path must include these neighbors. The next corollary follows immediately.

Corollary 2. *A 1-perfect coloring φ of $\mathbb{Z}^2$ with a coloring matrix equivalent to M_8 provides communication in at most one direction.*

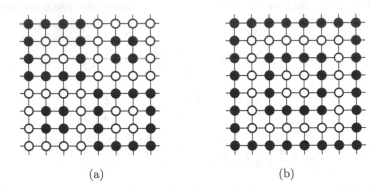

(a)   (b)

Fig. 4. Two distinct 1-perfect colorings which have coloring matrices equivalent to M_8.

Figure 4 shows two possible colorings corresponding to M_8. Observe that $\mathbb{Z}^2$ has finite communication under the coloring in Fig. 4(a) whereas the coloring in Fig. 4(b) is 1-directional. One can show, by increasing the sizes of the single color squares in Fig. 4(a), that for any $n \geq 0$, there exists a 1-perfect coloring with a coloring matrix equivalent to M_8 such that for all $v \in \mathbb{Z}^2$, the number of vertices in C_v^φ is $2^{j_v+3} - 4$, where $j_v \leq n$.

Corollary 3. *A 1-perfect coloring φ of $\mathbb{Z}^2$ with a coloring matrix equivalent to one of the matrices $M_2, M_5,$ or M_6 is 1-directional.*

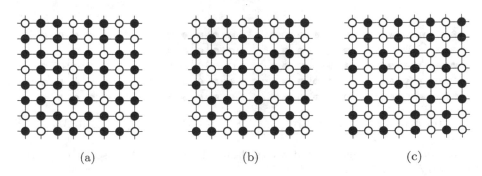

(a)   (b)   (c)

Fig. 5. The unique colorings for matrices (a) M_2, (b) M_5, and (c) M_6 [2].

Proof. Let φ be a coloring of $\mathbb{Z}^2$ that corresponds to a matrix equivalent to one of the matrices M_2, M_5, or M_6. By Proposition 1 there exists a unique (up to isomorphism) 1-perfect coloring corresponding to each of these matrices (see Fig. 5) [2]. Figure 6 depicts the communication graphs for these matrices. ∎

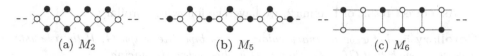

(a) M_2 (b) M_5 (c) M_6

Fig. 6. For $v \in \mathbb{Z}^2$, C_v^φ is depicted above the associated coloring matrix. Note that any vertex with a matching color may be chosen for v from each of the subgraphs above.

Corollary 4. *The only 1-perfect coloring of the integer lattice $\mathbb{Z}^2$ which provides communication in 2 directions is a checkerboard coloring. A checkerboard coloring is 2-directional.*

Proof. By Corollaries 1 through 3, all matrices M_i where $i \neq 3$ from Proposition 1 provide at most 1-directional communication. Note that φ has a coloring matrix equivalent to M_3 if and only if it is a checkerboard coloring. Let φ be a checkerboard coloring of $\mathbb{Z}^2$. For $v \in \mathbb{Z}^2$, the simple bi-infinite paths $\{v + (0,k)\}_{-\infty}^{\infty}$ and $\{v + (k,0)\}_{-\infty}^{\infty}$ are φ-alternating, and v is the only vertex in the intersection of p_1 and p_2, so φ provides communication in 2 directions at v. Because any coloring of $\mathbb{Z}^2$ can provide communication at most in 2 directions at a vertex ($\mathbb{Z}^2$ is four-regular graph), φ is 2-directional. ∎

4 Checkerboard Coloring and Directions of Communication

This section shows that d-directional communication for $d \geq 2$ may be possible at some vertices in tilings of the plane other than square tilings.

Definition 7. *Let $G = (V, E)$ be a (possibly infinite) graph. A binary coloring φ is called a* checkerboard coloring *if for every two adjacent vertices $v, u \in V$ we have that $\varphi(u) = 1 - \varphi(v)$.*

Observe that there exists a checkerboard coloring of G if and only if G is bipartite. Hence, when G is a bipartite graph, we assume a checkerboard coloring of G exists. Note that there are exactly two checkerboard colorings for any bipartite graph, one obtained from the other by switching the color at every vertex.

Lemma 2. *Let φ be a binary coloring of a bipartite graph G. A path $v_0, \ldots, v_n$ in G is φ-alternating if and only if for some checkerboard coloring γ of G, $\varphi(v_i) = \gamma(v_i)$ for all $0 \leq i \leq n$.*

Proof. By the definition of a checkerboard coloring γ, every path in G is γ-alternating. Suppose φ is a binary coloring of a bipartite graph G and the path $v_0, \ldots, v_n$ is φ-alternating. Note that $\varphi(v_0) = \gamma(v_0)$ for some checkerboard coloring γ of G. Then since the path is φ-alternating and γ is a checkerboard coloring, $\varphi(v_k) = 1 - \varphi(v_{k-1}) = 1 - \gamma(v_{k-1}) = \gamma(v_k)$, for all $1 \leq k \leq n$. ∎

As a direct result of Lemma 2, we have the following corollary.

Corollary 5. *Let φ be a binary coloring of a bipartite graph G. If there exists a vertex v such that $C_v^\varphi = G$, then φ is a checkerboard coloring.*

Recall that if there is a vertex v such that $C_v^\varphi = G$, then G is φ-connected and so $C_w^\varphi = G$ for all vertices w. Corollary 5 shows that for bipartite graphs, the only colorings φ under which G is φ-connected are the two checkerboard colorings. We provide an example of a non-bipartite graph which has only finitely many colorings φ making the graph φ-connected.

Let G_1, G_2 and G_3 be bipartite graphs. Fix vertices v_1, v_2 and v_3 in G_1, G_2 and G_3, respectively, and let $G = G_1 \cup G_2 \cup G_3 \cup \{\{v_1, v_2\}, \{v_2, v_3\}, \{v_1, v_3\}\}$ (see Fig. 7). Then (v_1, v_2, v_3) is an odd cycle in G, and therefore, the graph is non-bipartite.

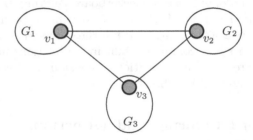

Fig. 7. A non-bipartite graph G constructed from bipartite graphs G_1, G_2 and G_3.

Observe that there exists a coloring φ, such that $C_{v_1} = G$. Indeed, if for the coloring φ we have $\varphi(v_1) = \varphi(v_2) = 0, \varphi(v_3) = 1$ and if φ coincides with checkerboard colorings on G_1, G_2 and G_3, then $C_{v_1} = G$.

Let v, w be vertices in G_1 and φ be any coloring of G under which G is φ-connected. Then there is a φ-alternating path $p = u_0, \ldots, u_n$ with $u_0 = v$ and $u_n = w$. If p travels through v_1 at most once, then all u_i are in G_1. If p travels through v_1 more than once, let i and j be the minimum and maximum indices, respectively, with $u_i = v_1$ and $u_j = v_1$, and let q be a path obtained from p by removal of $u_{i+1}, \ldots, u_j$. Then all vertices u_k of the path q are in G_1. Thus, G_1 is $\varphi|_{G_1}$-connected. By Corollary 5, the restriction $\varphi|_{G_1}$ is a checkerboard coloring. Similarly it holds that $\varphi|_{G_2}$ and $\varphi|_{G_3}$ are checkerboard colorings. Because there are only two checkerboard colorings for each of the G_i, there are only finitely many (in this case six) choices for φ.

The following theorem provides an example of a non-bipartite graph with uncountably many colorings φ under which the graph is φ-connected. We call the dual graph of the hexagonal tiling of the plane the *triangular grid* denoted with $\mathbb{T}$. The vertices of $\mathbb{T}$ are arranged as depicted in Fig. 8(a).

Theorem 1. *There are uncountably many binary colorings φ of the triangular grid $\mathbb{T}$ which make $\mathbb{T}$ φ-connected and provide communication in 3 directions at infinitely many, but not all, vertices.*

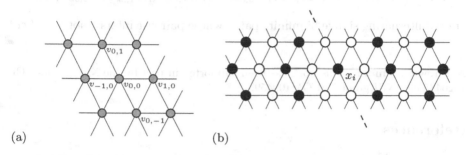

(a)   (b)

Fig. 8. Portions of the triangular grid (a) depicting the defined coordinate system and (b) one of the sets X_i, where $s_i = 1$ and the color of each remaining vertex depends on s_i and its distance to x_i.

Proof. Note that the square grid $\mathbb{Z}^2$ with addition of edges $\{(i,j),(i+1,j+1)\}$ is isomorphic to the triangular grid $\mathbb{T}$. Fix a vertex in $\mathbb{T}$ and denote it $v_{0,0}$. We label the rest of the vertices inductively such that for all $i,j \in \mathbb{Z}$ the horizontal neighbors of $v_{i,j}$ are $v_{i-1,j}$ to the left and $v_{i+1,j}$ to the right. The northwest and southeast neighbors of $v_{i,j}$ are $v_{i,j+1}$ and $v_{i,j-1}$, respectively (see Fig. 8(a)). Denote with V the set of vertices in $\mathbb{T}$. Set $x_0 = v_{0,0}$ and define a sequence of vertices by setting $x_k = v_{0,3k}$, for $k \in \mathbb{Z}^+$. We define sets $Y = \{v_{i,j} \in V \mid j < -1\}$ and $X_k = \{v_{i,j} \in V \mid 3k-1 \le j \le 3k+1, i \in \mathbb{Z}\}$, for $k = 0,1,2,\ldots$.

We prove the theorem by associating to every infinite binary sequence S a unique coloring φ_S which makes $\mathbb{T}$ φ_S-connected and provides communication in three directions at the vertices $x_0, x_1, x_2, \ldots$.

Let $S = s_0, s_1, s_2, \ldots$ be an infinite binary sequence. Define φ_S as follows. If $v_{i,j} \in Y$, then $\varphi_S(v_{i,j}) = i + j \mod 2$, that is, if one removes the edges $\{(i,j),(i+1,j+1)\}$ in Y, then φ_S is a checkerboard coloring of Y. Therefore Y is φ_S-connected.

For each $k = 0,1,2,\ldots$, if $v_{i,j} \in X_k$ then

$$\varphi_S(v_{i,j}) = \begin{cases} s_k & \text{if } dist(x_k, v_{i,j}) \text{ is even,} \\ 1 - s_k & \text{if } dist(x_k, v_{i,j}) \text{ is odd.} \end{cases}$$

Figure 8(b) depicts a portion of X_k. One can see that each of the X_k is φ_S-connected. For $k = 0,1,2,\ldots$, we have that $\varphi_S(v_{0,3k-1}) = 1 - \varphi_S(v_{1,3k-1})$, so that there is a φ_S-alternating path between $v_{0,3k-2}$ and either $v_{0,3k-1}$, or $v_{1,3k-1}$. Thus, there exists a φ_S-alternating path between vertices in X_k and

X_{k-1} for each $k \in \mathbb{Z}^+$ and also between vertices in X_0 and Y. Therefore, G is φ_S-connected.

Lastly, observe that for $k = 0, 1, 2, \ldots$, the paths

$$\ldots, v_{-2,3k+1}, v_{-1,3k+1}, v_{0,3k+1}, v_{0,3k}(= x_k), v_{1,3k+1}, v_{2,3k+1}, v_{3,3k+1}, \ldots$$

$$\ldots, v_{-3,3k}, v_{-2,3k}, v_{-1,3k}, v_{0,3k}(= x_k), v_{1,3k}, v_{2,3k}, v_{3,3k}, \ldots$$

$$\ldots, v_{-3,3k-1}, v_{-2,3k-1}, v_{-1,3k-1}, v_{0,3k}(= x_k), v_{0,3k-1}, v_{1,3k-1}, v_{2,3k-1}, \ldots$$

are φ_S-alternating simple bi-infinite paths whose pairwise intersections are $\{x_k\}$. ∎

Acknowledgement. This work has been supported in part by the NSF grants CCF-1526485 and NIH grant R01 GM109459.

References

1. Asanuma, H., Liang, X.G., Nishioka, H., Matsunaga, D., Liu, M.Z., Komiyama, M.: Synthesis of azobenzene-tethered DNA for reversible photo-regulation of DNA. Nat. Protoc. **2**(1), 203–212 (2007)
2. Axenovich, M.A.: On multiple coverings of the infinite rectangular grid with balls of constant radius. Discret. Math. **268**(1–3), 31–48 (2003)
3. Cook, M.: Universality in elementary cellular automata. Complex Syst. **15**(1), 1–40 (2004)
4. de Puig, H., Cifuentes Rius, A., Flemister, D., Baxamusa, S.H., Hamad-Schifferli, K.: Selective light-triggered release of DNA from gold nanorods switches blood clotting on and off. PLoS ONE **8**(7), 68511 (2013)
5. Evans, C.G.: Crystals that count! Physical principles and experimental investigations of DNA tile self-assembly. Ph.D. thesis, California Institute of Technology (2014)
6. Gu, H., Chao, J., Xiao, S.-J., Seeman, N.C.: A proximity-based programmable DNA nanoscale assembly line. Nature **465**(7295), 202–205 (2010)
7. Hamad-Schifferli, K., Schwartz, J.J., Santos, A.T., Zhang, S., Jacobson, J.M.: Remote electronic control of DNA hybridization through inductive coupling to an attached metal nanocrystal antenna. Nature **415**(6868), 152–155 (2002)
8. Isokawa, T., Peper, F., Kawamata, I., Matsui, N., Murata, S., Hagiya, M.: Universal totalistic asynchonous cellular automaton and its possible implementation by DNA. In: Amos, M., Condon, A. (eds.) UCNC 2016. LNCS, vol. 9726, pp. 182–195. Springer, Cham (2016). doi:10.1007/978-3-319-41312-9_15
9. Jonoska, N., Seeman, N.C.: Molecular ping-pong Game of Life on a two-dimensional DNA origami array. Philos. Trans. R. Soc. A: Math. Phys. Eng. Sci. **373**(2046), 20140215 (2015)
10. Jonoska, N., Karpenko, D., Seki, S.: Dynamic simulation of 1D cellular automata in the active aTAM. New Gener. Comput. **33**, 271–295 (2015)
11. Kawamata, I., Yoshizawa, S., Takabatake, F., Sugawara, K., Murata, S.: Discrete DNA reaction-diffusion model for implementing simple cellular automaton. In: Amos, M., Condon, A. (eds.) UCNC 2016. LNCS, vol. 9726, pp. 168–181. Springer, Cham (2016). doi:10.1007/978-3-319-41312-9_14

12. Liu, W., Zhong, H., Wang, R., Seeman, N.C.: Crystalline two-dimensional DNA-origami arrays. Angew. Chem. **50**(1), 264–267 (2011)
13. Mao, C., LaBean, T.H., Reif, J.H., Seeman, N.C.: Logical computation using algorithmic self-assembly of DNA triple-crossover molecules. Nature **407**(6803), 493–496 (2000)
14. Padilla, J.E., Sha, R., Kristiansen, M., Chen, J., Jonoska, N., Seeman, N.C.: A signal-passing DNA strand exchange mechanism for the active self-assembly of DNA nanostructures. Angew. Chem. **54**(20), 5939–5942 (2015)
15. Puzynina, S.A.: On periodicity of perfect colorings of the infinite hexagonal and triangular grids. Siberian Math. J. **52**(1), 91–104 (2011)
16. Richard, G.: Rule 110: universality and catenations. In: Journees Automates Cellulaires (Proceedings), pp. 141–160 (2008)
17. Rothemund, P.W.K.: Folding DNA to create nanoscale shapes and patterns. Nature **440**(7082), 297–302 (2006)
18. Rothemund, P.W.K., Papadakis, N., Winfree, E.: Algorithmic self-assembly of DNA Sierpinski triangles. PLoS Biol. **2**(12), e424 (2004)
19. Scalise, D., Schulman, R.: Emulating cellular automata in chemical reaction-diffusion networks. In: Murata, S., Kobayashi, S. (eds.) DNA 2014. LNCS, vol. 8727, pp. 67–83. Springer, Cham (2014). doi:10.1007/978-3-319-11295-4_5
20. Wu, G., Jonoska, N., Seeman, N.C.: Construction of a DNA nano-object directly demonstrates computation. BioSystems **98**(2), 80–84 (2009)
21. Yang, Y., Endo, M., Hidaka, K., Sugiyama, H.: Photo-controllable DNA origami nanostructures assembling into predesigned multiorientational patterns. J. Am. Chem. Soc. **134**(51), 20645–20653 (2012)

Self-assembly of Shapes at Constant Scale Using Repulsive Forces

Austin Luchsinger$^{(\boxtimes)}$, Robert Schweller, and Tim Wylie

Department of Computer Science, University of Texas - Rio Grande Valley,
Edinburg, TX 78539, USA
{austin.luchsinger01,robert.schweller,timothy.wylie}@utrgv.edu

Abstract. The algorithmic self-assembly of shapes has been considered in several models of self-assembly. For the problem of *shape construction*, we consider an extended version of the Two-Handed Tile Assembly Model (2HAM), which contains positive (attractive) and negative (repulsive) interactions. As a result, portions of an assembly can become unstable and detach. In this model, we utilize fuel-efficient computation to perform Turing machine simulations for the construction of the shape. In this paper, we show how an arbitrary shape can be constructed using an asymptotically optimal number of distinct tile types (based on the shape's Kolmogorov complexity). We achieve this at $O(1)$ scale factor in this straightforward model, whereas all previous results with sublinear scale factors utilize powerful self-assembly models containing features such as staging, tile deletion, chemical reaction networks, and tile activation/deactivation. Furthermore, the computation and construction in our result only creates constant-size garbage assemblies as a byproduct of assembling the shape.

1 Introduction

A fundamental question within the field of self-assembly, and perhaps the most fundamental, is how to efficiently self-assemble general shapes with the smallest possible set of system monomers. This question has been considered in multiple models of self-assembly. Soloveichek and Winfree [16] first showed that any shape S, if scaled up sufficiently, is self-assembled within the *abstract tile assembly model* (aTAM) using $O(\frac{K(S)}{\log K(S)})$ tile types, where $K(S)$ denotes the *Kolmogorov* or *descriptional* complexity of shape S with respect to some universal Turing machine, which matches the lower bound for this problem. This seminal result presented a concrete connection between the descriptional complexity of a shape and the efficiency of self-assembling the shape, and represents an elegant example of the potential connections between algorithmic processes and the self-assembly of matter. The only drawback with this result is the extremely large scale factor required by construction: the scale factor to build a shape S is at least linear

---

This research was supported in part by the National Science Foundation Grant CCF-1555626.

M.J. Patitz and M. Stannett (Eds.): UCNC 2017, LNCS 10240, pp. 82–97, 2017.
DOI: 10.1007/978-3-319-58187-3_7

in $|S|$, and is typically far greater in their construction. To lay claim as a true universal shape building scheme for potential experimental application, a much smaller scale factor is needed. Unfortunately, example shapes exist (long thin rectangles for example) which prove that the aTAM cannot build all shapes at $o(|S|)$ scale in the minimum possible $O(\frac{K(S)}{\log K(S)})$ tile complexity. This motivates the quest for small scale factors in more powerful self-assembly models.

The next result by Demaine, Patitz, Schweller, and Summers [5] considers general shape assembly within the *staged RNAse* self-assembly model. In this model, system tiles are separated into separate bins and mixed over distinct stages of the algorithm in a way that models realistic laboratory operations. In addition, each tile type in this model is of type DNA or RNA, and the staging permits the addition of an RNAse enzyme at any step in the staging, thereby dissolving all tiles of type RNA, leaving DNA tiles untouched. By adding the powerful operations of separate bins, sequential stages, and tile deletion, [5] achieves general shape construction within optimal $O(\frac{K(s)}{\log K(S)})$ tile complexity using only a constant number of bins and stages, and only a logarithmic scale factor. This leap in scale factor reduction constituted a great improvement, but required a very powerful model with both staging and tile dissolving. In addition, the holy grail of $O(1)$ scale factor remained elusive.

The next entry into the quest for Kolmogorov optimal shape assembly at small scale comes from a recent work by Schiefer and Winfree [14]. Schiefer and Winfree introduce the *chemical reaction network tile assembly model* (CRN-TAM) in which chemical reaction networks and abstract tile assembly systems combine and interact by allowing CRN species to activate and deactivate tiles, while tile attachments may introduce CRN species. This powerful interaction allowed the construction of Kolmogorov optimal systems for the assembly of general shapes at $O(1)$ scale. Although the result provides a great scale factor, the CRN-TAM constitutes a substantial jump in model complexity and power.

In this paper we study the optimal shape building problem within one of the simplest, and most well studied models of self-assembly: *the two handed tile assembly model* (2HAM), where system monomers are 4-sided tiles with glue types on each edge. Assembly in the 2HAM proceeds whenever two previously assembled conglomerations of tiles, or assemblies, collide along matching glue types whose strength sums to some temperature threshold. Our only addition to the model is the allowance of negative strength (i.e., *repulsive*) glues, an admittedly powerful addition based on recent work [6,9–11,15], but an addition motivated by biology [12] that maintains the *passive* nature of the model as system monomers are static, state-less pieces that simply attract or repulse based solely on surface chemistry (Fig. 1). While the negative glue 2HAM has been used for works such as fuel-efficient computation [15] and recently universal shape replication [1], it is also one of the simplest models where the general shape assembly problem has been considered. Our result is on par with the best possible result: we show that any connected shape S is self-assembled at $O(1)$-scale in the negative glue 2HAM within $O(\frac{K(S)}{\log K(S)})$ tile types, which is met by a matching lower bound.

Our Approach. We achieve our result by combining the *fuel efficient Turing machine* construction published in SODA 2013, [15], with a number of novel negative glue based gadgets. At a high level, the fuel efficient Turing machine system extracts a description of a path that walks the pixels of the constant-scaled shape from a compressed initial binary string. From there, the steps of the path are translated into *walker* gadgets which conceptually walk along the surface of the growing path and eventually deposit an additional pixel in the specified direction, with the aid of *path extension* gadgets. When all pixels have been placed, the path through the shape is filled, resulting in a scaled version of the original shape.

Additional Related Work. Additional work has considered assembly of $O(1)$-scaled shapes by breaking the assembly process up into a number of distinct stages. In particular, [3] introduce the *staged self-assembly* model in which intermediate tile assemblies grow in separate bins and are mixed and split over a sequence of distinct stages. This approach is applied to achieve $O(1)$-scaled shapes with $O(1)$ tiles types, but a large number of bins and stages which encode the target shape. In [4] this approach is pushed further to achieve tradeoffs in terms of bin complexity and stage complexity, while maintaining construction of a final assembly with no unbonded edges. In [8] similar constant-scale results are obtained in the *step-wise self-assembly* model in which tile sets are added in sequence to a growing seed assembly. Finally, in [17] $O(1)$-scaled shapes are assembled with $O(1)$ tile types by simply adjusting the temperature of a given system over multiple assembly stages. While each of above *staged* approaches offers important algorithmic insights, the large number of stages required by each makes the approaches infeasible for large shapes. Furthermore, the system complexity of these systems (which includes the staging algorithms) greatly exceeds the descriptional complexity of the goal shape in a typical case.

Paper Layout. Our construction consists of a number of detailed gadgets for specific tasks. Presentation is thus organized incrementally to walk through a version of each gadget (with symmetry there may be multiple). Section 2 gives the preliminary definitions and background. In Sect. 3 we provide a high-level overview of the entire process as a guide for the rest of the paper. Some of the details of our construction are shown in Sect. 4 with the construction gadgets and how to construct a line of the path. Section 5 provides the analysis of our construction, with the lower bound on tile complexity for shape assembly presented in Sect. 6, and details for pushing our construction to achieve a matching upper bound in Sect. 7. Then we conclude in Sect. 8.

2   Definitions and Model

In this section we first define the two-handed tile self-assembly model with both negative and positive strength glue types. We also formulate the problem of designing a tile assembly system that constructs a constant-scaled shape given the optimal description of that shape.

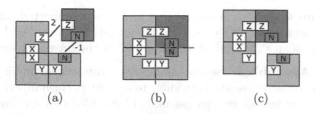

(a)   (b)   (c)

Fig. 1. This figure introduces notation for our constructions, as well as a simple example of negative glues. On each tile, the glue label is presented. Red (shaded) labels represent negative glues, and the relevant glue strengths for the tiles can be found in the captions. For caption brevity, for a glue type X we denote $str(X)$ simply as X (e.g., $X + Y = str(X) + str(Y)$). In this temperature $\tau = 1$ example, $X = 2$, $Y = 1$, $Z = 2$ and $N = -1$. (a) The three tile assembly on the left attaches with the single tile with strength $Z + N = 2 - 1 = \tau$ resulting in the 2×2 assembly shown in (b). However, this 2×2 assembly is unstable along the cut shown by the dotted line, since $Y + N = 1 - 1 < \tau$. Then the assembly is breakable into the assemblies shown in (c). (Color figure online)

Tiles and Assemblies. A tile is an axis-aligned unit square centered at a point in $\mathbb{Z}^2$, where each edge is labeled by a *glue* selected from a glue set Π. A *strength function* str : $\Pi \rightarrow \mathbb{N}$ denotes the *strength* of each glue. Two tiles equal up to translation have the same *type*. A *positioned shape* is any subset of $\mathbb{Z}^2$. A *positioned assembly* is a set of tiles at unique coordinates in $\mathbb{Z}^2$, and the positioned shape of a positioned assembly A is the set of those coordinates.

For a given positioned assembly Υ, define the *bond graph* G_Υ to be the weighted grid graph in which each element of Υ is a vertex and the weight of an edge between tiles is the strength of the matching coincident glues or 0.[1] A positioned assembly C is said to be τ-*stable* for positive integer τ provided the bond graph G_C has min-cut at least τ, and C is said to be *connected* if every pair of vertices in G_C has a connecting path using only positive strength edges.

For a positioned assembly A and integer vector $v = (v_1, v_2)$, let A_v denote the positioned assembly obtained by translating each tile in A by vector v. An *assembly* is a translation-free version of a positioned assembly, formally defined to be a set of all translations A_v of a positioned assembly A. An assembly is τ-stable if and only if its positioned elements are τ-stable. An assembly is *connected* if its positioned elements are connected. A *shape* is the set of all integer translations for some subset of $\mathbb{Z}^2$, and the shape of an assembly A is defined to be the set of the positioned shapes of all positioned assemblies in A. The *size* of either an assembly or shape X, denoted as $|X|$, refers to the number of elements of any positioned element of X.

Breakable Assemblies. An assembly is τ-*breakable* if it can be cut into two pieces along a cut whose strength sums to less than τ. Formally, an assembly C

---

[1] Note that only matching glues of the same type contribute a non-zero weight, whereas non-equal glues always contribute zero weight to the bond graph. Relaxing this restriction has been considered as well [2].

is *breakable* into assemblies A and B if A and B are connected, and the bond graph $G_{C'}$ for some assembly $C' \in C$ has a cut (A', B') for $A' \in A$ and $B' \in B$ of strength less than τ. We call A and B *pieces* of the breakable assembly C.

Combinable Assemblies. Two assemblies are τ-*combinable* provided they may attach along a border whose strength sums to at least τ. Formally, two assemblies A and B are τ-*combinable* into an assembly C provided $G_{C'}$ for any $C' \in C$ has a cut (A', B') of strength at least τ for some $A' \in A$ and $B' \in B$. We call C a *combination* of A and B.

Note that A and B may be combinable into an assembly that is not stable (and thus breakable). This is a key property that is leveraged throughout our constructions. See Fig. 1 for an example. For a system $\Gamma = (T, \tau)$, we say $A \to_1^\Gamma B$ for assemblies A and B if either A is τ-breakable into pieces that include B, or A is τ-combinable with some producible assembly to yield B, or if $A = B$. Intuitively this means that A may grow into assembly B through one or fewer combination or break reactions. We define the relation $\to^\Gamma$ to be the transitive closure of $\to_1^\Gamma$, i.e., $A \to^\Gamma B$ means that A may grow into B through a sequence of combination or break reactions.

Producibility and Unique Assembly. A *two-handed tile assembly system (2HAM system)* is an ordered pair (T, τ) where T is a set of single tile assemblies, called the *tile set*, and $\tau \in \mathbb{N}$ is the *temperature*. Assembly proceeds by repeated combination of assembly pairs, or breakage of unstable assemblies, to form new assemblies starting from the initial tile set. The *producible assemblies* are those constructed in this way. Formally:

Definition 1 (2HAM Producibility). *For a given 2HAM system $\Gamma = (T, \tau)$, the set of* producible assemblies *of Γ, denoted PROD$_\Gamma$, is defined recursively:*

- *(Base) $T \subseteq$ PROD$_\Gamma$*
- *(Combinations) For any $A, B \in$ PROD$_\Gamma$ such that A and B are τ-combinable into C, then $C \in$ PROD$_\Gamma$.*
- *(Breaks) For any assembly $C \in$ PROD$_\Gamma$ that is τ-breakable into A and B, then $A, B \in$ PROD$_\Gamma$.*

Definition 2 (Terminal Assemblies). *A terminal assembly of a 2HAM system is a producible assembly that cannot break and cannot combine with any other producible assembly. Formally, an assembly $A \in$ PROD$_\Gamma$ of a 2HAM system $\Gamma = (T, \tau)$ is terminal provided A is τ-stable (will not break) and not τ-combinable with any producible assembly of Γ (will not combine).*

Definition 3 (Unique Assembly - with bounded garbage). *A 2HAM system uniquely produces an assembly A if all producible assemblies have a forward growth path towards the terminal assembly A, with the possible exception of some $O(1)$-sized producible assemblies. Formally, a 2HAM system $\Gamma = (T, \tau)$ uniquely produces an assembly A provided that A is terminal, and for some constant c for all $B \in$ PROD$_\Gamma$ such that $|B| \geq c$, $B \to^\Gamma A$.*

Definition 4 (Unique Shape Assembly - with bounded garbage). *A 2HAM system uniquely produces a shape S if all producible assemblies have a forward growth path to a terminal assembly of shape S with the possible exception of some $O(1)$-sized producible assemblies. Formally, a 2HAM system $\Gamma = (T, \tau)$ uniquely assembles a finite shape S if for some constant c for every $A \in PROD_\Gamma$ such that $|A| \geq c$, there exists a terminal $A' \in PROD_\Gamma$ of shape S such that $A \to^\Gamma A'$.*

Definition 5 (Kolmogorov Complexity). *The Kolmogorov complexity (or descriptional complexity) of a shape S with respect to some fixed universal Turing machine U is the smallest bit string such that U outputs a list of exactly the positions in some translation of shape S when provided the bit string as input. We denote this value as $K(S)$.*

3 Concept/Construction Overview

This section presents a high-level overview of the shape construction process. First, we will present the conceptual overview, which explains the fundamental ideas behind our shape self-assembly process. Then, we will show a high-level look at how our construction implements this process.

3.1 Conceptual Overview

Starting with the Kolmogorov-optimal description of a shape (as a base b string, $b > 2$), we simulate a Turing machine which converts any base b string into its equivalent base 2 representation (Sect. 7) We then simulate another Turing machine that takes the binary description of a shape, finds a spanning tree for that shape, and outputs a path around that spanning tree as a set of instructions (forward, left, right) starting from a beginning node on the perimeter.

A simple depth-first search will find the spanning tree for any shape. Scaling the shape to scale 2 creates a perimeter *path* that outlines the spanning tree, and assembles the shape. Scaling again, this time by a multiple of 3, now allows space for the perimeter path with an equal-sized space buffer on both sides (Fig. 2). This buffer is required as it allows sufficient space for our construction gadgets to "walk" along the perimeter path being built.

Process Overview:

1. Given the Kolmogorov-optimal description of a shape, run a base conversion Turing machine to get its binary equivalent.
2. Given that binary string, run another Turing machine that outputs the description of a path around the shape's spanning tree as a set of instructions (forward, left, right).
3. Given those instructions, build the path. Our construction begins with a *tape* containing this *path* description for a scale 24 shape.

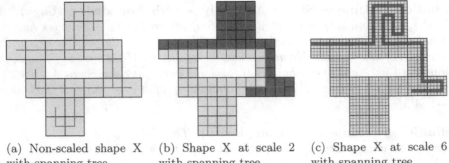

(a) Non-scaled shape X with spanning tree.

(b) Shape X at scale 2 with spanning tree.

(c) Shape X at scale 6 with spanning tree.

Fig. 2. The Turing machine calculates a spanning tree of the tiles in the shape (a), scales the shape in order to allow a path around the spanning tree (b), and further scales the shape for the gadgets (c).

3.2 Construction Overview

The construction overview begins at step 3 of the conceptual overview, using the output from step 2. Throughout this paper, we will be referring to this output as the *tape*, meaning the fuel-efficient Turing machine tape with *path*-building instructions encoded on it. This *tape* is detailed in Sect. 4.

Construction Steps Overview:

1. **Overlay.** The overlay process is the first step in shape construction. Figure 3a–c shows an abstraction of how the output from step 2 in the concept overview gets covered during the overlay process. The overlay initiator gadget can only attach to a completed tape. This begins a series of cooperative attachments that will cover the tape. Each bit of information on the tape is covered by its corresponding overlay piece, and thus is readable on the top of the overlay. The overlay process is finished once the entire tape is covered.
2. **Reading.** After the overlay process is complete, information can be extracted from the tape through the read process (Figs. 3d–f). Information can only be extracted from the covered leftmost section of the tape if it has not already been read. When a tape section is read, information is extracted from the tape and a corresponding information block is created.
3. **Information Walking.** Once the information block is created, it begins walking until it reaches the end of the tape/path (Figs. 3g–i). Walking gadgets allow the information to travel down the entire path.
4. **Path Extension.** When an information block cannot travel any further, the path is extended (Figs. 3j–l). The path can be extended forward, left, or right. The direction of the path extension is dependent on which information block is at the end of the path. After the path is extended, the information block is removed from the path.
5. **Tape Reduction.** Once information is extracted from the tape and sent down the path, one tape section is removed (Figs. 3j–l). Only tape sections

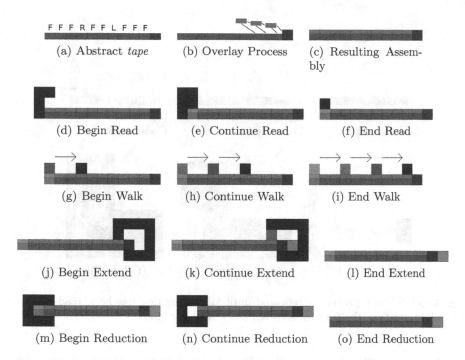

(a) Abstract *tape*

(b) Overlay Process

(c) Resulting Assembly

(d) Begin Read

(e) Continue Read

(f) End Read

(g) Begin Walk

(h) Continue Walk

(i) End Walk

(j) Begin Extend

(k) Continue Extend

(l) End Extend

(m) Begin Reduction

(n) Continue Reduction

(o) End Reduction

Fig. 3. (a)–(c) The *overlay* process covers the tape while making the data readable on top. (d)–(f) *Reading* the leftmost piece of data and creating an information block (depicted in green). (g)–(i) *Information Walking* on the path to the end where the information is used. (j)–(l) When the information block reaches the end of the path, the block triggers a *Path Extension*. (m)–(o) Once the information has been read, *Tape Reduction* removes that piece of the tape. (Color figure online)

that have been read are removed, which then allows the next section to be read. This process continues until every section of the tape is read/removed.

6. **Repeat.** Repeat the tape read, information walk, path extend, and tape reduction processes until all path instructions have been read (Figs. 4a–c).

7. **Path Filling.** The final tape section that gets read begins the shape fill process (Figs. 4d–f). In this process, the path is padded with tiles which fill it in and results in the final shape.

4   Construction Details

In this section, we detail the steps presented in the construction overview (Sect. 3.2). This is the process by which information is read from the *tape* and portions of the *path* are assembled.

We will also cover the gadgets required for each step, and review the tape construction from the fuel-efficient Turing machine used in [15]. This construction uses pre-constructed assemblies called gadgets. These gadgets are designed

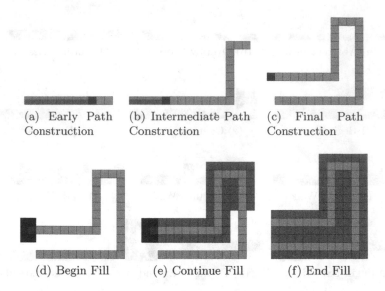

(a) Early Path Construction

(b) Intermediate Path Construction

(c) Final Path Construction

(d) Begin Fill

(e) Continue Fill

(f) End Fill

Fig. 4. (a)–(c) The process is repeated until all information has been read/removed from the tape. (d)–(f) The final step is *Path Filling* the shape.

to work in a temperature $\tau = 10$ system. In our figures, a perpendicular black line through the middle of the edge of two adjacent tiles indicates a unique $2\tau = 20$ strength bond[2]. Each gadget provides a different function to the shape creation process.

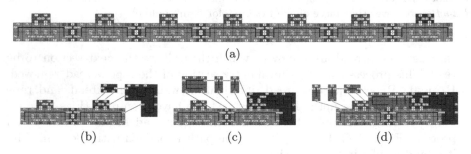

(a)

(b)   (c)   (d)

Fig. 5. (a) A completed *tape* consisting of all *forward* instructions. (b) Overlay Initiator gadget attaching to tape. (c–d) Overlay fillers begin covering all *tape* sections from right to left.

Turing Machine Tape. A detailed look at a fuel-efficient Turing machine *tape* is seen in Fig. 5a. Notice each tape section has a pair of tiles on top of it where

---

[2] The strongest detaching force used in our construction is a τ strength detachment, and since the internal bonds of our gadgets are meant to withstand even the strongest repulsive force, it follows that those bonds must be of strength at least 2τ.

the information is stored. When talking about the *tape* from Sect. 3.2, each pair of dark grey tiles on top of the tape sections represents a piece of information describing the *path*.

The Overlay Initiator Gadget attaches to the end of the completed *tape*, and begins the overlay process (Fig. 5b–d). Each bit of information on the tape is covered by a corresponding overlay section, allowing the information to be read on top of the overlay. This process continues, section by section, until the entire tape is covered. Once finished, the overlay layer will act as an interface, allowing the gadgets to use the information on the *tape*.

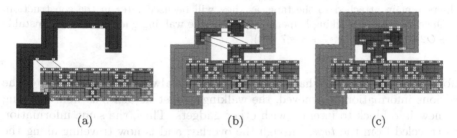

(a)   (b)   (c)

Fig. 6. (a) The Read Gadget attaches ($n + T + F = 2 + 7 + 1 \geq \tau$). In (b) the first form of an information block attaches ($F + F + J2 = 1 + 1 + 8 \geq \tau$). Since the *forward* version of the read gadget was used, the *forward* information block is placed. After the information block is placed, the penultimate read-helper attaches ($A2 + A2 + O1 = 2 + 2 + 7 \geq \tau$). (c) After all read helpers have attached, the read gadget becomes unstable ($F + F + M + n + T + F + Q = 1 + 1 + 1 + 2 + 7 + 1 - 7 \leq \tau$).

Read. The read gadget is required for "reading" the Turing machine *tape*. Essentially, this gadget extracts the information that is relayed from the *tape* through the overlay blocks. The read process (Fig. 6a–c) can only begin if the leftmost tape section has not previously been read. Once attached, the gadget allows the attachment of an information block (corresponding to the information being read) that will be used to carry the build instructions through the rest of our construction. Once the information block is present, the remaining read-helpers can attach. The final helper destabilizes the read gadget, allowing it to fall off and expose the newly attached information block. The read gadget was designed to produce this information block, alter the *tape* section that is being read (making it unreadable), and then detach from the assembly. This design ensures that each *tape* section is only read once, and allows us to transfer the instructions to other locations in our construction via the walking gadgets.

Information Walking. The walking gadgets begin the information walking process (Fig. 7), which allows instructions to travel throughout our construction. After a tape section has been read and an information block has been placed, a walking gadget can attach. Once attached, the walking gadget allows a new information block (of the same type) to attach, while also detaching the previous

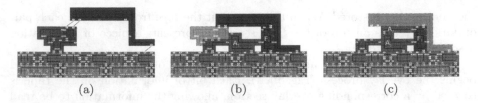

Fig. 7. (a) A Walking Gadget (specific to the information block) attaches to the overlay and the information block ($F + F + J1 = 1 + 1 + 8 \geq \tau$). (b) The negative interaction between the D glues destabilizes the old information block, along with the two walking-helpers ($J2 + A2 + A2 + F + F + D = 8 + 2 + 2 + 1 + 1 - 7 \leq \tau$). Notice that two helpers remain attached to the tape, as they will be used later in the construction. (c) Once the second walking-helper is attached, the walking gadget becomes unstable ($F + O2 + J1 + D = 1 + 7 + 8 - 7 \leq \tau$).

information block. Notice that this detachment will always be $O(1)$ size. After the previous information is removed, the walking gadget detaches as well, allowing the new info block to interact with other gadgets. Thus, the same information has traveled from the *tape*, through the overlay, and is now traveling along the *tape*. This process is repeated until the information has traveled to the end of the *path*, at which point it is used to construct the next *path* portion. This method is desirable because it does not allow duplicate readable instructions to be attached to the path at any time.

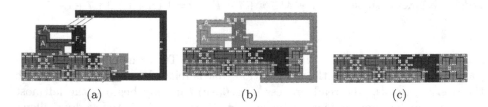

Fig. 8. (a) The forward-extension gadget attaches to the information block and Turing tape ($B + C + F + p = 3 + 4 + 1 + 2 \geq \tau$). (b) The second extension-helper comes with the negative D glue that causes targeted destabilization ($X + p + J1 + X + D = 2 + 2 + 8 + 2 - 7 \leq \tau$). The extension gadget and its helpers, along with the information block and its helpers are no longer stable along their tape-overlay edges. (c) The final result is a one path-pixel extension of the path.

Path Extension. After the information block has reached the end of the *path*, a path extension gadget can attach to the assembly. Once attached, the gadget allows the *path* extension process (Fig. 8) to begin, which extends the *path* in a given direction (forward, left, or right) based on the instruction carried by the information block. The extension gadget "reads" the information block, and then extends the path in the given direction. Afterwards, the extension helpers destabilize the information block and extension gadget, causing a $O(1)$ sized detachment. We designed the extension gadget to essentially replace an instruction block with a corresponding *path* portion. This design allows us to attach a $O(1)$ sized *path* portion for each instruction read from the *tape*.

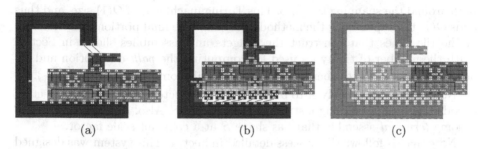

(a)   (b)   (c)

Fig. 9. (a) The tape reduction gadget attaches to the read-helpers ($A2+U = 2+8 \geq \tau$). (b) Filler tiles attach ($s+s = 8+8 \geq \tau$), and create a strong bond to the tape reduction gadget. (c) The two negative o glues cause a strong targeted destabilization of the previously read tape section ($e + u1 + u2 + o + o = 3 + 8 + 8 - 5 - 5 \leq \tau$).

Tape Reduction. After a tape section has been read, we no longer need it. Instead of continuing to grow the assembly, we can remove $O(1)$ size portions of the *tape* as it is being read. This is where the tape reduction gadget initiates the tape reduction process (Fig. 9) mentioned in Sect. 3.2. The attachments left behind by the read/walk processes allow the tape reduction gadget to attach to a tape section that has already been read. The gadget then removes itself, along with the previously read tape section, exposing the next section of the tape for reading. This technique is desirable because it allows us to break apart the *tape* into $O(1)$ sized pieces as we use it. As the *tape* is reduced, the *path* continues to grow until there are no more *tape* sections to be read.

Due to page constraints, some of the construction details have been omitted (such as turning and filling). For complete details, please see the arXiv version of this paper [7].

5   Constant Scaled Shapes

In this section, we formally state the results based on our construction.

Theorem 1. *For any finite connected shape S, there exists a 2HAM system $\Gamma = (T_S, 10)$ that uniquely produces S (with $O(1)$ size bounded garbage) at a $O(1)$ scale factor, and $|T_S| = O(\frac{K(S)}{\log K(S)})$.*

Proof. We show this by constructing a 2HAM system $\Gamma = (T_S, 10)$. One portion of T_S consists of the tile types which assemble a higher base Kolmogorov-optimal description of S (Sect. 7). This portion of T_S consists of $O(\frac{K(S)}{\log K(S)})$ tile types, as analyzed in Sect. 7. Another portion of T_S consists of the tile types needed to assemble a fuel-efficient Turing machine, as described by [15], that performs a simple base conversion to binary using $O(\frac{K(S)}{\log K(S)})$ tile types, as analyzed in Sect. 7. The next portion of T_S consists of the tile types required to assemble another fuel-efficient Turing machine that finds and outputs the description of a path around the spanning tree of S. This Turing machine is of $O(1)$ size, and thus adds $O(1)$ tile types using the method from [15]. The final portion of T_S consists of the tile types that construct the gadgets and assemblies shown in Sect. 4. With the number of tile types used for computing the *path* description and for our construction process being $O(1)$, our final tile complexity is $O(\frac{K(S)}{\log K(S)})$.

Now, consider assembly A to be the fully constructed *tape* assembly (Sect. 4) encoded with *path*-building instructions specific to S. Also, suppose assembly B is some *terminal* assembly that has shape S at a constant scale factor.

Note that Γ follows the process detailed in Sect. 4. This system was designed so that two assemblies are *combinable* only if at least one of those assemblies is at most a constant size (70 tiles), and every *breakable* assembly can only break into two subassemblies if one of those assemblies is at most another constant size (118 tiles). In our construction, the only non-constant size assemblies are A, B, or some intermediate assembly that consists of some portion of the *tape*, and some partially assembled section of the final shape. Of these, B is the only terminal assembly.

While A and the intermediate assemblies continue engaging in a series of attachments and detachments, the *tape* continues to get smaller and the *path* continues to grow. The attachment and detachment of $O(1)$ size pieces with these assemblies will continue until we reach the terminal assembly B, at which time A will have been disassembled into smaller constant garbage. Therefore, we see that $A \to^\Gamma B$.   □

6   Lower Bound

Here we present a brief argument for the lower bound of $\Omega(\frac{K(S)}{\log K(S)})$ on the tile types needed to assemble a scaling of a shape S. This argument is essentially the same as what is presented in [2,13,16], and we refer the reader there for a more detailed explanation.

Theorem 2. *The tile complexity in the 2HAM for self-assembling a scale-c version of a shape S at constant temperature and constant garbage is $\Omega(\frac{K(S)}{\log K(S)})$.*

Proof. Note that a 2HAM system $\Gamma = (T, \tau = O(1))$ can be uniquely represented with a string of $O(|T| \log |T|)$ bits. In particular, each tile may be encoded as a list of its 4 glues, and each glue may be represented by a $O(\log |T|)$-bit string taken from an indexing of the maximum possible $4|T|$ distinct glue types of the system. The constant bounded temperature incurs an additional additive constant. Given this representation, consider a 2HAM simulation program that inputs a 2HAM system, and outputs the positions of any uniquely produced scale-c shape (with up to $O(1)$ garbage), if one exists. This simulator, along with the $O(|T| \log |T|)$ bit encoding of a system Γ which assembles S at scale c, constitute a program which outputs the positions of S, and is thus lower bounded in bits by $K(S)$. Therefore $K(S) \leq d|T| \log |T|$ for some constant d, implying $|T| = \Omega(\frac{K(S)}{\log K(S)})$. □

7 Extension to $\frac{K(S)}{\log K(S)}$

The starting assembly for our shape construction algorithm is the *tape* assembly from [15] with a binary string as its value. For a binary string $A = a_0 \ldots a_{k-1}$, such an assembly can be constructed in a straightforward manner using $O(k)$ tile types (simply place a distinct tile for each position in the assembly, for example). However, by using a base conversion trick, we can take advantage of the fact that each tile type is asymptotically capable of representing slightly more than 1 bit in order to build the string in $O(k/\log k)$ tile types. To achieve this, first we consider the base-b representation $B = b_0 \ldots b_{d-1}$ of the string A for some higher base $b > 2$. Note that the number of digits of this string is $d \leq \lceil \frac{k}{\lfloor \log_2 b \rfloor} \rceil = O(\frac{k}{\log b})$. We are able to assemble this shorter string (by brute force with distinct tile types at each position) with only $O(d)$ tile types.

Next, we consider a Turing machine which converts any base b string into its equivalent base 2 representation. Such a Turing machine can be constructed using $O(b)$ transition rules. Therefore, we can apply the result of [15] to run this Turing machine on the initial tape assembly representing string B to obtain string A. The cost of this construction in total is $O(d)$ tiles to construct the initial tape assembly, plus $O(b)$ tiles to implement the rules of the conversion Turing machine[3], for a total of $O(d + b)$ tiles.

Finally, we select $b = \lceil \frac{k}{\log k} \rceil = O(\frac{k}{\log k})$, which yields $d = O(\frac{k}{\log k - \log \log k}) = O(\frac{k}{\log k})$, implying that the entire tile cost of setting up the initial tape assembly representing binary string B is $O(b + d) = O(\frac{k}{\log k})$ tile types. In our case $k = O(K(S))$ where $K(S)$ denotes the Kolmogorov complexity of shape S for some given universal Turing machine, and so we achieve our final tile complexity of $O(\frac{K(S)}{\log K(S)})$.

8 Conclusion

In this work, we considered the optimal shape building problem in the negative glue 2-handed assembly model, and provided a system that allows the self-assembly of general shapes at scale 24. Shape construction has been studied in more powerful self-assembly models such as the staged RNA assembly model and the chemical reaction network-controlled tile assembly model. However, our

---

[3] The formal theorem statement of [15] cites the product of the states and symbols of the Turing machine as the tile type cost. However, the actual cost is the number of transition rules, which is upper bounded by this product.

result constitutes the first example of optimal general shape construction at constant scale in a *passive* model of self-assembly where no outside experimenter intervention is required, and system monomers are state-less, static pieces which interact solely based on the attraction and repulsion of surface chemistry.

Our work opens up a number of directions for future work. We have not considered a runtime model for this construction, so analyzing and improving the *running time* for constant-scaled shape self-assembly in the 2-handed assembly is one open direction. Another is determining the lowest necessary temperature and glue strengths needed for $O(1)$ scale shape construction. We use temperature value 10 for the sake of clarity, and have not attempted to optimize this value.

References

1. Chalk, C., Demiane, E.D., Demaine, M.L., Martinez, E., Schweller, R., Vega, L., Wylie, T.: Universal shape replicators via self-assembly with attractive and repulsive forces. In: Proceedings of the 28th Annual ACM-SIAM Symposium on Discrete Algorithms (SODA 2017) (2017)
2. Cheng, Q., Aggarwal, G., Goldwasser, M.H., Kao, M.Y., Schweller, R.T., de Espanés, P.M.: Complexities for generalized models of self-assembly. SIAM J. Comput. **34**, 1493–1515 (2005)
3. Demaine, E.D., Demaine, M.L., Fekete, S.P., Ishaque, M., Rafalin, E., Schweller, R.T., Souvaine, D.L.: Staged self-assembly: nanomanufacture of arbitrary shapes with $O(1)$ glues. Nat. Comput. **7**(3), 347–370 (2008)
4. Demaine, E.D., Fekete, S.P., Scheffer, C., Schmidt, A.: New geometric algorithms for fully connected staged self-assembly. In: Phillips, A., Yin, P. (eds.) DNA 2015. LNCS, vol. 9211, pp. 104–116. Springer, Cham (2015). doi:10.1007/978-3-319-21999-8_7
5. Demaine, E.D., Patitz, M.J., Schweller, R.T., Summers, S.M.: Self-assembly of arbitrary shapes using RNAse enzymes: meeting the Kolmogorov bound with small scale factor (extended abstract). In: Proceedings of the 28th International Symposium on Theoretical Aspects of Computer Science (STACS 2011) (2011)
6. Doty, D., Kari, L., Masson, B.: Negative interactions in irreversible self-assembly. Algorithmica **66**(1), 153–172 (2013)
7. Luchsinger, A., Schweller, R., Wylie, T.: Self-assembly of shapes at constant scale using repulsive forces (2016). arXiv:1608.04791
8. Mauch, J., Stacho, L., Stoll, C.: Step-wise tile assembly with a constant number of tile types. Nat. Comput. **11**(3), 535–550 (2012)
9. Patitz, M.J., Rogers, T.A., Schweller, R.T., Summers, S.M., Winslow, A.: Resiliency to multiple nucleation in temperature-1 self-assembly. In: Rondelez, Y., Woods, D. (eds.) DNA 2016. LNCS, vol. 9818, pp. 98–113. Springer, Cham (2016). doi:10.1007/978-3-319-43994-5_7
10. Patitz, M.J., Schweller, R.T., Summers, S.M.: Exact shapes and turing universality at temperature 1 with a single negative glue. In: Cardelli, L., Shih, W. (eds.) DNA 2011. LNCS, vol. 6937, pp. 175–189. Springer, Heidelberg (2011). doi:10.1007/978-3-642-23638-9_15
11. Reif, J.H., Sahu, S., Yin, P.: Complexity of graph self-assembly in accretive systems and self-destructible systems. Theoret. Comput. Sci. **412**(17), 1592–1605 (2011)
12. Rothemund, P.W.K.: Using lateral capillary forces to compute by self-assembly. Proc. Nat. Acad. Sci. **97**(3), 984–989 (2000)

13. Rothemund, P.W.K., Winfree, E.: The program-size complexity of self-assembled squares (extended abstract). In: Proceedings of the 32nd Annual ACM Symposium on Theory of Computing, STOC 2000, pp. 459–468 (2000)
14. Schiefer, N., Winfree, E.: Universal computation and optimal construction in the chemical reaction network-controlled tile assembly model. In: Phillips, A., Yin, P. (eds.) DNA 2015. LNCS, vol. 9211, pp. 34–54. Springer, Cham (2015). doi:10.1007/978-3-319-21999-8_3
15. Schweller, R., Sherman, M.: Fuel efficient computation in passive self-assembly. In: SODA 2013: Proceedings of the 24th Annual ACM-SIAM Symposium on Discrete Algorithms, pp. 1513–1525. SIAM (2013)
16. Soloveichik, D., Winfree, E.: Complexity of self-assembled shapes. SIAM J. Comput. 36(6), 1544–1569 (2007)
17. Summers, S.M.: Reducing tile complexity for the self-assembly of scaled shapes through temperature programming. Algorithmica 63(1), 117–136 (2012)

Verification in Staged Tile Self-Assembly

Robert Schweller, Andrew Winslow$^{(\boxtimes)}$, and Tim Wylie

University of Texas - Rio Grande Valley, Edinburg, TX 78539, USA
{robert.schweller,andrew.winslow,timothy.wylie}@utrgv.edu

Abstract. We prove the unique assembly and unique shape verification problems, benchmark measures of self-assembly model power, are coNP^{NP}-hard and contained in PSPACE (and in Π^p_{2s} for staged systems with s stages). En route, we prove that unique shape verification problem in the 2HAM is coNP^{NP}-complete.

Keywords: DNA computing · Biocomputing · 2HAM · Hierarchical

1 Introduction

Here we consider the complexity of two standard problems in tile self-assembly: deciding whether a system uniquely assembles a given assembly or shape. These so-called *unique assembly* and *unique shape verification* problems are benchmark problems in tile assembly, and have been studied in a variety of models, including the aTAM [1,2], the q-tile model [6], and the 2HAM [3].

The unique assembly and unique shape verification problems ask whether a system behaves as expected: does a given system yield a unique given assembly or assemblies of a given unique shape? The distinct rules by which assemblies form in various tile assembly models yield the potential for such problems to have varying complexity. For instance, assuming P $\neq$ NP, the unique *assembly* verification problem is known to be a strictly easier problem in the aTAM than in the 2HAM.

However, several open questions remain. For instance, such a separation between the aTAM and 2HAM for the unique *shape* verification problem had not been known. Here we prove such a separation (see Table 1).

Additionally, a popular generalization of the 2HAM called the *staged tile assembly model* [7] has been shown to be capable of extremely efficient assembly across a range of parameters [4,7–9,14]. Does this power come from the increased complexity of verifying that systems assemble intended assemblies and shapes?

We achieve progress on these questions, proving a separation between the 2HAM and staged model for the unique assembly verification problem (coNP-complete versus coNP^{NP}-hard) utilizing a promising technique that may lead to proving a stronger separation for the unique shape verification problem (coNP^{NP}-complete versus a conjectured PSPACE-complete).

This research was supported in part by National Science Foundation Grants CCF-1117672 and CCF-1555626.

M.J. Patitz and M. Stannett (Eds.): UCNC 2017, LNCS 10240, pp. 98–112, 2017.
DOI: 10.1007/978-3-319-58187-3_8

Table 1. Known and new results on the unique assembly and unique shape verification problems.

Model	Unique assembly	Unique shape
aTAM	P [1]	coNP-complete [6]
2HAM	coNP-complete [5]	coNP^{NP}-complete (Sect. 3)
Staged	coNP^{NP}-hard (Sect. 5), in PSPACE (Sect. 6)	

The coNP^{NP}-hardness results are also interesting as the first, to our knowledge, verification problems in irreversible tile assembly that are decidable but not contained in NP or coNP.

2   The Staged Assembly Model

Tiles. A *tile* is a non-rotatable unit square with each edge labeled with a *glue* from a set Σ. Each pair of glues $g_1, g_2 \in \Sigma$ has a non-negative integer *strength*, denoted $\mathrm{str}(g_1, g_2)$. Every set Σ contains a special *null glue* whose strength with every other glue is 0. If the glue strengths do not obey $\mathrm{str}(g_1, g_2) = 0$ for all $g_1 \neq g_2$, then the glues are *flexible*. Unless otherwise stated, we assume that glues are not flexible.

Configurations, Assemblies, and Shapes. A *configuration* is a partial function $A : \mathbb{Z}^2 \to T$ for some set of tiles T, i.e., an arrangement of tiles on a square grid. For a configuration A and vector $\boldsymbol{u} = \langle u_x, u_y \rangle \in \mathbb{Z}^2$, $A + \boldsymbol{u}$ denotes the configuration $f \circ A$, where $f(x, y) = (x + u_x, y + u_y)$. For two configurations A and B, B is a *translation* of A, written $B \simeq A$, provided that $B = A + \boldsymbol{u}$ for some vector $\boldsymbol{u}$. For a configuration A, the *assembly* of A is the set $\tilde{A} = \{B : B \simeq A\}$. An assembly $\tilde{A}$ is a *subassembly* of an assembly $\tilde{B}$, denoted $\tilde{A} \sqsubseteq \tilde{B}$, provided that there exists an $A \in \tilde{A}$ and $B \in \tilde{B}$ such that $A \subseteq B$. The *shape* of an assembly $\tilde{A}$ is $\{\mathrm{dom}(A) : A \in \tilde{A}\}$ where $\mathrm{dom}()$ is the domain of a configuration. A shape S' is a *scaled* version of shape S provided that for some $k \in \mathbb{N}$ and $D \in S$, $\bigcup_{(x,y) \in D} \bigcup_{(i,j) \in \{0,1,\ldots,k-1\}^2} (kx + i, ky + j) \in S'$.

Bond Graphs and Stability. For a configuration A, define the *bond graph* G_A to be the weighted grid graph in which each element of $\mathrm{dom}(A)$ is a vertex, and the weight of the edge between a pair of tiles is equal to the strength of the coincident glue pair. A configuration is τ-*stable* for $\tau \in \mathbb{N}$ if every edge cut of G_A has strength at least τ, and is τ-*unstable* otherwise. Similarly, an assembly is τ-*stable* provided the configurations it contains are τ-stable. Assemblies $\tilde{A}$ and $\tilde{B}$ are τ-*combinable* into an assembly $\tilde{C}$ provided there exist $A \in \tilde{A}$, $B \in \tilde{B}$, and $C \in \tilde{C}$ such that $A \bigcup B = C$, $\mathrm{dom}(A) \bigcap \mathrm{dom}(B) = \emptyset$, and $\tilde{C}$ is τ-stable.

Two-Handed Assembly and Bins. We define the assembly process via bins. A bin is an ordered tuple (S, τ) where S is a set of *initial* assemblies and $\tau \in \mathbb{N}$ is the *temperature*. In this work, τ is always equal to 2 for upper bounds, and at most some constant for lower bounds. For a bin (S, τ), the set of *produced* assemblies $P'_{(S,\tau)}$ is defined recursively as follows:

1. $S \subseteq P'_{(S,\tau)}$.
2. If $A, B \in P'_{(S,\tau)}$ are τ-combinable into C, then $C \in P'_{(S,\tau)}$.

A produced assembly is *terminal* provided it is not τ-combinable with any other producible assembly, and the set of all terminal assemblies of a bin (S, τ) is denoted $P_{(S,\tau)}$. That is, $P'_{(S,\tau)}$ represents the set of all possible assemblies that can assemble from the initial set S, whereas $P_{(S,\tau)}$ represents only the set of assemblies that cannot grow any further.

The assemblies in $P_{(S,\tau)}$ are *uniquely produced* iff for each $x \in P'_{(S,\tau)}$ there exists a corresponding $y \in P_{(S,\tau)}$ such that $x \sqsubseteq y$. Unique production implies that every producible assembly can be repeatedly combined with others to form an assembly in $P_{(S,\tau)}$.

Staged Assembly Systems. An *r-stage b-bin mix graph* M is an acyclic r-partite digraph consisting of rb vertices $m_{i,j}$ for $1 \leq i \leq r$ and $1 \leq j \leq b$, and edges of the form $(m_{i,j}, m_{i+1,j'})$ for some i, j, j'. A *staged assembly system* is a 3-tuple $\langle M_{r,b}, \{T_1, T_2, \ldots, T_b\}, \tau \rangle$ where $M_{r,b}$ is an r-stage b-bin mix graph, T_i is a set of tile types, and $\tau \in \mathbb{N}$ is the temperature. Given a staged assembly system, for each $1 \leq i \leq r, 1 \leq j \leq b$, a corresponding bin $(R_{i,j}, \tau)$ is defined as follows:

1. $R_{1,j} = T_j$ (this is a bin in the first stage);
2. For $i \geq 2$, $R_{i,j} = \left(\displaystyle\bigcup_{k:\ (m_{i-1,k}, m_{i,j}) \in M_{r,b}} P_{(R_{(i-1,k)}, \tau_{i-1,k})} \right)$.

Thus, bins in stage 1 are tile sets T_j, and each bin in any subsequent stage receives an initial set of assemblies consisting of the terminally produced assemblies from a subset of the bins in the previous stage as dictated by the edges of the mix graph.[1] The *output* of a staged system is the union of the set of terminal assemblies of the bins in the final stage.[2] The output of a staged system is *uniquely produced* provided each bin in the staged system uniquely produces its terminal assemblies.

3   The 2HAM Unique Shape Verification Problem Is coNP^{NP}-Complete

This section serves as a warm-up for the format and techniques used in later sections. We begin by proving the 2HAM USV problem is in coNP^{NP} by providing

---

[1] The original staged model [7] only considered $O(1)$ distinct tile types, and thus for simplicity allowed tiles to be added at any stage (since $\mathcal{O}(1)$ extra bins could hold the individual tile types to mix at any stage). Because systems here may have super-constant tile complexity, we restrict tiles to only be added at the initial stage.

[2] This is a slight modification of the original staged model [7] in that there is no requirement of a final stage with a single output bin. This may be a slightly more capable model, and so it is considered here. However, all results in this paper apply to both variants of the model.

a (non-deterministic) algorithm for the problem that can be executed on such a machine. This is followed by a reduction from a SAT-like problem complete for coNP^{NP} ($\forall\exists$SAT).

Definition 1 (2HAM unique shape verification (2HAM USV) problem). *Given a 2HAM system Γ and shape S, does every terminal assembly of Γ have shape S?*

Theorem 1. *The 2HAM USV problem (for $\tau = 2$ systems) is* coNP^{NP}*-hard.*

Definition 2 ($\forall\exists$SAT). *Given a 3-SAT formula $\phi(x_1, x_2, \ldots, x_k, x_{k+1}, \ldots, x_n)$, is it true that for every assignment of $x_1, x_2, \ldots, x_k$, there exists an assignment of $x_{k+1}, x_{k+2}, \ldots, x_n$ such that $\phi(x_1, x_2, \ldots, x_n)$ evaluates to* T*?*

The $\forall\exists$SAT problem was shown to be coNP^{NP}-complete by Stockmeyer [13] (see [12] for further discussion).

Proof. The reduction is from $\forall\exists$SAT. Roughly speaking, the system output by the reduction behaves as follows. First, a distinct assembly encoding each possible assignment of the variables of the $\forall\exists$SAT instance is assembled. Further growth "tags" each assembly as either a *true* or *false* assembly, based upon the truth value of the input 3-SAT formula ϕ for the variable assignment encoded by the assembly.

False assemblies further grow into a slightly larger target shape S. A separate set of *test* assemblies are created, one for each variable assignment of the variables $x_1, \ldots x_k$. Each test assembly attaches to any true assembly with the same assignment of these variables to form an assembly with shape S - the same shape as false assemblies.

Terminal assemblies then consist of false assemblies and true-test assemblies with shape S, and possibly test assemblies. A test assembly is terminal if and only if there is no true assembly for it to attach to, i.e. the assignment of variables $x_1, \ldots, x_k$ has no corresponding assignment of the variables $x_{k+1}, \ldots, x_n$ such that $\phi(x_1, \ldots, x_n)$ is "true".

SAT Assemblies. Consider a given input formula C and input value k for the $\forall\exists$SAT problem. From this input we design a corresponding 2HAM system $\Gamma = (T, 2)$ and shape S such that the terminal assemblies of Γ share a common shape S if and only if the $\forall\exists$SAT instance is "true", i.e. each assignment of the variables x_1 through x_k can be combined with some assignment of the variables x_{k+1} through x_m such that the 3-SAT instance is satisfied.

The system has temperature 2, and the tile set T of the system output by the reduction is sketched in Fig. 1. The first subset of tiles is a minor modification of the commonly used 3-SAT solving system from [11].

For each variable x_i, the system has two tile subsets. These collections assemble into 1×4 assemblies with exposed north and south glues representing the values "0" and "1", respectively, encoding the assignment of a specific variable to true or false. These 1×4 assemblies further assemble into $1 \times 4n$ assemblies encoding complete assignments of the variables x_1 to x_n. The non-deterministic

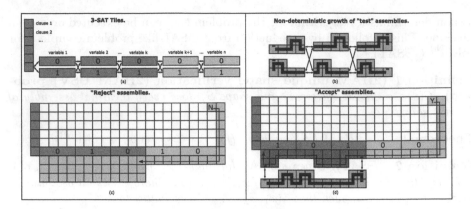

Fig. 1. Steps of the 2HAM USV coNP^{NP}-hardness reduction.

assembly process of 2HAM implies that such an assembly for every possible variable assignment will be assembled.

An additional column is attached to this bar of height equal to m, the number of clauses in the formula C (Fig. 1). An additional set of tiles are added that evaluate the 3-SAT formula ϕ based upon the variable assignments encoded by the initial $1 \times 4n$ assembly following the approach of [11]. These tiles place a tile in the upper right corner of the resulting assembly with exposed glue labeled "T" or "F", indicating the truth value of ϕ based upon the variable assignments.

The resulting assemblies are categorized as *true* and *false* assemblies. Additional tiles are added so that every false assembly further grows, extending the left $4k$ columns (corresponding to the variables x_1 to x_k) southward by 3 rows, and the remaining right $4(n-k)$ columns southward by 1 row (Fig. 1(c)). The resulting shape is the shape S output by the reduction, i.e. the only shape assembled by the system if the solution to the $\forall\exists$SAT instance is "true".

Test Assemblies. Additional tiles are also added so that true assemblies also grow southward, but extending the left $4k$ columns by various amounts based upon each variable assignment. The result is a sequence of geometric "bumps and dents" that encode the truth values of these variables.

A set of *test* assemblies with complementary geometry for each possible assignment of variables x_1 through x_k are assembled (Fig. 1(b)). Test assemblies use two strength-1 glues that cooperatively attach to any true assembly with a matching assignment of variables x_1 through x_k (Fig. 1(d)). The assembly formed by a test assembly attaching to a true assembly has shape S: the same shape as a false assembly.

Terminal Assemblies. If the solution to the $\forall\exists$SAT instance is "false", there is some truth assignment for variables $x_1 \ldots x_k$ with no corresponding assignment of the variables $x_{k+1} \ldots x_n$ such that $\phi(x_1, \ldots, x_n)$ is "true". Thus, the test assembly with this assignment of variables $x_1, \ldots, x_k$ has no compatible true assembly to attach to - and this test assembly is a terminal assembly of Γ with shape not equal to S.

On the other hand, if the solution to the $\forall\exists$SAT instance is "yes", every test assembly attaches to a true assembly and thus every terminal assembly (true-test assemblies and false assemblies) has shape S.

Theorem 2. *The 2HAM USV problem is in* $\mathsf{coNP}^{\mathsf{NP}}$.

Proof. The solution to an instance (Γ, S) of the 2HAM USV problem is "true" if and only if:

1. Every producible assembly of Γ has size at most $|S|$.
2. Every assembly of size at most $|S|$ and without shape S is not a terminal assembly.

Algorithm 1 solves the 2HAM USV problem by verifying each of these conditions, using an NP subroutine to verify the second condition. The algorithm is executed by a coNP machine, implying that "false" is returned if any of the non-deterministic branches return "false", and otherwise returns "true".

Algorithm 1. A $\mathsf{coNP}^{\mathsf{NP}}$ algorithm for the 2HAM USV problem

1: Non-deterministically select a τ-stable assembly A with $|S| < |A| \leq 2|S|$.
2: **if** A is producible **then**   ▷ In P by Theorem 3.2 of [10]
3:     **return** false.
4: **end if**
5: Non-deterministically select a τ-stable assembly B with $|B| \leq |S|$ and shape not equal to S.
6: **if** not $\mathcal{F}(\Gamma, B, |S|)$ **then**   ▷ Algorithm 2
7:     **return** false.
8: **end if**
9: **return** true.

Algorithm 2. An NP algorithm subroutine of Algorithm 1

1: **procedure** $\mathcal{F}(\Gamma, B, n)$ ▷ Returns whether B is *not* terminal.
2:     Non-deterministically select a τ-stable assembly C with $|C| \leq n$.
3:     **if** C cannot attach to B at temperature τ **then**
4:         **return** false.
5:     **end if**
6:     **if** C is a producible assembly of Γ **then**   ▷ In P by Theorem 3.2 of [10]
7:         **return** false.
8:     **end if**
9:     **return** true.
10: **end procedure**

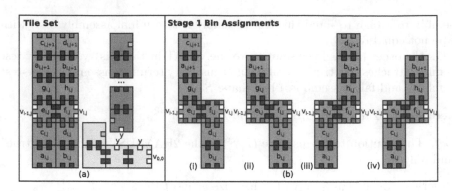

Fig. 2. (a) The tile set used in the staged coNP-hardness reduction. (b) The subsets of tiles included in separated initial bins within the first stage of the system. (Color figure online)

4 Staged Unique Assembly Verification Is coNP-Hard

Definition 3 (Staged unique assembly verification (Staged UAV) problem). *Given a staged system Γ and an assembly A, does Γ uniquely assemble A?*

Theorem 3. *The staged UAV problem (for $\tau = 2$ 4-stage systems) is coNP-hard.*

Proof. The reduction is from 3-SAT, outputting a staged system Γ and assembly A such that the 3-SAT instance is satisfiable if and only if A is *not* the unique terminal assembly of Γ. We reduce from 3-SAT: Given a 3-SAT formula ϕ, we design a staged assembly system and an assembly A such that ϕ is *not* satisfied if and only if A is uniquely assembled by Γ.

The Tileset. The tiles used in our construction are shown in Fig. 2(a). In particular, for each variable $x_i \in \{x_1, x_2, \ldots, x_n\}$ and clause $c_j \in \{c_1, c_2, \ldots, c_m\}$ in ϕ, there is a block of tiles labeled $a_{i,j}, b_{i,j}, c_{i,j}, d_{i,j}, e_{i,j}, f_{i,j}, g_{i,j}$. The set of tile types for each block is denoted block$_{i,j}$.

The strength-2 ($\tau = 2$) glues connecting adjacent tiles are unique with respect to adjacent tiles, and are unlabelled in the figures for clarity. Note that for each block (i,j), the top four tiles of the block occupy the same locations as the bottom four tiles of block $(i, j+1)$. Finally, the tileset includes a length $4m$ chain of *green* tiles, with each green tile sharing a strength-2 glue with its neighbors, along with four light-grey tiles which together attach to the green assembly.

Stage 1: Variable Assignments. The specific formula ϕ is encoded within the output staged system via the initial choice of tiles placed into a $O(1)$-sized collection of stage-1 bins. For each variable x_i and clause c_j combination, we select two subsets of the block$_{i,j}$ tileset. The first subset encodes a variable choice of "false" for x_i. The tile sets in Fig. 2(b)(i) and (iv) are used if x_i satisfies (and $\overline{x_i}$

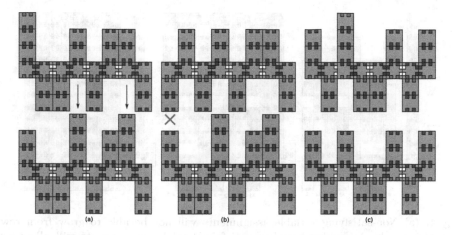

Fig. 3. In stage 2, rows non-deterministically form encoding each of the 2^n possible variable assignments. In stage 3 the rows are combined allowing for geometrically compatible, sequential rows with exposed red glue to attach. (a) Combinable rows. (b) Geometrically incompatible rows. (c) Rows with no glues for attachment. (Color figure online)

does not satisfy) clause c_j, respectively. Similarly, the tile sets in Fig. 2(b)(ii–iii) are used if x_i does not (and $\overline{x_i}$ does satisfy) clause c_j.

Beyond utilizing two types of $block_{i,j}$ tile sets, tile sets are further distinguished between odd and even values of i and j. In total, 16 distinct bins (satisfied or not, negated or not, odd or even i, odd or even j) are used.

We include the grey and green tiles of Fig. 2(a) separately in two additional bins. An additional four bins are used in the construction to maintain a set of single copies of all tiles used within the system. Separating these tile subsets into four bins ensures that the tiles do no interact (until mixed with other assemblies at a later stage).

Stage 2: Assembling Rows. In stage 2 we combine all $block_{i,j}$ assemblies for even j into one bin, and all $block_{i,j}$ assemblies for odd j into a second bin. Within each bin and for each value j, rows encoding each possible variable assignment assemble non-deterministically via attaching $0 - block_{i,j}$ and $1 - block_{i,j}$ assemblies for each $i \in \{1, 2, \ldots, n\}$. We refer to these assemblies as row_j assemblies. There are 2^n such assemblies for each j - one per variable assignment. Example row_j assemblies are shown in Fig. 3.

Stage 3: Combining Rows with Shared Assignments and Satisfied Clauses. Stage 3 is where the *real* action happens. All row_j assemblies are combined, along with the green and grey assemblies of Fig. 2.

Consider the possible assembly of a row_j and a row_{j+1} assembly. If the two respective rows encode distinct variable assignments, geometric incompatibility prohibits any possible connection (Fig. 3(b)). If the rows encode the same truth assignment, then the rows may attach if any of the row_j variable pieces expose the extended tip via the red $\tau = 2$ strength glues (Fig. 3(a)). Such an attachment indicates that the variable assignment of both rows satisfies c_j. If the variable

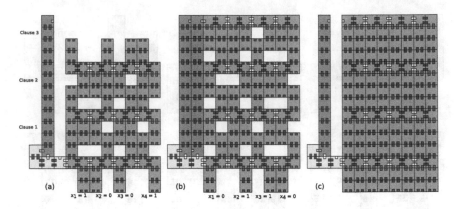

Fig. 4. (a) Non-satisfying variable assignments will not be able to grow from row 0 to row m. (b) Assemblies encoding satisfying variable assignments will allow for complete assemblies with all rows, allowing for a green assembly to attach. (c) The target assembly A given as output of the reduction. (Color figure online)

assignment encoding does not satisfy c_j, no extended tip exists and the rows cannot attach (Fig. 3(c)).

A satisfying assignment of ϕ corresponds to m rows attaching to form a complete "satisfying" assembly (Fig. 4(b)). The green assembly attaches cooperatively to such assemblies using the row_m assembly glue and a glue from the grey tiles, which attach uniquely to row_0. The attachment of a green assembly verifies that all rows are present and the variable assignment satisfies ϕ.

A second copy of the green assembly attaches to any assembly containing row_0, regardless of whether all rows are present or not (Fig. 4(a)). In a separate bin, the green assembly tiles and grey assemblies are combined, yielding a combined grey-green product (for mixing in stage 4).

Stage 4: Merging Assignments. In stage 4, the set of all $\text{block}_{i,j}$ individual tiles are added to the assemblies constructed in stage 3 as well as the grey-green assembly produced in the previous stage. Note that the green assembly is *not* an input assembly to this mixing.

Since all $\text{block}_{i,j}$ assemblies are included, each terminal assembly from stage 3 may grow into the unique terminal assembly shown in Fig. 4(c) with one exception: assemblies from stage 3 encoding satisfying variable assignments. These assemblies have one additional copy of the green bar assembly attached. Therefore, the assembly of Fig. 4(c) is uniquely assembled if an only if no such satisfying assembly exists.

5   Staged Unique Assembly Verification Is coNP^{NP}-Hard

Theorem 4. *The staged UAV problem (for $\tau = 2$ 7-stage systems) is* coNP^{NP}-*hard.*

Proof. We reduce from $\forall\exists$SAT by combining ideas from the reductions of Theorem 1 and 3.

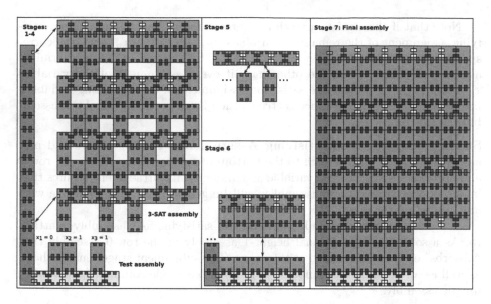

Fig. 5. The assemblies at respective stages for the coNP^{NP}-hardness reduction for the staged UAV problem. (Color figure online)

Stages 1–3: The SAT Assemblies. The first 3 stages follows those of the reduction in Theorem 3 but without the inclusion of the green assembly and light grey tiles. The result is a collection of assemblies encoding satisfying variable assignments with all m rows, as well as partial assemblies of less than m rows encoding non-satisfying assignments. For clarity, the bottom half of the $j = 0$ blocks for values $i > k$ are removed, exposing the "geometric teeth" only for the first k variables.

Stages 1–3: The Test Assemblies. Additionally, in a separate set of bins, we non-deterministically generate a set of *test* assemblies. The test assemblies are similar to row assemblies and generated in a similar fashion. An example test assembly is shown in Fig. 5 (Stages 1–4). A test assembly for each of the 2^k possible truth assignments of $x_1, x_2, \ldots, x_k$ is grown, and a green bar assembly is attached to the side of each test assembly.

Stage 4: The Magic Happens. The SAT assemblies and test assemblies are combined in a bin. Test assemblies attach to SAT assesmblies encoding satisfying variable assignments by utilizing cooperative bonding based on the two strength-1 green glues on the green assembly. SATassemblies encoding non-satisfying assignments must each lack the topmost or bottommost row, and therefore cannot attach to a test assembly.

Due to the geometric interlocking teeth from the test assembly and the bottom of SAT assemblies, test assemblies may only attach to SAT assemblies that encode the same variable assignment (of variables $x_1, x_2, \ldots, x_k$). Stages 1–4 of Fig. 5 show an example test assembly and a attaching SAT assembly.

Note that if there exists a truth assignment for $x_1, x_2, \ldots, x_k$ with no satisfying assignment of the remaining variables $x_{k+1}, x_{k+2}, \ldots, x_n$, then the corresponding test assembly does not attach to *any* SAT assembly and is a terminal assembly of this bin. On the other had, if every assignment of the variables $x_1, x_2, \ldots, x_k$ has at least one satisfying assignment of the remaining variables, i.e. the solution $\forall\exists$SAT instance is "true", then there are no terminal test assemblies of this bin.

Stage 5: Tagging Non-satisfying Assignments. In Stage 5, we add preassembled duples which attach to the bottom of any assembly containing row 0 and encodes a non-satisfying variable assignment. This attachment ensures that in subsequent stages, these assemblies will be geometrically incompatible with any remaining test assemblies from Stage 4.

It is possible that some duples have no non-satisfying SAT assembly to attach to. As a solution, an additional height-1 assembly of the row-0 assembly that "absorbs" each duple is added at this stage. The subsequent stages enable these, as well as all other SAT assemblies, to grow into a single common (potentially) unique assembly.

Stage 6: Attaching Test Assemblies. The result of Stage 5 is mixed with an assembly consisting of:

- The light-grey bar of the test assemblies.
- A second complete layer of dark grey tiles.
- The green bar.

This assembly attaches to any non-satisfying SAT assembly that includes row 0, ensuring that all assemblies containing row 0 now have a version of the test assembly attached (Stage 6 in Fig. 5).

Stage 7: Merging. In the final stage, every individual tile of the target assembly (seen in Stage 7 of Fig. 5) is added to the result of Stage 6, with the exception of the green tiles and the tiles in rows 1 through 5 of the SAT assemblies.

These tiles complete each SAT assembly in the assembly in Fig. 5 (Stage 7). Morever, the height-1 assembly used to absorb duples from Stage 5 grows into the assembly from Fig. 5 (Stage 7). However, because of the lack of tiles from rows 1 through 5, any leftover test assembly from Stage 4 remains terminal.

Thus the target assembly is the unique terminal assembly of the system if and only if the solution to the $\forall\exists$SAT instance is "yes".

Observe that every staged system output by the reduction has the property that if it does not have a unique terminal assembly, then it also does not have a unique terminal shape. Thus the same reduction suffices to prove that the staged USV problem is coNP^{NP}-hard.

Corollary 1. *The staged USV problem is* coNP^{NP}*-hard.*

6   Staged **PSPACE** Containment

Here we prove that the staged UAV and USV problems are in **PSPACE**. Parameterized versions of the results are also obtained; these prove that both problems restricted to systems with any *fixed* number of stages lie in the polynomial hierarchy. Both results are obtained via upper bounds on the complexities of the following three problems:

Definition 4 (Stage-s producible-in-bin verification (PIBV$_s$) problem). *Given a staged system Γ, a bin b in stage s of Γ, an assembly A, and an integer n:*

1. *is A a producible assembly of b?*
2. *and does every producible assembly of every bin in stage $s-1$ of Γ have size at most n?*

Definition 5 (Stage-s undersized-in-bin verification (UIBV$_s$) problem). *Given a staged system Γ, a bin b in stage s of Γ, and an integer n:*

1. *and does every producible assembly of b have size at most n?*
2. *and does every producible assembly of every bin in stage $s-1$ of Γ have size at most n?*

Definition 6 (Stage-s terminal-in-bin verification (TIBV$_s$) problem). *Given a staged system Γ, a bin b in stage s of Γ, an assembly A, and an integer n:*

1. *is A a terminal assembly of b?*
2. *and does every producible assembly of b have size at most n?*
3. *and does every producible assembly of every bin in stage $s-1$ of Γ have size at most n?*

The statements and proofs of the following results use terminology related to the polynomial hierarchy. For an introduction to the polynomial hierarchy, see Stockmeyer [13]. As a reminder, $\Sigma_{i+1}^P = \mathsf{NP}^{\Sigma_i^P}$, $\Pi_{i+1}^P = \mathsf{coNP}^{\Sigma_i^P}$, and $\Sigma_0^P = \Pi_0^P = \mathsf{P}$.

Lemma 1. *For all $s \in \mathbb{N}$:*

- *The PIBV$_s$ problem is in Σ_{2s-2}^P.*
- *The UIBV$_s$ and TIBV$_s$ problems are in Π_{2s-1}^P.*

Due to space limitations, the proof of this lemma is omitted.

Definition 7 (Stage-s unique assembly verification (Stage-s UAV) problem). *Given a staged system Γ with s stages and an assembly A, is A the unique terminal assembly of Γ?*

Theorem 5. *The stage-s UAV problem is in Π_{2s}^P.*

Proof. We give an algorithm for the stage-s UAV problem. The stage-s UAV problem may be restated as:

1. is every assembly B with $|B| \leq |A|$ and $B \neq A$ not a terminal assembly of any bin in stage s?
2. and does every producible assembly of every bin in stage $s - 1$ of Γ have size at most $|A|$?

In the algorithm below, $\mathcal{T}_s$ and $\mathcal{U}_s$ are algorithms for the TIBV$_s$ and UIBV$_s$ problems, respectively.

Algorithm 3. A Π_{2s}^P algorithm for the stage-s UAV problem

---

1: **procedure** $\mathcal{UAV}_s(\Gamma, A)$ ▷ Γ has s stages.
2:     Non-deterministically select an assembly B with $|B| \leq n$ and $A \neq B$.
3:     **for all** bins b in stage s of Γ **do**
4:         **if** $\mathcal{T}_s(\Gamma, b, B)$ **then**   ▷ Function call is in Π_{2s-1}^P
5:             **return** no.
6:         **end if**
7:     **end for**
8:     **if not** $\mathcal{U}_s(\Gamma, b, |A|)$ **then**   ▷ Function call is in Π_{2s-1}^P
9:         **return** no.
10:     **end if**
11:     **return** yes.
12: **end procedure**

The algorithm runs as a coNP machine, returning "no" unless every non-deterministic branch returns "yes". Lines 2–8 verify that A is a terminal assembly of bin b (subproblem 1): A is not a terminal assembly if and only if (1) A is not producible (lines 2–4), or (2) another producible assembly B can attach to A (lines 5–8).

Every staged system has some number of stages $s \in \mathbb{N}$, but there is no limit to the number of stages a staged system may have. Thus the staged UAV problem is not contained in any level of PH, but every instance can be solved by an algorithm that runs at a fixed level (Π_{2s}^P) of the hierarchy. Since it is a well-known that PH $\subseteq$ PSPACE, this gives the desired result:

Corollary 2. *The staged UAV problem is in* PSPACE.

Next, we move to shape verification:

Definition 8 (Stage-s unique shape verification (Stage-s USV) problem). *Given a staged system Γ with s stages and a shape S, is S the unique terminal shape of Γ?*

Theorem 6. *The stage-s USV problem is in* Π_{2s}^P.

Proof. The stage-s USV problem can be restated as:

1. is every assembly B with $|B| \leq |S|$ and shape not equal to S not a terminal assembly of any bin in stage s?
2. and does every producible assembly of every bin in stage $s - 1$ of Γ have size at most $|S|$?

Notice that the subproblems only differ from those of the stage-s UAV problem in that S replaces A and "equal shape" replaces "equals". Thus the algorithm differs from the Π_{2s}^P algorithm for the stage-s UAV problem on only line 5 (replace "$A \neq B$" with "shape not equal to S") and line 8 (replace $|A|$ with $|S|$).

As for the UAV problem, since the stage-s USV problem is in PH for each $s \in \mathbb{N}$, the USV problem is in PSPACE.

Corollary 3. *The staged USV problem is in* PSPACE.

7 Open Problems

The most direct problem left open by this work is closing the gap in the bottom row of Table 1 between the coNP^{NP}-hardness and PSPACE containment of the staged UAV and USV problems. We believe that the approach of differentiating between satisfying and non-satisfying assignments, then checking for the existence of various partial assignments (the $\forall$ portion of $\forall\exists$SAT) can be generalized to achieve hardness for any number of quantifier alternations, using a number of stages proportional to the number of alternations:

Conjecture 1. The staged UAV and USV problems are PSPACE-complete.

Conjecture 2. The stage-s UAV and stage-s USV problems are $\Pi_{\Omega(s)}^p$-hard.

The UAV and USV problems considered in this work are two variants of the generic challenge of *verification*; considering the same problems limited to temperature-1 systems or with different inputs is also interesting:

Problem 1. What are the complexities of the staged UAV and USV problems restricted to temperature-1 systems?

Problem 2. What is the complexity (in any model) of the following UAV-like problem: given a system Γ and an integer n, does Γ have a unique terminal assembly of size at most n?

Finally, the results and techniques presented here might find use in the study of other problems in staged and two-handed self-assembly, such as tile minimization. The aTAM USV problem is coNP-complete, while the *minimum tile set problem* of finding the minimum number of tiles that uniquely assemble into a given shape is NP^{NP}-complete [2]. We now know that the 2HAM USV problem is coNP^{NP}-complete (Sect. 3); does the corresponding optimization problem also rise in the hierarchy?

Conjecture 3. The 2HAM minimum tile set problem is NP$^{\mathsf{NP}^{\mathsf{NP}}}$-complete.

References

1. Adleman, L.M., Cheng, Q., Goel, A., Huang, M.-D., Kempe, D., de Espanés, P.M., Rothemund, P.W.K.: Combinatorial optimization problems in self-assembly. In: Proceedings of the Thirty-Fourth Annual ACM Symposium on Theory of Computing, pp. 23–32 (2002)
2. Bryans, N., Chiniforooshan, E., Doty, D., Kari, L., Seki, S.: The power of nondeterminism in self-assembly. Theory Comput. **9**(1), 1–29 (2013)
3. Cannon, S., Demaine, E.D., Demaine, M.L., Eisenstat, S., Patitz, M.J., Schweller, R.T., Summers, S.M., Winslow, A.: Two hands are better than one (up to constant factors): self-assembly in the 2HAM vs. aTAM. In: STACS 2013. LIPIcs, vol. 20, pp. 172–184. Schloss Dagstuhl (2013)
4. Chalk, C., Martinez, E., Schweller, R., Vega, L., Winslow, A., Wylie, T.: Optimal staged self-assembly of general shapes. In: Proceedings of the 24th European Symposium of Algorithms. LIPIcs, vol. 57, pp. 26:1–26:17. Schloss Dagstuhl (2016)
5. Chalk, C., Schweller, R., Winslow, A., Wylie, T.: Too hot 2HAMdle: high-temperature two-handed self-assembly (2017, under submission)
6. Cheng, Q., Aggarwal, G., Goldwasser, M.H., Kao, M.-Y., Schweller, R.T., de Espanés, P.M.: Complexities for generalized models of self-assembly. SIAM J. Comput. **34**, 1493–1515 (2005)
7. Demaine, E.D., Demaine, M.L., Fekete, S.P., Ishaque, M., Rafalin, E., Schweller, R.T., Souvaine, D.L.: Staged self-assembly: nanomanufacture of arbitrary shapes with $O(1)$ glues. Nat. Comput. **7**(3), 347–370 (2008)
8. Demaine, E.D., Eisenstat, S., Ishaque, M., Winslow, A.: One-dimensional staged self-assembly. In: Cardelli, L., Shih, W. (eds.) DNA 2011. LNCS, vol. 6937, pp. 100–114. Springer, Heidelberg (2011). doi:10.1007/978-3-642-23638-9_10
9. Demaine, E.D., Fekete, S.P., Scheffer, C., Schmidt, A.: New geometric algorithms for fully connected staged self-assembly. In: Phillips, A., Yin, P. (eds.) DNA 2015. LNCS, vol. 9211, pp. 104–116. Springer, Cham (2015). doi:10.1007/978-3-319-21999-8_7
10. Doty, D.: Producibility in hierarchical self-assembly. In: Ibarra, O.H., Kari, L., Kopecki, S. (eds.) UCNC 2014. LNCS, vol. 8553, pp. 142–154. Springer, Cham (2014). doi:10.1007/978-3-319-08123-6_12
11. Lagoudakis, M.G., Labean, T.H.: 2D DNA self-assembly for satisfiability. In: 5th International Meeting on DNA Based Computers (1999)
12. Schaefer, M., Umans, C.: Completeness in the polynomial-time hierarchy: a compendium. SIGACT News **33**(3), 32–49 (2002)
13. Stockmeyer, L.J.: The polynomial-time hierarchy. Theor. Comput. Sci. **3**(1), 1–22 (1976)
14. Winslow, A.: Staged self-assembly and polyomino context-free grammars. Nat. Comput. **14**(2), 293–302 (2015)

Self-Assembly of 4-Sided Fractals
in the Two-Handed Tile Assembly Model

Jacob Hendricks[1]([✉]) and Joseph Opseth[2]

[1] Department of Computer Science and Information Systems,
University of Wisconsin - River Falls, River Falls, USA
`jacob.hendricks@uwrf.edu`
[2] Department of Mathematics, University of Wisconsin - River Falls,
River Falls, USA
`joseph.opseth@my.uwrf.edu`

Abstract. In this paper, we consider the strict self-assembly of fractals in one of the most well-studied models of tile based self-assembling systems known as the Two-handed Tile Assembly Model (2HAM). We are particularly interested in a class of fractals called discrete self-similar fractals (a class of fractals that includes the discrete Sierpinski's carpet). We present a 2HAM system that strictly self-assembles the discrete Sierpinski's carpet with scale factor 1. Moreover, the 2HAM system that we give lends itself to being generalized and we describe how this system can be modified to obtain a 2HAM system that strictly self-assembles one of any fractal from an infinite set of fractals which we call 4-*sided fractals*. The 2HAM systems we give in this paper are the first examples of systems that strictly self-assemble discrete self-similar fractals at scale factor 1 in a purely growth model of self-assembly. Finally, we give an example of a 3-*sided fractal* (which is not a tree fractal) that cannot be strictly self-assembled by any 2HAM system.

1 Introduction

The study of fractals has both a mathematical and a practical basis, as these recursively self-similar patterns occur in nature in the form of circulatory systems and branch patterns. Evidently many fractals found in nature are the result of a process where a simple set of rules dictating how individual basic components (such as individual molecules) interact to yield larger complexes with recursive self-similar structure. One approach to understanding this process is to model such a process with artificial self-assembling systems.

One of the first and also one of the most studied mathematical models of self-assembling systems is Winfree's abstract Tile Assembly Model (aTAM) [39] where individual autonomous components are represented as tiles with glues on their edges. The aTAM was intended to model DNA tile self-assembly, where tiles are implemented using DNA molecules. There have been two main reasons for considering the self-assembly of fractals. First, in [16,36], DNA-based tiles are used to self-assemble Sierpinski's carpet, showing the potential for DNA tile self-assembly to be used for the controlled formation of

© Springer International Publishing AG 2017
M.J. Patitz and M. Stannett (Eds.): UCNC 2017, LNCS 10240, pp. 113–128, 2017.
DOI: 10.1007/978-3-319-58187-3_9

complex nanoscale structures. Second, there are have been many proposed theoretical models (and generalizations of these models) of DNA tile self-assembly (see [1,5,8,11,13,22,25,32,39] for some examples). While mathematical notions of simulation relations between systems in models continue to further elucidate how these various models relate [3,9,12,20,30,31], many "benchmark" problems have also been introduced, including the efficient self-assembly squares and/or general shapes [10,33,37,38], the capacity to perform universal computation [6,14,15,17,21,32,33], and the self-assembly of fractals [2,18,26,27,29,34,35]. When considering the self-assembly of discrete self-similar fractals (dssf) such as the Sierpinski triangle one can consider either "strict" self-assembly, wherein a shape is made by placing tiles only within the domain of the shape, or "weak" self-assembly where a pattern representing the shape forms as part of a complex of tiles that contains specially labeled tiles corresponding to points in the shape and possibly additional tiles not corresponding to points of the shape. In this paper, we only consider strict self-assembly of dssf's. Previous work (including [2,26,27,29,34,35]) has shown the difficulty of strict self-assembly of dssf's in the aTAM as no nontrivial dssf has been shown to self-assemble in the strict sense. In fact, the Sierpinski's triangle [28] and similar fractals [2] are known to be impossible to self-assemble in the aTAM; though it is possible to design systems which "approximate" the strict self-assembly of fractals [28,29,34]. Interestingly, it is unknown whether there exists a dssf which strictly self-assembles in the aTAM. This includes the Sierpinski's carpet dssf.

While the aTAM models single tile attachment at a time[1], a more generalized model and another of the most studied models of self-assembly called the 2-Handed Assembly Model [5] (2HAM, a.k.a. Hierarchical Assembly Model) allows pairs of large assemblies to bind together. The impossibility of strictly self-assembling the Sierpinski triangle [3] has been shown; this impossibility is due in part to the "tree-like" structure of Sierpinski's triangle. In [4] it is shown that Sierpinski's carpet self-assembles in the 2HAM at temperature 2, but with scale factor 3. That is, instead of self-assembling a structure with tiles corresponding to the points of Sierpinski's carpet, the structure that self-assembles contains a 3 by 3 block of tiles that corresponds to a single point of Sierpinski's carpet. Here we show that not only does Sierpinski's carpet self-assemble with no scale factor, but a general class of fractals, which we call the 4-sided fractals, self-assemble at temperature 2 in the 2HAM. Intuitively, 4-sided fractals are fractals that have a generator (the set of points in the first stage of the fractal) such that the generator is connected and consists of a rectangle of points and points "inside" this rectangle. Informally, a 4-sided fractal is a fractal with a generator that contains all 4 sides and one can define 0, 1, 2, and 3-sided fractals analogously. (Definitions are given in Sect. 2.) Moreover, we show that there exists a 3-sided fractal that cannot be strictly self-assembled by any 2HAM system at any temperature. This is especially interesting considering that 3-sided fractals are not tree fractals (a class of fractals that can be seen to not strictly self-assemble in the 2HAM with no scale factor.)

---

[1] or step in the self-assembly process.

Theorem 1 implies that one of the most well-known dssf's strictly self-assembles in one of the simplest and most studied models of self-assembly, the 2HAM. It should be noted that any dssf can strictly self-assemble [18] in the Signal-passing Tile Assembly Model (STAM) where tiles can change state and even disassociate from an existing assembly, "breaking" an assembly into two disconnected assemblies. That is, given any dssf, there is a STAM system that strictly self-assembles this fractal.[2] Additionally, in a model similar to the STAM, the Active Signal Tile Assembly Model [23], infinite, self-similar substitution tiling patterns which fill the plane have been shown to assemble [24]. This may be considered a testament to the power of active tiles. Here we show that it is still possible to strictly self-assemble an infinite class of fractals in the 2HAM even though tiles are not active and disassociation is not allowed. While the positive result presented here pertains only to 4-sided fractals, preliminary results discussed in Sect. 5 show that the techniques used here to prove this positive result may give rise to a much more general classification of which fractals strictly self-assemble in the 2HAM. Due to space limitation, detailed proofs of the results given here can be found in [19].

2   Preliminaries

Here we provide informal descriptions of the 2-Handed Tile Assembly Model (2HAM). For more details see [5,7]. We also give the definition of discrete self-similar fractals similar to the definitions found in [2,18].

2.1   Informal Description of the 2HAM

The 2HAM [5,7] is a generalization of the abstract Tile Assembly Model (aTAM) [39] in that it allows for two assemblies, both possibly consisting of more than one tile, to attach to each other. Since we must allow that the assemblies might require translation before they can bind, we define a *supertile* to be the set of all translations of a τ-stable assembly, and speak of the attachment of supertiles to each other, modeling that the assemblies attach, if possible, after appropriate translation. We now give a brief, informal, sketch of the 2HAM.

Given $V \subseteq \mathbb{Z}^2$, the *full grid graph* of V is the undirected graph $G_V^f = (V, E)$, such that for all $x, y \in V$, $\{x, y\} \in E$ iff $\|x - y\| = 1$, i.e., iff x and y are adjacent and the 2-dimensional integer Cartesian space.

A *tile type* is a unit square with each side having a *glue* consisting of a *label* (a finite string) and *strength* (a non-negative integer). We assume a finite set T of tile types, but an infinite number of copies of each tile type, each copy referred to as a *tile*. A *supertile* is (the set of all translations of) a positioning of tiles on the integer lattice $\mathbb{Z}^2$. Two adjacent tiles in a supertile *interact* if the glues on their abutting sides are equal and have positive strength. Each supertile induces a *binding graph*, a grid graph whose vertices are tiles, with an edge between two

---

[2] Additionally, in [18] it is shown that a large class of fractals strictly self-assembles in the STAM even with temperature restricted to 1.

tiles if they interact. The supertile is τ-*stable* if every cut of its binding graph has strength at least τ, where the weight of an edge is the strength of the glue it represents. That is, the supertile is stable if at least energy τ is required to separate the supertile into two parts. Note that throughout this paper, we will use the term *assembly* interchangeably with supertile.

A *(two-handed) tile assembly system (TAS)* is an ordered triple $\mathcal{T} = (T, S, \tau)$, where T is a finite set of tile types, S is the *initial state*, and $\tau \in \mathbb{N}$ is the temperature. For notational convenience we sometimes describe S as a set of supertiles, in which case we actually mean that S is a multiset of supertiles with one count of each supertile. We also assume that, in general, unless stated otherwise, the count for any single tile in the initial state is infinite. Commonly, 2HAM systems are defined as pairs $\mathcal{T} = (T, \tau)$, with the initial state simply consisting of an infinite number of copies of each singleton tile type of T, and throughout this paper this is the notation we will use.

Given a TAS $\mathcal{T} = (T, \tau)$, a supertile is *producible*, written as $\alpha \in \mathcal{A}[\mathcal{T}]$, if either it is a single tile from T, or it is the τ-stable result of translating two producible assemblies without overlap. A supertile α is *terminal*, written as $\alpha \in \mathcal{A}_\square[\mathcal{T}]$, if for every producible supertile β, α and β cannot be τ-stably attached. A TAS is *directed* if it has only one terminal, producible supertile. A set, or shape, X *strictly self-assembles* if there is a TAS $\mathcal{T}$ for which every assembly $\alpha \in \mathcal{A}_\square[\mathcal{T}]$ satisfies dom $\alpha = X$. Essentially, strict self-assembly means that tiles are only placed in positions defined by the shape. This is in contrast to the notion of *weak self-assembly* in which only specially marked tiles can and must be in the locations of X but other locations can perhaps receive tiles of other types. All results in this paper are for strict self-assembly of shapes via systems that are not directed.

2.2   Discrete Self-Similar Fractals

In order to state the main theorem, we need to provide a few definitions. The definition of a discrete self-similar fractals and some of the notation used here also appears in [2,18,34]. First we introduce some notation.

For $g \in \mathbb{N}$ and $G \subset \mathbb{N}_g^2$, let l_G, r_G, b_G, and t_G denote the integers: $l_G = \min_{(x,y)\in G} x$, $r_G = \max_{(x,y)\in G} x$, $b_G = \min_{(x,y)\in G} y$, and $t_G = \max_{(x,y)\in G} y$. Moreover, let $w_G = r_G - l_G + 1$ and $h_G = t_G - b_G + 1$ denote the *width* and *height* of G respectively. Finally, let $L_G = \{(l_G, y) \mid b_G \leq y \leq t_G\}$, $R_G = \{(r_G, y) \mid b_G \leq y \leq t_G\}$, $T_G = \{(x, t_G) \mid l_G \leq x \leq r_G\}$, and $B_G = \{(x, b_G) \mid l_G \leq x \leq r_G\}$. In other words, L_G, R_G, T_G, and B_G are the left, right, top, and bottom line segments of a "bounding box" of G. We also use $\mathbb{N}_g$ to denote the subset $\{0, \ldots, g-1\}$ of $\mathbb{N}$. Finally, if A and B are subsets of $\mathbb{N}^2$ and $(x,y) \in \mathbb{N}^2$, then $A + (x,y)B = \{(x_a, y_a) + (x \cdot x_b, y \cdot y_b) \mid (x_a, y_a) \in A \text{ and } (x_b, y_b) \in B\}$. First we give the definition of a discrete self-similar fractal.

Definition 1. *Let* $\mathbf{X} \subset \mathbb{N}^2$. *We say that* $\mathbf{X}$ *is a* discrete self-similar fractal *(or* dssf *for short), if there is a set* $\{(0,0)\} \subset G \subset \mathbb{N}_g^2$ *with at least one point in every row and column, such that*

1. the full grid-graph of G *is connected,*

2. $w_G > 1$ and $h_G > 1$,
3. $G \subsetneq \mathbb{N}_{w_G} \times \mathbb{N}_{h_G}$, and
4. $\boldsymbol{X} = \cup_{i=1}^{\infty} X_i$, where X^i, the ith stage of $\boldsymbol{X}$, is defined by $X^1 = G$ and $X^{i+1} = X^i + (w_G^i, h_G^i)G$.

Moreover, we say that G is the generator *of $\boldsymbol{X}$.*

A connected discrete self-similar fractal is one in which every component is connected in every stage, i.e. there is only one connected component in the grid graph formed by the points of the shape.

Definition 2. *[n-sided fractals] Let $n \in \{0,1,2,3,4\}$, $1 < g \in \mathbb{N}$ and $\boldsymbol{X} \subset \mathbb{N}^2$. We say that $\boldsymbol{X}$ is a n-sided fractal iff $\boldsymbol{X}$ is a g-discrete self-similar fractal with generator G such that:*

1. *the full grid graph of G is connected,*
2. *$S \cap G = S$ for at least n distinct sets S in $\{L_G, R_G, T_G, B_G\}$.*

Intuitively, the second condition in Definition 2 is saying that the fractal generator contains all points of at least n of the left, right, top, and bottom line segments of a "bounding box" of G. In particular, the generator of a 4-sided fractal contains all of the points along the left, right, top, and bottom "sides" of the fractal generator. Finally, for a fractal $\boldsymbol{X}$ with generator G, an enumeration of the points in a generator $G = \{v_i\}_{i=1}^{|G|}$, and $j \in \mathbb{N}$, the stages of $\boldsymbol{X}$ are $S^1 = G$ and $S^{j+1} = S^j + (w_G^j, h_G^j)G$. For $i \in N$ such that $1 \leq i \leq |G|$, we call the points of the $j+1$ stage given by $S_j + (w_G^j, h_G^j)v_i$ the jth *stage at position i*.

3   Four Sided Fractals

In this section we show how to strictly self-assemble the class of 4-sided discrete self-similar fractals in the 2HAM (with scale factor of 1). The most well-known example of a 4-sided fractal is Sierpinski's carpet. This is the first example of a non-trivial dssf shown to self-assemble in either the 2HAM (or the aTAM) with no scale factor. Here we give an overview of the construction for the Sierpinski's carpet and the modifications needed to the Sierpinski's carpet construction to show that any 4-sided fractal strictly self-assembles in the 2HAM. For more detail (including a depiction of the complete tile set for Sierpinski's carpet) see [19]. Also, figures in this section contain color. Figures with color can be found in the online version of the proceedings or in [19].

Theorem 1. *Let $\boldsymbol{X}$ be a 4-sided fractal. Then, there exists a 2HAM TAS $\mathcal{T}_X = (T, 2)$ that strictly self-assembles $\boldsymbol{X}$. Moreover, if G is the generator for $\boldsymbol{X}$ and $|G| = g$, $|T|$ is $O(g^3)$.*

We build intuition for a construction showing Theorem 1 by showing that Sierpinski's carpet strictly self-assembles in the 2HAM at scale factor 1. We then describe the modifications needed to extend the construction for the carpet to give an algorithm for obtaining a tile set T given a generator for a 4-sided fractal, $\boldsymbol{X}$, such that the 2HAM TAS $(T, 2)$ strictly self-assembles $\boldsymbol{X}$.

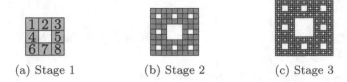

(a) Stage 1   (b) Stage 2   (c) Stage 3

Fig. 1. Three stages of Sierpinski's carpet

3.1   Sierpinski's Carpet Construction Overview

The Sierpinski's carpet dssf is the dssf with generator $G = \{(0,0), (0,1), (0,2), (1,0), (1,2), (2,0), (2,1), (2,2)\}$. Fig. 1a depicts this generator, while Fig. 1b and c depict the 2nd and 3rd stages of the dssf respectively. We denote this carpet by S and for $i \in \mathbb{N}$, we denote the ith stage of S as S^i. We enumerate the points of S^1 as depicted in Fig. 1a and use this enumeration to reference the positions of some substage within a subsequent stage of the carpet.

We now describe the tile set, T, that is used to strictly self-assemble S in the 2HAM at temperature $\tau = 2$ at scale factor 1.

Overview of Stage 2 Assembly. We begin by distinguishing between two classes of tile types called `grout` tile types (or `grout` tiles when referring to actual tiles) and `initializer` tile types (or `initializer` tiles). Informally, `initializer` tiles self-assemble to form 8 different super-tiles, the domains of which are contained in the portion of S^2 depicted in Fig. 2. We call these 8 supertiles C_i^2 for $1 \le i \le 8$. The main idea is that tiles that self-assemble C_i^2 have been "hard-coded" (i.e. for any glue on the edge of some tile, there exists a single matching glue on another tile) to ensure that for each i, all tiles of C_i^2 self-assemble before C_i^2 can be a subassembly in any other strictly larger assembly. In other words, referring to Fig. 4a, the gray tiles self-assemble one of the 8 different supertiles C_i^2 before any of the the aqua tiles can attach. Figure 3 depicts C_i^2 for each i. Note that for each i, C_i^2 subassemblies may expose glues of type g^d or $\hat{g}^d$ for d either n, s, e, or w, as well as possibly g^k or $\hat{g}^k$ for $1 \le k \le 8$. Informally, these glues encode which position (1 through 8) each C_i^2 assembly will end up in an assembly corresponding to stage 3 of Sierpinski's carpet, where C_i^2 will be in position i. We now explain the purpose of these glues in more detail.

Fig. 2. The shape of the portion of S^2 that is self-assembled by `initializer` tiles.

Overview of Stage 3 Assembly. For each i, C_i^2 exposes glues that allow for the attachment of `grout` tiles. In Fig. 4, `grout` tiles are depicted in aqua. The `grout` supertiles that bind to some C_i^2 before any other `grout` supertiles are called `start-gadgets`. See Fig. 5. There are 8 different classes of `grout` tile

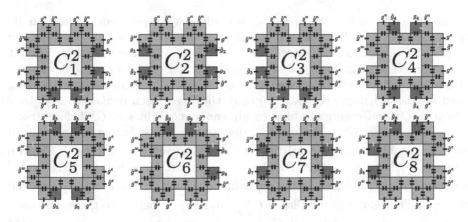

Fig. 3. The tiles that self-assemble a stage 2 supertile C_i^2. The unlabelled strength 1 and 2 black and yellow glues shown on edges of two adjacent tiles in each of the 8 supertiles are defined to have matching type. Moreover, these glues do not match any other glues of other tile types in T. (Color figure online)

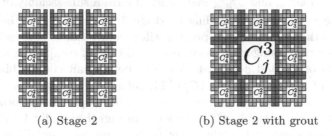

(a) Stage 2   (b) Stage 2 with grout

Fig. 4. For i, j such that $1 \leq i, j \leq 8$, **grout** tiles bind to C_i^2 and expose glues in precise locations that allow the resulting assemblies (shown in (a)) to bind to form C_j^3. Moreover, j is determined by the **grout** class that binds to the assemblies C_i^2.

types (with corresponding **grout** tiles) which we enumerate with 1 through 8. Let $j \in \mathbb{N}$ such that $1 \leq j \leq 8$ refer to a class of **grout**. Glues of **grout** tiles have been defined so that **grout** supertiles cooperatively bind to C_i^2 assemblies, eventually surrounding such an assembly. The **grout** super-tiles other than **start-gadgets** that cooperatively bind to C_i^2 are called **c-rawlers**. Glues labeled g_k or $\hat{g}_k$ for $1 \leq k \leq 8$ are called **indicator** glues and these have a special purpose. A **grout** tile that binds to an **indica-tor** glue via a south glue (likewise

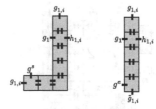

Fig. 5. Left: The supertile that starts the growth of **grout** for C_1^2. Right: The super-tile that starts the growth of **grout** for C_1^s for $s > 2$. Note that for each $s \geq 2$, only one of these supertiles can bind to tiles of C_1^s. Moreover, the supertile depicted on the left can bind to some C_1^s iff $s = 2$, and the supertile depicted on the right can bind to some C_1^s iff $s > 2$.

for north, east, and west) of the grout tile may expose (depending on its grout class) a strength-1 glue on its north edge that will eventually take part in a cooperative binding event between C_i^2 and $C_{i'}^2$ with a sufficient number of grout tiles attached to each. The type of glue and whether or not a grout tile exposes such a glue depends on the grout tiles class. We call these glues stage-binding glues for the 3rd stage. For each i, grout tiles have been defined so that they attach to C_i^2 and eventually bind to all indicator glues of C_i^2 before grout tiles can no longer bind. We let $C_{(i,j)}^2$ denote the largest supertile (in terms of the subassembly relation) consisting of C_i^2 and grout tiles of class j. Figure 6 depicts $C_{(i,j)}^2$ for $i = 1$ and 2 and j between 1 and 8. Moreover, for i, j, i' and j' between 1 and 8 (inclusive), glues are defined so that $C_{(i,j)}^2$ and $C_{(i',j')}^2$ can bind iff $j = j'$. That is the grout tiles of $C_{(i,j)}^2$ and $C_{(i',j')}^2$ belong to the same class.

As grout tiles attach to each C_i^2 assembly, stage-binding glues are exposed on specially designated grout tiles so that the supertiles $C_{(i,j)}^2$ can bind to form the portion of S^3 depicted in Fig. 4b. Note that stage-binding glues may be exposed before $C_{(i,j)}^2$ completely assembles and therefore for some i and i', two subassemblies of $C_{(i,j)}^2$ and $C_{(i',j)}^2$ may bind to form a subassembly of an assembly, which we call C_j^3, corresponding to stage 3. We define glues belonging to grout tiles so that this does not prevent tiles from binding in locations corresponding to points of stage 2 at positions i and i' from completing assembly as a subassembly of C_j^3 and note that this does not permit tiles to bind in locations outside of locations in dom (C_j^3). Therefore, we assume that each $C_{(i,j)}^2$ completely assembles before binding to some other supertile to become a subassembly of a larger assembly. C_j^3 is depicted in Fig. 4b. Finally, for i' such that $1 \leq i' \leq 8$, the glues that might allow (depending on i and i') some supertile $C_{(i,j)}^2$ to bind to another supertile $C_{(i',j)}^2$ are strength 1 glues separated by a distance of $3^{2-1} = 3$. This distance is ensured by the locations of the indicator glues and will prevent supertiles corresponding to different fractal

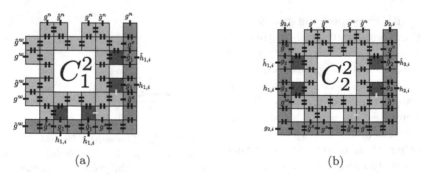

(a)   (b)

Fig. 6. (a) A depiction of $C_{(1,i)}^2$ with stage-binding glues $h_{1,i}$ and $\hat{h}_{1,i}$. (b) A depiction of $C_{(2,i)}^2$ with stage-binding glues $h_{1,i}$, $\hat{h}_{1,i}$, $h_{2,i}$, and $\hat{h}_{2,i}$. Notice that the stage-binding glues of $C_{(1,i)}^2$ and $C_{(2,i)}^2$ allow for the cooperative binding of $C_{(1,i)}^2$ and $C_{(2,i)}^2$. Intuitively, the distance between these glues ensures proper assembly of each stage of Sierpinski's carpet.

stages from binding. Moreover, we define the grout tiles such that the $C^2_{(i,j)}$ supertiles bind before the "next iteration" of grout tiles can attach. In other words, $C^2_{(i,j)}$ supertiles bind for all i between 1 and 8 before a start-gadget can bind to the resulting assembly C^3_j.

Overview of Stage s assembly for $s \geq 4$. For each j and all i, the supertiles $C^2_{(i,j)}$ bind to form a supertile C^3_j corresponding to a portion of S^3. Just as i corresponds to the position where the C^2_i supertile will bind when C^3_j forms, j corresponds to the position where C^3_j will bind when a supertile corresponding to a portion of S^4 self-assembles. This portion of S_4 is essentially, S^4 without northernmost, southernmost, easternmost, and westernmost points, the absence of which makes room for the assembly of more grout tiles. Informally, the position in the C^3_j supertiles of each C^2_i supertile is determined by the glues exposed by the supertiles C^2_i. Moreover, the grout class j determines the grout tiles that will bind to C^3_j, which will in turn determine the position of the C^3_j supertile in S^4. Finally, just as some super tile C^2_i exposes some indicator glues the supertile C^3_j for $i = j$ expose the same strength-1 indicator glues, only at a distance of $3^2 = 9$.

Repurposing i, we now let C^3_j be denoted by C^3_i. Now, for each i and j with $1 \leq i,j \leq 8$, the 8 different classes of grout tile types can attach to each C^3_i supertile to give supertiles $C^3_{(i,j)}$, and the glues of each different class of grout tiles determine where the supertiles consisting of $C^3_{(i,j)}$ attach to self-assemble supertiles, C^4_j, corresponding to a portion of S^4. C^4_j is depicted in Fig. 7.

Moreover, the glues that allow some supertile $C^3_{(i,j)}$ to bind to another supertile $C^3_{(i',j)}$, for some i' say, are strength 1 glues separated by a distance of 9.

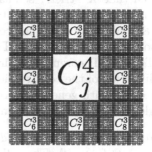

Repeating this process, we see that for any $i,j,s \in \mathbb{N}$ such that $1 \leq i,j \leq 8$ and $s > 2$, we can self-assemble supertiles C^{s-1}_i corresponding to a portion of S^{s-1} (again, we are leaving room for grout tiles), and supertiles $C^{s-1}_{(i,j)}$ corresponding to C^{s-1}_i with the attachment of grout tiles all belonging to the jth class of grout tile types. Moreover, the supertiles $C^{s-1}_{(i,j)}$ expose strength 1 glues that are at a distance of 3^{s-2} apart that allow for the stable binding of these supertiles to form

Fig. 7. A depiction of the portion of S^4 that is self-assembled by supertiles denoted by $C^3_{(i)}$ for i and j between 1 and 8 (inclusive) and some class j of grout tiles.

a supertile C^s_i corresponding to S^s. For $i' \in \mathbb{N}$ such that $1 \leq i' \leq 8$, since the distance between the 2 glues that allow for two supertiles $C^{s-1}_{(i,j)}$ and $C^{s-1}_{(i',j)}$ to bind is 3^{s-2}, one can observe that no erroneous supertiles can self-assemble. In particular, glue distances ensure that for $p,q \in \mathbb{N}$ such that $p,q > 2$, $C^p_{(i,j)}$ subassemblies can bind to some $C^q_{(i,j)}$ subassemblies iff $p = q$. Hence, one can show that each supertile is a subassembly of such a C^n_i for some $n \in \mathbb{N}$, and

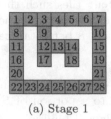   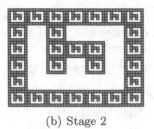

(a) Stage 1   (b) Stage 2

Fig. 8. Two stages of a 4-side fractal.

therefore for any producible assembly $\alpha \in \mathcal{A}[\mathcal{T}]$, there exists a stage $s > 1$ such that dom $\alpha \subset S^s$. Moreover, one can observe that for any stage $s \geq 1$, $S^s \subset C_i^{s+1}$. Therefore, as this hierarchical growth continues indefinitely, the domain of the terminal assembly of the 2HAM TAS $\mathcal{T} = (T, 2)$ is S. Thus, $\mathcal{T}$ strictly self-assembles S.

3.2   4-Sided Fractals Construction Overview

The construction that shows that any 4-sided fractal strictly self-assembles in the 2HAM at scale factor 1 (Theorem 1) is a generalization of the construction given in Sect. 3.1. Let G be the generator for a 4-sided fractal and recall the notation of L_G, R_G, B_G, and T_G. Moreover, let $|G| = r$, let X denote the dssf with generator G, and let X_s be the s stage of X. We will describe a tile set T such that X strictly self-assembles in the 2HAM system $\mathcal{T} = (T, 2)$. As an example, consider the generator in Fig. 8a. Stage 2 of this fractal is depicted in Fig. 8b. We also choose the convention of ordering the positions in G from top to bottom and left to right. This enumeration is depicted in Fig. 8a.

To show Theorem 1, we first show the following lemma that follows from a modification of the construction given in Sect. 3.1. Intuitively, this lemma states that dssf's with generators consisting only of points on the perimeter of a rectangle strictly self-assemble in the 2HAM.

Lemma 1. *Let X be a 4-sided fractal with generator G such that $G \setminus (L_G \cup L_G \cup T_G \cup B_G) = \emptyset$. Then, there exists a 2HAM TAS $\mathcal{T}_X = (T, 2)$ that strictly self-assembles X.*

To show Lemma 1, we show how to modify the construction given in Sect. 3.1. Given a 4-sided fractal X with generator that satisfies the assumptions of Lemma 1 (for example, the generator depicted in Fig. 9), one can see that each step in the construction in Sect. 3.1 generalizes to give a tile set T such that the 2HAM TAS $\mathcal{T}_X = (T, 2)$ strictly self-assembles X. The basic idea for proving Lemma 1 is to "elongate" the **initializer**

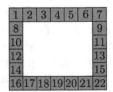

Fig. 9. An example generator for the 4-sided fractals considered in Lemma 1.

and **grout** supertiles given in the Sierpinski's carpet construction and most of the remaining details are analogous.

We now give a high-level overview of the proof of Theorem 1. To prove Theorem 1, given any 4-sided fractal X with generator G, we consider a set that consists of the points only on the perimeter of G and call this set G'. Then, the fractal X' with generator G' strictly self-assembles in the 2HAM by Lemma 1 and we denote the tile set given by this lemma by T'. Then, to give a tile set T such that the 2HAM TAS strictly self-assembles X we add additional tiles to the set T' to account for points of G that are not on the perimeter of G and modify the tiles of T' by adding strength-2 glues to particular edges of the tiles of T' that allow for these additional tiles to attach. Additional **initialize-r** tiles are added to T' to ensure that tiles are placed at points of G that are not on the perimeter of G during the self-assembly of **initializer** supertiles. For example, the gray tiles in Fig. 10 are the tiles of an **initializer** supertile. Note the tiles corresponding to points of G that are not on the perimeter of G. Additional **grout** tiles can be added so that as **grout** supertiles attach to an assembly, tiles can attach in locations corresponding to points of G not on the perimeter of G. For an example, consider the aqua tiles in Fig. 10. These are tiles of **grout** supertiles. Note that as **grout** supertiles attach along the northernmost tiles of the **initializer** supertile (shown in gray), strength-2 glue allow for the self-assembly of complete stage-1 subassemblies.

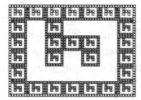

Fig. 10. A depiction of supertile that represents stage 2 of the fractal with generator given in Fig. 8a after grout supertiles have attached. (Color figure online)

Moreover, to ensure that stages at a position, p say, corresponding to points that are not on the perimeter of G correctly assemble, additional **grout** tiles are added such that these additional **grout** supertiles always surround an entire assembly corresponding to a stage, i say, and expose glues such that the resulting supertile will bind to an assembly that (possibly after the binding of other supertiles) corresponds to an assembly corresponding to stage $i+1$. Figure 10 depicts a supertile that will bind at position 12 as a supertile corresponding to stage 3 of the dssf self-assembles. Note the glues that are exposed on tiles adjacent to red tiles. These glues will permit this supertile to bind in position 12 as a supertile corresponding to stage 3 of the dssf self-assembles. Finally, we note that with these modification to the tiles set given by Lemma 1 give a tile set that satisfies Theorem 1. To see that the tile complexity is $O(g^3)$, note that hard-coding **initializer** supertiles, **corner-gadgets**, **crawler** supertiles, and **start-gadgets** each require $O(g^3)$ tile types each. For example, **initializer** supertiles require

$O(g^2)$ tiles to hard-code their stage 2 shape and g of them must assembly (one for each point in G). For tile types making up `corner-gadgets`, `crawler` supertiles, and `start-gadgets`, note that none of these supertiles consists of more than g tiles. Therefore, to hard-code one of these these supertiles (requiring $O(g)$ types) that can bind to some C_i^s for i between 1 and 8 (requiring $O(g)$ times more types) that also belongs to one of g classes of `grout` (requiring $O(g)$ times more types), $O(g^3)$ tile types are required. Hence in total, $O(g^3)$ tiles types are required.

4   A 3-Sided Fractal that Does Not Strictly Self-Assemble

In this section we give a high-level sketch of the proof that there exist 3-sided fractals that do not strictly self-assemble in the 2HAM. A detailed proof is given in [19].

Theorem 2. *There exists a 3-sided fractal $\mathbf{X}$ for which there is no 2HAM TAS $\mathcal{T}_{\mathbf{X}} = (T, \tau)$ that strictly self-assembles $\mathbf{X}$.*

To prove Theorem 2, we consider the fractal with generator given by the points in Fig. 11a. Stage 2 of this fractal is shown in Fig. 11b. We refer to this fractal as $\mathbf{X}$ and, similar to the convention in Sect. 3.1, we refer to the sth stage of $\mathbf{X}$ as X^s. We refer to the ith position of X^s as X_i^s where $1 \le i \le 13$ (Fig. 11a). We call the assembly γ_i^s for which dom $\gamma_i^s = X_i^s$.

Consider any 2HAM TAS $\mathcal{T}_{\mathbf{X}} = (T, \tau)$. Let g be the number of tiles in $\mathcal{T}_{\mathbf{X}}$. Consider a producible assembly α such that $X^{g+2} \subseteq$ dom α, and specifically the subassembly γ_6^{g+2}, which is an assembly γ^{g+1}. One can then show that γ^{g+1} contains a sequence of $g+1$ strength τ cuts consisting of a single glue (Fig. 11b).

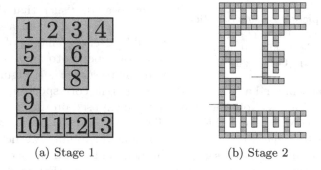

(a) Stage 1   (b) Stage 2

Fig. 11. The assemblies that form the first two stages of $\mathbf{X}$. Strength τ cuts are shown on Stage 2.

Let β_k be the subassembly below the kth cut in this sequence. Essentially, because the cuts are strength τ, the β_k subassemblies can be removed and the resulting subassemblies are still producible, so the β_k subassemblies cannot be guaranteed to attach before any point in the construction of α.

However, since there are $g + 1$ cuts and only g tiles, there is some β_i, β_j with $|\beta_i| > |\beta_j|$ that attach with the same glue, and if other β_k subassemblies have not yet attached, it is possible for β_i to bind where β_j is needed (Fig. 12). Since the domain of the resulting assembly $\notin X$, $\mathcal{T}_X$ does not strictly self-assemble X.

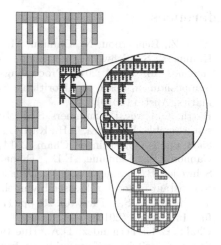

Fig. 12. An example of erroneous binding within γ^5. Because of the large number of tiles some of the γ^3 subassemblies are shown as rectangles.

5   Conclusion

Theorem 1 shows that any 4-sided dssf strictly self-assembles in the 2HAM at temperature 2 and with no scale factor. Theorem 2 shows that there exists a 3-sided fractal that does not strictly self-assemble in any 2HAM system at any temperature. Preliminary results seem to show that similar techniques to those described in Sect. 3.2 can be used to give an example of a 3-sided fractal that can strictly self-assemble in the 2HAM and though still just an early investigation, the techniques used to give a tile set that strictly self-assembles a given 4-sided fractal

Fig. 13. Do fractals with generators like the one depicted in this figure strictly self-assemble in the 2HAM?

may be modifiable to show that a much more general class of fractals strictly self-assembles. In particular, a fractal belonging to this class can be described as having a generator with a *generating cycle*.

Informally, a simple cycle C in G (technically defined in the full-grid graph of G) is a *generating cycle* iff (1) G contains 2 distinct east points of contact p_1 and p_2 with corresponding west points of contact p_3 and p_4, and 2 distinct north points of contact p_5 and p_6 with corresponding south points of contact p_7 and p_8, and (2) for $i \in \mathbb{N}$ such that $1 \leq i \leq n$, C contains points p_i' and paths P_i from p_i' to p_i, (3) moreover, $P_i \cap P_{i+1} = \emptyset$ for $i \in \{1, 3, 5, 7\}$. Figure 13 depicts one of the simplest generators (for a dssf which we have been calling the *hashtag fractal*) with a generating cycle.

References

1. Abel, Z., Benbernou, N., Damian, M., Demaine, E., Demaine, M., Flatland, R., Kominers, S., Schweller, R.: Shape replication through self-assembly, RNAse enzymes. In: SODA 2010: Proceedings of the Twenty-first Annual ACM-SIAM Symposium on Discrete Algorithms, Society for Industrial and Applied Mathematics, Austin (2010)
2. Barth, K., Furcy, D., Summers, S.M., Totzke, P.: Scaled tree fractals do not strictly self-assemble. In: Ibarra, O.H., Kari, L., Kopecki, S. (eds.) UCNC 2014. LNCS, vol. 8553, pp. 27–39. Springer, Cham (2014). doi:10.1007/978-3-319-08123-6_3
3. Cannon, S., Demaine, E.D., Demaine, M.L., Eisenstat, S., Patitz, M.J., Schweller, R.T., Summers, S.M., Winslow, A.: Two hands are better than one (up to constant factors): self-assembly in the 2HAM vs. aTAM. In: Portier, N., Wilke, T. (eds.) STACS, LIPIcs, vol. 20, pp. 172–184. Schloss Dagstuhl - Leibniz-Zentrum fuer Informatik (2013)
4. Chalk, C.T., Fernandez, D.A., Huerta, A., Maldonado, M.A., Schweller, R.T., Sweet, L.: Strict self-assembly of fractals using multiple hands. Algorithmica 1–30 (2015)
5. Cheng, Q., Aggarwal, G., Goldwasser, M.H., Kao, M.-Y., Schweller, R.T., de Espanés, P.M.: Complexities for generalized models of self-assembly. SIAM J. Comput. **34**, 1493–1515 (2005)
6. Cook, M., Fu, Y., Schweller, R.T.: Temperature 1 self-assembly: deterministic assembly in 3D and probabilistic assembly in 2D. In: SODA 2011: Proceedings of the 22nd Annual ACM-SIAM Symposium on Discrete Algorithms. SIAM (2011)
7. Demaine, E.D., Demaine, M.L., Fekete, S.P., Ishaque, M., Rafalin, E., Schweller, R.T., Souvaine, D.L.: Staged self-assembly: nanomanufacture of arbitrary shapes with $O(1)$ glues. Nat. Comput. **7**(3), 347–370 (2008)
8. Demaine, E.D., Demaine, M.L., Fekete, S.P., Patitz, M.J., Schweller, R.T., Winslow, A., Woods, D.: One tile to rule them all: simulating any tile assembly system with a single universal tile. In: Esparza, J., Fraigniaud, P., Husfeldt, T., Koutsoupias, E. (eds.) ICALP 2014. LNCS, vol. 8572, pp. 368–379. Springer, Heidelberg (2014). doi:10.1007/978-3-662-43948-7_31
9. Demaine, E.D., Patitz, M.J., Rogers, T.A., Schweller, R.T., Summers, S.M., Woods, D.: The two-handed tile assembly model is not intrinsically universal. Algorithmica (to appear)
10. Demaine, E.D., Patitz, M.J., Schweller, R.T., Summers, S.M.: Self-assembly of arbitrary shapes using RNAse enzymes: meeting the kolmogorov bound with small scale factor (extended abstract). In: Schwentick, T., Dürr, C. (eds.) 28th International Symposium on Theoretical Aspects of Computer Science (STACS 2011), volume 9 of Leibniz International Proceedings in Informatics (LIPIcs), pp. 201–212, Dagstuhl, Germany, 2011, Schloss Dagstuhl–Leibniz-Zentrum fuer Informatik
11. Doty, D., Kari, L., Masson, B.: Negative interactions in irreversible self-assembly. In: Sakakibara, Y., Mi, Y. (eds.) DNA 2010. LNCS, vol. 6518, pp. 37–48. Springer, Heidelberg (2011). doi:10.1007/978-3-642-18305-8_4
12. Doty, D., Lutz, J.H., Patitz, M.J., Schweller, R.T., Summers, S.M., Woods, D.: The tile assembly model is intrinsically universal. In: Proceedings of the 53rd Annual IEEE Symposium on Foundations of Computer Science, FOCS 2012, pp. 302–310 (2012)
13. Doty, D., Patitz, M.J., Reishus, D., Schweller, R.T., Summers, S.M.: Strong fault-tolerance for self-assembly with fuzzy temperature. In: Proceedings of the 51st Annual IEEE Symposium on Foundations of Computer Science (FOCS 2010), pp. 417–426 (2010)

14. Doty, D., Patitz, M.J., Summers, S.M.: Limitations of self-assembly at temperature 1. In: Proceedings of the Fifteenth International Meeting on DNA Computing and Molecular Programming (Fayetteville, Arkansas, USA, 8–11 June 2009), pp. 283–294 (2009)
15. Fekete, S.P., Hendricks, J., Patitz, M.J., Rogers, T.A., Schweller, R.T.: Universal computation with arbitrary polyomino tiles in non-cooperative self-assembly. In: Proceedings of the Twenty-Sixth Annual ACM-SIAM Symposium on Discrete Algorithms (SODA 2015), San Diego, CA, USA, 4–6 January 2015, pp. 148–167 (2015)
16. Fujibayashi, K., Hariadi, R., Park, S.H., Winfree, E., Murata, S.: Toward reliable algorithmic self-assembly of DNA tiles: a fixed-width cellular automaton pattern. Nano Lett. 8(7), 1791–1797 (2007)
17. Gilber, O., Hendricks, J., Patitz, M.J., Rogers, T.A.: Computing in continuous space with self-assembling polygonal tiles. In: Proceedings of the Twenty-Seventh Annual ACM-SIAM Symposium on Discrete Algorithms (SODA 2016), Arlington, VA, USA, 10–12 January 2016, pp. 937–956 (2016)
18. Hendricks, J., Olsen, M., Patitz, M.J., Rogers, T.A., Thomas, H.: Hierarchical self-assembly of fractals with signal-passing tiles (extended abstract). In: Proceedings of the 22nd International Conference on DNA Computing and Molecular Programming (DNA 22), Ludwig-Maximilians-Universität, Munich, Germany, 4–8 September 2016, pp. 82–97 (2016)
19. Hendricks, J., Opseth, J.: Self-assembly of 4-sided fractals in the two-handed tile assembly model. Technical Report 1703.04774, Computing Research Repository (2017). http://arxiv.org/abs/1703.04774
20. Hendricks, J., Patitz, M.J., Rogers, T.A.: Universal simulation of directed systems in the abstract tile assembly model requires undirectedness. In: Proceedings of the 57th Annual IEEE Symposium on Foundations of Computer Science (FOCS 2016), New Brunswick, New Jersey, USA, 9–11 October 2016 (2016 to appear)
21. Hendricks, J., Patitz, M.J., Rogers, T.A.: Reflections on tiles (in self-assembly). In: Phillips, A., Yin, P. (eds.) DNA 2015. LNCS, vol. 9211, pp. 55–70. Springer, Cham (2015). doi:10.1007/978-3-319-21999-8_4
22. Jonoska, N., Karpenko, D.: Active tile self-assembly, self-similar structures and recursion. Technical Report 1211.3085, Computing Research Repository (2012)
23. Jonoska, N., Karpenko, D.: Active tile self-assembly, part 1: universality at temperature 1. Int. J. Found. Comput. Sci. 25(02), 141–163 (2014)
24. Jonoska, N., Karpenko, D.: Active tile self-assembly, part 2: self-similar structures and structural recursion. Int. J. Found. Comput. Sci. 25(02), 165–194 (2014)
25. Kao, M.-Y., Schweller, R.T.: Reducing tile complexity for self-assembly through temperature programming. In: Proceedings of the 17th Annual ACM-SIAM Symposium on Discrete Algorithms (SODA 2006), Miami, Florida, January 2006, pp. 571–580 (2007)
26. Kautz, S., Shutters, B.: Self-assembling rulers for approximating generalized Sierpinski carpets. Algorithmica 67(2), 207–233 (2013)
27. Kautz, S.M. Lathrop, J.I.: Self-assembly of the Sierpinski carpet and related fractals. In: Proceedings of the Fifteenth International Meeting on DNA Computing and Molecular Programming (Fayetteville, Arkansas, USA, 8–11 June 2009), pp. 78–87 (2009)
28. Lathrop, J.I., Lutz, J.H., Summers, S.M.: Strict self-assembly of discrete Sierpinski triangles. Theor. Comput. Sci. 410, 384–405 (2009)
29. Lutz, J.H., Shutters, B.: Approximate self-assembly of the Sierpinski triangle. Theory Comput. Syst. 51(3), 372–400 (2012)

30. Meunier, P.-E., Patitz, M.J., Summers, S.M., Theyssier, G., Winslow, A., Woods, D.: Intrinsic universality in tile self-assembly requires cooperation. In: Proceedings of the ACM-SIAM Symposium on Discrete Algorithms (SODA 2014), (Portland, OR, USA, 5–7 January 2014), pp. 752–771 (2014)
31. Meunier, P.-É., Woods, D.: The non-cooperative tile assembly model is not intrinsically universal or capable of bounded Turing machine simulation. In: STOC 2017: Proceedings of the Thirty-Second Annual ACM Symposium on Theory of Computing (2017, to appear)
32. Padilla, J.E., Patitz, M.J., Schweller, R.T., Seeman, N.C., Summers, S.M., Zhong, X.: Asynchronous signal passing for tile self-assembly: fuel efficient computation and efficient assembly of shapes. Int. J. Founda. Comput. Sci. 25(4), 459–488 (2014)
33. Patitz, M.J., Schweller, R.T., Summers, S.M.: Exact shapes and turing universality at temperature 1 with a single negative glue. In: Proceedings of the 17th International Conference on DNA Computing and Molecular Programming, DNA 2011, pp. 175–189 (2011)
34. Patitz, M.J., Summers, S.M.: Self-assembly of discrete self-similar fractals. Nat. Comput. 1, 135–172 (2010)
35. Rothemund, P.W., Papadakis, N., Winfree, E.: Algorithmic self-assembly of DNA Sierpinski triangles. PLoS Biol. 2(12), 2041–2053 (2004)
36. Rothemund, P.W.K., Papadakis, N., Winfree, E.: Algorithmic self-assembly of DNA Sierpinski triangles. PLoS Biol. 2(12), e424 (2004)
37. Rothemund, P.W.K., Winfree, E.: The program-size complexity of self-assembled squares (extended abstract). In: STOC 2000: Proceedings of the Thirty-Second Annual ACM Symposium on Theory of Computing, pp. 459–468. ACM, Portland, Oregon, United States (2000)
38. Summers, S.M.: Reducing tile complexity for the self-assembly of scaled shapes through temperature programming. Algorithmica 63(1–2), 117–136 (2012)
39. Winfree, E.: Algorithmic self-assembly of DNA. Ph.D. thesis, California Institute of Technology, June 1998

Self-assembled DC Resistive Circuits
with Self-controlled Voltage-Based Growth

Russell Deaton[✉], Rojoba Yasmin, Tyler Moore, and Max Garzon

Electrical Engineering and Computer Science, The University of Memphis,
Memphis, TN 38152, USA
{rjdeaton,ryasmin,tgmoore,mgarzon}@memphis.edu

Abstract. A new model for analog self-assembly is introduced, the circuit Tile Assembly model (cTAM), in which a supply voltage creates electric "glues" that attach small resistive circuits to a seed to form larger circuits. Component circuits can only attach to the growing circuit if the voltage across the output terminals of the partial assembly exceeds a given threshold. Thus, as the circuit grows, the supply voltage progressively dissipates until additional circuit components can no longer attach. Thus, the supply voltage acts as a finite resource that is used up as the circuit assembles, like nutrientfor bacterial colonies. Assemblies in the shape of resistive ladders and grids are analyzed. For ladder-like circuits, the size of the assembled circuits remain within the order of the logarithm of the ratio of the supply voltage to the threshold, and is inversely proportional to the golden ratio ϕ, a universal constant pervasive in architecture, engineering, and biology. For grids, empirical results are presented showing bounded growth and unique terminal assemblies. The model exhibits intriguing properties, such as *self-controlled growth* without glue or seed programming, and *communication at a distance* within the assembly without signaling programming. In addition, a generalization of the model is proposed in which construction is driven by energy minimization in response to boundary conditions on the perimeter of the assembly.

1 Introduction

Self-assembly is the unsupervised aggregation of component parts through local interactions to construct a material that is structured to have useful properties, and promises new methods for manufacturing new materials. Algorithmic models of self-assembly treat its products as the output of a computation. Because target structures can be programmed with DNA sequence selection, DNA-guided self-assembly is one of the more promising techniques to achieve asymmetric patterns for a wide range of applications [16,20]. The assembly executes an algorithm that is implemented through specific local interactions, for example, DNA template matching reactions [16]. When cooperative effects are present in DNA tile assembly, called temperature 2, the system is capable of universal computation [6,22]. Cooperation, however, is difficult to achieve and enforce experimentally. Systems

© Springer International Publishing AG 2017
M.J. Patitz and M. Stannett (Eds.): UCNC 2017, LNCS 10240, pp. 129–143, 2017.
DOI: 10.1007/978-3-319-58187-3_10

that do not rely on cooperation to achieve pattern formation would be easier to implement in practice, but it is not known whether they are computationally universal in two dimensions [4]. More seriously, they frequently exhibit the problem of uncontrolled growth and uncertain outcomes [6].

Motivated by Tile Assembly Models (aTAM) and their power and challenges, a new assembly model and mechanism are proposed here, the circuit Tile Assembly Model (cTAM), in which DC resistive circuits self-assemble under voltage control. This model exhibits both self-assembly and self-control, in the sense that attachments are controlled by local voltage differences and, as the assembly grows, there always exists locations (binding domains) to which new components might attach, but they do not because the external resource (voltage) that is necessary for growth has been depleted. The resource can be thought of as a source of energy that the growth reaction needs in order to proceed, and is analogous to a source of energy or nutrient for a biological organism.

Electric phenomena are important in several examples of biological self-assembly and organization. Galvanotaxis is the movement of cells under the influence of an electric field, and is a mechanism for both wound healing, as well as embryonic cell migration within embryos [17]. The biological molecules that inspire artificial approaches to self-assembly, namely lipids, nucleic acids, and amino acids, are charged molecules, and electric phenomena are directly involved in their formation and stability [18], as in the role of counterion condensation in the formation of a stable DNA helix. Electric fields and associated effects are used in additive manufacturing [5], electrospray technology [8], and other nanomanufacturing technologies [9]. In addition, the study of networks of resistors has a long history, from Kirchhoff [12] to present day. They have applicability not only to electrical engineering, but also to the theory of random media and random walks [7], as well as properties of materials like graphene [3]. Therefore, incorporating electrical effects into models of assembly inspired by biology might elucidate alternative mechanisms for the algorithmic control of growth. Moreover, if our conjecture below is true that the proposed cTAM may be generalized into an assembly system that corresponds to a discrete version of a Dirichlet (boundary value) problem [7,11], then, the range of platforms for assembly and their applications substantially widens from electromagnetism to gravitational, fluid, thermal, and mechanical systems.

In this paper, we introduce the cTAM and derive bounds on the sizes of the circuits that it can assemble. The main result is that the assembled circuits exhibit growth that is controlled by a voltage source, a threshold for attachment, and the geometry of the assembled circuit. The paper is organized as follows. In Sect. 2, some circuit analysis fundamentals are given. In Sect. 3, the cTAM is formally defined. In Sects. 3.1 and 3.2, bounds on the size of self-assembled circuits for resistive ladders and grids are characterized. In addition, in Sect. 3.1, our general approach to solving this type of circuit is outlined. In Sect. 4, a generalization of the assembly model is proposed to correspond to a discrete Dirichlet problem, and empirical evidence is presented to support this generalization. Finally, conclusions and open questions are discussed in Sect. 5.

2   Circuit Theory Background

For what follows we will consider DC resistive circuits exclusively.

Definition 1 (Circuit). *Borrowing some notation from [2], a circuit is a graph consisting of nodes N and edges E. For a connected path of edges $\{e_1, e_2, \ldots, e_k\} \subseteq E$, there are mappings that identify the source $s : E \to N$ and target $t : E \to N$ of the path, and for each edge, a label $R : E \to (0, \infty) \cup \{V_0, \text{GND}\}$ that gives the value of the resistance on that edge, or identifies it as one of two special circuits, a voltage source V_0 or a point of zero potential (ground GND.) Moreover, two finite subsets N_{in}, $N_{out} \subseteq N$ identify the inputs and outputs to the circuit, respectively. The boundary or terminals of the circuit are $\partial N = N_{in} \cup N_{out}$. Thus, a circuit is given by a tuple $\gamma = (N, E, s, t, R, N_{in}, N_{out})$.*

Voltage is the electric potential energy difference per unit charge between two nodes in a circuit. The ground node in the circuit has a potential of zero. Thus, a voltage $\nu : N \to \mathbb{R}$ relative to ground is associated with each node in the circuit. It is analogous to pressure in a water pipe because just as pressure causes water to flow, voltage causes *current* to flow. Voltage is related to the work necessary to move a positive charge against an electric field, and thus, voltage gives rise to current in a circuit, *i.e.* the movement of charge per unit time, with positive charge moving from regions of high voltage to those of low voltage. Electrical *resistance* is analogous to the resistance produced by different diameter pipes in a water system. Resistors are units of dielectric material that impede current flow.

The voltage between two nodes in a circuit joined by a path $\epsilon = \{e_1, e_2, \ldots, e_k\}$ is

$$V(\epsilon) = \nu(s(e_1)) - \nu(t(e_k)), \tag{1}$$

which we will denote $V(s, t)$, $s, t \in N$. The choice of the source s and target t is somewhat arbitrary but should be consistent with the current flow $s \to t$ from points of high voltage s to points of low voltage t. According to *Kirchhoff's voltage law* (KVL), the sum of the voltages around a closed circuit must be zero, which is a statement of conservation of energy. Kirchhoff's current law, which is an expression for conservation of charge, holds for all nonterminal nodes $k \in N \setminus \partial N$,

$$\sum_{l \in N} I_{k,l} = 0,$$

where $I_{k,l}$ is the current flowing from node k to l. The relationship between voltage (V) across a resistor and current (I) through a resistor R is given by Ohm's law, $V = IR$, where the units of current/resistance are the Ampere/Ohm (A/Ω), respectively.

In this paper, two additional techniques are used for circuit analysis. Thévenin's theorem states that an electrical network can be replaced by an equivalent voltage source V_{oc} and a resistor in series R_{th}. Finally, circuits in a Δ shape can be converted to an equivalent circuit in the shape of a Y through the transformation in Fig. 1, where $R_A = (R_1 R_3)/(R_1 + R_2 + R_3)$, and similarly, for R_B and R_C. A key topology for the self-assembled circuits which follow is the voltage divider in Fig. 2. The two resistors, R_1 and R_2, divide the voltage V_0 as $V_{R_1} = V_0 \frac{R_1}{R_1 + R_2}$ and $V_{R_2} = V_0 \frac{R_2}{R_1 + R_2}$. In the remainder, $R_1 = R_2 = R$ are assumed and units will be omitted where unnecessary. In addition, the equivalent resistance as the circuit gets large will be denoted R^{eq}. Circuit simulations were done using PSpice [1].

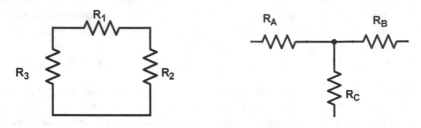

Fig. 1. $\Delta - Y$ transformation in which $R_A = (R_1 R_3)/(R_1 + R_2 + R_3)$, and similarly, for R_B and R_C.

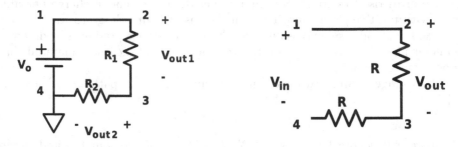

Fig. 2. Seed circuit tile for all assemblies. V_0 is the supply voltage. See text for definition

Fig. 3. Circuit tile for the ladder circuit. See text for a precise definition.

3   Circuit Self-assembly Model

Since circuit assembly is inspired by tile assembly models, the notation for the cTAM is adapted from aTAM notation [4,21]. Like tiles in aTAM models, rotation is not allowed.

Definition 2 (Circuit Tile Assembly System). *A circuit tile assembly system is a tuple* $\mathcal{C} = (\Gamma, S, \tau, \nu, \zeta)$, *where* Γ *is a finite set of circuit tile types,* $S \subseteq \Gamma$ *is a set of seed circuit tiles that includes a source and ground, and* $\tau \in \mathbb{R}$ *is the threshold voltage for attachment.* $\nu : N \to \mathbb{R}$ *is the electric potential energy at a node relative to ground in the circuit, and* $\zeta : N_{in} \to N_{out}$ *maps input nodes to output nodes.*

A diode is a switch, which is one when the voltage across its terminals is greater than a threshold voltage that is typically about $1\,V$. Therefore, the threshold function can be implemented with diodes in series with the first resistor in the voltage divider R_1. Each diode in series would add about $1\,V$ to the threshold voltage τ.

Definition 3. *An configuration of a cTAM is a mapping* $\alpha : \mathbb{Z}^2 \to \Gamma \cup \{\lambda\}$. *Thus, the circuit tile type at location* $(i,j) \in \mathbb{Z}^2$ *is denoted* $\alpha(i,j)$. λ *is the null circuit tile representing a vacancy. An* assembly *is a circuit that is obtained from the seed tiles by a finite number of successive circuit tile attachments.*

Thus, an assembly α describes an electric circuit. Intuitively, a new circuit tile attaches to the circuit assembly if its chosen location is empty, and the voltage difference between its input terminals would be greater than or equal to τ *after* attachment. The assembly proceeds from the seed circuit tile, which in this paper, will always refer to the source and ground. Input nodes of new circuit tiles attach to output nodes of the assembly.

An assembly proceeds asynchronously and nondeterministically with new circuit tiles $\gamma \in \Gamma$ attaching to eligible locations (i,j). An eligible location is unoccupied (contains the null tile λ) and one of its neighbors offers a significant voltage difference between its output nodes to attach new circuit tiles, *i.e.*, $\alpha_{i,j} = \lambda$ and $V(\epsilon) \geq \tau$, where $V(\epsilon)$ (Eq. 1) is the voltage difference between the input nodes of γ along the path ϵ at the grid location (i,j), assuming it is electrically connected to an assembly α.

The mapping ζ identifies which input nodes connect to which output nodes, and thus, serves a similar purpose to glues in the aTAM. In general, this is $\zeta : N_{in}^c \to N_{out}^b$ where $b, c \in \Gamma$, and c is the circuit tile attaching to the assembly via output nodes on circuit tile $b \in \alpha$. Moreover, the output node of the circuit tile b should be a terminal of α, *i.e.*, $b \in \partial N^\alpha$. In general for the Euclidean grid, if $i = 1$ (the first row), c is connected to the output nodes of the circuit tile in the previous column $(1, j-1)$, $N_{out}^{\alpha(1,j-1)}$, and if $j = 1$ (the first column), c is connected to the output nodes of the circuit tile in the previous row $(i-1,1)$, $N_{out}^{\alpha(i-1,1)}$. Otherwise, c connects to $N_{out}^{\alpha(i,j-1)}$ and $N_{out}^{\alpha(i-1,j)}$. The notation $k_{(i,j)}$ will represent ζ where $k \in \partial N$ is the set of terminal nodes for the circuit tile at grid location (i,j). Whether it is an input or output node will be clear from the context, but in general will be given as INPUT $\to$ OUTPUT. For example, referring to Fig. 3, suppose this circuit tile were attaching at the grid location $(1,4)$. The input nodes for the circuit tile are $N_{in} = \{1,4\}$. Therefore, the voltage difference is across the path $\epsilon = \{e_{(1,2)}, e_{(2,3)}, e_{(3,4)}\}$ with $V(1,4) = V(\epsilon) = \nu(s(e_{(1,2)})) - \nu(t(e_{(3,4)}))$. The voltage across the input nodes of the attaching circuit tile will be equal to that across the output nodes of the circuit tile in the assembly to which it attaches. The set of assemblies is $\mathbf{A}[\mathcal{C}]$. An assembly $\alpha \in \mathbf{A}[\mathcal{C}]$ is terminal if no tile can be added that is stable under the attachment conditions. The set of terminal assemblies is $\mathbf{A}_\square[\mathcal{C}] \subset \mathbf{A}[\mathcal{C}]$.

3.1 Resistive Ladder

In order to demonstrate the model, the first example is a resistive ladder. Richard Feynman in his *Lectures on Physics* [10] talked about this circuit. For an infinite ladder, the equivalent resistance is related to ϕ, the golden ratio. The seed circuit tile (Fig. 2) consists of the DC voltage source V_0 in series with two resistors, R_1 and R_2, with node 4 connected to ground. The configuration of the seed, as well as the other circuit tiles, is a voltage divider, which results in a $V_0/2$ drop across both resistors R. The seed circuit tile only has output nodes, which are $N_{out}^{seed} = \{2, 3, 4\}$. In what follows, a wire with resistance 0 is denoted R_0, and $R_1 = R_2 = R > 0$. In addition to the seed, there is one circuit tile $c = \{N = \{1, 2, 3, 4\}, \{e_{1,2} = R_0, e_{2,3} = R, e_{3,4} = R\}, N_{in}^c = \{1, 4\}, N_{out}^c = \{2, 3\}\}$ (Fig. 3). The assembly proceeds with the ladder tile c attaching to the seed according to the rules $\{1\}_{(1,2)} \rightarrow \{2\}_{(1,1)}$ and $\{4\}_{(1,2)} \rightarrow \{3\}_{(1,1)}$, with the successful attachment if $V^c(1, 4) \geq \tau$. The subsequent attachment rules are $\{1\}_{(1,j)} \rightarrow \{2\}_{(1,j-1)}$ and $\{4\}_{(1,j)} \rightarrow \{3\}_{(1,j-1)}$, with $V_{in}^c(1, 4) = V_{out}^c(2, 3) \geq \tau$. In these circuit calculations, we need to know the equivalent resistance at different points in the assembly in order to calculate the voltage differences and determine if a new circuit tile attaches or not. An important point is that as new circuit tiles are added anywhere, the equivalent resistances and voltages in the circuit change *everywhere* with essentially, the speed of light. First, as the circuit assembly grows, we need to know how the equivalent resistances change. Therefore, a recurrence relationship $R^{eq}(m) = f(R^{eq}(m-1))$ is determined, as depicted in Fig. 5. This recurrence starts at the growing interface and proceeds toward the voltage source V_0. In order to determine if the assembly grows, we need to know the voltage across the nodes at the growing interface. Therefore, using the expression for $R^{eq}(m)$, a recurrence is calculated for the voltage at nodes on the active boundary of the assembly in terms of the preceding nodes, $N(i) = N(i-1)$, where for a circuit of size n, $m = n - i$ with $m \in \{1, 2, \ldots n-1\}$ and $i \in \{0, 1, \ldots, n\}$ (Fig. 4). Thus, the recurrences for resistance and voltage proceed in opposite directions from the exterior to the interior of the circuit, and back out again. The calculation of the voltage might involve the determination of Thévenin Equivalents and $\Delta - Y$ transformations. This is in general how we proceed.

Theorem 1. *The maximum size for a self-assembled ladder circuit is bounded by $B = \lceil \log(V_0/\tau)/\log(1 + \phi) \rceil$ where ϕ is the golden ratio, V_0 is the source voltage in the seed, and τ is the threshold voltage for attachment.*

Proof. The proof proceeds by characterizing the equivalent resistance, and then, the voltage for attachments as the size n (number of circuit tiles including the seed) increases.

Referring to Fig. 5,

$$R^{eq}(m) = \frac{R(R + R^{eq}(m-1))}{2R + R^{eq}(m-1)}, \tag{2}$$

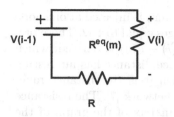 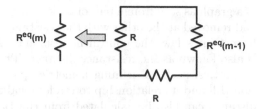

Fig. 4. Circuit to compute voltage recurrence for the ladder.

Fig. 5. Circuit to compute equivalent resistance for the ladder.

with $R^{eq}(0) = R$. The circuit has $R^{eq}(m-1)$ in series with R. This series combination is then in parallel with R resulting in $R^{eq}(m)$. Letting $x(m) = R^{eq}(m)/R$, and taking the limit so that $x = R^{eq}/R$, then, $x = \frac{1+x}{2+x}$. Solving the quadratic equation, and knowing that resistance cannot be negative, then, $x = \frac{-1+\sqrt{5}}{2} = 1/\phi$, and with $x = R^{eq}/R$, then, $R^{eq} = R/\phi$, where ϕ is the golden ratio. Furthermore, referring to Fig. 4,

$$V(i) = \frac{R^{eq}(m)}{R + R^{eq}(m)} V(i-1), \tag{3}$$

where $m = n - i$, $m = \{0, 1, \ldots, n-1\}$, and $i = \{0, 1, \ldots, n\}$, with $V(0) = V_0$. Assuming the circuit is large so that $R^{eq}(m) \to R^{eq}$, then, $V(n) = \frac{1}{1+\phi} V(n-1)$. Finally, the condition on the voltage to stop growth at the nth circuit tile attachment, including the seed, is $V(n) = (1/(\phi+1))^n V_0 < \tau$. Solving for n yields the result. $\qquad \square$

Simulations with PSpice indicated that self-assembled circuits conform to the predicted bound B. Figure 6 shows a self-assembled circuit with $V_0 = 50$ and $\tau = 1$. The size is $n = 5$, which matches the bound value $B = \lceil 4.1 \rceil$. At size $n = 4$, the voltage is still above the threshold; hence, one more tile will attach. When the threshold voltage for growth is taken across only one resistor in the voltage divider, the bound should hold for other circuits, such as column ladders, diagonal ladders, and meandering paths.

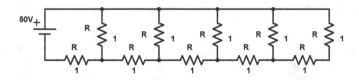

Fig. 6. Ladder circuit assembly with $V_0 = 50$ and $\tau = 1$. The maximum size is $n = 5$, which matches the predicted value of $B = \lceil 4.1 \rceil$.

3.2 Resistive Grid

The problems of calculating the resistance between two arbitrary points in a resistor grid has a long history and continues to generate interest, whether the grid is finite [23] or infinite [19]. These results relate to the equivalent resistance of a graph as seen from a pair of nodes when 1 A of current is injected at one node and removed at the other with the resistance of all edges equal to 1 Ω. Therefore, from Ohm's law, the equivalent resistance $R_{ij} = \nu(i) - \nu(j)$ is derived, which is also known as the resistance distance. The resistance distance has interesting properties, such as defining a metric space for which it is the distance function [13] and its relationship to random walks on the network [7]. The resistance distance can also be calculated from the Laplacian matrix of the graph of the electrical network. It seems clear that for highly symmetric graphs, the resistance distance can be characterized combinatorially as a function of size, but it is not clear how this relates to our assembly model. Our problem is slightly different as we not only have to know the resistances, but also the voltage at a potential attachment point.

To begin, we will consider a symmetric diagonal circuit assembly that is no longer strictly one-dimensional, like the ladder, and requires that the threshold voltage appears across two distinct circuit tiles, and both resistors in the voltage divider (Fig. 8). The circuit tiles for this assembly are shown in Fig. 7. As with the ladder, the seed (Fig. 2) is the circuit tile with the source voltage V_0, the voltage divider consisting of two identical resistors R, and ground. The three other circuit tiles are $c_1 = \{N_{c_1} = \{1,2,3,4\}, \{e_{1,2} = R_0, e_{2,3} = R, e_{3,4} = R\}, N_{in}^{c_1} = \{1,4\}, N_{out}^{c_1} = \{3\}\}$, $c_2 = \{N_{c_2} = \{1,2,3,4\}, \{e_{1,2} = R, e_{2,3} = R, e_{3,4} = R_0, N_{in}^{c_2} = \{1,4\}, N_{out}^{c_2} = \{2\}\}$, and $c_3 = \{N_{c_3} = \{1,2,3\}, \{e_{1,2} = R, e_{2,3} = R\}, N_{in}^{c_3} = \{1,3\}, N_{out}^{c_3} = \{1,2,3\}\}$. The connection rules are

$$\{1\}_{c_1(i,j)} \to \{1\}_{c_3(i,j-1)}, \qquad \{4\}_{c_1(i,j)} \to \{2\}_{c_3(i,j-1)},$$
$$\{1\}_{c_3(i,j)} \to \{3\}_{c_1(i-1,j)}, \qquad \{3\}_{c_3(i,j)} \to \{2\}_{c_2(i,j-1)},$$
$$\{1\}_{c_2(i,j)} \to \{2\}_{c_3(i-1,j)}, \qquad \{4\}_{c_2(i,j)} \to \{3\}_{c_3(i-1,j)},$$

with corresponding voltage calculations. Figures 9 and 10 show the method for calculating equivalent resistance and voltages, respectively. Moreover, for this circuit, Thévenin's theorem and several $\Delta - Y$ transformations were applied for the calculation of the voltage for the nth attachment, V_n.

Theorem 2. *The maximum size n of the self-assembled symmetric diagonal circuit assembly is bounded by $B = \lceil \log(V_0/\tau)/\log(2 + \sqrt{3}) \rceil$ where V_0 is the source voltage in the seed, and τ is the threshold voltage for attachment.*

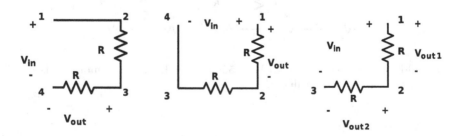

Fig. 7. Circuit tiles for the symmetric diagonal circuit and grid circuit, c_1, c_2, and c_3. See text for definition.

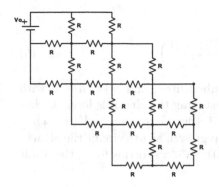

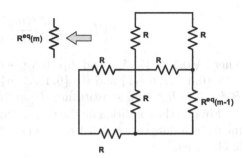

Fig. 8. Symmetric diagonal circuit.

Fig. 9. Circuit to compute equivalent resistance for the circuit in Fig. 8.

Proof. Following the same general procedure, the proof proceeds by first computing the equivalent resistance, and then, the voltages for attachments as the size n (in this case, the number of diagonal steps) increases.

Referring to Fig. 9,

$$R^{eq}(m) = \frac{4R(R + R^{eq}(m-1))}{4R + 3R^{eq}(m-1)} \tag{4}$$

with $R^{eq}(0) = 2R$. Calculation of the equivalent resistance begins with a $\Delta - Y$ transformation of the two Δ's composed of three R resistors in symmetric positions in the upper right and lower left of the circuit. $R^{eq}(m)$ follows. Letting $x(m) = R^{eq}(m)/R$, and taking the limit so that $x = R^{eq}/R$, then, $x = \frac{4+4x}{4+3x}$. Solving the quadratic equation, and knowing that resistance cannot be negative, then, $x = \frac{2}{\sqrt{3}}$: and with $x = R^{eq}/R$, then, $R^{eq} = 2R/\sqrt{3}$.

To calculate the voltage relationship, the circuit in Fig. 10 is converted to a Thévenin equivalent with a voltage source $V_{oc} = V(n-1)/2$, which is the voltage present when the load is open circuit (location of $V(n)$) in series with $R_{th} = R$, which is calculated with the input short circuited, (the location of $V(n-1)$ replaced with a wire with resistance 0). Then, for a diagonal circuit of

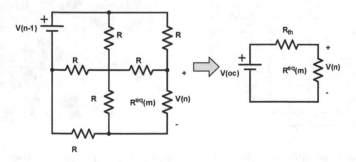

Fig. 10. Circuit to compute voltage recurrence for the circuit in Fig. 8.

size n and at the ith subcircuit,

$$V(i) = \frac{R^{eq}(m)}{R^{eq}(m) + R}\left(\frac{V(i-1)}{2}\right), \tag{5}$$

where $V(0) = V_0$, V_{oc} and R_{th} have been substituted, and $m = n - i$, with $m = \{0, 1, \ldots, n-1\}$ and $i = \{0, 1, \ldots, n\}$. Assuming the circuit is large so that $R^{eq}(m) \to R^{eq}$, and substituting $R^{eq} = 2R/\sqrt{3}$, then, $V(n) = \frac{1}{2+\sqrt{3}}V(n-1)$.

Finally, the condition on the voltage to stop growth at nth circuit tile attachment, including the seed, is $V(n) = (1/(2+\sqrt{3}))^n V_0 < \tau$. Solving for n, the result is obtained. $\square$

The bound was again verified by PSpice simulations.

We do not have a result, yet, that characterizes the size and shape of the resistive grid with supply and threshold voltage. Nevertheless, there is little doubt that the circuit assemblies are bounded since the supply voltage V_0 is distributed along the growing interface of the grid. As the grid grows, this interface gets longer, producing lower voltages across each resistor. Eventually, the perimeter will get long enough that each voltage is below threshold, and growth will cease. Our simulations also indicated that the terminal assemblies appear to be generally unique. In addition, because of the way the circuit tiles are defined for the interior of the grid, there is no node (terminal) to which a new circuit tile can attach unless the circuit has first grown by attachment in the first row or column. Therefore, the bounding box of the grid is determined by the length of the first row and column, and thus, those voltages at the boundary are important to characterize. For example, using KVL, for the 3×3 grid, $V(1,3) = V_0/3$, and for the 4×4 grid, $V(1,4) = 0.241V_0$. Simulations reveal an approximately linear relation between size of the first row and the supply voltage $n \approx 0.8V_0$, and for $V_0 = 12$ and $\tau = 1$ produced the circuit assembly in Fig. 11, which shows the

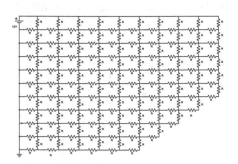

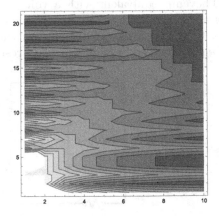

Fig. 11. Grid assembly with $V_0 = 12$, $\tau = 1$, and resistor value R.

Fig. 12. Contour map of voltages for Grid assembly with $V_0 = 12$ and $\tau = 1$. The seed is at the lower left corner at the origin. The upper right region is zero voltage.

general shape of the truncated square that we observe. A contour map of the voltages for this circuit is shown in Fig. 12. Study of the grid problem, however, has produced a proposal for a more general model that is discussed in the next section.

4   Discrete Dirichlet Assembly Model

The Dirichlet principle states that a real-valued function $f(x)$ over a region of space Υ that satisfies Dirichlet boundary conditions $f(x) = g(x)$ on $\partial\Upsilon$ is a harmonic function with the lowest energy in Υ that satisfies Laplace's equation $\Delta f = 0$, and expresses the physical principle that systems at equilibrium seek the lowest energy state. In a discrete setting [7,11], the combinatorial Laplacian defined over a graph is

$$L_{ij} = \begin{cases} d_i & : \text{if } i = j, \\ -w_{ij} & : \text{if } i, j \text{ adjacent}, \\ 0 & : \text{otherwise}, \end{cases} \qquad (6)$$

where d_i is the degree of node i, and $-w_{ij}$ is the negative of the weight on the edge (i, j). The harmonic function $f(x)$ minimizes

$$D[f] = \frac{1}{2} \sum_{e_{ij} \in E} w_{ij}(f_i - f_j)^2, \qquad (7)$$

subject to boundary conditions at certain nodes ∂N of the graph. In circuit problems, as is well known [7], the voltage ν is a harmonic function that is a solution to the Dirichlet problem for a resistive circuit. In particular, a cTAM assembly should be a solution to a Dirichlet problem over the space of assemblies $\mathbb{A}[\mathcal{C}]$ where on the boundary $\partial\mathbb{A}$, $\nu = V_0$ at the source node, $\nu = 0$ at the ground node, and $V(e) < \tau$ at the boundary of terminal assemblies $\partial\mathbb{A}_\square$.

Therefore, we propose a discrete Dirichlet Assembly system (dDAS), of which the CTAM is a particular case, as follows.

Definition 4 (Discrete Dirichlet Assembly System). *A discrete Dirichlet assembly system (dDAS) is a tuple $\mathcal{D} = (\Gamma, S, \tau, \nu, \zeta)$, where Γ is a finite set of weighted graph types, $S \subseteq T$ is a set of initial graphs connected according to ζ, and $\tau \in \mathbb{R}$ is the threshold value of ν for attachment. ν is a real valued function defined over the space of assemblies $\mathbb{A}[\mathcal{D}]$ and defined for each graph in Γ. Thus, $\nu : N \to \mathbb{R}$ where N are the nodes in the graphs of Γ; ζ specifies the attachment rules for the graphs in Γ (glues).*

In the dDAS, the types Γ are weighted graphs, as are the assemblies $\mathbb{A}[\mathcal{D}]$. The potential function ν should satisfy $\Delta\nu = 0$ by minimizing Eq. (7), subject to boundary conditions on the terminal assemblies $\partial\mathbb{A}_\square[\mathcal{D}]$, and thus, ν is hypothesized to be a harmonic function on the assembly space.

It is an interesting possibility to have an assembly system in which the shape, response in terms of ν, as well as dynamic behavior could be controlled by

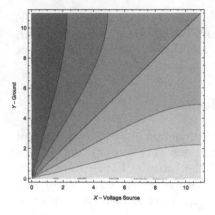

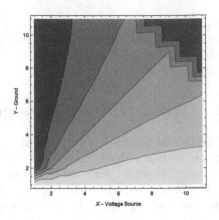

Fig. 13. Contour plot of ν in the plane as continuous solution to Laplace's equation.

Fig. 14. Contour plot of ν (node voltages) in the plane for assembly in Fig. 11.

conditions on the boundary. In addition, we present a couple of conjectures that depend upon ν being a harmonic function [7]. The first is that assemblies produced by a dDAS would always terminate, or be controlled, based on the fact that harmonic functions attain their minima and maxima on the boundary. As a consequence, the second is that the assemblies produced by a dDAS would be unique because ν, as a harmonic function, would be unique for a given set of boundary conditions.

Finally, we present some empirical evidence that the proposed dDAM is valid. In Fig. 13, we present the continuous solution to $\Delta\nu = 0$ in the $x - y$ plane with boundary conditions $\nu = 0$ for $x = 0$ and $\nu = 12V$ for $y = 0$. This is the continuous version of the grid assembly shown in Fig. 11, for which in Fig. 14, the node voltages ν are shown. Taking into account discretization and truncation because of τ, the results are similar. Thresholding the voltage on the perimeter is seen to affect the equipotential lines in the discrete (Fig. 14) as compared to the continuous version (Fig. 13).

5   Conclusions and Open Questions

In the aTAM, an assembly is terminal if no tile can be added that is stable at threshold. Typically, since tile attachment is governed by the presence of compatible glues on the sides of the tile, this is achieved programmatically so that the terminal arrangement of tiles does not present a valid binding site for further tile attachment at the given temperature. By contrast, in the cTAM valid binding sites always exist. There is no programmatic control of the extent of the assembly through a set of glues. For circuit tiles, the connections between input and output nodes could be considered as "glues," and in fact, for example, the ladder is built with a single circuit tile with one set of glues. In aTAM terminology, which may be strained in this case, the cTAM has similarities to a temperature 1 assembly system, but with a different kind of control and cooperation. Control of growth is determined by the source voltage, which represents a finite resource that supplies the necessary energy for an attachment, and the threshold, which represents the minimal rate at which the supply is depleted. Cooperation emerges from the physical properties of electricity, which travels at the speed of light throughout the circuit, *modifying the properties everywhere when the circuit is changed anywhere.*

It is an open question how the cTAM relates in power to various aTAM models, or how this "action at a distance" in the cTAM circuits can be controlled in a programmatic way. In aTAM's, cooperation (temperature 2) seems to be a necessary feature for increased power, such as computation [4] universality in two dimensions and intrinsic universality [15]. In the aTAM, a tile assembly system is *directed* if there is a unique terminal assembly. It is conjectured that in the dDAM, assemblies are unique. Complicating factors to understanding the power of the cTAM are the fact that its voltages and equivalent resistances are real numbers. Therefore, an interesting question might be, what is the computational power of the cTAM by restricting its voltages and resistances to rational voltages and thresholds. Another factor to consider is that the voltages and equivalent resistances can be solved in polynomial time using the standard analysis tools of linear circuit theory.

As presented here, the model uses a lumped circuit model in which the electrical components are "lumped" into circuit elements. As far as potential implementation in nanoscale systems, a distributed circuit model might be more appropriate, such as transmission lines, in which properties like resistance are distributed per unit length or area. One could imagine a nanoscale assembly system consisting of components with designed electrical properties assembling in the presence of an electric field, which dDAM would approximate. This also might present a possible way to implement things like negative glues in restricted glue tile assembly system [14] in which temperature 1 assembly is computation universal, or if combined with DNA tiles, a way to enhance cooperation.

In this paper, voltage controls the growth of the circuit assembly in terms of size. Only one fundamental circuit building block, the voltage divider with equal resistances, has been presented. Preliminary simulations indicate that using different resistor values in the resistor divider produces different shapes. Certainly, there are many circuits available within the cTAM. Therefore, it is an open question as to the degree of control that can be exercised in the cTAM by varying resistor values and the topology of the fundamental circuit tile. In addition, the cTAM could be extended to other passive elements, inductors and capacitors, time-varying voltage sources, or even active, nonlinear elements, like diodes and transistors, or additional sources. Finally, in this paper, once an element attached, detachment was not allowed. The model could be extended to allow dynamic detachment and attachment when the voltage across a circuit tile fell below threshold, even if it is not on the boundary, resulting in oscillatory behavior or rewriting of blocks of the circuit.

Finally, an assembly model is proposed, the dDAM, that describes assembly systems, such as in the cTAM, as solving a discrete Dirichlet boundary value problem, in which an energy source is depleted to match given boundary conditions. Remaining unresolved questions include how the solutions to the discrete Laplacian for the potential function ν can be systematically related to threshold voltages, and thus, sizes and shapes of assembled structures. Nevertheless, it is an intriguing possibility to have assembly systems "programmed" by boundary conditions. Moreover, the dDAM extends discrete assembly models toward important systems that are described by differential equations with boundary conditions, such as electromagnetic, gravitational, thermal, fluid, and mechanical systems. The dDAM also presents the opportunity for assembly systems to describe dynamic assembly of time-varying systems by, for example in the cTAM, supplying a time-varying voltage source to circuits containing active, energy-storing elements, like inductors and capacitors.

Acknowledgements. This work was supported by the National Science Foundation "EAGER: Self-Assembly of Complex Systems" (CCF-1049719) and "Engineering Nano-Building Block Toolboxes for Programmable Self-Assembly of Nanostructures with Arbitrary Shapes and Functions" (CMMI-1235100). We also thank the reviewers for their comments.

References

1. PSPICE. www.pspice.com
2. Baez, J.C.: A Compositional framework for passive linear networks. arXiv:1504.05625 [math.CT]
3. Cheianov, V.V., Falako, V.I., Altshuler, B.L., Aleiner, I.L.: Random resistor network model of minimal conductivity in graphene. Phys. Rev. Lett. **99**(17), 176801 (2007)
4. Cook, M., Fu, Y., Schweller, R.T.: Temperature 1 self-assembly: deterministic assembly in 3D and probabilistic assembly in 2D. In: Proceedings of the 22nd Annual ACM-SIAM Symposium on Discrete Algorithms, SODA 2011. SIAM (2011)
5. Decker, B.Y., Gan, Y.X.: Electric field-assisted additive manufacturing polyaniline based composites for thermoelectric energy conversion. J. Manuf. Sci. Eng. **137**(2), 024504 (2015)
6. Doty, D., Patitz, M.J., Summers, S.M.: Limitations of self-assembly at temperature 1. Theoret. Comput. Sci. **412**, 145–158 (2011)
7. Doyle, P.G., Snell, J.L.: Random Walks and Electric Networks. Mathematical Association of America, Washington, DC (1984). https://math.dartmouth.edu/doyle/docs/walks/walks.pdf
8. El-Khoury, P.Z., Khon, E., Gong, Y., Joly, A.G., Abellan, P., Evans, J.E., Browning, N.D., Hu, D., Zamkov, M., Hess, W.P.: Electric field enhancement in a self-assembled 2D array of silver nanospheres. J. Chem. Phys. **141**(21), 214308 (2014)
9. Englander, O., Christensen, D., Kim, J., Lin, L., Morris, S.J.: Electric-field assisted growth and self-assembly of intrinsic silicon nanowires. Nano Lett. **5**(4), 705–708 (2005)

10. Feynman, R.P., Leighton, R.B., Sands, M.L.: The Feynman lectures on physics. Addison-Wesley, Redwood City (1989). http://opac.inria.fr/record=b1131031
11. Grady, L.: Random walks for image segmentation. IEEE Trans. Pattern Anal. Mach. Intell. **28**(11), 1768–1782 (2014)
12. Kirchhoff, G.: Ueber die auflösung der gleichungen, auf welche man bei der untersuchung der linearen vertheilung galvanischer ströme geführt wird. Ann. Phys. **148**(12), 497–508 (1847)
13. Klein, D.J., Randic, M.: Random distance. J. Math. Chem. **12**, 81 (1993)
14. Patitz, M.J., Schweller, R.T., Summers, S.M.: Efficient squares and turing universality at temperature 1 with a unique negative glue. arXiv:1105.1215v2 (2012)
15. Meunier, P.E., Patitz, M.J., Summers, S.M., Theyssier, G., Winslow, A., Woods, D.: Intrinsic universality in tile self-assembly requires cooperation. In: Proceedings of the ACM-SIAM Symposium on Discrete Algorithms (SODA 2014), Portland, OR, USA, 5–7 January 2014 (2014, to appear)
16. Mirkin, C., Letsinger, R.L., Mucic, R.C., Storhoff, J.J.: A DNA-based method for rationally assembling nanoparticles into macroscopic materials. Nature **382**, 607–609 (1996)
17. Nuccitelli, R.: A role for endogenous electric fields in wound healing. Curr. Top. Dev. Biol. **58**, 1–26 (2003)
18. Pereira, R.N., Souza, B.W., Cerqueira, M.A., Teixeira, J.A., Vicente, A.A.: Effects of electric fields on protein unfolding and aggregation: influence on edible films formation. Biomacromolecules **11**(11), 2912–2918 (2010)
19. Venezian, G.: On the resistance between two points on a grid. Am. J. Phys. **62**(11), 1000–1004 (1994)
20. Winfree, E., Liu, F., Wenzler, L.A., Seeman, N.C.: Design and self-assembly of two-dimensional DNA crystals. Nature **394**, 539–544 (1998)
21. Winfree, E., Rothemund, P.: The program-size complexity of self-assembled squares. In: Proceedings of the Thirty-Second Annual ACM Symposium on Theory of Computing, STOC 2000, pp. 459–468. ACM, New York (2000)
22. Winfree, E.: Algorithmic self-assembly of DNA. Ph.D. thesis, California Institute of Technology, June 1998
23. Wu, F.Y.: Theory of resistor networks: the two-point resistance. J. Phys. A: Math. Gen. **37**(26), 6653 (2004)

Morphogenetic and Homeostatic Self-assembled Systems

Petr Sosík[2]([✉]), Vladimír Smolka[2], Jan Drastík[2], Tyler Moore[1],
and Max Garzon[1]

[1] The University of Memphis, Memphis, TN, USA
[2] Research Institute of the IT4Innovations Centre of Excellence,
Faculty of Philosophy and Science, Silesian University, Opava, Czech Republic
petr.sosik@fpf.slu.cz

Abstract. As a natural evolution of developments in membrane computing and self-assembly, the time appears ripe to hybridize their principles to explore models capable of exhibiting further properties exhibited by living organisms, while preserving the primary advantages of models in physics, chemistry and computer science, e.g. arising from local interactions of their components and implementable *in silico* and/or *in vitro*. We introduce an abstract model named **M system**, capable of self-assembly and a developmental process, that strikes a balance between these conflicting goals, namely biological realism, physical-chemical realism and computational realism. We demonstrate that such systems are capable of being assembled from scratch from some atomic components, undergo a process of morphogenesis by the unfolding of the self-assembly rules defined by their local interactions, exhibit crucial properties of living cells as the self-healing property or mitosis (cell division), and eventually enter a stable equilibrium of adulthood in which they will continue to function as long as certain conditions in their environment remain. We present some theoretical results on the model, as well as preliminary simulations and experimental results of an M system simulator we have developed to explore this kind of model.

1 Introduction

The relationship between the macrosciences (such as biology) and the microsciences (such as quantum mechanics and physics) has been a topic of increasing interest for decades. In a pioneering work, Schrödinger [21] explored this connection and pointed to the future developments of a molecular basis for biology, later fully validated by the discovery of the structure of DNA [25] in the 1950s, the development of biotechnology in the 1980s, the genome projects (HGPs, www.ornl.gov) of the 1990s, and the subsequent *-omics of the 21st century.

A fundamental distinction between biology and the other natural sciences is that while physics and chemistry, for example, are governed by interactions

Electronic supplementary material The online version of this chapter (doi:10.1007/978-3-319-58187-3_11) contains supplementary material, which is available to authorized users.

© Springer International Publishing AG 2017
M.J. Patitz and M. Stannett (Eds.): UCNC 2017, LNCS 10240, pp. 144–159, 2017.
DOI: 10.1007/978-3-319-58187-3_11

that appear immutable and perennial over time, the basic unit of life, a biological organism, is conceived in the physics and chemistry of the world, undergoes a growth process that turns it into an idiosyncratic adult, but eventually dies back into the material world. In the process, the organism produces offspring that inherit some of its uniqueness and perpetuate it over time, but in a very mutable way that creates some sort of living memory and gives rise to evolution. Understandably, the significance of the answers and the complexity of evolution have led computer scientists, and perhaps even biologists, to focus their work on the latter (primarily, natural selection and *-omics), which has resulted in relatively poor attention devoted to the organisms themselves, e.g., the morphogenetic growth processes, which may nonetheless play an equally important role in the adult organism itself. A major aim of this work is to focus on models of morphogenesis and the transition into what we term *homeostasis*, i.e., a sustainable, balanced functioning state as a "productive" organism.

The development of higher biological organisms from a fertilized zygote can be logically split into three kinds of processes, namely, cellular differentiation, control of cell growth and morphogenesis (e.g., how biological organisms develop their specific shape). Morphogenesis is a classical, critical, yet underdeveloped area in biology, computational studies and mathematical models, although its importance was realized by the early founding fathers of computer science [12,24]. Turing's paper [24] is perhaps the original most famous attempt at producing a model to explain the memory pattern formation and their resilience in biological organisms, such as the spots in a leopard skin [24].

There have been two notable attempts to address this gap, namely membrane computing and virtual cells [23]. The original inspiring idea of *membrane computing*, now usually referred to as P systems [17], was to develop models that could begin to shed light on the role of membranes in the process of morphogenesis of the living cell, while obtaining new insights and approaches to solving difficult problems in computer science. A survey of membrane computing (see [18]) shows a number of works hinting at this kind of model. [7] studies synchronized colonies of membrane-inspired agents, including their behavioural robustness in cases of agent loss or rule failure. A *Spatial P system* embedded in a 2D lattice, partly resembling cellular automata, appears in [2]. The same authors introduced the *Spatial Calculus of Looping Sequences* (Spatial CLS) [1], where membranes may have assigned exclusive positions in 2D/3D space. Membrane systems allowing self-assembly of graphs representing interconnected systems of cells at their vertices were studied in [3]. A model of morphogenesis of a multicellular body based on abstract membranes displacement and attachment in 3D space was presented in [10] and applied to simulate the growth of colonies of *Dictyostelium discoideu*. However, all these models assume an abstract cell as an atomic assembly unit of an abstract nature. Here, we are interested in exploring the developmental process from scratch, i.e., through self-assembly of 1D or 2D primitives allowing for self-assembly of 3D cell-like forms. To be sure, we are not interested in cloning biological organisms (an exercise that sheds little understanding of the key mechanisms at play), but in a deeper examination of potential mechanisms or strategies whereby they may be achieved through a complexification process distributed in space and time, emerging from the bottom-up through local interactions among atomic components naturally available in an environment. Specifically, the objective is to explore higher functions such as internal dynamical homeostasis, self-reproduction, self-healing, for example, and their relationships. (We must point out that, to the best of our knowledge, the actual etiology of these process in biology is not fully known, but even if they were, knowledge of such mechanisms or strategies may prove useful both within biology and other fields such as artificial life.)

Perhaps the most appealing feature of membranes is that they bring into the picture an obvious but most fundamental ingredient in the formation of a biological cell, namely the walls that separate it from the external world or the various parts of it. Less known is the more general and primary role of other spatial relationships and constraints in the organization of biological systems, let alone the role of *geometric shape*. An attempt at a general approach to formalization of spatial and geometrical interaction in complex (biological) systems is the 3π calculus [6] based on process algebra.

Recent research points to an increasingly important role in biological morphogenesis of topological and geometric features such as crevices and wrinkles (see e.g., [22]). Another example of current interest is the formation of the mammalian brain cortex. Mechanical and biochemical models have been used. Mechanical models hypothesize that gyris (foldings) in the brain are the results of anisotropic differential growth, while numerical solutions to chemically reaction-diffusion (RD) systems have produced qualitatively approximate patterns in cortex formation, both in 2D and 3D models. Genetic factors, particularly the protein β-catenin recently, are also implicated in the process. These models can be used for prognosis of brain malformations during development in terms of coefficients in the RD model (e.g., polymicrogyria and lissencephaly). Biologists are also now beginning to discover the importance of the role of even more elementary physical phenomena, such as electric fields and chemical gradients, including their role in chemical signaling in the living cell [20], e.g. in critical mechano-sensitive channels [4].

In parallel, from a separate direction, computational ideas from the field of DNA Computing have developed models and theories of DNA self-assembly that capture more directly a "morphogenetic" process of sorts in the form of models of self-assembly of patterns and families of patterns and afford clues as to the nature of and capabilities of morphogenesis [9]. However, once again, these models do not directly afford new knowledge on the fundamental biological problem of morphogenesis and homeostasis that would bring them anywhere near the kind of contribution that other models in natural sciences like physics and chemistry provide us about motion and matter transformation.

Inspired by these developments, the time appears ripe to hybridize P systems and geometric self-assembly in order to explore models of morphogenesis and homeostasis, balancing three somewhat conflicting properties to the best degree possible: biological realism, physical-chemical realism and computational realism. To achieve physical-chemical realism, very critical components and the corresponding dynamic process occurring in a living cell will be specifically represented in the model by appropriate data structures and algorithmic interactions. To achieve computational realism, all components and processes must be modeled at the appropriate level of granularity in both time and resources in order to maintain the computational feasibility of the model. To achieve biological realism, the aggregate observables accumulated over time and space in the model must reflect, to some degree, the corresponding macroscopic observables, e.g., must reflect to some level of scale or granularity known properties of biological organisms at the observable (nano, micro or macro) level, independently of whether they faithfully describe factual processes in biological organisms.

Therefore, the desirable features of the model are self-assembly, self-controlled growth and emerging global behavior that is consistent with observable properties of biological organisms, but which arise from nondeterministic local interactions of elementary components, also consistent with self-assembly and P systems. We present the definition of the model, referred to as **M** systems, in Sect. 2, as well as the relevant known biological knowledge (fairly incomplete and mostly unavailable) that guided it. In Sect. 3, we discuss arguments that show how these properties may be guaranteed or to what extent, including a theoretical result and experimental evidence that these properties actually do emerge with very high probability, and provide a characterization of their behavior, consistent with recent probabilistic analysis of self-assembly systems [11]. Section 4 completes the view by demonstration of computational power of the model in the Turing sense even under severe restrictions. Finally, in Sect. 5, we present some discussion on the significance of the model, some of its implications, and some interesting further problems that could be addressed with plausible extensions of it.

2   M Systems

As mentioned above, introducing geometric features in P systems is a natural an interesting idea of its own. First, it is an intriguing question that may help realize the potential of the original idea of membrane computing, as spatial arrangement is critical for information processing in living cells, colonies, tissues and organisms. Second, it may also further our understanding of computation beyond the scope of traditional computer science, where shape and geometry are not native concepts, but rather that require enormous amounts of effort to build back in, while on the other hand, our understanding of the world is inherently dependent on it. Besides being able to compute in the Turing sense, a model should be able to interact with and "sense" its physical environment, so as to be capable of self-modification and unenthropical evolution, i.e., to increase its fitness (however defined) in its embedding environment. Membrane systems seem to be a good candidate, but a sufficient level of self-modification and evolution of new features is hardly possible in the current amorphous level.

The basic model of a P system generally consists of a structure of (possibly nested) *membranes* which delimit *regions* precisely identified by the membranes.

In addition, the system contains objects from a set O placed inside membranes or in the surrounding environment, but which do not bear any information about their location or shape within the membranes. Several copies of the same object can be present in a region, so we work with *multisets* of objects. A primary biological carrier of shape is a protein. This feature is explicitly used in P systems with proteins on membranes [13,14].

The **M system** extends this concept with explicit geometric features and self-assembly capabilities. The whole system is embedded in an nD Euclidean space $\mathbb{R}^n$ (assume 3D space unless stated otherwise). There are three types of objects present in the system: *proteins*, *tiles* and *floating objects*.

Floating objects are small shapeless atomic objects floating freely within the environment, but having at each moment their specified position in space. They can pass through protein channels and participate in mutual reactions with other types of objects, in *discrete time steps*. This latter property ensures that, if started empty, membranes will always contain a finite number of objects regardless of time allowed to operate, and makes unnecessary the specification of the finite volume they would occupy.

Tiles have their pre-defined size and shape, together with specified position and orientation in space at each moment. Tiles can stick together along their edges or at selected points. These edges/points are called *connectors* and they are covered with *glues*. Their connection is controlled by a pre-defined *glue relation*. Thus the tiles can self-assemble into interconnected structures.

Proteins are placed on tiles and, apart from acting as protein channels letting floating objects pass through, they also catalyze their reactions.

Unlike current models of membrane systems, *membranes* are not present even implicitly, but they can only be formed of tiles during the evolution of the M system. Therefore, at the beginning of the evolution, typically *no membranes* are present and they must be subsequently self-assembled. The connected tiles can be also disconnected and/or destroyed under certain conditions. The following definitions provide the elements to capture these properties in a formal model (they can be skipped without hindering understanding of Sect. 3).

2.1   Polytopic Tiling

The cornerstone of our concept of morphogenetic self-assembly is an nD tile shaped as a bounded convex polytope (n-polytope) [28], with faces of dimension $n-1$ called *facets*. Hence, a 1D tile is an edge/rod whose facets are its endpoints, a 2D tile is a convex polygon with its edges as facets, a 3D tile is a convex polyhedron with polygons as facets, and so forth. Furthermore, tile may contain connectors defining its connection to other tiles. Let G be a finite set of *glues*. A *connector* of a tile forming an n-polytope Δ is a triple (Δ_c, g, φ), where

$\Delta_c \subset \Delta$ is a bounded convex k-polytope where $0 \leq k < n$,
$g \in G$ is a glue,
$\varphi \in (-\pi, \pi\rangle$ is the connecting angle.

We distinguish

- *facet connectors* with $k = n - 1$ where Δ_c is a facet of the polytope Δ;
- *non-facet connectors* with $k < n - 1$ placed anywhere on the tile.

Two or more connectors can share the same position on a tile. Formally, an *n-dimensional tile* is defined as

$$t = (\Delta, \{c_1, \ldots, c_k\}, g_s), \text{ for } k \geq 0,$$

where Δ is a bounded convex n-polytope, $c_1, \ldots, c_k$ are connectors and $g_s \in G$ is the *surface glue* covering the entire surface of the tile except where connectors are placed.

For an $(n - 1)$-dimensional tile embedded in $\mathbb{R}^n$ we denote its two sides by *in* and *out*. A *non-facet* connector with positive connecting angle is placed on side *in*, one with negative angle is placed on side *out*, and one with zero angle can only be located on some facet of the tile.

Definition 1. *A polytopic tile system in $\mathbb{R}^n$ is a construct $T = (Q, G, \gamma, d_g, S)$, where*

Q is the set of tiles of dimensions less than n;
G is the set of glues;
$\gamma \subseteq G \times G$ is the glue relation;
$d_g \in \mathbb{R}_0^+$ is the gluing distance (assumed to be small compared to the size of tiles);
S is the finite multiset of seed tiles from Q randomly distributed in space.

A tile t_2 with a connector c_2 *can connect* to a connector c_1 on a tile t_1 at the connecting angle of c_1 if the following conditions are met:

- c_1 and c_2 are unconnected and have the same dimension and size;
- their glues g_1 and g_2 satisfy $(g_1, g_2) \in \gamma$;
- at least one of c_1 or c_2 is a facet connector.

If both t_1 and t_2 are $(n - 1)$-polytopes, then their *in* and *out* faces must match and the connecting angle precisely determines their mutual position. Otherwise, the connecting angle may provide one degree of freedom to t_2 whose orientation is then semi-random.

If t_2 attaches to t_1 and it still has free connectors now positioned within the distance d_g from free connectors on other tiles already in place, then the pairs which can connect together would do so. Similarly, if a free connector $c = (\Delta_c, g_c, \varphi)$ of t_2 lies within the distance d_g from an existing tile t_3 with surface glue g_s such that $(g_c, g_s) \in \gamma$, then t_2 connects to the surface of t_3.

Note that the relation γ is generally non-symmetric. So if c_2 can connect to c_1 does not imply that also c_1 can connect to c_2. This is in accordance with natural morphogenetic processes which are often irreversible [5].

Example 1. Consider a polytopic tile system in $\mathbb{R}^3$ with a single glue g and the glue relation $\gamma = \{(g, g)\}$. Let Q contain a 2D tile q shaped as a regular pentagon, with five facet connectors on its edges, each with the glue g and with the connecting angle $\varphi = 2.0345$ radians, which is the inner angle between two faces in a dodecahedron. Let finally $S = \{q\}$ be the only seed tile, see the leftmost image. Then, provided that q is available in enough copies, the system assembles as follows.

1. Five tiles q would connect to the five connectors of the seed tile in the first phase, connecting also their five edges starting at vertices of the seed tile as they stick together. The connecting angle determines them to shape as cup with zig-zag rim with 10 edges (central-left image).
2. Another five tiles would connect to these edges, determined by the connecting angle to form an almost-closed shape (central-right image).
3. Finally, the last attached tile encloses the dodecahedral "soccer-ball". All connectors on the tiles match and connect together, hence no further assembly is possible (rightmost image).

2.2 Morphogenetic Systems

An M system naturally merges principles of both self assembly and membrane computing. Geometrical structure and growth of each M system is determined by its underlying polytopic tile system. Unlike usual tiling systems, the M system does not assume availability of an unlimited number of copies of each tile. The M system life cycle starts in an initial configuration where only seed tiles are present. Further structures can only be created by the application of rules of the M system.

Formally, for a multiset M we denote by $|M|_a$ the multiplicity of elements a in M. A multiset M with the underlying set O can be represented by a string $x \in O^*$ (by O^* we denote the free monoid generated by O with respect to the concatenation and the identity λ) such that the number of occurrences of $a \in O$ in x represents the value $|M|_a$.

Definition 2. *A morphogenetic system (M system) in $\mathbb{R}^n$ is a tuple*

$$\mathcal{M} = (F, P, T, \mu, R, r, \sigma),$$

where

$F = (O, m, e)$ *is the catalogue of floating objects, where:*

O is the set of floating objects;

$m : O \longrightarrow \mathbb{R}^+$ *is the mean mobility of each floating object in the environment;*

$e : O \longrightarrow \mathbb{R}_0^+$ *is the concentration of each floating object in the environment:*
  $e(o)$ copies of object o per spatial unit 1^n;

P is the set of proteins;

$T = (Q, G, \gamma, d_g, S)$ *is a polytopic tile system in $\mathbb{R}^n$, with O, P, Q, G all pairwise disjoint;*

μ *is the mapping assigning to each tile $t \in Q$ a multiset of proteins placed on t together with their positions: $\mu(t) \subset P \times \Delta$ where Δ is the underlying polytope of t;*

R is a finite set of reaction rules;

$r \in \mathbb{R}_0^+$ *is the reaction radius; a reaction rule can be applied when all objects entering the reaction are positioned within this radius;*

$\sigma : \gamma \longrightarrow O^*$ *is the mapping assigning to each glue pair $(g_1, g_2) \in \gamma$ a multiset of floating objects which are released to the environment within the reaction radius from a new connection with (g_1, g_2), when the connection is established.*

Unless stated otherwise, we consider M systems in $\mathbb{R}^3$ in the rest of the paper.

A *reaction rule* from the set R has the form $u \to v$, where u and v are strings containing floating objects, proteins, glues and tiles due to types of rules specified bellow. The necessary condition to apply the rule is that all objects in u are present in the environment within radius r, while certain rules may specify further conditions on the location of objects.

Metabolic Rules

Metabolic rules are of several types: *simple* and *catalytic rules* allowing mutual reactions of floating objects, similarly as cooperative and catalytic rules in membrane systems [16, 17].

Symport and *antiport* rules allow the floating objects to pass through protein channels, similarly as in P systems with proteins on membranes [13, 14]. Let $u, v \in O^+$ be non-empty multisets of floating objects and $p \in P$ be a protein. The rules containing the symbol [are applicable only when p is placed on an $(n-1)$-dimensional tile, where object to the left of [in the string correspond to the side "out" and those to the right correspond to the side "in" of the tile.

Type	Rule	Effect
Simple	$u \to v$	Objects in multiset u react to produce v
Catalytic	$pu \to pv$	Objects in u react in presence of p to produce v;
	$u[p \to v[p$	Eventually, u, v must both appear on the side "out"
	$[pu \to [pv$	Or on the side "in" of the tile on which p is placed
Symport	$u[p \to p[u$	Passing of u through protein channel p
	$[pu \to u[p$	To the other side of the tile
Antiport	$u[pv \to v[pu$	Interchange of u and v through protein channel p

Note that these rules are rather powerful and we will mostly consider some restrictions when studying M systems from the computational power point of view.

Creation rules $u \to t$,

where $t \in Q$ and $u \in O^+$. The rule creates tile t while consuming the floating objects in u. It can be applied if the following holds:

(i) there already exists a tile (say s) in the environment with a free connector c_s such that t can connect to c_s by some of its connectors, and
(ii) floating objects in u exist in the environment within the distance r from c_s.

Then an attempt is made to create tile t and connect it to c_s as specified in Sect. 2.1. If t would intersect another existing tile, say s', then s' (together with all tiles interconnected with it) is pushed away to make room for t. This may cause a chain reaction of mutual pushing of tiles in the way. If it is impossible to make enough room for t and t is a polygon, the rule is not applied, otherwise t is shortened so that it just touches s'. Its connector(s) at the shortened end (if any) are preserved.

Finally, free connectors of t automatically connect to existing tiles as described in Sect. 2.1.

Destruction rules $ut \to v$,

where $t \in Q, u, v \in O^+$. Tile t is destroyed in the presence of the "destructor" multiset of floating objects u. All connectors on other tiles connected to t are released. The objects in u are consumed and the multiset v of "waste" objects is produced.

Division rules $g \xrightarrow{u} h \to g, h$,

where $g - h$ is a pair of glues on connectors of two connected tiles. The connection is released in the presence of the multiset $u \in O^+$. The multiset u is consumed. The tiles remain in their position but the pair of connectors is released so that new tiles can possibly attach to them.

Configuration of the M system is determined by

- positions and Euler angles of all tiles in the environment;
- interconnection graph of connectors on these tiles;
- positions of all floating objects within the finite part of the environment occupied by tiles; the rest of the (infinite) environment contains floating objects randomly distributed due to their concentrations e.

The initial configuration contains only (unconnected) seed tiles in S and a random distribution of floating objects given by their concentration e.

Computation of the M System

The system transits between configurations by application of rules in the set R. At each step, each floating object can be subject to at most one rule, each connector can be subject to at most one creation or division rule, and each tile can be subject to at most one destruction rule. Since there may be trade-offs between applicable rules, their selection is done in the following order: 1. metabolic rules, 2. destruction rules, 3. creation rules, 4. division rules. The rules within each group are chosen nondeterministically until their maximum applicable multiset is obtained, so that no more rules can be added to it. Then all the selected rules are applied in parallel to the actual configuration.

Finally, each floating object o with mean mobility $m(o)$ changes randomly its position at each step due to the Maxwell-Boltzmann distribution [27] with parameter $a = \sqrt{\pi/8}\, m(o)$ corresponding to Brownian motion of particles in liquid media.

A sequence of transitions of an M system between configurations is called a *computation*. The computation can be finite (if an M system cannot apply any rule, it halts) or infinite, and it is, by definition, nondeterministic. The reader is referred to the proof of Proposition 2 for a simple example, or to supplementary material for a more complex one (follow the link in the proof of Proposition 1).

We will mostly be interested in the general dynamics of the M system, as the probability of reaching certain equilibrium or oscillatory states, growth of certain spatial structures, evolution and emergence of new properties, mitosis and division of cell-like structures. However, numerical input and output of the system can be defined, too, demonstrating its computational capability in Turing sense, as we show in Sect. 4.

3   Computational Morphogenesis and Homeostasis

In this section we demonstrate that M systems are indeed capable of being assembled from scratch from some atomic components, undergo a process of morphogenesis by the unfolding of the self-assembly rules defined by their local interactions as given by the catalytic, creation and destruction rules, and eventually enter a stable dynamical equilibrium of adulthood in which they will continue to function as long as certain conditions in their environment remain.

We illustrate with an example of an M system $\mathcal{M}_0$ shown at Fig. 1, that demonstrates the ability of creation and self-reproduction (*mitosis*) of elementary cells and simultaneously building an internal cytoskeleton structure. The geometrical structure of $\mathcal{M}_0$ builds on two sets of 2D pentagonal tiles: larger tiles self-assembling in a cell-like membrane, and smaller tiles assembling a nuclear membrane. These tiles are much alike that in Example 1 but with different glues on their edges. Some of the larger tiles contain also point connectors on their inner surface, connecting to rod-shaped 1D tiles. Endpoints of rods bear one (straight-oriented) or two (fork-oriented) connectors, allowing the rods to assemble a tree-like structure of cytoskeleton.

Proposition 1. *Assuming discrete time and bounded finite resources in the environment, an arbitrary run of the M system $\mathcal{M}_0$ crosses a critical time at which it stops growing and enters a period of homeostasis, where it will remain in functional equilibrium despite certain fluctuations in the environment and/or damage to its internal structure.*

Proof. (Sketch; full description of the M system and more proof details are provided as a supplementary material at url sosik.zam.slu.cz/Msystem.html *or* bmc.memphis.edu/cytos.)

As pointed out above, discrete time interactions guarantee that at any given time, only a finite number of membranes and objects are contained therein throughout the life of the model, (although they could potentially contain an uncountable number of objects as a continuum). In the terminology of self-assembly systems, $\mathcal{M}_0$ is locally deterministic and attachment of tiles proceeds as in the aTAM model [26]. As illustrated by Example 1, the geometric structure of the tiles forces them to curve as they are attached and to close upon themselves to eventually form a dodecahedron and present plain geometric blocking for further growth, which thus finishes the membrane building phase when the last keystone tile is attached. Simultaneously an analogous process creates a much smaller nuclear membrane.

The attached tiles bear proteins triggering the formation of cytoskeleton by rods, which can grow nondeterministically in various directions from both "poles" of the membrane. Eventually, addition of rods is no longer possible for excluded volume reasons, so the cytoskeleton, and hence morphogenesis is now complete and $\mathcal{M}_0$ enters the "adult" homeostatic phase.

Even before this phase is fully completed, the contact of growing rods with the nuclear membrane triggers the process of mitosis which proceeds to create two copies of the cells and separate it into two identical parts, which will then begin anew the entire process and continue while enough supplies and room for growth remain. All this is fully controlled only by local interactions of tiles and floating objects.

At any point in the morphogenetic process, any damage will either simply undo a previous state, or detach a piece of the systems altogether, which will reset it back to a previous state, from which it will further develop as it did before, *perhaps through a different run as a nondeterministic system.* Because the stable equilibrium is achieved again with similar characteristics, perhaps the same original individual will not be formed again, but the new individual will bear the characteristic features of the original one. Therefore, the original organism is capable of sustaining injuries to some degree of severity to its internal structure, without changing the overall structure of the adult organism.   □

This result has been verified experimentally using our M system simulator (follow the link in the proof), some snapshots are provided at Fig. 1.

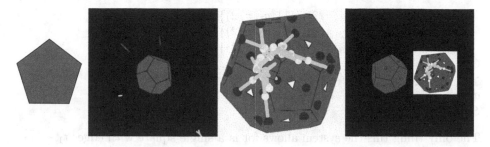

Fig. 1. (Left) A cell wall tile, (middle-left) a completed cell wall structure in a membrane context among free-floating objects, (middle-right) an interior view of a cell where yellow rods grow inward from dark grey connectors on the cell wall in order to support an interior nuclear membrane, and (right) two complete cells emerging from a single complete cell that divided by mitosis in a membrane context. (Color figure online)

4   Computational Universality

Although M systems are primarily designed to study natural computing in a broad sense (see Sect. 1), and not as a tool for solving "classical" computational problems, we show that the model is theoretically capable of universal computing in the Turing sense too.

We define the result of a computation of an M system as the number of floating objects produced by the M system at the halting configuration. Only objects not present originally in the environment (with $e(o) = 0$) are considered. The result is undefined if $\mathcal{M}$ never halts. Collecting all possible results, we obtain a set of nonnegative integers denoted by $N(\mathcal{M})$. The family of all sets of integers computed by M systems of a certain *type* is denoted by $NOM(type)$. Particularly, if the M system uses only creation rules and metabolic rules restricted to forms $a \to u$ and $pa \to pu$, for $p \in P, a \in O$ and $u \in O^*$, we denote the resulting family $NOM(cat_k, crea)$, where k is the number of proteins. Let further NRE denote the family of all recursively enumerable sets of nonnegative integers.

The following result relies on a simulation of a catalytic P system by an M system. *Catalysts* in P systems are a specific kind of objects which allow for reactions of objects but remain themselves unchanged. Recall that a *catalytic P system* [8] uses evolution rules of the forms $a \to v$ and $ca \to cv$ where c is a catalyst, a is an object from $O \setminus C$, and $v \in (O \setminus C)^*$ are objects produced by the rule.

Proposition 2. *For any catalytic P system Π with a single membrane and $k \geq 1$ catalysts there is a 2D M system $\mathcal{M}$ with k proteins, using only metabolic rules of the form $a \to u, pa \to pu$ and creation rules, such that $N(\Pi) \cup \{0\} = N(\mathcal{M})$.*

Proof. Consider a polytopic tile system $T = (Q, G, \gamma, d_g, S)$ in $\mathbb{R}^2$, where

Q contains three types of equally-shaped segments of length 1, each with a connector with connecting angle $\pi/2$ at each endpoint. Formally, let

$$t_1 = (\langle 0, 1 \rangle, \{(\{0\}, g_1, \pi/2), (\{1\}, g_1, \pi/2)\}, g_s);$$
$$t_2 = (\langle 0, 1 \rangle, \{(\{0\}, g_2, \pi/2), (\{1\}, g_2, \pi/2)\}, g_s);$$
$$t_3 = (\langle 0, 1 \rangle, \{(\{0\}, g_3, \pi/2), (\{1\}, g_4, \pi/2)\}, g_s);$$
$$G = \{g_1, g_2, g_3, g_4, g_s\};$$
$$\gamma = \{(g_1, g_2), (g_2, g_3), (g_4, g_2)\};$$
$$d_g = 0.1;$$
$$S = \{t_1\}.$$

The only tiling this tile system allows for is a single square with edges $t_1 - t_2 - t_3 - t_2$. This tiling provides the geometrical base for the M system we construct in the next step.

Let Π be a catalytic P system with a set of objects O, a set of catalysts C, a set of rules R, a single membrane containing initially a multiset of objects $w \in (O \setminus C)^*$. We show how to simulate Π by morphogenetic systems. Consider the M system $\mathcal{M} = (F, P, T, \mu, R', r, \sigma)$ in $\mathbb{R}^2$, where:

$F = (O', m, e)$, where:
  $O' = O \setminus C \cup \{a, b\}$, where $a, b \notin O$ are new floating objects;
  $m(o) = 1$ for each $o \in O'$;
  $e(a) = 1000$ and $e(o) = 0$ for all other $o \in O'$;
$P = C$;
T is the polytopic tile system described above;
$\mu(t_1) = P$, the set of proteins arbitrarily positioned on the tile, and
$\mu(t_2) = \mu(t_3) = \emptyset$;
$R' = \{d \to u \mid d \to u \in R\} \cup \{\ [cd \to [cu \mid cd \to cu \in R\} \cup \{aaa \to t_2, aaa \to$
  $t_3, [pb \to [pw\}$, where p is a single protein arbitrarily chosen from P;
$r = 2$;
$\sigma(g_4, g_2) = \{b\}$ and $\sigma(g_i, g_j) = \emptyset$ for all other $(g_i, g_j) \in \gamma$.

The initial configuration of the M system $\mathcal{M}$ contains the seed tile (segment) t_1 and a high concentration of objects a in the environment. Typical computation proceeds in the following steps:

1. Two instances of the rule $aaa \to t_2$ are applied, adding two perpendicular segments t_2 to both ends of the seed segment t_1 (as the connecting angle is $\pi/2$. No other rule is applicable.
2. Rule $aaa \to t_3$ adds segment t_3 bridging both loose ends of segments t_2 and enclosing a square. No further growth of segments is possible as all their connectors are occupied. All their sides in are facing inwards the square, as determined by the assembly principles in Sect. 2.1. At that moment, since $\sigma(g_4, g_2) = \{b\}$, object b is released in the proximity of the square corner connecting t_2 and t_3.
3. If the object b appears outside the square, the computation halts with result 0. Otherwise, rule $[pb \to [pw$ is applied and the initial multiset w of the P system Π is produced inside the square.

4. From this step on, the system $\mathcal{M}$ applies inside the square the rules of Π in exactly the same manner as Π would, while proteins in P act as catalysts of Π. This happens with certainty as the reaction radius encompasses the whole interior of the square. No rule is applicable outside the square as there are only objects a not appearing in these rules.

Hence, if Π eventually halts, so does $\mathcal{M}$, with equal content of objects within the square, and so $N(\Pi) \cup \{0\} = N(\mathcal{M})$. Note that $\mathcal{M}$ (as any other M system) uses random distribution of floating objects, so in an unlikely case no object a is located within reaction radius from existing tiles at steps 1 and 2, hence no rule is applicable and the system may halt prematurely with result 0.   □

Let us denote by NRE_0 the class of all recursively enumerable set of integers containing 0, i.e., $NRE_0 = \{A \cup \{0\} \mid A \in NRE\}$.

Corollary 1. $NOM(cat_2, crea) = NRE_0$.

Proof. It is demonstrated in [8] that a catalytic P system Π with a single membrane and two catalysts can generate any recursively enumerable set of integers. Then the statement follows by Proposition 2.   □

Note that, from the computational complexity point of view, the M system $\mathcal{M}$ in the above proof is inefficient as it simulates the P system Π which, in turn, simulates a register machine. However, we conjecture that a more efficient way of computation is possible, allowing to simulate a Turing machine or a cellular automaton in polynomial time. Proof of Proposition 1 even suggests an unlimited exponential growth of cells which might eventually allow the model to solve NP-hard problems in polynomial time. This, however, is subject of further research.

5   Conclusions

We have introduced a geometric model, *M systems*, that exhibit properties of self-assembly and controlled growth akin to those observed in cell biology. The model is inspired by P systems and the new properties are obtained by introducing geometric concepts of shape and arrangement of atomic objects at specific locations. Basic abstract operations in the model include reactions among objects, their transport through protein channels, and their mutual interconnection, leading to construction and destruction of complex geometric structures, which are cell-inspired in the examples we have provided, but which can adopt virtually any geometric forms.

We have shown that M systems are computationally universal in the Turing sense, even if restricted to very simple shape and operations, based on similar results in P systems. This result suggests many research avenues in this direction, as the relation of M systems to other models of P systems, e.g., with symport/antiport [15], with proteins on membranes [13] or with active membranes [19]. How can the geometrical and morphological structure of the M system increase/restrict its computational potential? This question is especially relevant in connection with an unlimited membrane division in P systems, which the M system is capable of, but with more realistic spatial and concentration constraints.

We have also shown that M systems are universal in a perhaps more restricted but more biological sense, i.e., they exhibit a morphogenetic and homeostatic structure in their life cycle and can live forever by replication. We have also demonstrated their capability to grow complex cell-inspired information processing structures, providing a model of the cytoskeleton growth which in turn controls a process akin to biological mitosis. We have also developed a software simulator of M systems to continue research on this models that is available at url sosik.zam.slu.cz/Msystem.html or bmc.memphis.edu/cytos.

This direction of research raises some interesting questions. First, can other systems exhibit similar characteristics with simpler rules? Second, what is the extent of their self-repair properties? What kind of "injuries" will harm the model beyond repair? How exactly can injury be properly defined to establish more specific properties and limitations of self-healing? Third, adding evolutionary properties to the model is an intriguing possibility – the capability to evolve unenthropically towards more efficient behavior related to its specific goals, which can be of many kinds. To this end, the model should be equipped with a kind of abstract genetic code defining shapes of tiles and placement of connectors and other proteins on them. Perhaps the evolution of new floating objects and proteins and their mutual reactions should be allowed, too, reflecting the evolution of new "organic" molecules. This evolution may produce new development of models *in silico*, a kind of artificial life closer to biological life as we know it.

Acknowledgements. This work was supported by the Ministry of Education, Youth and Sports Of the Czech Republic from the National Programme of Sustainability (NPU II) project IT4Innovations Excellence in Science - LQ1602, and by the Silesian University in Opava under the Student Funding Scheme, project SGS/13/2016. We are grateful to anonymous reviewers whose valuable comments helped to improve the paper.

References

1. Barbuti, R., Maggiolo-Schettini, A., Milazzo, P., Pardini, G.: Spatial calculus of looping sequences. Theor. Comput. Sci. **412**(43), 5976–6001 (2011)
2. Barbuti, R., Maggiolo-Schettini, A., Milazzo, P., Pardini, G., Tesei, L.: Spatial P systems. Nat. Comput. **10**(1), 3–16 (2011)
3. Bernardini, F., Brijder, R., Cavaliere, M., Franco, G., Hoogeboom, H.J., Rozenberg, G.: On aggregation in multiset-based self-assembly of graphs. Nat. Comput. **10**(1), 17–38 (2011)
4. Blount, P., Sukharev, S.I., Moe, P.C., Schroeder, M.J., Guy, H., Kung, C.: Membrane topology and multimeric structure of a mechanosensitive channel protein of escherichia coli. EMBO J. **15**(18), 4798–4805 (1996)
5. Bourgine, P., Lesne, A.: Morphogenesis: Origins of Patterns and Shapes. Springer Complexity. Springer, Heidelberg (2010)

6. Cardelli, L., Gardner, P.: Processes in space. In: Ferreira, F., Löwe, B., Mayordomo, E., Mendes Gomes, L. (eds.) CiE 2010. LNCS, vol. 6158, pp. 78–87. Springer, Heidelberg (2010). doi:10.1007/978-3-642-13962-8_9
7. Cavaliere, M., Mardare, R., Sedwards, S.: A multiset-based model of synchronizing agents: computability and robustness. Theoret. Comput. Sci. **391**(3), 216–238 (2008)
8. Freund, R., Kari, L., Oswald, M., Sosík, P.: Computationally universal P systems without priorities: two catalysts are sufficient. Theoret. Comput. Sci. **330**, 251–266 (2005)
9. Krasnogor, N., Gustafson, S., Pelta, D., Verdegay, J.: Systems Self-Assembly: Multidisciplinary Snapshots. Studies in Multidisciplinarity. Elsevier Science, Amsterdam (2011)
10. Manca, V., Pardini, G.: Morphogenesis through moving membranes. Nat. Comput. **13**(3), 403–419 (2014)
11. Moore, T., Garzon, M., Deaton, R.: Probabilistic analysis of pattern formation in monotonic self-assembly. PLoS One **10**(9), 1–23 (2015). doi:10.1371/journal.pone.0137982
12. von Neumann, J.: Probabilistic logics and the synthesis of reliable organisms from unreliable components. Ann. Math. Studies **34**, 43–98 (1956)
13. Păun, A., Popa, B.: P systems with proteins on membranes. Fundamenta Informaticae **72**(4), 467–483 (2006)
14. Păun, A., Popa, B.: P Systems with proteins on membranes and membrane division. In: Ibarra, O.H., Dang, Z. (eds.) DLT 2006. LNCS, vol. 4036, pp. 292–303. Springer, Heidelberg (2006). doi:10.1007/11779148_27
15. Păun, A., Păun, G.: The power of communication: P systems with symport/antiport. New Gener. Comput. **20**(3), 295–305 (2002)
16. Păun, G.: Computing with membranes. J. Comput. System Sci. **61**, 108–143 (2000)
17. Păun, G.: Membrane Computing - An Introduction. Springer, Berlin (2002)
18. Păun, G., Rozenberg, G., Salomaa, A. (eds.): The Oxford Handbook of Membrane Computing. Oxford University Press, Oxford (2010)
19. Păun, G.: P systems with active membranes: attacking NP-complete problems. J. Automata Lang. Comb. **6**(1), 75–90 (2001)
20. Robinson, K., Messerli, M.: Left/right, up/down: the role of endogenous electrical fields as directional signals in development, repair and invasion. BioEssays **25**, 759–766 (2003)
21. Schrödinger, E.: What Is Life? The Physical Aspect of the Living Cell. Trinity College, Dublin (1944)
22. Tangirala, K., Caragea, D.: Generating features using burrows wheeler transformation for biological sequence classification. In: Pastor, O., et al. (ed.) Proceedings of the International Conference on Bioinformatics Models, Methods and Algorithms, pp. 196–203. SciTePress (2014)
23. Tomita, M.: Whole-cell simulation: a grand challenge of the 21st century. Trends Biotechnol. **19**(6), 205–210 (2001)
24. Turing, A.: The chemical basis of morphogenesis. Philos. Trans. R. Soc. Lond. B **237**, 7–72 (1950)
25. Watson, J., Crick, F.: A structure for deoxyribose nucleic acid. Nature **171**, 737–738 (1953)
26. Winfree, E.: Models of experimental self-assembly. Ph.D. thesis, Caltech (1998)
27. Maxwell-Boltzmann distribution, Wikipedia (cit 2017-1-29). https://en.wikipedia.org/wiki/Maxwell-Boltzmann_distribution
28. Ziegler, G.: Lectures on Polytopes. Graduate Texts in Mathematics. Springer, New York (1995)

Superposition as Memory: Unlocking Quantum Automatic Complexity

Bjørn Kjos-Hanssen[✉]

University of Hawai'i at Mānoa, Honolulu, HI 96822, USA
Bjoern.Kjos-Hanssen@hawaii.edu
https://math.hawaii.edu/wordpress/bjoern/

Abstract. We define the semi-classical quantum automatic complexity $Q_s(x)$ of a word x as the infimum in lexicographic order of those pairs of nonnegative integers (n, q) such that there is a subgroup G of the projective unitary group $\mathrm{PU}(n)$ with $|G| \leq q$ and with $U_0, U_1 \in G$ such that, in terms of a standard basis $\{e_k\}$ and with $U_z = \prod_k U_{z(k)}$, we have $U_x e_1 = e_2$ and $U_y e_1 \neq e_2$ for all $y \neq x$ with $|y| = |x|$. We show that Q_s is unbounded and not constant for strings of a given length. In particular,

$$Q_s(0^2 1^2) \leq (2, 12) < (3, 1) \leq Q_s(0^{60} 1^{60})$$

and $Q_s(0^{120}) \leq (2, 121)$.

Keywords: Finite automata · Security · Quantum automata · Automatic complexity

1 Introduction

Quantum Locks. Imagine a lock with two states, "locked" and "unlocked", which may be manipulated using two operations, called 0 and 1. Moreover, the only way to (with certainty) unlock using four operations is to do them in the sequence 0011, i.e., $0^n 1^n$ where $n = 2$. In this scenario one might think that the lock needs to be in certain further states after each operation, so that there is some memory of what has been done so far. Here we show that this memory can be entirely encoded in superpositions of the two basic states "locked" and "unlocked", where, as dictated by quantum mechanics, the operations are given by unitary matrices. Moreover, we show using the Jordan–Schur lemma that a similar lock is not possible for $n = 60$.

Quantum Security. A problem with traditional padlocks is that a clever lock-breaker can seek to detect what internal state the lock is in part-way through the entering of the lock code. This problem disappears when the internal states are just superpositions of "locked" and "unlocked". Of course, there may be a positive probability that the system when observed part-way through the entering of the lack code is observed in the "unlocked" state. To remedy this, one could use a sequence of many locks, say 10^k for a suitable positive integer k,

© Springer International Publishing AG 2017
M.J. Patitz and M. Stannett (Eds.): UCNC 2017, LNCS 10240, pp. 160–169, 2017.
DOI: 10.1007/978-3-319-58187-3_12

and add a third "permanently locked" state which, once reached, cannot be left. Then observing the lock will likely eventually result in landing in the permanently locked state. (In the case of the code $0^n 1^n$, the permanently locked state might be implemented as having a probability related to the difference in the number of 0s and 1s entered in the code so far.) Note that in theory this is a purely quantum phenomenon: any simulation of the quantum device using classical hardware will be subject to the original problem that a lock-breaker may try to discern the internal states of the classical hardware.

Quantum Automata. One of the fascinating aspects of quantum mechanics is how our understanding of states is enriched, with observable states, pure states, and mixed states. The notion of *state* of a finite automaton begs for a generalization to the quantum realm. Indeed, quantum finite automata have been studied already [1].

On the other hand automatic complexity introduced by Shallit and Wang [2] has been related it to model selection in statistics [3] and to pseudorandomness generation with linear feedback shift registers [4]. Other approaches to automatic complexity [5–7] yield better insight into infinite words.

We shall consider complexity with respect to an arbitrary semigroup before considering the quantum case of the projective unitary group $PU(n)$.

Definition 1. *Let T_X denote the set of all transformations of the set X; $T_X = \{f \mid f : X \to X\}$. The complexity of a string $x \in \{0,1\}^n$, $n \geq 0$, is the class of all semigroup actions $\varphi : G \to T_X$ for semigroups G and sets X, with*

- *two[1] elements $\delta_0, \delta_1 \in G$, inducing $\delta_y = \prod_{k=1}^{|y|} \delta_{y(k)}$ for each $y \in \{0,1\}^n$, $y = y(1) \cdots y(|y|)$;*
- *an initial state $\alpha \in X$; and*
- *a final state $\omega \in X$,*

such that x is the only $y \in \{0,1\}^n$ for which $\delta_y \alpha := \varphi(\delta_y)\alpha = \omega$.

In this case we say that x has complexity at most φ, *or, if φ is understood,* complexity at most G.

1.1 Quantum Automatic Complexity

Let $e_j^{(n)}$, $1 \leq j \leq n$ be the standard basis for $\mathbb{C}^n$. Let $U(n)$ be the group of unitary complex $n \times n$ matrices and let $PU(n)$ be the projective unitary group.

For $n \times n$ matrices U_0 and U_1 and a binary string x, we define

$$U_x = \prod_{k=1}^{|x|} U_{x(k)}.$$

---

[1] Noncommuting, unless x is a unary string like 0^n.

Definition 2. *A quantum deterministic finite automaton (quantum DFA) M with q states consists of an initial state $\alpha \in \mathbb{CP}^q$, a final state ω, and $\delta_0, \delta_1 \in$ PU(q). We say that M accepts a word $x \in \{0,1\}^n$, $n \geq 0$ if*

$$\delta_x \alpha = \omega.$$

Let $x \in \{0,1\}^n$, $n \geq 0$. The quantum automatic complexity *of x, Q(x), is the least q such that there exists a quantum DFA M with q states such that for all $y \in \{0,1\}^n$, M accepts y iff $y = x$.*

- *If we additionally require that δ_0, δ_1 generate a finite subgroup of PU(q), we obtain the* finite quantum automatic complexity $Q_f(x)$.
- *If we require $\alpha = e_1$ and $\beta = e_2$ then we obtain* semi-classical quantum automatic complexity Q_s.
- *If we require both of the extra requirements for Q_s and Q_f, we get Q_{sf}.*

We can write $Q_s(x) \leq (n, \infty)$ if $Q_s(x) \leq n$, and $Q_s(x) \leq (n, f)$ if $Q_{sf}(x) \leq n$ as witnessed by a finite group of order f. This way we see A_{perm}, the automatic complexity [2] with the added restriction that the transition functions be permutations, as an upper bound for n and a lower bound for f. Ordering these pairs lexicographically, we shall show that

$$(3, 121) \leq Q_s(0^{60}1^{60}) \leq (121, \infty)$$

assuming the following conjecture.

Conjecture 3. $A_{\text{perm}}(x) = |x| + 1$ *for all x.*

Remark 4. *We have verified Conjecture 3 for binary strings of length up to 9.*

Theorem 5. *(1) If $Q_s(x) > (n, \infty)$ then $Q_s(x) \geq (n + 1, A_{\text{perm}}(x))$. (2) We always have $Q_s(x) \leq (A_{\text{perm}}(x), A_{\text{perm}}(x))$.*

Proof. For (1) we note that the quantum states can be considered as states, so that the Cayley graph of any group witnessing Q_{sf} can be thought of as a witness for A_{perm}. For (2) we note that we can restrict attention to only the states $e_j^{(q)}$, $1 \leq j \leq q$, refusing to use superposition.

Matrices M of dimension $n \times n$ whose entries are 0 and 1, with exactly one 1 per column, act on $X = [n] = \{1, \ldots, n\}$ by matrix multiplication in the following way:

$$\varphi(M)(j) = k, \qquad \text{where } M e_j^{(n)} = e_k^{(n)}.$$

If M is additionally invertible then it thus induces an element of the symmetric group S_n and belongs to O(n), the group of orthogonal matrices M (satisfying $M^{-1} = M^T$).

Theorem 6. *For each string x, $Q_f(x)$ is finite.*

Proof. By the embedding of S_n into $O(n)$ above, and then inclusion of $O(n)$ into $U(n)$ (simply because $U^{-1} = U^T$ for a real matrix U implies $U^{-1} = U^\dagger$), we have $Q_f(x) \leq (A_{\mathrm{perm}}(x), A_{\mathrm{perm}}(x)) \leq (x+1, x+1)$.

We also have $Q \leq Q_f \leq Q_{sf}$ and $Q \leq Q_s \leq Q_{sf}$. For our quantum lock analogy we want distinct initial and final states, whereas for automatic complexity $A(x)$ or $A_{\mathrm{perm}}(x)$ it is natural to not require that.

2 Bounds on Q_s

Arbitrary q-state DFA transition functions δ_0, δ_1 can be considered to belong to the matrix algebra M_q of all $q \times q$ matrices. They are then exactly the matrices whose entries are 0 and 1, with exactly one 1 per column. And the nondeterministic case just corresponds to 0–1 valued matrices with *not necessarily* exactly one 1 per column. Moving to arbitrary real matrices we can significantly reduce the required dimension, from $n/2 + 1$ [8] to 2, as we now explain.

The following Theorem 7 indicates how any binary string can be encoded, in a sense, by two 2×2 matrices.

Theorem 7. *For each binary string x there exist $U_0, U_1 \in \mathrm{GL}_2(\mathbb{R})$ such that $U_x e_1 = e_2$ and for any $y \neq x$, $|y| = |x|$, $U_y e_1 \neq e_2$.*

We omit the proof.

Theorem 8. $Q(x) \leq 2$ *for all strings x.*

Proof. It suffices to show that there is a free group generated by two unitary matrices. It is well-known [9] that a generic pair of unitaries in $U(2)$ generates a free group. Indeed, the existence of free subgroups of $SO(3)$ (and hence its double cover $SU(2)$) was already known to Hausdorff [10]; see also [11] and explicit examples in [12].

Unfortunately, perhaps, free groups are incompatible with the "semi-classical" $e_1 \mapsto e_2$ property in the following way:

Theorem 9. *There is no word x of length >0 and pair of unitary matrices U_0, U_1 such that U_0 and U_1 generate a free group and $U_x e_1 = e_2$ in projective space.*

3 Unboundedness of Q_f

As usual we denote by $H \trianglelefteq G$ that H is a normal subgroup G, and by $[G : H]$ the index of H in G.

Theorem 10 (Jordan–Schur). *There is a function $f(n)$ such that given a finite group G that is a subgroup of $M_n(\mathbb{C})$, there is an abelian subgroup $H \trianglelefteq G$ such that $[G : H] \leq f(n)$.*

Corollary 11. *For each n there exists an m such that for any $u, v \in U(n)$ which generate a finite group, we have $[u^m, v^m] = 1$, i.e., $u^m v^m = v^m u^m$.*

Proof (Proof of Corollary from Theorem). If G is a finite group generated by u and v, and H a normal abelian subgroup of index $[G : H] = m$, then $u^m H = H$ and $v^m H = H$ (since any group element raised to the order of the group is the identity) and so u^m and v^m belong to H, hence, H being abelian, they commute.

Theorem 12. *For each n there is a binary string x with $Q_f(x) > n$.*

Proof. Let $x = 0^m 1^m$ where m is as in Corollary 11. Given $\delta_0, \delta_1 \in \mathrm{PU}(n) = U(n)/U(1)$, choose x and y in $U(n)$ such that $\delta_0 = xU(1)$ and $\delta_1 = yU(1)$. Then $\delta_{0^m 1^m} - (xU(1))^m (yU(1))^m = x^m y^m U(1) = y^m x^m U(1) - \delta_{1^m 0^m}$.

The extent to which 2×2 matrices suffice for quantum automatic complexity is indicated in Table 1.

Table 1. Supremum of quantum automatic complexity over all strings. In the case where $e_1 \mapsto e_2$ is required (semi-classical quantum automatic complexity Q_s) but finiteness (Q_f) is not, we at least know that free groups cannot answer the question, by Theorem 9.

	$e_1 \mapsto e_2$ required	Not required
Finite group required	∞	∞
Not required	Unknown	2

Theorem 13. $Q_{sf}(0^{60} 1^{60}) > 2$.

Proof. Note that we may assume our finite subgroups are primitive as there is no point in having a separate automaton disconnected from the witnessing one. Collins [13] then shows that for $n = 2$, the optimal value is $m = 60$.

On the other hand, we show below in Theorem 19 that $Q_{sf}(0^2 1^2) = 2$, leaving a gap $(2, 60)$ for the least n such that $Q_{sf}(0^n 1^n) > 2$. The state of our knowledge of finiteness of quantum automatic complexity is given in Table 1.

4 Calculating $Q_s(0011) \leq (2, 12)$

The group $SU(2)$ is the group of unit quaternions with the matrix representation [14]

$$1 = \begin{bmatrix} 1 & 0 \\ 0 & 1 \end{bmatrix}, \qquad \mathbf{i} = \begin{bmatrix} i & 0 \\ 0 & -i \end{bmatrix}, \qquad \mathbf{j} = \begin{bmatrix} 0 & 1 \\ -1 & 0 \end{bmatrix}, \qquad \mathbf{k} = \begin{bmatrix} 0 & i \\ i & 0 \end{bmatrix}$$

where i is the imaginary unit. We shall consider its order 24 subgroup the binary tetrahedral group

$$\left\{ \pm 1, \pm \mathbf{i}, \pm \mathbf{j}, \pm \mathbf{k}, \frac{1}{2}(\pm 1 \pm \mathbf{i} \pm \mathbf{j} \pm \mathbf{k}) \right\},$$

also known by isomorphism as $SL(2, 3)$. Moreover we shall consider the order 12 quotient $PSL(2, 3)$ which is isomorphic to the alternating group $\mathrm{Alt}(4)$.

Theorem 14. *There exist* $\mathbf{a}, \mathbf{b} \in SU(2)$ *such that*

$$\mathbf{aabb} \notin \{\mathbf{a}, \mathbf{b}\}^4 \setminus \{\mathbf{aabb}\}.$$

Proof. It turns out we can use the binary tetrahedral group to realize 0011 within $SU(2)$. Namely, let

$$\mathbf{a} = \delta_0 = (1 + i + j - k)/2, \qquad \mathbf{b} = \delta_1 = (1 + i + j + k)/2$$

in the quaternion representation,

$$\mathbf{a} = \frac{1}{2} \begin{bmatrix} 1+i & 1-i \\ -i-1 & 1-i \end{bmatrix}, \qquad \mathbf{b} = \frac{1}{2} \begin{bmatrix} 1+i & 1+i \\ i-1 & 1-i \end{bmatrix}.$$

We can check that $\mathbf{aabb} = -\mathbf{j}$ is unique among 4-letter words in $\mathbf{a}, \mathbf{b}$.

Theorem 15. *For* $x = 0011$, *there exist* $\delta_0, \delta_1 \in SO(3)$ *such that for all* $y \in \{0, 1\}^4$, $\delta_y = \delta_x$ *iff* $y = x$.

Proof. Another way to express $\mathbf{a}$ and $\mathbf{b}$ in Theorem 14 is as

$$e^{i\varphi} \begin{bmatrix} e^{i\Psi} & 0 \\ 0 & e^{-i\Psi} \end{bmatrix} \begin{bmatrix} \cos\theta & \sin\theta \\ -\sin\theta & \cos\theta \end{bmatrix} \begin{bmatrix} e^{i\Delta} & 0 \\ 0 & e^{-i\Delta} \end{bmatrix}$$

where $\varphi = 0$, $\theta = \pi/4$, and $\mathbf{a}$ has $(\Psi, \Delta) = (0, \pi/4)$ and $\mathbf{b}$ has $(\Psi, \Delta) = (\pi/4, 0)$. Thus

$$\mathbf{a} = \frac{1-i}{2} \begin{bmatrix} 1 & 1 \\ -1 & 1 \end{bmatrix} \begin{bmatrix} i & 0 \\ 0 & 1 \end{bmatrix} = \left(\frac{1}{\sqrt{2}} \begin{bmatrix} 1 & 1 \\ -1 & 1 \end{bmatrix} \right) \left(\frac{1-i}{\sqrt{2}} \begin{bmatrix} i & 0 \\ 0 & 1 \end{bmatrix} \right)$$

is a product of two matrices $\mathbf{rs}$ in $SU(2)$. The first one, $\mathbf{r}$, corresponds [15] to the $SO(3)$ rotation

$$\begin{bmatrix} 0 & 0 & -1 \\ 0 & 1 & 0 \\ 1 & 0 & 0 \end{bmatrix}$$

which is a 90-degree rotation in the xz-plane, and the second one, $\mathbf{s}$, to a 90-degree rotation

$$\begin{bmatrix} 0 & -1 & 0 \\ 1 & 0 & 0 \\ 0 & 0 & 1 \end{bmatrix}$$

in the xy-plane in $SO(3)$. We have

$$\mathbf{b} = \frac{1-i}{2} \begin{bmatrix} i & 0 \\ 0 & 1 \end{bmatrix} \begin{bmatrix} 1 & 1 \\ -1 & 1 \end{bmatrix} = \mathbf{sr}.$$

One remaining wrinkle, taken care of in Theorem 19, is to make sure the other words are not only distinct from $\mathbf{aabb}$, but map the start state to distinct vectors from what $\mathbf{aabb}$ does.

Theorem 16. (well known). *The order 24 group* $\mathrm{SL}(2,3)$ *is given by* $a^3 = b^3 = c^2 = abc$, *or equivalently* $a^3 = b^3 = abab$.

Theorem 17. [16]. $\mathrm{SL}(2,3)$ *is isomorphic to the binary tetrahedral group, a subgroup of* $\mathrm{U}(2)$.

The group $\mathrm{Alt}(4)$ does serve as complexity bound for 0011. It is not a subgroup of $\mathrm{U}(2)$ [16], but:

Theorem 18. *There is a faithful, irreducible representation of* $\mathrm{Alt}(4) \cong \mathrm{PSL}$ $(2,3)$ *as a subgroup of* $\mathrm{SL}(2,3)$ *of index 2 and as a subgroup of* $\mathrm{PU}(2)$.

Proof. Let a be as in Theorem 16. We define an equivalence relation $\equiv$ by $u \equiv v \iff u \in \{v, a^3v\}$. It is required to show that each element of our $\mathrm{SL}(2,3)$ is equivalent to an element of $\mathrm{Alt}(4)$. This is done in detail in Fig. 1.

The representation from Theorem 18 is used in the proof of Theorem 19.

$$1, \tag{1}$$
$$a, \tag{2}$$
$$b, \tag{3}$$
$$a^2 = bab, \tag{4}$$
$$ab, \tag{5}$$
$$ba, \tag{6}$$
$$b^2 = aba, \tag{7}$$
$$a^3 = b^3 = baba = abab \equiv 1, \tag{8}$$
$$a^2b = bab^2, \tag{9}$$
$$ab^2 = a^2ba, \tag{10}$$
$$ba^2 = b^2ab = aba^2b, \tag{11}$$
$$b^2a = aba^2 = ab^2ab, \tag{12}$$
$$a^4 = ab^3 = b^3a = a^2bab = ababa \equiv a, \tag{13}$$
$$a^3b = ba^3 = b^4 = abab^2 \equiv b, \tag{14}$$
$$a^2b^2 = a^3ba \equiv ba, \tag{15}$$
$$ab^2a = a^2ba^2, \tag{16}$$
$$ba^2b \equiv abba, \tag{17}$$
$$b^2a^2 = a^4b = aba^3 = ab^4 \equiv ab, \tag{18}$$
$$a^5 = a^2b^3 = ab^3a \equiv a^2, \tag{19}$$
$$a^3b^2 \equiv b^2, \tag{20}$$
$$a^2b^2a \equiv baa, \tag{21}$$
$$ab^2a^2 \equiv aab, \tag{22}$$
$$ba^2b^2 \equiv bba, \tag{23}$$
$$b^2a^2b \equiv abb. \tag{24}$$

Fig. 1. The 24 elements of $\mathrm{SL}(2,3)$. All strings of length at most 2 are unique of their length. By symmetry, words of length 5 starting with b are not written down.

Theorem 19. $Q_{sf}(0011) = 2$.

Proof. Let $v = \begin{bmatrix} v_1 \\ v_2 \end{bmatrix}$ with $v_1, v_2 \in \mathbb{R}$. Let

$$E_0 = \mathbf{a} = \frac{1}{2}\begin{bmatrix} 1+i & 1-i \\ -1-i & 1-i \end{bmatrix}, \qquad E_1 = \mathbf{b} = \frac{1}{2}\begin{bmatrix} 1+i & 1+i \\ -1+i & 1-i \end{bmatrix}.$$

Let

$$D = \begin{bmatrix} v_1 & -v_2 \\ v_2 & v_1 \end{bmatrix} = [v \mid E_{0011}v], \qquad C = \frac{1}{\sqrt{\det D}}D.$$

Let

$$U_j = C^{-1}E_jC, \qquad j \in \{0,1\}.$$

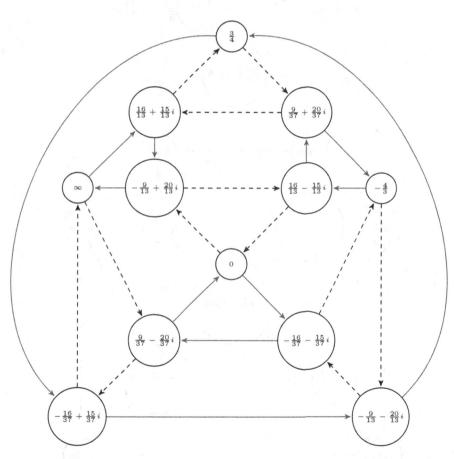

Fig. 2. Quantum complexity witness having the shape of a cuboctahedron. The label α represents the projective point $[1 : \alpha]$. The initial state is $[1 : 0]$ denoted by 0 and the accept state is $[0 : 1]$ denoted by ∞. Dashed lines indicate multiplication by U_0. Solid lines indicate multiplication by U_1.

Then it follows that

$$CU_{0011} \begin{bmatrix} 1 \\ 0 \end{bmatrix} = E_{0011}C \begin{bmatrix} 1 \\ 0 \end{bmatrix} = E_{0011} \begin{bmatrix} v_1 \\ v_2 \end{bmatrix} = C \begin{bmatrix} 0 \\ 1 \end{bmatrix}.$$

Hence

$$U_{0011} \begin{bmatrix} 1 \\ 0 \end{bmatrix} = \begin{bmatrix} 0 \\ 1 \end{bmatrix}.$$

Since fortunately our E_0 and E_1 satisfy $E_{0011} = -\mathbf{j}$, C is orthogonal, and in particular C is unitary. If we now choose $v = \begin{bmatrix} 1 \\ 2 \end{bmatrix}$, then v is sufficiently generic that $U_y e_1 \neq e_2$ as elements of $\mathbb{CP}^1$ for all $y \in \{0,1\}^4 \setminus \{x\}$. We have verified as much with an Octave computation (see Figs. 2 and 3). We have

$$C = \frac{1}{\sqrt{5}} \begin{bmatrix} 1 & -2 \\ 2 & 1 \end{bmatrix}, \qquad C^{-1} = \frac{1}{\sqrt{5}} \begin{bmatrix} 1 & 2 \\ -2 & 1 \end{bmatrix},$$

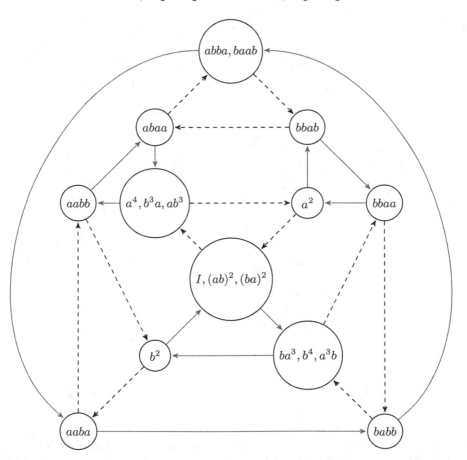

Fig. 3. Another view of the quantum complexity witness having the shape of a cuboctahedron of Fig. 2.

$$U_0 = \frac{1}{10} \begin{bmatrix} 5+i & 5+7i \\ -5+7i & 5-i \end{bmatrix} \quad \text{and} \quad U_1 = \frac{1}{10} \begin{bmatrix} 5-7i & 5+i \\ -5+i & 5+7i \end{bmatrix}.$$

Remark 20. *It is still a question what the nature of the "complexity" Q and Q_s are picking out is. If it is anything like A_{perm} it may be less than intuitive. However, there is some reason to believe that quantum automatic complexity is better than permutation automatic complexity at distinguishing strings of the same length. For permutation automatic complexity we do not know any example of strings of the same length having distinct complexity, but for quantum automatic complexity, $0^{60}1^{60}$ and 0^{120} form such an example. The latter has complexity at most 2 whereas the former does not (Theorem 13).*

References

1. Kondacs, A., Watrous, J.: On the power of quantum finite state automata. In: 38th Annual Symposium on Foundations of Computer Science, FOCS 1997, Miami Beach, Florida, USA, 19–22 October 1997, pp. 66–75 (1997). http://dx.doi.org/10.1109/SFCS.1997.646094
2. Shallit, J., Wang, M.-W.: Automatic complexity of strings. J. Autom. Lang. Comb. **6**(4), 537–554 (2001). 2nd Workshop on Descriptional Complexity of Automata, Grammars and Related Structures, London, ON, 2000
3. Kjos-Hanssen, B.: Few paths, fewer words: model selection with automatic structure functions. Exp. Math. (2018). Conditionally accepted. arXiv:1608.01399
4. Kjos-Hanssen, B.: Shift registers fool finite automata. ArXiv e-prints, July 2016
5. Shen, A.: Automatic Kolmogorov complexity and normality revisited. ArXiv e-prints, January 2017
6. Becher, V., Carton, O., Heiber, P.A.: Normality and automata. J. Comput. Syst. Sci. **81**(8), 1592–1613 (2015). http://dx.doi.org/10.1016/j.jcss.2015.04.007
7. Calude, C.S., Salomaa, K., Roblot, T.K.: Finite state complexity. Theor. Comput. Sci. **412**(41), 5668–5677 (2011). http://dx.doi.org/10.1016/j.tcs.2011.06.021
8. Hyde, K., Kjos-Hanssen, B.: Nondeterministic automatic complexity of overlap-free and almost square-free words. Electron. J. Comb. **22**(3), paper 3.22, 18 p. (2015)
9. Thom, A.: Convergent sequences in discrete groups. Canad. Math. Bull. **56**(2), 424–433 (2013). http://dx.doi.org/10.4153/CMB-2011-155-3
10. Hausdorff, F.: Bemerkung über den Inhalt von Punktmengen. Math. Ann. **75**(3), 428–433 (1914). http://dx.doi.org/10.1007/BF01563735
11. Świerczkowski, S.: On a free group of rotations of the Euclidean space. Nederl. Akad. Wetensch. Proc. Ser. A 61 = Indag. Math. **20**, 376–378 (1958)
12. Świerczkowski, S.: A class of free rotation groups. Indag. Math. (N.S.) **5**(2), 221–226 (1994). http://dx.doi.org/10.1016/0019-3577(94)90026-4
13. Collins, M.J.: On Jordan's theorem for complex linear groups. J. Group Theory **10**(4), 411–423 (2007). http://dx.doi.org/10.1515/JGT.2007.032
14. Yuan, Q.: SU(2) and the quaternions, February 2011. https://qchu.wordpress.com/2011/02/12/su2-and-the-quaternions/
15. Gelfand, I.M., Minlos, R.A., Sapiro, Z.J.: Predstavleniya gruppy vrashcheni i gruppy Lorentsa, ikh primeneniya. Gosudarstv. Izdat. Fiz.-Mat. Lit., Moscow (1958)
16. Parattu,K.M., Wingerter, A.: Tribimaximal mixing from small groups (2011). https://arxiv.org/pdf/1012.2842v2.pdf

Solving the Bin-Packing Problem by Means of Tissue P System with 2-Division

Hepzibah A. Christinal[1]([⊠]), Rose Rani John[1], D. Abraham Chandy[1], and Miguel A. Gutiérrez-Naranjo[2]

[1] Karunya University, Coimbatore, Tamilnadu, India
hepzia@yahoo.com, roseranijohn@karunya.edu, abrahamdchandy@gmail.com
[2] Department of Computer Science and Artificial Intelligence,
University of Seville, 41012 Seville, Spain
magutier@us.es

Abstract. The ability of tissue P systems with 2-division for solving **NP** problems in polynomial time is well-known and many solutions can be found in the literature to several of such problems. Nonetheless, there are very few papers devoted to the Bin-packing problem. The reason may be the difficulties for dealing with different number of bins, capacity and number of objects by using exclusively division rules that produce two offsprings in each application. In this paper we present the design of a family of tissue P systems with 2 division which solves the Bin-packing problem in polynomial time by combining design techniques which can be useful for further research.

1 Introduction

Membrane computing was born from the assumption that the processes taking place within the compartmental structure of a living cell can be interpreted as computations [26]. From the beginning, the computational complexity of the membrane algorithms has been a vivid research area [25]. In particular, there is a large amount of papers dealing with the **P** versus **NP** problem in the framework of membrane computing [22]. The **P** versus **NP** problem is one of the most important unsolved problem in computer science and it was chosen as one of the seven Millennium Prize Problems [11]. The precise statement of the problem was introduced in 1971 by Stephen Cook [1], although it was essentially mentioned in a personal communication between Gödel and von Neumann [10].

The problem of deciding whether **P** and **NP** complexity classes are same or not is not yet solved but the efforts for solving it have contributed to the development of new research areas full of interesting open questions. One of them is the research of *frontiers of tractability*, i.e., to identify some features of the computational models such that the corresponding device is able to solve **NP** problems or not depending on the endowment of such features.

In membrane computing there exists an extensive literature devoted to this type of problem (see [22] and the references therein) and the present paper is a novel contribution in such research line. We consider here a variant of one of the

© Springer International Publishing AG 2017
M.J. Patitz and M. Stannett (Eds.): UCNC 2017, LNCS 10240, pp. 170–181, 2017.
DOI: 10.1007/978-3-319-58187-3_13

most popular P systems architectures: tissue P systems. Such model was firstly presented in [16,17] by placing the cells in a general graph instead of a tree-like graph as in the cell-like model. Under the hypothesis $\mathbf{P} \neq \mathbf{NP}$, Zandron *et al.* [33] established the limitations of P systems that do not use membrane division concerning the efficient solution of $\mathbf{NP}$-complete problems.

From this premise, Păun *et al.* presented in [28] the model of tissue P systems endowed with cell division, which can solve $\mathbf{NP}$-problems. Since then, many other variants have been presented, e.g., [6,12,13,18,19]. In this way, all solutions of $\mathbf{NP}$-complete problems in membrane computing rely on the possibility of P systems to obtain *exponential space* in polynomial time[1]. Besides creating an exponential amount of cells in polynomial time, to solve $\mathbf{NP}$-complete problems, we need to be able to effectively use that workspace, by making objects interact. For instance, it is known that, even with membrane division, without polarizations and without dissolution only problems in $\mathbf{P}$ may be solved [9].

The cell division proposed in [28] was inspired in the *mitosis* of alive cells and consists on the division of one cell into two offsprings. The most extended use of this type of rules is obtaining an exponential amount of cells in linear time, since 2^n cells can be obtained from an initial one after n steps. The ability of tissue P systems with 2-division for solving $\mathbf{NP}$ problems is well known [19], nonetheless, the study of new problems requires the effort of solving specific designs which, on the one hand, makes stronger the theory and on the other hand, can provide new ideas for unsolved problems in membrane computing.

In particular, the design of a solution for the Bin-packing problem by using 2-division presents important subproblems whose solution can be useful for further development of the theory. The intrinsic difficulty of this problem explains that there are very few papers [23,24] devoted to this problem in the vast literature of solutions for $\mathbf{NP}$ problems in membrane computing.

The problem can be stated as follows: *Given a set $A = \{s_1, \dots, s_n\}$, a weight function $\omega : A \to \mathbb{N}$ and two constants $b \in \mathbb{N}$, $c \in \mathbb{N}$ decide whether or not there exists a partition of A into b subsets such that their weights do not exceed c.* The traditional strategy for designing a solution of an $\mathbf{NP}$-problem has a first stage where an exponential amount of cells is created and each feasible candidate to be a solution is placed into one of the exponential amount of available cells. In the Bin-packing problem, this generation of feasible candidates consists on considering all the possibilities for distributing the n objects among the b bins. This means that b^n feasible candidates should be encoded in the corresponding multisets and placed into b^n different cells.

The 2-division proposed in [28] fits perfectly when the exponential growth of the number of candidates is on basis 2, as in the SAT problem (e.g., [2,7]) or the Partition problem [5,8] or even on basis 3 by performing a new division on

---

[1] Such solutions are technically correct, but, of course, the exponential generation of new working space has evident limits from a practical point of view. Any practical implementation of P systems solving $\mathbf{NP}$-problems with physical support only could solve small instances of the problem.

one of the offsprings, as in the 3-COL problem [4]. In our case, the problem is different, since the number of necessary membranes depends on the parameter b. In this way, the designed family of tissue P systems must be able to build b^n membranes in polynomial time on b and n for each b and n by using 2-division.

This leads us to solve two subproblems: The first one is place each of the n objects in one of the b bins (if the distribution condition of objects is satisfied). This means that we need to represent each of the symbols in $\{0, \ldots, b-1\}$ with a 2-division process for each object s_i with $i \in \{1, \ldots, n\}$. And the second problem is to implement such distribution of n objects, one for each object in the set A. In the next sections, we explain the details of the corresponding solutions.

The paper is organized as follows. In Sect. 2, the formal description of the used model of P systems is recalled. Section 3 is devoted to the main ideas related to recognizer P systems, the framework for solving decision problems. Our solution is presented in Sect. 4 and the paper ends with some conclusions and hints for future work.

2   Tissue P Systems with Cell Division

In the first definition of the model of tissue P systems [16,17] the membrane structure did not change along with the computation. Based on the biological *mitosis*, Păun *et al.* presented in [28] a tissue P system model endowed with 2-division is one of the most used and well-known P system models nowadays. We briefly recall their syntax and semantics.

Formally[2], a *tissue P system with cell division* of degree $q \geq 1$ is a tuple of the form

$$\Pi = (\Gamma, \mathcal{E}, \Sigma, w_1, \ldots, w_q, \mathcal{R}, i_{in}, i_{out}),$$

where:

1. Γ is a finite *alphabet*, whose symbols will be called *objects*.
2. $\mathcal{E} \subseteq \Gamma$ is the alphabet of the environment.
3. $\Sigma \subset \Gamma$ is the input alphabet.
4. $w_1, \ldots, w_q$ are strings over Γ.
5. $\mathcal{R}$ is a finite set of rules of the following form:
   (a) *Communication rules*: $(i, u/v, j)$, for $i, j \in \{0, 1, 2, \ldots, q\}, i \neq j, u, v \in \Gamma^*$.
   (b) *Division rules*: $[a]_i \rightarrow [b]_i[c]_i$, where $i \in \{1, 2, \ldots, q\}$ and $a, b, c \in \Gamma$.
6. $i_{in}, i_{out} \in \{0, 1, 2, \ldots, q\}$ are the input and output labels, respectively.

A tissue P system with cell division of degree $q \geq 1$ can be seen as a set of q cells (each one consisting of an elementary membrane) labelled by $1, 2, \ldots, q$. We shall use 0 as the label of the environment, and i_{in} and i_{out} denote, respectively, the input and output regions (which can be a region inside a membrane or the environment).

---

[2] The reader is supposed to be familiar with the basic concepts of membrane computing. See [29] for details.

The communication rules determine an implicit net of channels, where the nodes are the cells and the edges indicate if it is possible for pairs of cells to communicate directly. This is a dynamic graph, in which new nodes can be produced by the application of division rules. Note also that the connections only depend on the label of the cell, and thus when a cell is divided, the two new cells will have identical connections. Nevertheless, this graph is just an intuition, we shall not handle it explicitly along the computations.

The strings $w_1, \ldots, w_q$ describe the multisets of objects placed in the q cells of the system. We interpret that $\mathcal{E} \subseteq \Gamma$ is the set of objects placed in the environment, each one of them in an arbitrary large amount of copies.

The communication rule $(i, u/v, j)$ can be applied over two cells i and j such that u is contained in cell i and v is contained in cell j. The application of this rule means that the objects of the multisets represented by u and v are interchanged between the two cells.

The division rule $[a]_i \to [b]_i [c]_i$ can be applied over a cell i containing object a. The application of this rule divides this cell into two new cells with the same label. All the objects in the original cell are replicated and copied in each of the new cells, with the exception of the object a, which is replaced by the object b in the first new cell and by c in the second one.

Rules are used as usual in the framework of membrane computing, that is, in a maximally parallel way. In one step, each object in a membrane can only be used for one rule (non-deterministically chosen when there are several possibilities), but any object which can participate in a rule of any form must do it, i.e., in each step we apply a maximal set of rules. This way of applying rules has only one restriction when a cell is divided, the division rule is the only one which is applied for that cell in that step; the objects inside that cell do not evolve in that step.

3 Recognizer P Systems

The notion of recognizer P system is general enough to cover many P system variants. Such P systems are a well-known model of P systems which are basic for the study of complexity aspects in membrane computing. Roughly speaking, a recognizer P system is a P system which takes some information as *input* and outputs a distinguished object which can be considered as a *decision* on the input. Of course, some other conditions are imposed, but the general framework does not depend on the type of rules or the membrane structure of the P system.

Next, we briefly recall some basic ideas related to them. A detailed description, is given in [21,22]. In recognizer P systems all computations halt; there are two distinguished objects traditionally called **yes** and **no** (used to signal the result of the computation), and exactly one of these objects is sent out to the environment (only) in the last computation step.

Let us recall that a decision problem X is a pair (I_X, θ_X) where I_X is a language over a finite alphabet (the elements are called *instances*) and θ_X is a predicate (a total Boolean function) over I_X. Let $X = (I_X, \theta_X)$ be a decision problem. A *polynomial encoding* of X is a pair (cod, s) of polynomial time computable functions over I_X such that for each instance $w \in I_X$, $s(w)$ is a natural number representing the *size* of the instance and $cod(w)$ is a multiset representing an encoding of the instance. Polynomial encodings are stable under polynomial time reductions.

Let $\mathcal{R}$ be a class of recognizer P systems with input membrane. A decision problem $X = (I_X, \theta_X)$ is solvable in a uniform way and polynomial time by a family $\Pi = (\Pi(n))_{n \in \mathbb{N}}$ of P systems from $\mathcal{R}$ – we denote this by $X \in \mathbf{PMC}_{\mathcal{R}}$ – if the family Π is polynomially uniform by Turing machines, i.e., there exists a polynomial encoding (cod, s) from I_X to Π such that the family Π is polynomially bounded with regard to (X, cod, s); this means that there exists a polynomial function p such that for each $u \in I_X$ every computation of $\Pi(s(u))$ with input $cod(u)$ is halting and, moreover, it performs at most $p(|u|)$ steps; the family Π is sound and complete with regard to (X, cod, s).

4   The Solution to Bin Packing Problem

In this section we provide a family of tissue P systems with 2-division which solves the Bin-packing problem in polynomial time. Before giving the formal description of the P system, we provide some hints about how the problem has been solved.

As pointed out in the Introduction, each of the n objects can potentially be placed on one of the b bins. In such way, b^n candidates (and hence b^n cells) should be built in polynomial time by using 2-division. The solution needs the pre-process of the parameter m, where m is the least integer which satisfies $b \leq 2^m$, i.e., $m = \lceil log_2 b \rceil$. In the same way, by generating 2^m cells with m 2-division steps we can assure that at least b cells are generated. The idea of considering a number of logarithmic steps is not new in the design of membrane computing solutions (see, e.g., [3]). Nevertheless, the mere generation of b (or more) cells are not enough. Each object s_i of the set $A = \{s_1, \ldots, s_n\}$ must be placed in one of the bins $\{0, \ldots, b-1\}$, where each membrane encoding a different bin has been generated by 2-division. In this way, the natural encoding of each number in $\{0, \ldots, b-1\}$ is performed by a binary representation $C_{m-1}C_{m-2} \ldots C_0$ where[3] $C_i \in \{T_i, F_i\}$ for $i \in \{0, \ldots, b-1\}$. In this way, each 2-division will produce an object T_i or F_i in each offspring and the value i will control the number of the division in the iterative process of building 2^m cells. This process will be controlled by the set of rules **R1** (see below).

From the 2^m generated cells, only b of them are necessary in our solution. The remaining $2^m - b$ cells (if any) will remain inactive. This means that we only need rules for control b different values $\{0, \ldots, b-1\}$. Such values are originally represented via a binary representation by using m objects. Nonetheless, for the sake of readability, in our solution we propose to take a decimal representation by a unique symbol object b_j with $j \in \{0, \ldots, b-1\}$. The trick for recovering such notation is controlled by the set of rules **R2** (see below).

---

[3] T_i and F_i stand for *True* and *False* in the $i - th$ position and, as usual, represents 1 and 0 in a binary representation.

The key idea of such set of rules consists of keeping in each cell of label 1 an object b_k which acts as an accumulator in the index i (with b_0 at the beginning). The different values of the binary representation $C_{m-1}C_{m-2}\ldots C_0$ with $C_i \in \{T_i, F_i\}$ arrive sequentially to the cell:

- If the object T_i arrives and $k + 2^i$ does not exceed the value $b - 1$ then, the objects T_i and b_k are traded against a new object b_{k+2^i}. If $k + 2^i \geq b$, then the corresponding membrane does not encode one of the possible bins (enumerated from 0 to $b - 1$) and it stays inactive during the remaining computation steps.
- If the object F_i arrives, nothing is added to the accumulator and the object b_k does not change.

Bearing in mind these considerations, the proposed solution can be split in to the following stages:

- *Generation and Calculation stage:* In this stage the b^n candidates for solution are generated (each of the n objects in $A = \{s_1, \ldots, s_n\}$ can go to one of the b bins). For each s_i, $2m + 3$ steps are performed and the number of steps in this stage is $O(m \cdot n)$.
  During the generation stage, the process of assigning an object s_i to a bin is performed n times. After each assignment, the free capacity of the corresponding bin (represented by objects p_j) is decreased in an amount equal to the weight $w(s_i)$ if it is possible. This decrement is performed by the set of rules **R4** which send pairs of objects representing unit of weights and units of free capacity to the environment. If there is no free capacity enough for such assignment, some objects representing weights will not be sent to the environment.
- *Checking stage:* This stage is performed in parallel in the all b^n cells which represent candidates (let us recall that the $2^m - b$ cells extra generated in each construction process keep inactive). This stage consists on checking if all the objects representing weights have been sent to the environment. If there is no such objects in the corresponding cell, then the candidate placed in such membrane represents a solution to the Bin-packing problem. Otherwise, if there is one or more object in the cell, then the assignment of objects to cells does not satisfy the restriction and it is not a solution to the problem.
- *Output stage:* Finally, the output stage controls that only one object *yes* or only one object *no* is sent to the output cell in the last step of computation.

Each instance of the Bin-packing Problem is stated by a set of n objects, $A = \{s_1, \ldots, s_n\}$, a set of weights $\omega(A) = \{\omega(s_1), \ldots, \omega(s_n)\}$ and two constants $b \in \mathbb{N}$ (the number of bins) and $c \in \mathbb{N}$ (the capacity). We propose a family of tissue P systems with 2-division which solves the Bin-packing Problem where each tissue P system of the family depends on the parameters n, b and c. For the sake of simplicity, we will consider a pre-computed extra parameter $m = \lceil log_2 b \rceil$ which only depends on b. Let us notice that the set of objects $A = \{s_1, \ldots, s_n\}$ is encoded as the multiset $s_1^{w(s_1)}, \ldots, s_n^{w_{s_n}}$, i.e., the weight of the object s_i is represented in its multiplicity. Such multiset is placed in the input cell in the initial configuration and the computation starts.

Each tissue P system of the family is of the following form[4]:

$$\Pi(n, b, c, m) = (\Gamma, \mathcal{E}, \Sigma, w_1, w_2, R, i_{in}, in_{out})$$

where:

- Γ is the alphabet of objects used in the computation

$$\Gamma = \mathcal{E} \cup \Sigma \cup \{A_0, b_0, d_1, z_1, x_0\} \cup \{p_i : i \in \{0, \ldots, b-1\}\}$$

- $\mathcal{E}$ is the set of objects initially placed in the environment.

$$\mathcal{E} = \{yes, no, g, f_0, f_1, y_0, y_1, \#\}$$
$$\cup \{T_i, k_i \, k_i, r_i : i \in \{0, \ldots, m-1\}\}$$
$$\cup \{A_i : i \in \{0, \ldots, m\}\}$$
$$\cup \{b_i : i \in \{0, \ldots, b-1\}\}$$
$$\cup \{q_i, h_i : i \in \{0, \ldots, b-1\}\}$$
$$\cup \{z_i, d_i : i \in \{2, \ldots, n\}\}$$
$$\cup \{x_i : i \in \{1, \ldots, n*(2m+3)+1\}$$
$$\cup \{k_{i,j} : i \in \{0, \ldots, b-1\} \, j \in \{0, 1\}\}$$

- $\Sigma = \{s_i : i \in \{1, \ldots, n\}\}$ is the input alphabet.
- Initially, the initial configuration has only two cells. The initial multisets are

$$w_1 = A_0 \, b_0 \, d_1 \, z_1^c \, p_0^c \ldots p_{b-1}^c \quad \text{and} \quad w_2 = x_{0,1}$$

- The following are the set of rules R :

R1. $[A_i]_1 \to [T_i]_1 [F_i]_1 : 0 \le i \le m-1$

These rules control the generation of new membranes by division. Since $b \le 2^m$, it is guaranteed that after m applications of 2-division rules, the number of membranes is enough for encoding b bins. Each of the offsprings has an object T_i or F_i of the corresponding number in binary encoding. $C_{m-1} C_{m-2} \ldots C_0$ with $C_i \in \{T_i, F_i\}$.

R2. $(1, T_i \, b_{k-2^i} / b_k \, A_{i+1}, 0) : 0 \le i \le m-1, \quad 0 \le k \le min\{b - 2^i, 2^i\} - 1$
$(1, F_i / A_{i+1}, 0) : 0 \le i \le m-1$

As pointed out above, the binary number $C_{m-1} C_{m-2} \ldots C_0$ with $C_i \in \{T_i, F_i\}$ is not stored in such form in the cells. Each cell with label 1 has an object b_k (initially b_0) which can be considered as an accumulator for the decimal representation of the number $C_{m-1} C_{m-2} \ldots C_0$ with $C_i \in \{T_i, F_i\}$. If a new object T_i arrives to the cell by the application of a division rule, then T_i and b_k are traded against one object b_{k+2^i} if b_{k+2^i} is the index of one of the bins,

---

[4] As usual, we omit the parameters in the description for the sake of readability.

i.e., if it belongs to $\{0, \ldots, b-1\}$. Let us remark that the application of the rule also brings an object A_{i+1} and the cell is prepared for a new division. If $k + 2^i \geq b$, then the rule is not applied, the object A_{i+1} is not brought into the cell and the cell remains inactive. If an object F_i arrives, the accumulator b_k is not modified.

R3. $(1, A_m \, b_r / q_r^c \, k_{r,0}) : r \in \{0, \ldots, b-1\}$

When the object A_m arrives to a cell 1, the calculus of b_r has finished. This means that the corresponding object s_i from $A = \{s_1, \ldots, s_n\}$ is placed on the $r - th$ bin. In order to help in the subtraction of the weight of the object s_i from the free capacity of the bin r, c objects q_r are brought into the cell. An object $k_{r,0}$ is also brought for technical reasons.

R4. $(1, z_i \, s_i \, q_r \, p_r / \#) : i \in \{1, \ldots, n\} \quad r \in \{0, \ldots, b-1\}$

This set of rules is the key in the calculus of the total weigh associated to each bin. Its usage exploits the massive parallelism of P systems and the maximal application of the rules. Let us notice that in each application of the rule only one object of the four kind z_i, s_i, q_r and p_r is sent out of the cell, so the number of applications correspond to the minimum of amounts of these objects. Since there are exactly c objects of type z_i and q_r, the number of applications corresponds to the minimum between the multiplicities of s_i and p_r. Let us remark that if the weight of the object s_i (encoded in their multiplicity) is greater than the free capacity of the r-th bin (encoded in the multiplicity of objects p_r) then at least one object s_i will remain in the cell after the application of these rules.

R5. $\left.\begin{array}{l} (1, k_{r,0}/h_r^c, k_{r,1}, 0) \\ (1, h_r \, q_r / \#, 0) \end{array}\right\}$ for $r \in \{0, \ldots, b-1\}$.

These rules can be considered as *cleaning* rules. After the subtraction performed by the set of rules **R4**, the leftovers objects q_r (if any) must be sent out of the cells with label 1 in order to avoid undesired interactions. This is the technical reason of the objects $k_{r,0}$ and $k_{r,1}$.

R6. $(1, k_{r,1} \, d_i / A_0 \, b_0 \, z_{i+1}^c \, d_{i+1}, 0) : i \in \{1, \ldots, n-1\} \quad r \in \{0, \ldots, b-1\}$
$(1, k_{r,1} \, d_n / f_0 \, g, 0) : r \in \{0, \ldots, b-1\}$

When the object $k_{r,1}$ appears in a cell with label 1, the cleaning process performed by the set of rules **R5** has finished and the cell is prepared for starting the process of a new object s_{i+1} This set of rules **R6** brings the objects A_0 and b_0 for starting newly the division together with the objects z_{i+1} and d_{i+1}. When all the objects s_i, $i \in \{1, \ldots, n\}$ are processed, the objects f_0 and g are brought into the cells 1 which remain active.

R7. $(2, x_i / x_{i+1}, 0) : 0 \leq i \leq n * (2m+3) - 1$
$(2, x_{n*(2m+3)} / x_{n*(2m+3)+1}, y_0, 0)$

The objects x_i in the cell 2 act as a counter. When it reaches $x_{n*(2m+3)+1}$, a new object y_0 is also brought into the cell 2 for controlling the output process.

R10. $(1, g\, s_i/\#, 0) : i \in \{1, \ldots, n\}$
$(1, f_0/f_1, 0)$
$(1, f_1\, g/x_{n*(2m+3)+1}, 2)$
$(2, y_0/y_1, 0)$
$(2, g, y_1/yes, 0)$
$(2, x_{n*(2m+3)+1}\, no, 0)$

These rules control the output process. Two cases must be considered:

- **Case 1:** In all the active cells with label 1, there is at least one object s_i. This means that all the possible assignment of objects to bins exceed the capacity. In this case, a rule $(1, g\, s_i/\#, 0)$ is applied in such membranes and g is sent out to the environment, the rule $(1, f_1\, g/x_{n*(2m+3)+1}, 2)$ is not applied and finally, the rule $(2, x_{n*(2m+3)+1}\, no, 0)$ sends an object no to the cell with label 2.

- **Case 2:** There is at least one of the cells with label 1, where there are no objects s_i. This means that all the assignment of objects encoded in such membrane does not exceed the capacity and it represents a solution for the problem. In this case, a rule $(1, g\, s_i/\#, 0)$ is not applied in such membrane and, in the next step of computation, the rule $(1, f_1\, g/x_{n*(2m+3)+1}, 2)$ is applied, the object g is sent to the cell with label 2 and finally, the application of $(2, g, y_1/yes, 0)$ sends an object yes to the output cell.

– Finally, the input cell has label 1, $i_{in} = 1$ and the output cell has label 2, $i_{out} = 2$.

4.1   A Short Overview

Next, we provide some hints on the computation. The initial configuration $\mathbb{C}_0$ contains an object A_0 which starts the division process, an object b_0 which works as an accumulator initially set to 0 and objects d_1 and z_1, where the index a denotes that the first object in the set $A = \{s_1, \ldots, s_n\}$ will be process at the beginning. According to the process described above, the cells with label 1 are divided and, in parallel, the counted b_r is increased. The configuration $\mathbb{C}_{2m}$ contains an object A_m and an object b_r encoding that the first object of the set A is placed into the r-th bin. In the next three steps, rules from the sets **R3**, **R4** and **R5** perform the subtraction between the weight of the processed object and the free capacity of the r-th bin (represented by the multiplicity of the object p_r). The first set of rules from **R6** is also applied and in $\mathbb{C}_{2m+3}$ the corresponding cells 1 contain new objects A_0 and b_0 and objects d_2 and z_2, denoting that the second object of the set A will be processed.

This sequence of $2m + 3$ steps is repeated n times (as many times as objects in A). In the configuration $\mathbb{C}_{n*(2m+3)}$ all the objects in A have been processed and the objects f_0 and g appear. Only three steps later, in output stage with two possible cases described above, the halting configuration $\mathbb{C}_{n*(2m+3)+3}$ is reached.

4.2   Computational Resources

Each tissue P system of the family described above depends on three parameters: n, the number of object to distribute among the bins; c, the capacity of the bins;

and b the number of the bins. For the sake of simplicity, the description also includes a forth parameter m, which only depends on the parameter b, $m = \lceil log_2 b \rceil$. Each P system $\Pi(n, b, c, m)$ processes all the input set $A = \{s_1, \ldots, s_n\}$ regardless the weight function $\omega : A \rightarrow \mathbb{N}$.

Initially, the P system has only two membranes and the number of objects of the alphabet is $O(nm + b)$. The set of rules is $O(nb)$ and the number of steps of the computation is $O(nm)$. Let us remark the special case of rules of the set **R2**. In spite of a potential exponential number of cells can be built, not all of them encode an object b_r with $r \in \{0, \ldots, 2^m - 1\}$, which would lead to an exponential amount of initial resources. In our solution, we only deal with objects b_i with $i \in \{0, \ldots, b - 1\}$, so the initial amount of resources are polynomial function on the input parameters.

5 Conclusions

The complexity theory of membrane computing is full of interesting open problems. The most important is the *Păun conjecture* [14,20,27] which ask if a concrete P system model is able to solve or not **NP**-problems in polynomial time. The question has been open for more than ten years and even today nobody knows the answer. If the answer is that **NP**-problems can be solved in the such model, a simple way to prove is by providing the design of a family which effectively solves an **NP**-complete problem. In this way, or it is impossible to find such design or we need to make new efforts and finding new techniques for designing solutions to **NP**-problems which allow us to get the skills for solving the conjecture. In this research line, the design presented in this paper can help to make the theory stronger and provide new ideas for dealing with open questions.

Finally, let us remark the important role of the definition for recognizer P systems we have used in this paper. On the one hand, this definition is quite restrictive, since only one object *yes* or *no* is sent to the environment in any computation. In the literature one can find other definitions of recognizer P systems and therefore other definitions of what it means *to solve* a problem in the framework of Membrane Computing. On the second hand, the synchronization of the processes in the different membranes plays a key role in the design presented in this paper, but in the literature one can find some solutions to **NP**-problems in time free membrane computing models (e.g., [15,30–32]). The study of the complexity classes in membrane computing deserves a deep revision under these new definitions.

References

1. Cook, S.A.: The complexity of theorem-proving procedures. In: Proceedings of the Third Annual ACM Symposium on Theory of Computing, STOC 1971, NY, USA, pp. 151–158. ACM, New York (1971)
2. Cordón-Franco, A., Gutiérrez-Naranjo, M.A., Pérez-Jiménez, M.J., Sancho-Caparrini, F.: A prolog simulator for deterministic P systems with active membranes. New Gener. Comput. **22**(4), 349–363 (2004)

3. Díaz-Pernil, D., Gutiérrez-Naranjo, M.A., Pérez-Jiménez, M.J., Riscos-Núñez, A.: A logarithmic bound for solving subset sum with P systems. In: Eleftherakis, G., Kefalas, P., Păun, G., Rozenberg, G., Salomaa, A. (eds.) WMC 2007. LNCS, vol. 4860, pp. 257–270. Springer, Heidelberg (2007). doi:10.1007/978-3-540-77312-2_16
4. Díaz-Pernil, D., Gutiérrez-Naranjo, M.A., Pérez-Jiménez, M.J., Riscos-Núñez, A.: A uniform family of tissue P systems with cell division solving 3-COL in a linear time. Theoret. Comput. Sci. **404**(1–2), 76–87 (2008)
5. Díaz-Pernil, D., Gutiérrez-Naranjo, M.A., Pérez-Jiménez, M.J., Riscos-Núñez, A.: A linear time solution to the partition problem in a cellular tissue-like model. J. Comput. Theor. Nanosci. **7**(5), 884–889 (2010)
6. Freund, R., Păun, G., Pérez-Jiménez, M.J.: Tissue P systems with channel states. Theoret. Comput. Sci. **330**(1), 101–116 (2005)
7. Gazdag, Z., Kolonits, G.: A new approach for solving SAT by P systems with active membranes. In: Csuhaj-Varjú, E., Gheorghe, M., Rozenberg, G., Salomaa, A., Vaszil, G. (eds.) CMC 2012. LNCS, vol. 7762, pp. 195–207. Springer, Heidelberg (2013). doi:10.1007/978-3-642-36751-9_14
8. Gutiérrez-Naranjo, M.A., Pérez-Jiménez, M.J., Riscos-Núñez, A.: A fast P system for finding a balanced 2-partition. Soft. Comput. **9**(9), 673–678 (2005)
9. Gutiérrez-Naranjo, M.A., Pérez-Jiménez, M.J., Riscos-Núñez, A., Romero-Campero, F.J.: On the power of dissolution in P systems with active membranes. In: Freund, R., Păun, G., Rozenberg, G., Salomaa, A. (eds.) WMC 2005. LNCS, vol. 3850, pp. 224–240. Springer, Heidelberg (2006). doi:10.1007/11603047_16
10. Hartmanis, J.: Gödel, von Neumann and the P =? NP problem. In: Rozenberg, G., Salomaa, A. (eds.) Current Trends in Theoretical Computer Science - Essays and Tutorials, World Scientific Series in Computer Science, vol. 40, pp. 445–450. World Scientific, Singapore (1993)
11. Jaffe, A.M.: The millennium grand challenge in mathematics. Not. Am. Math. Soc. **53**(6), 652–660 (2006)
12. Krishna, S.N., Lakshmanan, K., Rama, R.: Tissue P systems with contextual and rewriting rules. In: PĂun, G., Rozenberg, G., Salomaa, A., Zandron, C. (eds.) WMC 2002. LNCS, vol. 2597, pp. 339–351. Springer, Heidelberg (2003). doi:10.1007/3-540-36490-0_22
13. Lakshmanan, K., Rama, R.: On the power of tissue P systems with insertion and deletion rules. In: Alhazov, A., Martín-Vide, C., Păun, G. (eds.) Preproceedings of the Workshop on Membrane Computing, pp. 304–318, Tarragona, 17–22 July 2003
14. Leporati, A., Manzoni, L., Mauri, G., Porreca, A.E., Zandron, C.: Simulating elementary active membranes - with an application to the P conjecture. In: Membrane Computing - 15th International Conference, CMC 2014, Prague, Czech Republic, 20–22 August 2014, Revised Selected Papers, pp. 284–299 (2014)
15. Liu, X., Suo, J., Leung, S.C.H., Liu, J., Zeng, X.: The power of time-free tissue P systems: attacking NP-complete problems. Neurocomputing **159**, 151–156 (2015)
16. Martín-Vide, C., Pazos, J., Păun, G., Rodríguez-Patón, A.: A new class of symbolic abstract neural nets: tissue P systems. In: Ibarra, Oscar H., Zhang, Louxin (eds.) COCOON 2002. LNCS, vol. 2387, pp. 290–299. Springer, Heidelberg (2002). doi:10.1007/3-540-45655-4_32
17. Martín-Vide, C., Pazos, J., Rodríguez-Patón, A.: Tissue P systems. Theoret. Comput. Sci. **296**(2), 295–326 (2003)
18. Pakash, V.: On the power of tissue P systems working in the maximal-one mode. In: Alhazov, A., Martín-Vide, C., Păun, G. (eds.) Preproceedings of the Workshop on Membrane Computing, pp. 356–364, Tarragona, 17–22 July 2003

19. Pan, L., Pérez-Jiménez, M.J.: Computational complexity of tissue-like P systems. J. Complex. **26**(3), 296–315 (2010)
20. Pérez-Hurtado, I., Pérez-Jiménez, M.J., Riscos-Núñez, A., Gutiérrez-Naranjo, M.A., Rius-Font, M.: On a partial affirmative answer for a Păun's conjecture. Int. J. Found. Comput. Sci. **22**(1), 55–64 (2011)
21. Pérez-Jiménez, M.J.: An approach to computational complexity in membrane computing. In: Mauri, G., Păun, G., Pérez-Jiménez, M.J., Rozenberg, G., Salomaa, A. (eds.) WMC 2004. LNCS, vol. 3365, pp. 85–109. Springer, Heidelberg (2005). doi:10.1007/978-3-540-31837-8_5
22. Pérez-Jiménez, M.J., Riscos-Núñez, A., Romero-Jiménez, A., Woods, D.: Complexity - membrane division, membrane creation. In: Păun et al. [29], pp. 302–336
23. Pérez-Jiménez, M.J., Romero-Campero, F.J.: An efficient family of P systems for packing items into bins. J. Univ. Comput. Sci. **10**(5), 650–670 (2004)
24. Pérez-Jiménez, M.J., Romero-Campero, F.J.: Solving the binpacking problem by recognizer P systems with active membranes. In: Păun, G., Riscos-Núñez, A., Romero-Jiménez, Á., Sancho-Caparrini, F. (eds.) Second Brainstorming Week on Membrane Computing, pp. 414–430. Fénix Editora, Sevilla (2004)
25. Pérez-Jiménez, M.J., Romero-Jiménez, Á., Sancho-Caparrini, F.: Complexity classes in models of cellular computing with membranes. Nat. Comput. **2**(3), 265–285 (2003)
26. Păun, G.: Membrane Computing: An Introduction. Springer, Berlin (2002)
27. Păun, G.: Further twenty six open problems in membrane computing. In: Third Brainstorming Week on Membrane Computing, pp. 249–262. Fénix Editora, Sevilla, Spain (2005)
28. Păun, G., Pérez-Jiménez, M.J., Riscos-Núñez, A.: Tissue P systems with cell division. Int. J. Comput. Commun. Control **3**(3), 295–303 (2008)
29. Păun, G., Rozenberg, G., Salomaa, A. (eds.): The Oxford Handbook of Membrane Computing. Oxford University Press, Oxford (2010)
30. Song, B., Song, T., Pan, L.: A time-free uniform solution to subset sum problem by tissue P systems with cell division. Math. Struct. Comput. Sci. **27**(1), 17–32 (2017)
31. Song, T., Luo, L., He, J., Chen, Z., Zhang, K.: Solving subset sum problems by time-free spiking neural P systems. Appl. Math. Inf. Sci. **8**(1), 327–332 (2014)
32. Song, T., Macías-Ramos, L.F., Pan, L., Pérez-Jiménez, M.J.: Time-free solution to SAT problem using P systems with active membranes. Theoret. Comput. Sci. **529**, 61–68 (2014)
33. Zandron, C., Ferretti, C., Mauri, G.: Solving NP-complete problems using P systems with active membranes. In: Antoniou, I., Calude, C.S., Dinneen, M.J. (eds.) UMC 2000. DMTCS, pp. 289–301. Springer, London (2000). doi:10.1007/978-1-4471-0313-4_21

Universal Matrix Insertion Grammars with Small Size

Henning Fernau[1], Lakshmanan Kuppusamy[2], and Sergey Verlan[3(✉)]

[1] Fachbereich 4 – Abteilung Informatikwissenschaften, Universität Trier,
54286 Trier, Germany
fernau@uni-trier.de
[2] School of Computer Science and Engineering, VIT University,
Vellore 632 014, India
klakshma@vit.ac.in
[3] Laboratoire d'Algorithmique, Complexité et Logique,
Université Paris Est - Créteil Val de Marne, 94010 Créteil, France
verlan@u-pec.fr

Abstract. We study matrix insertion grammars (MIS) towards representation of recursively enumerable languages with small size. We show that pure MIS of size $(3; 1, 2, 2)$ (*i.e.*, having ternary matrices inserting one symbol in two symbol context) can characterize all recursively enumerable languages. This is achieved by either applying an inverse morphism and a weak coding, or a left (right) quotient with a regular language or an intersection with a regular language followed by a weak coding. The obtained results complete known results on insertion-deletion systems from DNA computing area.

Keywords: Insertion grammars · Matrix insertion grammars · Recursively enumerable sets · Homomorphism · Regular intersection and quotient

1 Introduction

Insertion grammars were initially known as *semi-contextual grammars* introduced by Galiukschov [8], as opposed to context-sensitive grammars (rewriting nonterminals in given contexts) and Marcus contextual grammars (contexts are adjoined to given strings). In an insertion grammar, strings are inserted in given contexts. Beside the motivation from the linguistics, such grammars have a biological inspiration. As pointed out in [26], the process of mismatched annealing of DNA strands can be seen as an insertion or a deletion of a string in a specified context. A similar process happens in the case of the RNA editing [1], where the uracil base U is inserted or deleted in some left context. These observations led to the intense study of *insertion-deletion* systems (considering insertion and deletion operations together) in the framework of DNA computing [13, 15, 19, 20, 27, 28].

© Springer International Publishing AG 2017
M.J. Patitz and M. Stannett (Eds.): UCNC 2017, LNCS 10240, pp. 182–193, 2017.
DOI: 10.1007/978-3-319-58187-3_14

There are several related models using a similar principle of insertion or deletion of a string in a specified context. We cite guided-insertion systems [2] used to model RNA editing, leftist grammars [21] used to model accessibility problems in protection systems, restarting automata [12] used to model the analysis by reduction and the insertion operation from [10] introduced as a generalization of the concatenation (and which corresponds to a context-free insertion grammar).

We consider here matrix insertion grammars, where the insertion rules are given in a matrix form and if a matrix is chosen for application in a derivation, then all the rules of the matrix are applied in the given order. This model was first considered in [18]. Related models like *matrix insertion-deletion systems* and *graph-controlled insertion-deletion systems* were considered in [3,4,16,17,24,26].

Given an insertion grammar, the size of the system is defined as (i, l, r), where i is the maximal length of the insertion string of all rules and l (r, respectively) is the maximal length of the left (right, respectively) context of all rules.

In the literature, there are several results related to characterization of recursively enumerable languages using insertion grammars. As observed in [26], insertion grammars form a subclass of context-sensitive languages. So, in order to obtain a characterization of recursively enumerable languages additional squeezing mechanisms are used. Traditionally, an inverse morphism and a weak coding are used, as well as an intersection with a (sub-)regular language, followed by a weak coding. Another used possibility is the left or right quotient with a regular language.

In [26], it is shown that insertion grammars of size $(4, 7, 6)$ can generate any recursively enumerable language (using an inverse morphism and a weak coding). In [22], this result was improved to the size $(3, 5, 4)$. The size was further decreased to $(3, 3, 3)$ in [14,23]. A related result was obtained in [25], where it is shown that any recursively enumerable language can be obtained as the intersection of a Dyck language (with arbitrarily many parenthesis types) with the language generated by a context-free insertion grammar of size $(3, 0, 0)$.

In [16], graph-controlled insertion grammars were considered, where rules are grouped into components. A characterization of the recursively enumerable languages was obtained with rules of size $(2, 2, 2)$, grouped into three components.

We consider insertion grammars along with matrix control. Alongside the above discussed size of an insertion grammar, the length parameter is added, which refers to the maximal number of rules of any matrix. We show a characterization of the recursively enumerable languages by matrix insertion grammars with size $(3; 1, 2, 2)$ by applying an inverse morphism and weak coding to the generated language. We also show that the same result can be obtained by using an intersection with a regular language from LOC(2), the family of locally testable languages of size 2, and a weak coding, as well as using a left/right quotient with a regular language from LOC(2).

2 Definitions

We introduce the basic notations and definitions that are necessary for understanding the paper. Given a alphabet V (finite set of symbols), let V^* denote the set of all strings over V, i.e., the free monoid generated by V; the operator symbol $\cdot$ (for concatenation) is mostly omitted. For a string $x \in V^*$, we denote the length of x by $|x|$ and the empty string is written as λ. If not explicitly stated otherwise, the notion of a morphism refers to a (homo)morphism mapping from the free monoid over some alphabet to the free monoid over some (other) alphabet. Weak codings are special morphisms $h : V^* \to W^*$, where $W \subseteq V$ and the restriction of h to W is the identity, and $h(x) = \lambda$ for $x \in V \setminus W$. We write $|x|_W$ if we first apply the weak coding $h : V^* \to W^*$ to $x \in V^*$ and then the length function $|\cdot|$. Following [6], let LOC(2) denote the class of *strictly two-testable languages*, a quite restricted form of regular languages. $L \in \mathrm{LOC}(2), L \subseteq T^*$, if there is a triple (P, I, S), with $P, I, S \subseteq T^2$, such that $w \in L$ iff the prefix of length two of w is in P, the suffix of length two of w is in S, and all factors (or infixes) of length two of w lie in I.

We now discuss the normal form for type-0 grammar needed in our proofs.

Following [5, 11, 24], based on [9], a type-0 grammar $G = (N, T, S, P)$ is said to be in *special Geffert normal form*, or SGNF for short, if the set of non-terminals N decomposes as $N = N' \cup N'', N' \cap N'' = \varnothing$, where $N'' = \{A, B, C, D\}$ and N' is the set of non-terminals containing S, S' and some other auxiliary non-terminals, and if it only has two (non-context-free) erasing rules, $AB \to \lambda$ and $CD \to \lambda$, and several context-free rules of one of the following forms:

$$X \to bY, \quad \text{where } X, Y \in N', b \in T \cup N'', X \neq Y,$$
$$X \to Yb, \quad \text{where } X, Y \in N', b \in N'', X \neq Y,$$
$$S' \to \lambda.$$

Moreover, it may be assumed without loss of generality that, for any two rules $X \to w$ and $U \to w$ in P, where the first symbol of w is different from S or S', we have $U = X$. We remark that the terminals are generated at the left-hand side of the string. This observation is necessary for proving the main theorem later. Moreover, the generation of a string using a grammar in SGNF is performed in two stages. During the first stage, only context-free rules can be applied; in the second stage, only context-sensitive deletion rules are applied. The transition between the stages is done by the rule $S' \to \lambda$. All sentential forms are always of form $T^*\{A, C\}^*(N' \cup \{\lambda\})\{C, D\}^*$.

We are now going to define the crucial notions of this paper.

Definition 1. *Let V be an alphabet. An* insertion rule *over V is given by a triple $r = (u, x, v)$, where $u, x, v \in V^*$. We can associate to r the derivation relation $\Rightarrow_r \subseteq V^* \times V^*$ by defining, for $y, z \in V^*$, $y \Rightarrow_r z$ iff there are $y_1, y_2 \in V^*$ such that $y = y_1 u v y_2$ and $z = y_1 u x v y_2$.*

In terms of rewriting rules, this is equivalent to specify $uv \to uxv$.

Definition 2. *A pure insertion grammar is described by a triple $\gamma = (V, A, R)$, where V is an alphabet, $A \subseteq V^*$ is the finite set of axioms, R is a finite set of insertion rules of form $r_i = (u_i, x_i, v_i), 1 \leq i \leq t$. We define $\Rightarrow_\gamma := \bigcup_{r \in R} \Rightarrow_r$ and write $\Rightarrow_\gamma^*$ for the reflexive transitive closure of $\Rightarrow_\gamma$. Now, $L(\gamma) := \{w \in V^* \mid \exists z \in A \ (z \Rightarrow_\gamma^* w)\}$.*

Definition 3. *A pure matrix insertion grammar with matrices of size at most n is described by a triple $\Pi = (V, A, \mathcal{M})$, where*

- *V is an alphabet,*
- *$A \subseteq V^*$ is the finite set of axioms,*
- *$\mathcal{M}$ is a finite set of sequences of rules, also called matrices, of the form $m = [r_1, \ldots, r_{n(m)}]$, where each $r_i = (u_i, x_i, v_i)$, $1 \le i \le n(m) \le n$ is an insertion rule over V; $n(m)$ is also called the length of m.*

For a matrix $m = [r_1, \ldots, r_{n(m)}]$, we will also write $m.i = r_i$. Let $R_\Pi = \{m.i \mid m \in \mathcal{M}, 1 \le i \le n(m)\} \subseteq 2^{V^* \times V^*}$. Recall that $(2^{V^* \times V^*}, \circ, \mathrm{id})$ forms a monoid. Consider the monoid morphism given by $m.i \mapsto \Rightarrow_{m.i}$ that allows to identify sequences of rules with some derivation relation, hence defining in particular $\Rightarrow_m$ for $m \in \mathcal{M}$. This way, we can set $\Rightarrow_\Pi := \bigcup_{m \in \mathcal{M}} \Rightarrow_m$ and write $\Rightarrow_\Pi^*$ for the reflexive transitive closure of $\Rightarrow_\Pi$. Now, $L(\Pi) := \{w \in V^* \mid \exists z \in A(z \Rightarrow_\Pi^* w)\}$.

The descriptive complexity measures of a matrix insertion system $\Pi = (V, A, \mathcal{M})$ are defined by the parameters $(n; i, l, r)$, also called the *size* of Π, where

$$n = \max\{n(m) : m \in \mathcal{M}\}, \quad i = \max\{|x| : (u, x, v) \in R_\Pi\},$$
$$l = \max\{|u| \mid (u, x, v) \in R_\Pi\}, r = \max\{|v| \mid (u, x, v) \in R_\Pi\}.$$

The family of languages generated by matrix insertion grammars of size $(n; i, l, r)$ (and sometimes also the grammar family itself) is denoted by $\mathrm{MIS}(n; i, l, r)$.

The next example shows the power of matrix insertion grammars compared to (pure) insertion grammars.

Example 1. The language $L_1 = \{a^n b a^n \mid n \ge 1\}$ can be generated by the matrix insertion grammar $\Pi_1 = (\{a, b\}, \{aba\}, m_1 = [(\lambda, a, b), (b, a, \lambda)])$. Starting from the axiom aba, one can apply m_1 repeatedly, which will introduce every time one a to the left of b and one a to the right of b. It is easy to see that $L(\Pi_1) = L_1$. Note that L_1 cannot be generated by any insertion grammar [26]. The size of the grammar Π_1 is $(2; 1, 1, 1)$. □

3   Main Results

Before presenting the proof of the main result, we would like to discuss the *mark-and-migration* technique introduced in [26] to obtain the computational completeness result. This technique is based on simulating a type-0 grammar, in some special normal form. The main idea is that the deletion of a non-terminal symbol X is simulated by adding special marker \$ to its left (in [26] two markers #\$ were used). Such a sequence can be later easily filtered by an inverse morphism. The contexts of the insertion rules verify that symbol X from the sequence \$$X$ is not considered for any grammar derivation anymore, so it is treated as non-existing. We will also call a symbol X with a \$ to its left a *dead symbol*. Such an approach works perfectly for the simulation of context-free rules.

However, for context-sensitive rules like $AB \to \lambda$ (and $CD \to \lambda$), it may happen that symbols A and B (likewise, C and D) are separated by a sequence of dead symbols. To address this issue, the "migration" of B towards the left until it is placed right to its partner A is performed (likewise, D is moved towards left until it is placed right to its partner C). During this migration, a substring $\$XB$ is transformed to $Bw_1\$Xw_2\$B$, with $w_1, w_2 \in (\$Z)^*$, with Z being an alphabet of some additional symbols. The iteration of this process allows to obtain an adjacent pair of symbols A and B (likewise, C and D is paired) that can be further used for the simulation of an application of the corresponding rule $AB \to \lambda$, by turning the neighboring symbols A, B into dead symbols (similarly with C, D).

As shown in [14, 23], contexts of size 3 allow to implement the aforementioned technique. Two stages are used for the migration of B over $\$X$: "jumping" over $\$X$ and marking B as dead. When decreasing the size of contexts down to 2, an additional constraint is added – it is not possible anymore to "jump" over the sequence $\$X$, as there is no sufficient context. We solve this problem by splitting the corresponding "jump" into two sub-stages, so finally we need three stages to perform this operation. In order to ensure the integrity of the operation (that inserts only one symbol), matrices of size 3 are used. During the first two stages $\$XB$ is transformed to $\$\bar{B}_1\$X\$B$, where the sequence $\$\bar{B}_1$ denotes that we are in the process of migrating B to the left. Next, $\$\bar{B}_1\$X\$B$ is transformed to $B\$\nabla\$\bar{B}_2\$\bar{B}_1\$X\$B$, where ∇ is a new separator symbol. Hence, the migration of B over $\$X$ was performed. However, such a migration introduced the sequence $\bar{\$}\bar{B}_i, 1 \le i \le 2$. A symmetrical group of rules allows to perform a migration over sequences $\bar{\$}\bar{X}$.

Now we are ready to state the main result of the paper.

Theorem 1. *For each recursively enumerable language L there exists a morphism h, a weak coding g and a language $L_1 \in \mathrm{MIS}(3; 1, 2, 2)$ such that $L = g(h^{-1}(L_1))$.*

Proof. Let $G = (N' \cup N'', T, P, S)$ be a type-0 grammar in SGNF. We construct the following matrix insertion grammar $\Pi = (V, A, \mathcal{M})$. We define the alphabet V as follows (we assume that all added symbols are new and do not belong to $N' \cup N'' \cup T$).

$$V = N' \cup N'' \cup T \cup \{\mathcal{c}, K_{AB}, K_{CD}\} \cup \{x, \bar{x} \mid x \in \{\nabla, \$, B_1, B_2, D_1, D_2\}\}.$$

The set of axioms is defined as $A = \{\mathcal{c}\mathcal{c}S\}$.
Consider following sets:

$$\begin{aligned}
\mathcal{L} &= T \cup \{A, C, \mathcal{c}\}, \\
\mathcal{N} &= N' \cup N'' \cup \{K_{AB}, K_{CD}, \nabla, B_1, B_2, D_1, D_2\}, \\
\bar{\mathcal{N}} &= \{\bar{B}_1, \bar{D}_1, \bar{B}_2, \bar{D}_2, \bar{\nabla}\}, \\
\mathcal{F} &= \mathcal{L}^2 \cup \{\$X \mid X \in \mathcal{N}\} \cup \{\$\bar{Y} \mid \bar{Y} \in \bar{\mathcal{N}}\}.
\end{aligned}$$

We assume that $\bar{\bar{X}} = X$.

The rules $\mathcal{M}$ of the matrix insertion system are given as follows:

- For any rule $X \to bY \in P$, we add the following matrix to $\mathcal{M}$:

$$m_{1.\alpha} = [(\alpha, Y, X), (Y, \$, X), (\alpha, b, Y)], \alpha \in \mathcal{L}.$$

- For any rule $X \to Yb \in P$, we add the following matrix to $\mathcal{M}$:

$$m_{2.\alpha} = [(\alpha, Y, X), (Y, \$, X), (\alpha Y, b, \$)], \alpha \in \mathcal{L}.$$

- Rule $S' \to \lambda$ is simulated by the following matrix:

$$m_{3.\alpha} = [(\alpha, \$, S')], \alpha \in \mathcal{L}.$$

- The move of symbols B and D to the left of the sequence $\$X$, where $X \in \mathcal{N}$, is performed using following matrices ($Z \in \{B, D\}$ and $\alpha \in \mathcal{F}$):

$$m_4 = [(\$, \bar{Z}_1, XZ), (\bar{Z}_1 X, \$, Z), (\$\bar{Z}_1, \$, X\$)].$$
$$m_{5.\alpha} = [(\$, \bar{Z}_2, \bar{Z}_1), (\alpha, Z, \$\bar{Z}_2), (\$, \nabla, \bar{Z}_2)].$$
$$m_6 = [(\nabla, \bar{\$}, \bar{Z}_2 \bar{Z}_1), (\bar{\$}\bar{Z}_2, \bar{\$}, \bar{Z}_1)].$$

- The move of symbols B and D to the left of the sequence $\bar{\$}\bar{Y}$, where $\bar{Y} \in \bar{\mathcal{N}}$, is performed using following matrices ($Z \in \{B, D\}$ and $\alpha \in \mathcal{F}$):

$$m'_4 = [(\bar{\$}, Z_1, \bar{Y}Z), (Z_1\bar{Y}, \$, Z), (\bar{\$}Z_1, \bar{\$}, \bar{Y}\$)].$$
$$m'_{5'.\alpha} = [(\bar{\$}, Z_2, Z_1), (\alpha, Z, \bar{\$}Z_2), (\bar{\$}, \bar{\nabla}, Z_2)].$$
$$m'_6 = [(\bar{\nabla}, \$, Z_2 Z_1), (\$Z_2, \$, Z_1)].$$

We remark that matrices $m'_4 - m'_6$ are very similar to $m_4 - m_6$ (basically, the $^-$ operator is applied to most of the symbols in the contexts and the insertion string).

- Rules $AB \to \lambda$ and $CD \to \lambda$ are simulated by the following matrices, where $(Z, Z') \in \{(A, B), (C, D)\}$ and $\alpha \in \mathcal{L}$. As no deletion takes place in the matrix insertion grammar, the factor ZZ' is replaced by $\$Z\$K_{ZZ'}\$Z'$ and hence marked as dead.

$$m_{7.\alpha} = [(\alpha Z, K_{ZZ'}, Z'), (ZK_{ZZ'}, \$, Z'), (\alpha, \$, ZK_{ZZ'})],$$
$$m_8 = [(Z, \$, K_{ZZ'})].$$

Finally, let $h : T \cup \{\cent\} \cup \mathcal{N} \cup \bar{\mathcal{N}} \to V^*$ be the morphism defined by

$$h(x) = \begin{cases} \$x, & x \in \mathcal{N}, \\ \bar{\$}x, & x \in \bar{\mathcal{N}}, \\ x, & x \in T, \\ \cent, & x = \cent. \end{cases}$$

and $g : T \cup \{\cent\} \cup \mathcal{N} \cup \bar{\mathcal{N}} \to T$ be the weak coding defined by

$$g(x) = \begin{cases} x, & x \in T, \\ \lambda, & \text{otherwise}. \end{cases}$$

Now we show that $L(G) = g(h^{-1}(L(\Pi)))$.

We start with the inclusion $L(G) \subseteq g(h^{-1}(L(\Pi)))$. In the matrix rules $m_{i.\alpha}$, whenever α is not a matter for discussion, we refer the matrix without the α. By using matrices $m_1 - m_3$, Π simulates all derivations of the first stage of G, the sequence \$$X$ meaning that the symbol X is erased. Now in order to simulate the second stage, matrices m_8 and m_9 are used, allowing to erase adjacent symbols AB or CD. Because of the derivation in the first stage, the first pair A, B or C, D is separated by a sequence of \$$X$. Thus, we need to move the symbols B and D (in order of their appearance) to the left of \$$S'$ and to match them with their partner A or C. Matrices $m_4 - m_6$ allow to move the symbols $Z \in \{B, D\}$ to the left over a sequence \$$X$, $X \in \mathcal{N}$. In fact, in m_4, we copy the Z to be $\bar{Z}_1$ and in m_5 we copy the $\bar{Z}_1$ to Z (see $m_5.2$) and place it to the left of \$. The dummy symbol ∇ is introduced between \$ and $\bar{Z}$ (see $m_5.3$) in order to avoid the repetition of using m_5 again and $\bar{\$}$ is introduced to the left of $\bar{Z}$ to mark $\bar{Z}$ as dead (see m_6). Thus, an application of matrices $m_4 - m_6$ to a (sub)string \$$XZ$ derives the following:

$$\$XZ \Rightarrow_{m_4} \$\bar{Z}_1\$X\$Z \Rightarrow_{m_5} Z\$\nabla\bar{Z}_2\bar{Z}_1\$X\$Z \Rightarrow_{m_6} Z\$\nabla\bar{\$}\bar{Z}_2\bar{\$}\bar{Z}_1\$X\$Z.$$

Since such a derivation introduces a pair of symbols $\bar{\$}\bar{Z}_i$, $1 \leq i \leq 2$, it should be also necessary to be able to move B or D over such a barred pair. This is done using matrices $m'_4 - m'_6$, which work in a symmetrical manner:

$$\bar{\$}\bar{Y}Z \Rightarrow_{m'_4} \bar{\$}Z_1\bar{\$}\bar{Y}\$Z \Rightarrow_{m'_5} Z\bar{\$}\bar{\nabla}Z_2Z_1\$\bar{Y}\$Z \Rightarrow_{m'_6} Z\bar{\$}\bar{\nabla}\$Z_2\$Z_1\$\bar{Y}\$Z.$$

We can notice from the two derivations above that \$ is placed to the left of the symbols of $N' \cup \{B, D, \nabla\}$ (except for the copied Z) and $\bar{\$}$ is placed to the left of the symbols of $\bar{\mathcal{N}}$. The purpose of placing \$ and $\bar{\$}$ and ∇ is to inactivate the symbols $N' \cup \bar{\mathcal{N}}$ temporarily in the substring and these symbols have to wait till some other B or D are copied from the right to get the substring to one of the forms \$$XZ$ or \$$\nabla Z$ or $\bar{\$}\bar{X}Z$ or $\bar{\$}\bar{\nabla}Z$ for activation.

Using the above discussed rules, the symbol B or D is moved up to A or C that can be seen to the left of \$$S'$ (or up to the last matched pairs). Now the task is to match B or D with its partner and then place \$ in between symbols to mark them dead. The partner matching is done by introducing a $K_{ZZ'}$ in between the pair Z and Z' and then \$ is placed between the symbols (so that when the next Z is copied from the right, it can move across these symbols, too). The application of matrices m_7 and m_8 for the matched string ZZ' is shown below:

$$\alpha ZZ' \Rightarrow_{m_7} \alpha\$ZK_{ZZ'}\$Z' \Rightarrow_{m_8} \alpha\$Z\$K_{ZZ'}\$Z', \alpha \in \mathcal{L}.$$

Now, having the morphism and weak coding defined above, with the help of inverse morphism, we can see that $L(G) \subseteq g(h^{-1}(L(\Pi)))$.

In the following, we prove the converse inclusion, $g(h^{-1}(L(\Pi))) \subseteq L(G)$. We will show that no additional, unintended words can be generated.

Consider following regular languages:

$$L_0 = \{\$X \mid X \in \mathcal{N}\} \cup \{\$\bar{Y} \mid \bar{Y} \in \bar{\mathcal{N}}\}.$$
$$L_1 = L_0 \{B, D, \lambda\}.$$
$$L_2 = \{\$\bar{Z}_1, \bar{\$}Z_1 \mid Z \in \{B, D\}\}.$$
$$L_3 = \{\$\nabla \bar{Z}_2 \bar{Z}_1, \bar{\$}\bar{\nabla} Z_2 Z_1 \mid Z \in \{B, D\}\}.$$
$$L_4 = \{\$ZK_{ZZ'} \mid (Z, Z') \in \{(A, B), (C, D)\}\}.$$
$$L_b = \{\text{¢¢}\} T^* \{A, C\}^*$$
$$L_e = (L_1 \cup L_2 \cup L_3)^*$$
$$L_5 = L_b N'\{B, D, \lambda\} L_e$$
$$L_6 = L_b (L_4 \cup \{\lambda\})\{B, D, \lambda\} L_e$$

The computation in Π follows the two computational stages from SGNF. The transition between the stages is performed by the matrix m_3, corresponding to the simulation of the rule $S' \to \lambda$. However, during both stages the total or partial migration to the left of symbols B and D can be performed. However, neither of the matrices m_7 or m_8 can be applied without prior application of m_3.

We claim that during the first stage (using matrices m_1, m_2, but also $m_4 - m_6$, $m'_4 - m'_6$) the string is of a form given by L_5, i.e., $\text{¢¢}S \Rightarrow^* w$ implies that $w \in L_5$. We will prove this statement by induction. The axiom $\text{¢¢}S$ is contained in L_5. Let $w_1 \in L_5$ and $w_1 \Rightarrow_{m_k} w_2$, $1 \leq k \leq 7$. We will consider the case of each matrix in the following to prove the induction step.

Recall that in SGNF, only one non-terminal from N' is present during the first phase. This corresponds exactly to the N' part of the L_5 expression. All other non-terminals from N' are preceded by a $ symbol, marking them as dead.

The Case of m_1: By the remark above, the unique site for the application of the first rule from the matrix is the leftmost non-terminal X from N' which has the required context $\mathcal{L}X$ (below $\alpha \in L_b$ and $\beta \in \{B, D, \lambda\}L_e$):

$$\alpha\, X\, \beta \Rightarrow_{m_{1.1}} \alpha\, YX\, \beta \Rightarrow_{m_{1.2}} \alpha\, Y\$X\, \beta \Rightarrow_{m_{1.3}} \alpha\, bY\$X\, \beta$$

We recall that according to the Geffert normal form construction, the terminals are generated before A and C. Hence, $b \in T$ implies that $|\alpha|_{\{A,C\}} = 0$.

The sites of the application of the second and third rules of the matrix: YX, $X, Y \in N'$ and $\mathcal{L}Y$ are also unique. It can be easily seen that the resulting string belongs to L_5.

The Case of m_2: As in the previous case, the matrix can be applied to the leftmost non-terminal from N' (the context $\mathcal{L}X$). Next, the contexts YX, $X, Y \in N'$ and $\mathcal{L}Y\$$ are unique in the string, which proves the assertion (below $\alpha \in L_b$ and $\beta \in \{B, D, \lambda\}L_e$):

$$\alpha\, X\, \beta \Rightarrow_{m_{2.1}} \alpha\, YX\, \beta \Rightarrow_{m_{2.2}} \alpha\, Y\$X\, \beta \Rightarrow_{m_{2.3}} \alpha\, Yb\$X\, \beta$$

The Case of m_4: Clearly, for a string $w_1 \in L_5$, if the string $\$XZ, X \in \mathcal{N}, Z \in \{B, D\}$ is a factor of w_1 then it is a factor of L_e. But this implies that this string is a factor of L_1 (*i.e.*, there could not be the situation where $\$XZ$ is not the prefix of L_1L_k, with $1 \leq k \leq 3$).

The string can have several sites matching $\$XZ$ (because there can be several copies of B and D generated using the rules from m_2). Consider one of them. Then we can have the following derivation (below, $\alpha \in L_bN'\{B, D, \lambda\}L_e$ and $\beta \in L_e$):

$$\alpha\$XZ\beta \Rightarrow_{m_4.1} \alpha\$\bar{Z}_1XZ\beta \Rightarrow_{m_4.2} \alpha\$\bar{Z}_1X\$Z\beta \Rightarrow_{m_4.3} \alpha\$\bar{Z}_1\$X\$Z\beta.$$

We claim that this is the only possible derivation. Indeed, the application of $m_4.1$ yields to the insertion of $\bar{Z}_1$, producing the substring $\bar{Z}_1XZ$, which is used as a context for rule $m_4.2$. Clearly, this context is unique (no other place from L_e can have 3 consecutive symbols not containing the symbols $\$$ or $\bar{\$}$). The application of $m_4.2$ produces the substring $\$\bar{Z}_1X\$$, which is also unique in the string (L_2 should be followed by $\$$ or $\bar{\$}$). Observe that the resulting string is from L_5.

The Case of m_5: Using similar arguments as above, we deduce that a factor $\$\bar{Z}_1$ can be only in the L_2 part of L_e. Now consider the following derivation (below, $\alpha \in L_bN'\{B, D, \lambda\}L_e$ and $\beta \in L_e$):

$$\alpha\$\bar{Z}_1\beta \Rightarrow_{m_5.1} \alpha\$\bar{Z}_2\bar{Z}_1\beta \Rightarrow_{m_5.2} \alpha Z\$\bar{Z}_2\bar{Z}_1\beta \Rightarrow_{m_5.3} \alpha Z\$\nabla\bar{Z}_2\bar{Z}_1\$X\$Z\beta.$$

The use of $m_2.2$ implies that $\alpha = \alpha'\alpha''$, with $\alpha' \in L_bN'\{B, D, \lambda\}L_e$ and $\alpha'' \in L_1$. We claim that this is the only possible derivation. Indeed, the application of $m_5.1$ yields to the insertion of $\bar{Z}_2$, producing the substring $\$\bar{Z}_2$, which is used as a context for rules $m_5.2$ and $m_5.3$. Clearly, this context is unique (no other place from L_e can have such a sequence). We also remark that the application of $m_5.2$ requires $\mathcal{F}$ as its left context. Since $\mathcal{F} \cap L_e = L_1$, this application guarantees the context L_1 at the left of $\$\bar{Z}_2$. Hence, the resulting string is from L_5.

The Case of m_6: Using similar arguments as above, we deduce that a factor $\$\bar{Z}_1$ can be only in the L_3 part of L_e. Now consider the following derivation (below, $\alpha \in L_bN'\{B, D, \lambda\}L_e$ and $\beta \in L_e$):

$$\alpha\$\nabla\bar{Z}_2\bar{Z}_1\beta \Rightarrow_{m_6.1} \alpha\$\nabla\$\bar{Z}_2\bar{Z}_1\beta \Rightarrow_{m_6.2} \alpha\$\nabla\$\bar{Z}_2\bar{\$}\bar{Z}_1\beta.$$

We claim that this is the only possible derivation. Indeed, the application of $m_6.1$ yields to the insertion of $\$$ producing the substring $\$\bar{Z}_2\bar{Z}_1$, which is used as a context for rule $m_6.2$. It can be easily seen that this context is unique (the sequence $\bar{Z}_2\bar{Z}_1$ can be only present in L_3, but it does not have symbol $\$$ in front of it). Finally, we remark that the resulting string is from L_5.

The Case of $m_4' - m_6'$: The corresponding matrices are similar to $m_4 - m_6$ (changing $\$$ to $\bar{\$}$ and Z_k to $\bar{Z}_k$), $1 \leq k \leq 2$, so similar arguments hold.

This concludes the inductive proof for the claim concerning stage one. We now consider the transition from stage one to stage two.

The Case of m_3: The application of this rule (m_3) on a string from L_5 yields a string in L_6.

We are now in the discussion of stage two. As before we show by induction that any string in L_6 using matrices m_7, m_8 and $m_4 - m_6, m_4' - m_6'$ also yields a string in L_6. We do not discuss the case of the last six matrices, as it is the same as in the discussion above, because the presence of a symbol from N' was immaterial.

The Case of m_7: Using similar arguments as above, we deduce that a factor ZZ' can be obtained only when the L_4 part is absent. Now consider the following derivation (below, $\alpha \in L_b$ and $\beta \in L_e$):

$$\alpha\, ZZ'\, \beta \Rightarrow_{m_7.1} \alpha\, ZK_{ZZ'}Z'\, \beta \Rightarrow_{m_7.2} \alpha\, ZK_{ZZ'}\$Z'\, \beta \Rightarrow_{m_7.3} \alpha\, \$ZK_{ZZ'}\$Z'\, \beta.$$

We claim that this is the only possible derivation. Indeed, the application of $m_7.1$ yields to the insertion of $K_{ZZ'}$ producing the substring $ZK_{ZZ'}Z'$, which is used as a context for rule $m_7.2$. Clearly, this context is unique. Next, the context $\mathcal{L}ZK_{ZZ'}$ is used for rule $m_7.3$. Because of $\mathcal{L}$, it can only be present at the beginning of the string, which concludes the argument.

The Case of m_8: Using similar arguments as above, we deduce that a factor $ZK_{ZZ'}$ can be obtained only when the L_4 part is present. Now, consider the following derivation (below, $\alpha \in L_b$ and $\beta \in L_e$):

$$\alpha\, \$ZK_{ZZ'}\, \beta \Rightarrow_{m_8.1} \alpha\, \$Z\$K_{ZZ'}\, \beta$$

Hence, all strings that can be obtained in Π and that can be arguments of h^{-1} are of form $\mathop{\text{¢¢}}wL_0$, where $w \in L(G)$. This concludes the proof.   □

As in [14,26] we show that the inverse morphism and the weak coding can be replaced by a right (left) quotient with a regular language.

Theorem 2. *For each recursively enumerable language L there exists a language $L_1 \in \text{MIS}(3; 1, 2, 2)$ and a language $R_{L_1} \in \text{LOC}(2)$ such that $L = L_1 R_{L_1}^{-1}$.*

Proof. Let G be a grammar in SGNF such that $L(G) = L$. The construction from Theorem 1 shows that for any $w \in L$ the word $\mathop{\text{¢¢}}wL_0$ is produced in Π. It can be easily verified that $L_0 \in \text{LOC}(2)$. Now we will show that the leading symbols ¢¢ can be omitted. Indeed, let $L_2' = \{w \in L \mid |w| \leq 2\}$ and let

$$F = \{wSw' \mid S \Rightarrow^* wSw', w \in T^*, |w| \geq 2 \text{ and there is no derivation}$$
$$S \Rightarrow^* uSu' \Rightarrow^* wSw' \text{with } u \in T^* \text{ and } |u| \geq 2\}$$

Observe that F is finite. Then it is clear that by replacing the axiom $\mathop{\text{¢¢}}S$ by the axiom set $L_2' \cup F$ the corresponding insertion grammar Π' will generate the words $wL_0, w \in L$. Hence, $L = L(\Pi')L_0^{-1}$. Notice that the language L_0 is dependent on the number of non-terminal symbols from Π and hence from G.   □

Following [6,7] we consider another squeezing mechanism consisting of an intersection with a regular language followed by a weak coding.

Theorem 3. *For each recursively enumerable language L there exists a language* $L_1 \in \text{MIS}(3;1,2,2)$, *a language* $R_{L_1} \in \text{LOC}(2)$ *and a weak coding g such that* $L = g(L_1 \cap R_{L_1})$.

Proof. Consider the construction from Theorem 1. In addition to the matrices of $\mathcal{M}$, we add the matrices $m_{t.\alpha.\beta} = [(\alpha, \$, \beta)]$ to $\mathcal{M}$, where $\alpha, \beta \in T \cup \{\textcent\}$.

We also replace the axiom by $\$\textcent\textcent S$ and denote the obtained system Π'. Let $R = \{\$X \mid X \in \mathcal{N} \cup \mathcal{L}\} \cup \{\$\bar{Y} \mid \bar{Y} \in \bar{\mathcal{N}}\}$. Clearly, R allows to test if the computation in Π' arrived at the end. Hence, it is sufficient to take a weak coding keeping terminals only to obtain the result.   □

4 Conclusion

We considered insertion grammars with matrix control and we have shown that $\text{MIS}(3;1,2,2)$ is computationally complete using different squeezing mechanisms. We introduced a novel technique based on the mark-and-migration technique that allowed us to perform the migration using contexts of size two.

A natural open question is whether a similar result can be obtained using only binary matrices. Another open question concerns the power of insertion grammars with contexts of size 2: can our technique be also helpful in this case?

References

1. Benne, R. (ed.): RNA Editing: The Alteration of Protein Coding Sequences of RNA. Series in Molecular Biology. Ellis Horwood, Chichester (1993)
2. Biegler, F., Burrell, M.J., Daley, M.: Regulated RNA rewriting: modelling RNA editing with guided insertion. Theoret. Comput. Sci. **387**(2), 103–112 (2007)
3. Fernau, H., Kuppusamy, L., Raman, I.: Descriptional complexity of graph-controlled insertion-deletion systems. In: Câmpeanu, C., Manea, F., Shallit, J. (eds.) DCFS 2016. LNCS, vol. 9777, pp. 111–125. Springer, Cham (2016). doi:10. 1007/978-3-319-41114-9_9
4. Fernau, H., Kuppusamy, L., Raman, I.: Generative power of matrix insertion-deletion systems with context-free insertion or deletion. In: Amos, M., Condon, A. (eds.) UCNC 2016. LNCS, vol. 9726, pp. 35–48. Springer, Cham (2016). doi:10. 1007/978-3-319-41312-9_4
5. Freund, R., Kogler, M., Rogozhin, Y., Verlan, S.: Graph-controlled insertion-deletion systems. In: McQuillan, I., Pighizzini, G. (eds.) Proceedings Twelfth Annual Workshop on Descriptional Complexity of Formal Systems, DCFS. EPTCS, vol. 31, pp. 88–98 (2010)
6. Fujioka, K.: Morphic characterizations of languages in Chomsky hierarchy with insertion and locality. Inf. Comput. **209**(3), 397–408 (2011)
7. Fujioka, K.: Morphic characterizations with insertion systems controlled by a context of length one. Theoret. Comput. Sci. **469**, 69–76 (2013)
8. Galiukschov, B.S.: Semicontextual grammars (in Russian). In: Matematika Logica i Matematika Linguistika, pp. 38–50. Kalinin University (1981)
9. Geffert, V.: Normal forms for phrase-structure grammars. RAIRO Informatique théorique et Applications/Theor. Inform. Appl. **25**, 473–498 (1991)

10. Haussler, D.: Insertion languages. Inf. Sci. **31**(1), 77–89 (1983)
11. Ivanov, S., Verlan, S.: Random context and semi-conditional insertion-deletion systems. Fundamenta Informaticae **138**, 127–144 (2015)
12. Jančar, P., Mráz, F., Plátek, M., Vogel, J.: Restarting automata. In: Reichel, H. (ed.) FCT 1995. LNCS, vol. 965, pp. 283–292. Springer, Heidelberg (1995). doi:10.1007/3-540-60249-6_60
13. Kari, L., Păun, G., Thierrin, G., Yu, S.: At the crossroads of DNA computing, formal languages: characterizing recursively enumerable languages using insertion-deletion systems. In: Rubin, H., Wood, D.H. (eds.) DNA Based Computers III. DIMACS Series in Discrete Mathematics and Theretical Computer Science, vol. 48, pp. 329–338 (1999)
14. Kari, L., Sosík, P.: On the weight of universal insertion grammars. Theoret. Comput. Sci. **396**(1–3), 264–270 (2008)
15. Kari, L., Thierrin, G.: Contextual insertions/deletions and computability. Inf. Comput. **131**(1), 47–61 (1996)
16. Krassovitskiy, A.: On the power of insertion P systems of small size. In: Martínez del Amor, M.A., Orejuela-Pinedo, E.F., Păun, G., Pérez-Hurtado, I., Riscos-Núñez, A. (eds.) Seventh Brainstorming Week on Membrane Computing, vol. II, pp. 29–43. Fénix Editora, Sevilla (2009)
17. Kuppusamy, L., Mahendran, A.: Modelling DNA and RNA secondary structures using matrix insertion-deletion systems. Int. J. Appl. Math. Comput. Sci. **26**(1), 245–258 (2016)
18. Marcus, M., Păun, G.: Regulated Galiukschov semicontextual grammars. Kybernetika **26**(4), 316–326 (1990)
19. Margenstern, M., Păun, G., Rogozhin, Y., Verlan, S.: Context-free insertion-deletion systems. Theoret. Comput. Sci. **330**(2), 339–348 (2005)
20. Matveevici, A., Rogozhin, Y., Verlan, S.: Insertion-deletion systems with one-sided contexts. In: Durand-Lose, J., Margenstern, M. (eds.) MCU 2007. LNCS, vol. 4664, pp. 205–217. Springer, Heidelberg (2007). doi:10.1007/978-3-540-74593-8_18
21. Motwani, R., Panigrahy, R., Saraswat, V., Ventkatasubramanian, S.: On the decidability of accessibility problems (extended abstract). In: Proceedings of the Thirty-Second Annual ACM Symposium on Theory of Computing, STOC, pp. 306–315. ACM (2000)
22. Mutyam, M., Krithivasan, K., Reddy, A.S.: On characterizing recursively enumerable languages by insertion grammars. Fundamenta Informaticae **64**(1–4), 317–324 (2005)
23. Onodera, K.: A note on homomorphic representation of recursively enumerable languages with insertion grammars. Trans. Inf. Process. Soc. Japan **44**(5), 1424–1427 (2003)
24. Petre, I., Verlan, S.: Matrix insertion-deletion systems. Theoret. Comput. Sci. **456**, 80–88 (2012)
25. Păun, G., Pérez-Jiménez, M.J., Yokomori, T.: Representations and characterizations of languages in Chomsky hierarchy by means of insertion-deletion systems. Int. J. Found. Comput. Sci. **19**(4), 859–871 (2008)
26. Păun, G., Rozenberg, G., Salomaa, A.: DNA Computing: New Computing Paradigms. Springer, New York (1998)
27. Takahara, A., Yokomori, T.: On the computational power of insertion-deletion systems. Nat. Comput. **2**(4), 321–336 (2003)
28. Verlan, S.: On minimal context-free insertion-deletion systems. J. Autom. Lang. Comb. **12**(1–2), 317–328 (2007)

Deduplication on Finite Automata and Nested Duplication Systems

Da-Jung Cho, Yo-Sub Han[(✉)], and Hwee Kim

Department of Computer Science, Yonsei University, 50 Yonsei-Ro, Seodaemun-Gu,
Seoul 03722, Republic of Korea
{dajungcho,emmous,kimhwee}@yonsei.ac.kr

Abstract. Motivated by work on bio-operations on DNA sequences, a
string duplication system S consists of an initial string over Σ and a set
of duplication functions that iteratively generate new strings from existing strings in the system. As the main result we introduce the concept of
a deduplication—a reverse function of duplication—on an nondeterministic finite-state automaton (NFA) and propose the deduplication operation on an NFA that transforms a given NFA to a smaller NFA while
generating the same language in the string duplication system. Then,
we introduce a nested duplication, which is similar to tandem duplication but depends on the information of the nested duplication in the
previous step. We propose an NFA construction for an arbitrary nested
duplication system, analyze its properties and present an algorithm that
computes the system capacity.

Keywords: Bio-inspired operations · Tandem duplication · String
duplication systems · Capacity · Automata theory

1 Introduction

A tandem duplication—a subsequence of a DNA sequence is placed next to the
original position of a DNA sequence—occurs during DNA replication, indeed,
more than half of the human genome consists of repetitive sequences [4]. Tandem duplications are well-studied in both DNA computing and formal language
theory. From a formal language framework, a tandem duplication of a string xyz
generates a new string $xyyz$, where $x, y, z \in \Sigma^*$. Many researchers [1–3,7,8,11,
13,15–17,20] considered the duplication operation and investigated their properties under formal language theory. Searls [17] introduced a formal representation
of DNA recombination events. Dassow et al. [2,3] and Ito et al. [7] considered the
duplication operation and investigated their closure properties of languages in
the Chomsky hierarchy. Several researchers [8,11,13,14] considered (uniformly-)
bounded duplication, which has an restriction on the length of duplicated factor and investigated closure properties with several conditions on the size of
alphabet and length of duplicated factor. Both Martín-Vide and Păun [15] and
Mitrana and Rozenberg [16] investigated the generative power of context-free

© Springer International Publishing AG 2017
M.J. Patitz and M. Stannett (Eds.): UCNC 2017, LNCS 10240, pp. 194–205, 2017.
DOI: 10.1007/978-3-319-58187-3_15

and context-sensitive duplication grammars. Recently, Cho et al. [1] defined an extended variant of duplication and investigated their closure properties.

From an information theory viewpoint, Jain et al. [9] and Farnoud et al. [5] investigated the *string duplication system* that generates all strings obtained by applying the duplication function to an initial string a finite number of times, and computed the exact or bounded capacity of duplication systems considering several different alphabets, initial string and length of duplication. They suggested a concept of the *deduplication operation*, which is a reverse function of a duplication operation, on a regular expression.

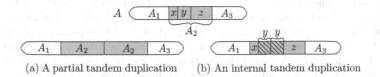

(a) A partial tandem duplication   (b) An internal tandem duplication

Fig. 1. Given a gene sequence $A = A1A2A3$, (a) an internal tandem duplication duplicates a subsequence y generating $A1xyyzA3$, internal to $A2$, (b) a partial duplication duplicates a junction $A2$ to the end of $A2$.

In molecular biology, a tandem duplication is classified to a *partial tandem duplication* (PTD) or an *internal tandem duplication* (ITD) [18]. Figure 1 shows an example of partial and internal tandem duplications on a gene. The internal tandem duplication has an restriction on the position of duplicated factor, and it motivates us to define a *nested duplication*, which can be viewed as a generalization of an internal tandem duplication. A nested duplication considers the position and the size of the duplication segment of the previous duplications while general tandem duplications occur independently. Figure 2 shows that when duplication segments overlap each other, the size of nested duplication segments decreases over time whereas tandem duplication segments do not. Note that the size of a nested duplication segment is dependent on the nested duplication segment of the previous duplication step.

We can compute the capacity of a language L using Perron-Frobenius theory [6] if L is regular, or Chomsky-Schützenberger enumeration theorem [10] if L is unambiguously context-free. However, the language generated from a tandem duplication system turns out to be context-free in general cases [14]. On the other hand, a nested duplication system with an arbitrary seed and (fixed) duplication lengths always gives a regular language L even with the expanded cases of seed and duplication length.

We suggest the concept of deduplication on NFAs that reduces the size of an NFA while maintaining the same resulting language from the duplication system and give a formal construction, which was implicit in the previous research [9]. Then, we suggest an NFA construction that recognizes the language generated from a nested duplication system, and prove that there exists the case when the constructed NFA is the minimal DFA. We also propose an algorithm that computes the capacity of a nested duplication system using the construction.

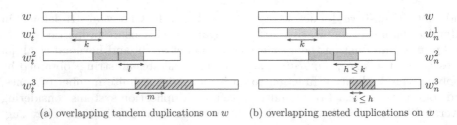

(a) overlapping tandem duplications on w (b) overlapping nested duplications on w

Fig. 2. An example of overlapping tandem and nested duplications on an initial string w of length n. Let w_t^i be the string generated by the ith tandem duplication from w, and w_n^i be the string generated by the ith nested duplication from w, where $i = \{1, 2, 3\}$. (a) For a string w, a tandem duplication segment of length k is duplicated w_t^1, where $k \leq n$. The second and third duplications, w_t^2 and w_t^3, show that a duplication segment that overlaps the previous duplication segment is not dependent to the size of previously duplicated segment. (b) A nested duplication segment of length k is duplicated w_n^1, where $k \leq n$. The second and the third nested duplications have a smaller fragment size than the first and the second duplications, respectively. In other words, let h, i be the size of the second and the third duplication fragment, respectively. Then, $1 \leq i \leq h \leq k \leq n$.

2 Preliminaries

The reader may refer to Wood [19] for more knowledge in finite automata and formal languages. The symbol Σ denotes a finite alphabet, Σ^* is the set of strings over Σ, $|w|$ is the length of a string $w \in \Sigma^*$ and λ is the empty string. A string $x = x[1]x[2] \cdots x[n] \in \Sigma^n$ is a finite sequence of n symbols over $x[i] \in \Sigma$. We denote a string $x = x[1] \cdots x[n]$ by $x[1 : n]$ according to indices of each characters of x. For two strings $x = x[1 : n]$ and $y = y[1 : m]$ we denote the *catenation* of x and y by $x[1 : n] \cdot y[1 : m]$. We use w^n to denote the string resulted from catenation of n consecutive w's. We refer to a string $x \in \mathbb{N}^n$ as a *natural number array*, or simply an array, where $\mathbb{N}$ is the set of non-negative integers. A nondeterministic finite-state automaton (NFA) is a tuple $M = (Q, \Sigma, \delta, q_0, F)$, where Q is the finite set of states, Σ is the alphabet, $\delta \subseteq Q \times \Sigma \rightarrow 2^Q$ is the multivalued transitions function, $q_0 \in Q$ is the initial state and $F \subseteq Q$ is the set of final states. Note that we can regard states as vertices and $\delta(p, a) = q$ as a labeled directed edge between two vertices p and q. Let $|Q|$ be the number of states in Q and $|\delta|$ be the number of transitions in δ. Then, the size of M is $|M| = |Q| + |\delta|$. Given a transition $\delta(p, a) = q$, we say that q has an *in-transition* and p has an *out-transition*. A string w is accepted by A if there is a labeled path from q_0 to a final state and we call this path an *accepting path*. The language accepted by M is $L(M) = \{w \in \Sigma^* \mid \delta(q_0, w) \cap F \neq \emptyset\}$. The automaton M is a deterministic finite-state automaton (DFA) if δ is a single valued partial function. A sequence $q_0, q_1, \cdots, q_n$ of states denotes a *path*, and a path has a *cycle* if it has an occurrence of the same state twice in the path. We define the *size* of a cycle by the number of distinct states in the cycle.

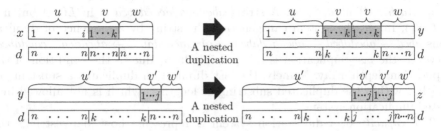

Fig. 3. An example of nested duplications on $x = uvw$, where $|u| = i, |v| = k, |x| = n$, and $d[1 : n] = n \cdots n$. A substring $v = x[i{+}1 : i{+}k]$ is duplicated if $d[i{+}1] \geq k$, which implies that $x = uvw$ transforms into $y = uvvw$ and the corresponding array d is updated as $d[i{+}1 : 2k] = k^{2k}$. From $y = u'v'w'$, a nested duplication of length j occurs on the position $i' + 1$ of y, where $|u'| = i', |v'| = j$ and $d[i' + 1] \geq j$. Then, the corresponding array $d[i'{+}1 : i'{+}j]$ is updated to j^{2j}.

A *tandem duplication* function $\mathbb{D}_{i,k}^{tan}$ is defined as follows:

$$\mathbb{D}_{i,k}^{tan}(x) = \begin{cases} uvvw & \text{for } x = uvw, |u| = i, |v| = k, \\ x & \text{otherwise.} \end{cases}$$

Note that $\mathbb{D}_{i,k}^{tan}(x)$ allows substring of length k starting at position $i + 1$ to be duplicated next to its original position. Similarly, $\mathbb{D}_{\leq k}^{tan}$ allows substring of length at most k to be duplicated.

We propose a new duplication function called the *nested duplication*. A nested duplication function has two inputs—a string x to duplicate and an array d indicating the duplication depth of each character in the string (See Fig. 3 for an example). The function $\mathbb{D}_{i,k}^{nes}$ is defined as follows:

$$\mathbb{D}_{i,k}^{nes}(x, d) = \begin{cases} (uvvw, d[1 : |u|] \cdot |v|^{2|v|} \cdot d[|u|+|v|+1 : |x|]) \\ \quad \text{for } x = uvw, |u| = i, |v| = k, \\ \quad d[j] \geq |v| \text{ for } |u| + 1 \leq j \leq |u| + |v|, \\ (x, d) \text{ otherwise.} \end{cases}$$

A *string duplication system* consists of three tuples $S = (\Sigma, s, \tau)$, where $s \in \Sigma^*$ is a finite length string called *seed*, an initial string of finite length, and τ is the set of rules that generate new strings from existing strings in the system [5]. We call the set of all strings generated by the system S *the language generated by the system*, and denote the language by $L(S)$. In the rest of paper, the nested duplication function $\mathbb{D}_{\leq k}^{nes}$ refers to the rule τ, and the term *nested duplication system* refers to the string duplication system over nested duplication function. We assume that the duplication length array for the seed is initialized as $|s|$ for all indices. We call a system $S = (\Sigma, s, \mathbb{D}_{\leq k}^{nes})$ a *bounded system* if $k \leq n$. We extend the nested duplication system to a language $S = (\Sigma, L, \mathbb{D}_{\leq k}^{nes})$ that generates all duplicated strings from a given initial language L. Note that $L(\Sigma, s, \mathbb{D}_{\leq k}^{nes}) \subseteq L(\Sigma, s, \mathbb{D}_{\leq k}^{nes})$. For example, let $S_1 = (\{a, b, c, d\}, abcd, \mathbb{D}_{\leq 4}^{nes})$ and

$S_2 = (\{a, b, c, d\}, abcd, \mathbb{D}_{\leq 4}^{tan})$. A string $abcdacadacacdabcd$ is in $L(S_2)$ but not in $L(S_1)$. In S_2, the system can generate the string by a sequence of duplications $abcd \rightarrow abcdabcd \rightarrow abcdacdabcd \rightarrow abcdacacdabcd \rightarrow abcdacadacacdabcd$. However, the last duplication is not possible in S_1 due to the condition of the duplication depth array. Namely, the last duplication duplicates a substring of length 4 within the duplicated substring of length 2, which is not allowed in a nested duplication system.

The *capacity* of a duplication system S represents how many strings the system produces compared to Σ^n, where n goes to infinity, and it is defined by

$$\operatorname{cap}(S) = \lim_{n \to \infty} \sup \frac{\log_{|\Sigma|} |S \cap \Sigma^n|}{n}.$$

3 $\mathbb{D}$-Cycle Deduplication on Finite Automata

A duplication (both tandem and nested) on a string $w = xyz$ allows a substring y to be duplicated next to its original position in w and generate a string $w' = xyyz$, where $x, y, z \in \Sigma^*$. A *deduplication* of length k is an operation that transforms a substring yy into y, where $|y| = k$. Namely, a deduplication of $w' = xyyz$ is $w = xyz$. The operation was defined in various names by researchers [7,12]. Note that both duplication systems with the same duplication rule and different seeds w' and w generates the same language, where $|w'| > |w|$. Based on these aspects, a deduplication on a language is defined as follows: Given a language L_1, $L_1 \xrightarrow{dd_{\leq k}} L_2$ denotes a deduplication on L_1 when two duplication systems with duplication length up to k and two seeds L_1 and L_2 are same, and there is a metric $\mathbb{S}$ to measure the size of the language such that $\mathbb{S}(L_1) > \mathbb{S}(L_2)$. For instance, $L(a^+)$ can be transformed into $L(a)$ by $L(a^+) \xrightarrow{dd_{\leq 3}} L(a)$ when the size of the language is measured by the number of states of the minimal DFA that recognizes the language.

Though a deduplication on a string is straightforward, it is hard to do a deduplication on infinite languages such as regular languages or context-free languages. Now, we introduce a special deduplication on an NFA called $\mathbb{D}$-*cycle deduplication* that transforms a given NFA to a smaller NFA while generating the same language in the duplication system by removing cycles in the NFA that satisfies special conditions. For the following description, we assume that a given NFA has no λ-transition and all states are reachable. For a cycle C in an NFA, we call the cycle $\mathbb{D}$-cycle if C satisfies the following conditions:

(i) The cycle C is defined by a sequence of states $(q_{in}, q_1', q_2', \ldots, q_i', q_{out}, q_1, q_2, \ldots, q_j, q_{in})$, where $i, j \geq 0$. All states except q_{in} and q_{out} have one in-transition from the previous state and one out-transition to the following state. The state q_{in} has more than one in-transition, which implies that there exists an in-transition from a state outside of the cycle. The state q_{out} has also more than one out-transition.

(ii) There exist positive integers k and l that satisfy the following conditions:
- (a) All paths of size $k + 1$ from q_{out} yield a same set of strings.
- (b) All paths of size $l + 1$ to q_{in} yield a same set of strings.
- (c) $k + l = j+1$.

We are now ready to introduce $\mathbb{D}$-cycle deduplication on an NFA (See Fig. 4 for an example).

Definition 1. *Given an NFA $M = (Q, \Sigma, \delta, s, F)$ with a $\mathbb{D}$-cycle $(q_{in}, q'_1, q'_2, \ldots,$*

$q'_i, q_{out}, q_1, q_2, \ldots, q_j, q_{in})$, we define a $\mathbb{D}$-cycle deduplication by $M \xrightarrow{\mathbb{D}^{-1}_{\leq h}} M'$, where $i + j = h$ to be

$$M' = (Q \setminus \{q_1, q_2, \ldots, q_j\}, \Sigma, \{\delta(p, \sigma) \to q \mid p, q \notin \{q_1, q_2, \ldots, q_j\}\}, s, F).$$

We say that the cycle $(q_{in}, q'_1, q'_2, \ldots, q'_i, q_{out}, q_1, q_2, \ldots, q_j, q_{in})$ is removed from M.

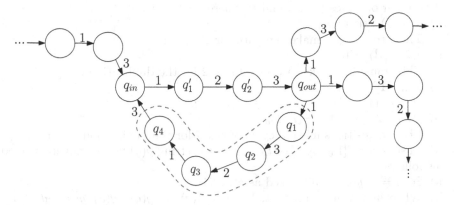

Fig. 4. An example of a $\mathbb{D}$-cycle $(q_{in}, q'_1, q'_2, q_{out}, q_1, q_2, q_3, q_4, q_{in})$. All states of the cycle except q_{in} and q_{out} have one in-transition from the previous state and one out-transition to the following state. All paths of size 4 from q_{out} yield the same string 132 and all paths of size 3 to q_{in} yield the same string 13. Also, the size of the path from q_{out} to q_{in} in the cycle is 6. Then, all states and transitions in the dashed line can be eliminated.

We use $\mathcal{S}(L(M)) = |M| = |Q| + |\delta|$. By this measure, it is straightforward that the size of the automaton is reduced. We now prove that the resulting automaton generates the same language in the tandem duplication system. Let $S^{tan}_{\leq h}(A) = (\Sigma, L(A), \mathbb{D}^{tan}_{\leq h})$ be the tandem duplication system for an NFA M.

Lemma 1. *Given an NFA $M = (Q, \Sigma, \delta, s, F)$ and its deduplication M' such that $M \xrightarrow{\mathbb{D}^{-1}_{\leq h}} M'$, $L(S^{tan}_{\leq h}(M)) = L(S^{tan}_{\leq h}(M'))$.*

From Lemma 1, we prove that $\mathbb{D}$-cycle deduplication satisfies the conditions of deduplication on a language. Using $\mathbb{D}$-cycle deduplication, we can reduce the size of the seed regular language for a tandem duplication system.

4   An NFA Construction for a Nested Duplication System

We introduce an NFA construction for a nested duplication system with an arbitrary seed and (fixed) duplication lengths. First, we show that the construction can be applied to a system with a designated set of duplication lengths, not only for a bounded system. Second, we show that the construction can be applied to a system with the maximum duplication length greater than the length of the seed. Then, we give a procedure of computing the capacity of a nested duplication system.

We first introduce an NFA construction for a nested duplication system with an arbitrary seed s and duplication length up to $k = |s|$. For a bounded nested duplication system $S = (\Sigma, s, \mathbb{D}_{\leq n}^{nes})$ where $|s| = n$, we define an NFA $M_S = (Q, \Sigma, \delta, 0_0, \{n_0\})$ as follows: The set of states is defined as $Q = \{q = l[1]_{d[1]} l[2]_{d[2]} \cdots l[t]_{d[t]} \mid 1 \leq t \leq n, d[1] = 0, d[i] = n - i + 2, l[i] < d[i]$ for $2 \leq i \leq n\}$, and transitions are defined by the following.

(i) For a pair of states $(i-1)_0$ and i_0 where $1 \leq i \leq n$,
   (a) $\delta((i-1)_0, s[i]) = i_0$.
   These transitions make the path for the seed.
   (b) $\delta(2_0, s[1]) = 1_0$.
   This transition makes a cycle of size 2 for the duplication of $s[1 : 2]$.
   (c) $\delta(i_0, s[1]) = i_0 1_i$.
   (d) $\delta(i_0(j-1)_i, s[j]) = i_0 j_i$ for $1 \leq j \leq i - 2$.
   (e) $\delta(i_0(i-2)_i, s[i-1]) = (i-1)_0$.
   These transitions make a cycle of size i for the duplication of $s[1 : i]$.
(ii) For a state $q = l[1]_0 l[2]_{d[2]} \cdots l[t]_{d[t]}$, let the string $y(q)$ be recursively defined as follows:
   (a) For $i = 1$, $y(q)$ is initialized as $s[1 : l[1]]$.
   (b) While increasing i up to t, let new $y(q)$ be $y(q) \cdot y(q)[|y(q)|-d[i]+1 : |y(q)|-d[i]+l[i]]$.
   For example, if $s = abcd$ and $q = 4_0 2_4 1_3$, then $y(q) = abcdabd$.
   Then, for an integer $d' \leq n$,
   (a) $\delta(q, y(q)[|y(q)|-d'+1]) = l[1]_0 l[2]_{d[2]} \cdots l[t]_{d[t]} 1_{d'}$ when $d' < d[t]$ or $t = 1$.
   (b) $\delta(l[1]_0 l[2]_{d[2]} \cdots l[t]_{d[t]} (j-1)_{d'}, y(q)[|y(q)|-d'+j]) = l[1]_0 l[2]_{d[2]} \cdots l[t]_{d[t]} j_{d'}$ for $2 \leq j \leq d' - 1$.
   (c) $\delta(l[1]_0 l[2]_{d[2]} \cdots l[t]_{d[t]} (d'-1)_{d'}, y(q)[|y(q)|]) = q$.
   These transitions make a cycle of size $d' < d[t]$ for the duplication of a string $y(q)$.
   (d) $\delta(q, y(q)[|y(q)|]) = q$ except for $q = 0_0$.
   These transitions make a self loop for the duplication of single character.

We give a description for the semantics of the states. For a state $q = l[1]_{d[1]} l[2]_{d[2]} \cdots l[t]_{d[t]}$, t represents the depth of a duplication. For each depth i, there can be arbitrary many duplications of length $d[i]$, and $l[i]$ represents how many characters are so far duplicated by the last duplication in depth i. Note that $d[i] > d[i+1]$ for $i > 1$, which indicates that the duplication length decreases as the depth increases. This property indicates that the automaton accepts the language generated from a nested duplication system, not a tandem duplication system. The first length $d[1]$ is always 0, which indicates the original seed. Once the construction is given, $y(q)$ is equal to the string that is yielded by the shortest path from the start state. For a state q, we define the *largest duplication length (LDL)* to be the size of the largest simple cycle that includes the state. If $q = l[1]_0$, then $LDL(q) = l[1] + 1$ except for the start state, where $LDL(0_0) = 0$. In all other cases, $LDL(q) = d[t]$ (See Fig. 5 for an example).

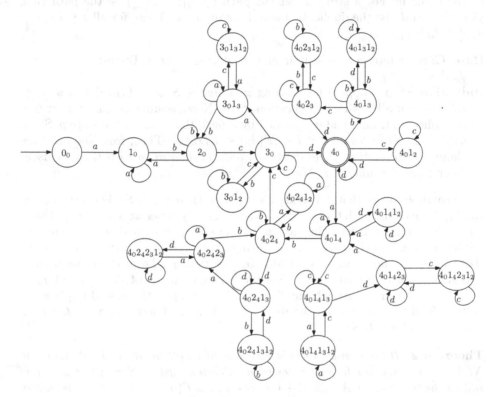

Fig. 5. An example of an NFA $M_S = (Q, \Sigma, \delta, 0_0, \{4_0\})$ for $S = (\Sigma, abcd, \mathbb{D}_{\leq 4}^{nes})$. Note that $y(4_0 2_4 1_3) = abcdabd$, which is equal to the string that is yielded by the shortest path from the start state. Also note that $LDL(3_0) = 4$ and $LDL(4_0 1_4 1_3) = 3$.

Theorem 1. *For a string s of length n, the NFA $M_S = (Q, \Sigma, \delta, 0_0, \{n_0\})$ recognizes the language generated by the nested duplication system $S = (\Sigma, s, \mathbb{D}_{\leq n}^{nes})$. Namely, $L(M_S) = L(S)$.*

Proof. We first prove that if a string $x \in L(S)$, then $x \in L(M_S)$. We start from the following claim:

Claim. For a state q in Q, let y be a string yielded by a path of length less than or equal to $LDL(q)$ that ends at q. Then there always exists a cyclic path from q to q that yields y.

We have two observations from the construction: First, for each string y yielded by a non-cyclic path p of length less than or equal to $LDL(q)$ to q, there always exists a cyclic path p' from q to q that yields y. Second, for each string y' yielded by a cyclic path p_c of length less than or equal to $LDL(q)$ with a state in p, there always exists a cyclic path p'_c that yields y with a state in p'. From two observations, we know that the claim holds.

Now, we use induction on the duplication step of x. We add another claim to the theorem: For a string x, let the path $(q_0, q_1, \ldots, q_{|x|})$ be the path that yields x and d_x be the duplication length array for x. Then, for all $1 \leq i \leq |x|$, $d_x[i] \leq LDL(q_i)$.

Base Case. Suppose $x = s$. It implies that $x \in L(M_S)$. For all $1 \leq i \leq |x|$, $d_x[i] = LDL(q_i) = n$.

Inductive Step. Suppose for a string $x = uvz \in S$, $x \in L(M_S)$ and $d_x[i] \leq LDL(q_i)$ for all x with k duplication steps. Now, assume that $x' = uvvz \in S$ is duplicated from x and v is yielded by a path that ends at the state p. Since $d_x[i] \leq LDL(q_i)$ for all $1 \leq i \leq |x|$, $|v| \leq LDL(p)$. Thus, from the previous claim, we know that there exists a cyclic path from p to p that yields v. Therefore, $x' = uvvz \in L(M_S)$.

Second, we prove that if a string $x \in L(M_S)$, then $x \in L(S)$. For a string $x \in L(M_S)$, let p be the path that yields x. We recursively generate a series of paths p_i and strings x_i as follows: The path p_1 is the string generated by removing all self loops in p, and the path p_i is the string generated by removing all cycles of size i in p_{i-1}. The string x_i is yielded by the path p_i. From the construction, it is straightforward that $x_n = s$. Now, let d_i be an array of size $|x_i|$ and $d_n = n^n$. Then, we can successfully duplicate x_i from x_{i+1} in the nested duplication system S, since i represents the duplication length. Therefore, $x_i \in L(S)$ for $1 \leq i \leq n$ and $x \in L(S)$.   □

Theorem 2. *If all characters in a string s of length n are distinct, then the NFA M_S constructed from the nested duplication system $S = (\Sigma, s, \mathbb{D}_{\leq n}^{nes})$ is indeed the minimal DFA with $n! + 1$ states and $en\Gamma(n, 1) + 1$ transitions, where Γ is the partial Gamma function.*

Proof. Let s be a string where $s[i] \neq s[j]$ if $i \neq j$. Note that the number of out-transitions from a state q is equal to $LDL(q)$. Thus, if $LDL(p) \neq LDL(q)$, then p and q are distinct. We also observe that for any simple cycle in M_S, all transitions in the cycle have pairwise distinct labels. Thus, any pair of states in a simple cycle (with the same LDL) is distinct. Now, suppose there are two states p and q where $LDL(p) = LDL(q)$, p and q are in a different simple cycle and p and q are equivalent. Then there should be two paths from p and q that end at the same state r and yields the same string. Since all characters in s are pairwise distinct, states before r in two paths should have different LDLs. Then, there exists two paths from p and q that end at distinct states and yield the same string. Thus, p and q are distinct.

We now compute the number of states and transitions in M_S by induction on a given n. We call the constructed DFA $M_S(n)$.

Base Case. For $n = 2$, $|Q| = 3 = 2! + 1$ and $|\delta| = 5 = 2e \times \frac{2}{e} + 1$.

Inductive Step. Assume that the statement holds for $n = k$. For $n = k + 1$, there exists one simple cycle of size $k + 1$ in the DFA, where each state in the cycle has the same topologic structure as $M_S(k)$ without 0_0. Therefore, the number of the states becomes $(k + 1)(k! + 1 - 1) + 1 = (k + 1)! + 1$, and the number of the transitions becomes $(k + 1)(ek\Gamma(k, 1) + 1 - 1) + (k + 1) + 1 = (k + 1)e(k\Gamma(k, 1) + \frac{1}{e}) - (k + 1) + (k + 1) + 1 = (k + 1)e\Gamma(k + 1, 1) + 1$. □

Theorem 2 shows that there exists a case where M_S is the minimal DFA that recognizes $L(S)$. Note that for all other cases, where there exist i, j such that $w[i] = w[j]$, M_S is an NFA.

The construction of M_S for the system S can be generalized to the following cases:

1. The seed can be given as a finite seed language. Since L is finite, we can construct NFAs for all strings in L and make an union NFA for S.
2. The bound k can be generalized to any positive integer. When $k \leq |s|$ and all characters in a string s of length n are distinct, the NFA M_S becomes the minimal DFA with $k!(n = k + 1) + 1$ states and $ek(n - k + 1)\Gamma(k, 1) + n - k + 1$ transitions, where n is the length of the seed.
3. The duplication length can be given as a set $\mathcal{L}$ of possible duplication lengths, not an inequality. Suppose $k_i \leq n$ and $k_{i-1} < k_i$ for $L = \{k_i\}$, $2 \leq i \leq m = |L|$. If all characters in a string s of length n are distinct, the NFA M_S becomes the minimal DFA with $(n - k_m + 1)k_m \prod_{i=1}^{m-1}(k_i - 1) +$

$$\sum_{i=1}^{m-1}\left(k_i\alpha_i \prod_{j=1}^{i-1}(k_j - 1)\right) + k_1 - 1 \text{ states and } k_m(n - k_m + 1) + \sum_{i=1}^{m-1}$$

$$\left(k_i\left((n - k_m + 1)k_m \prod_{j=1}^{i-1}(k_j - 1) + \sum_{j=1}^{i-1}\left(k_j\alpha_j \prod_{l=1}^{j-1}(k_l - 1)\right) + \alpha_i\right)\right) + n - m$$

transitions, where

$$\alpha_i = \begin{cases} 1 & \text{if} k_{i+1} - k_i > 1, \\ 0 & \text{otherwise.} \end{cases}$$

Using the construction, we can design an algorithm to compute the capacity of S. Once the NFA M_S is generated, we first construct an equivalent DFA by the subset construction, and modify the DFA so that the DFA has at most one transition for every pair of states. This modification can be done by making copies of states that have multiple in-transitions from a state. From the resulting DFA, we can compute the capacity of the language recognized by the DFA using Perron-Frobenius Theory [6, 9].

Procedure. ComputeCap(s)

1 Construct an NFA M_S for $S = (\Sigma, s, \mathbb{D}_{\leq n}^{tan})$. /* s is a seed of length n */
2 Convert M_S to a DFA M', where there exists at most one transition for every pair of states.
3 Find the maximal connected component in M' and compute its adjacency matrix M.
4 Return the maximum eigenvalue of M.

5 Conclusions

We have suggested the concept of deduplications—removing duplications—in an NFA and proposed an example of deduplications. Then, we have proposed a new duplication operation called the nested duplication: The operation is motivated by the internal tandem duplication phenomenon, which restricts the duplication length and position according to the previous duplication step. For a nested duplication system, we proposed an NFA construction that recognizes the system, and proved that this construction can be expanded to systems with various conditions. Using the constructed NFA, we have also proposed a procedure to compute the capacity of the given nested duplication system.

Although the concept of deduplications in an NFA is proposed, it is still open to find more duplication conditions applicable in an NFA. Finding deduplication conditions for other classes of FA, including pushdown automata, is one of the future works. For the nested duplication system, the tight bound of the size of the minimal DFA is an open problem. Inspection of subword closure properties on a nested duplication system is also one of the possible future works.

References

1. Cho, D.-J., Han, Y.-S., Kim, H., Palioudakis, A., Salomaa, K.: Duplications and pseudo-duplications. Int. J. Unconv. Comput. **12**, 145–167 (2016)
2. Dassow, J., Mitrana, V., Paun, G.: On the regularity of duplication closure. Bull. EATCS **69**, 133–136 (1999)
3. Dassow, J., Mitrana, V., Salomaa, A.: Operations and language generating devices suggested by the genome evolution. Theoret. Comput. Sci. **270**(1–2), 701–738 (2002)
4. de Koning, A.J., Gu, W., Castoe, T.A., Batzer, M.A., Pollock, D.D.: Repetitive elements may comprise over two-thirds of the human genome. PLoS Genet. **7**(12), e1002384 (2011)
5. Farnoud, F., Schwartz, M., Bruck, J.: The capacity of string-duplication systems. IEEE Trans. Inf. Theory **62**(2), 811–824 (2016)
6. Immink, K.: Codes for Mass Data Storage Systems. Shannon Foundation Publishers, Denver (2004)
7. Ito, M., Kari, L., Kincaid, Z., Seki, S.: Duplication in DNA sequences. In: Ito, M., Toyama, M. (eds.) DLT 2008. LNCS, vol. 5257, pp. 419–430. Springer, Heidelberg (2008). doi:10.1007/978-3-540-85780-8_33

8. Ito, M., Leupold, P., Shikishima-Tsuji, K.: Closure of language classes under bounded duplication. In: Ibarra, O.H., Dang, Z. (eds.) DLT 2006. LNCS, vol. 4036, pp. 238–247. Springer, Heidelberg (2006). doi:10.1007/11779148_22

9. Jain, S., Farnoud, F., Bruck, J.: Capacity and expressiveness of genomic tandem duplication. In: Proceedings of the 23rd IEEE International Symposium on Information Theory, pp. 1946–1950 (2015)

10. Kuich, W., Salomaa, A.: Semirings, Automata and Languages. Springer, New York, Inc. (1985)

11. Leupold, P.: Languages generated by iterated idempotencies. Ph.D. thesis, University Rovira i Virgili (2006)

12. Leupold, P.: Duplication roots. In: Harju, T., Karhumäki, J., Lepistö, A. (eds.) DLT 2007. LNCS, vol. 4588, pp. 290–299. Springer, Heidelberg (2007). doi:10.1007/978-3-540-73208-2_28

13. Leupold, P., Martín-Vide, C., Mitrana, V.: Uniformly bounded duplication languages. Discret. Appl. Math. 146(3), 301–310 (2005)

14. Leupold, P., Mitrana, V., Sempere, J.M.: Formal languages arising from gene repeated duplication. In: Jonoska, N., Păun, G., Rozenberg, G. (eds.) Aspects of Molecular Computing. LNCS, vol. 2950, pp. 297–308. Springer, Heidelberg (2003). doi:10.1007/978-3-540-24635-0_22

15. Martín-Vide, C., Păun, G.: Duplication grammars. Acta Cybern. 14(1), 151–164 (1999)

16. Mitrana, V., Rozenberg, G.: Some properties of duplication grammars. Acta Cybern. 14(1), 165–177 (1999)

17. Searls, D.B.: The computational linguistics of biological sequences. Artif. Intell. Mol. Biol. 2, 47–120 (1993)

18. Swanson, L., Robertson, G., Mungall, K.L., Butterfield, Y.S., Chiu, R., Corbett, R.D., Docking, T.R., Hogge, D., Jackman, S.D., Moore, R.A., et al.: Barnacle: detecting and characterizing tandem duplications and fusions in transcriptome assemblies. BMC Genom. 14(1), 550 (2013)

19. Wood, D.: Theory of Computation. Wiley, New York (1987)

20. Yokomori, T., Kobayashi, S.: DNA evolutionary linguistics, RNA structure modeling: a computational approach. In: Proceedings of the 1st International Symposium on Intelligence in Neural and Biological Systems, pp. 38–45 (1995)

Descrambling Order Analysis in Ciliates

Nazifa Azam Khan[(✉)] and Ian McQuillan

Department of Computer Science, University of Saskatchewan,
Saskatoon, SK, Canada
nak310@mail.usask.ca, mcquillan@cs.usask.ca

Abstract. Certain genera of ciliates undergo a large genomic transformation, where many segments get rearranged and removed. A topic of interest is to predict a (partial) order on the rearrangement of segments to descramble. Similar to phylogenetic analysis, this prediction can be based on the principle of parsimony, whereby the smallest sequence of operations is likely close to the actual number. The *Oxytricha trifallax* genome is analyzed, providing evidence that multiple parallel recombination operations occur during descrambling, with alignment of interleaving segments in a manner that can be captured with the shuffle operation. Two similar systems involving shuffle are created, an optimal algorithm for each is created, and executed on the genomic data. One system can descramble 96.63% of the scrambled micronuclear chromosome fragments by 1 or 2 applications of shuffle, and every sequence can be descrambled with at most seven operations.

Keywords: Ciliates · Macronucleus · Micronucleus · Scrambled genes · Shuffle · Parsimony

1 Introduction

Ciliated protozoa are a group of unicellular organisms, where each cell has two types of nuclei; the *micronucleus* (MIC) and the *macronucleus* (MAC). When two cells mate, they exchange haploid micronuclei, destroy their own macronuclei, and then develop a new MAC from the genetic material in the new MIC. In the MIC of stichotrichs (a group of ciliates), less than 5% of the DNA actually encodes genes, with a large amount of non-coding DNA both between genes, and also within genes. In contrast, the MAC largely consists of single gene chromosomes, and the intragenic spacer is not present. Indeed, certain segments get removed when converting to MAC chromosomes, called *internal eliminated segments* (IESs), while certain segments remain, called *macronuclear destined segments* (MDSs); see Fig. 1. Even stranger, many genes have the MDSs in a different order between the MIC and MAC version of a gene, and these MDSs become rearranged, or descrambled, during the conversion of the MIC to the MAC in a process known as the gene assembly process [17].

I. McQuillan—Supported, in part, by a grant from the Natural Sciences and Engineering Council of Canada.

M.J. Patitz and M. Stannett (Eds.): UCNC 2017, LNCS 10240, pp. 206–219, 2017.
DOI: 10.1007/978-3-319-58187-3_16

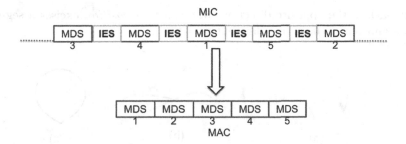

Fig. 1. Simplified conversion of a MAC chromosome fragment from a MIC chromosome fragment.

The process of gene assembly is a fascinating example of computing taking place in nature [17]. An extensive amount of parallel computation occurs during the gene assembly process. In fact, descrambling MDSs is a computationally hard problem, as even the problem of aligning a micronuclear gene to a macronuclear gene to partition it into segments is an NP-complete problem [8], meaning that very likely no optimal polynomial time algorithm exists to solve it. Knowledge about how nature is solving these computationally complex problems may assist computer scientists to construct new algorithms and techniques, and conversely, computational results could be used to infer biological conclusions.

There are a variety of biological and computational models and hypotheses that have been created to explain the gene assembly process in ciliates. Originally, a model known as the intermolecular model viewed this gene descrambling as a computational process, consisting of one intramolecular and two intermolecular operations of DNA recombination on pointers [10]. Another theoretical model for gene assembly, known as the intramolecular model was introduced by Prescott et al. [16] and Ehrenfeucht et al. [5]. It consists of three unary molecular operations based on pointers: loop excision, hairpin excision, and double loop deletion, that explains IES excision and MDS rearrangements during gene assembly. In 2009, the notion of assembly graphs was introduced to model the DNA structure during the recombination process [1]. They introduced another model in 2012 that describes rearrangement pathways of DNA recombination events with three rewriting rules: insertion, deletion, and inversion [2].

In 1980, Meyer et al. studied *Stylonychia mytilus* by means of electron microscopy and observed that at the very beginning of the gene assembly process, IESs are eliminated in the form of chromatin rings (loops) [12]. Then, micronuclear chromatin becomes organised into coiled, lampbrush patterns, or loop-like structures (Fig. 2) that might be a necessary prerequisite for later IES elimination and MDS rearrangement [13,14]. Chromatin consists of DNA that is tightly coiled around proteins called histones that condenses to form chromosomes. In 2008, Matthias et al. concluded that multiple descrambling pathways may produce functional macronuclear molecules [15], and that there are occurrences of multiple parallel inversion and transposition events through each pathway during assembly [15]. *Inversion* takes a particular segment of MDSs in a MIC gene and puts it back in the opposite direction, whereas *transposition* excises a segment of DNA and puts it back in a different position.

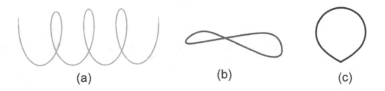

(a)   (b)   (c)

Fig. 2. Coiled structure (a) lampbrush pattern (b) loop, or ring shape (c).

The *Oxytricha trifallax* MIC genome has been recently sequenced, allowing for deeper analysis that what was previously possible. Very recently, Burns et al. investigated the scrambled gene architectures in the *Oxytricha trifallax* genome [3]. For scrambled genes, they identified the precursor scrambled patterns with so-called sequence rearrangement maps, and assembly graph representations. From their analysis of the MIC and MAC genes, they deduced that 87.2% of the MIC loci is non-scrambled, and among the scrambled MIC contigs, 81.7% follow a pattern involving either a sequence of consecutive odd numbered MDSs, followed by a sequence of consecutive even numbered MDSs, or vice versa [3]. These statistics are very similar to those we independently calculated [9].

The order of MDSs in the MIC genome provides evidence that multiple parallel transpositions occur, where the structure allows for interleaving between two sections that can be captured with a string operation called *shuffle*. The shuffle operation on two strings results in new strings by weaving together the first two, preserving the order within each string. For example, if $x = 2\ 4\ 5\ 6\ 7$ and $y = 1\ 3\ 8\ 9$ are two strings of numbers, then the shuffle of x and y is any permutation r of $1\ 2\ 3 \cdots 9$ where the order of the members of x and y is followed in r as well (for example $r = 2\ 4\ 1\ 3\ 5\ 6\ 7\ 8\ 9$). The sequences in Fig. 3a can be rearranged computationally by shuffle between two segments, $1\ 3\ 5\ 7\ 10\ 12$ and $2\ 4\ 6\ 8\ 9\ 11\ 13\ 14\ 15\ 16\ 17$, as $1\ 2\ 3 \cdots 17$ is one of the results of the shuffle of the two segments. Figure 3b is even more complex, but the result can be obtained by splitting the whole sequence into two segments and applying shuffle once.

Shuffle is nondeterministic, and therefore multiple strings can be in the shuffle of two strings, however it is thought that structural components allow the developing MAC to align in a shuffle-like fashion, similar to the coiled and lampbrush patterns in Fig. 2. Furthermore, the sheer number of genes that can be rearranged with very few applications — as seen in Sects. 3 and 4 — yields evidence that this type of behaviour is occurring.

Predicting the order to descramble a gene or chromosomal segment, can be based on the principle of parsimony, whereby the smallest sequence of operations is likely close to the actual number of operations that occurred [7,15]. The genome rearrangement problem similarly uses the principle of parsimony for predicting genomic rearrangement operations [7]. This is now a well-studied

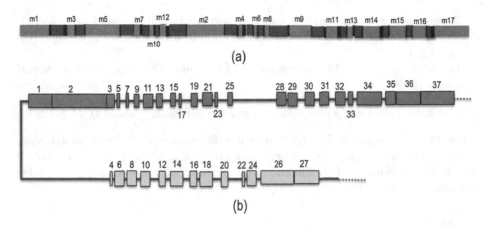

Fig. 3. (a) MDS organization found in the scrambled alpha-telomere-binding protein genes of *Oxytricha trifallax* [15]. (b) A schematic alignment of the micronuclear genes encoding the large catalytic subunit of DNA-polymerase α in *Oxytricha nova* [11] (inverted MDSs indicated by green MDSs). (Color figure online)

problem, and indeed is quite similar to gene assembly [6]. Similarly, maximum parsimony is also an established method for phylogeny reconstruction.

This study aims to determine the order of parallel rearrangements by examining the number of applications of shuffle needed to assemble MIC genes.

2   Preliminaries

First, some notation that is used will be described.

An *alphabet* is a finite, non-empty set of symbols. Given an alphabet A, A^* is the set of all words over A, and A^+ is the set of all non-empty words over A. Let $\mathbb{N}$ be the natural numbers. Let $n \in \mathbb{N}$. Then $\mathbb{Z}_+(n) = \{1, 2, \ldots, n\}$ and $\mathbb{Z}_-(n) = \{-n, \ldots, -1\}$, and $\mathbb{Z}_{+-}(n) = \mathbb{Z}_+(n) \cup \mathbb{Z}_-(n)$ (0 is not in this set). For $i \in \mathbb{Z}_{+-}(n)$, let $sgn(i)$ be $+1$ if $i > 0$ and -1 otherwise. It is also common to examine sequences of numbers represented in the form of words with numbers for the alphabet. Therefore, $\mathbb{Z}_{+-}(n)^+$ is the set of all non-empty strings over the alphabet $\mathbb{Z}_{+-}(n)$. A string $\pi = \pi_1 \cdots \pi_n, \pi_1, \ldots, \pi_n \in \mathbb{Z}_{+-}(n)$ is *positive* if $\pi \in \mathbb{Z}_+(n)^+$, and *negative* if $\pi \in \mathbb{Z}_-(n)^+$. Also, π is *increasing* if $\pi_1 < \pi_2 < \cdots < \pi_n$, and is *decreasing* if $\pi_1 > \pi_2 > \cdots > \pi_n$ (here, $<$ and $>$ are the usual orderings of the integers). A *subword* of π is any word $\pi_i \pi_{i+1} \cdots \pi_j, 1 \le i \le j \le n$. The *inversion* of π, π^I, is the string obtained by reversing π and switching the sign of each number (this is the reverse complement). For $i \in \mathbb{Z}_{+-}(n)$, let $\Psi(\pi, i)$ be the number of i's in π. If $\pi \in \mathbb{Z}_+(n)^+ \cup \mathbb{Z}_-(n)^+$, then let $\bar{\pi}$ be equal to π if π is positive, and the inversion of π if π is negative (by reversing the numbers and making them all positive). Then $\bar{\pi}$ is always positive for every such π. For $n \in \mathbb{N}$, let $id_n = 1\,2 \cdots n$, which we call the *identity permutation*.

A sequence $\pi \in \mathbb{Z}_{+-}(n)^+$ is called a *permutation* if, for each $i \in \mathbb{Z}_+(n)$, $\Psi(\pi, i) + \Psi(\pi, -i) = 1$. π is a partial permutation if, for each $i \in \mathbb{Z}_+(n)$, $\Psi(\pi, i) + \Psi(\pi, -i) \leq 1$.

Let $u, v \in \mathbb{Z}_{+-}(n)^+$ be two sequences of integers. Then the *shuffle* of u and v, $u \circ v$, is the set

$$\{x_1 y_1 x_2 y_2 \cdots x_r y_r \mid u = x_1 x_2 \cdots x_r, v = y_1 y_2 \cdots y_r, \ x_i, y_i \in \mathbb{Z}_{+-}(n)^*, 1 \leq i \leq r\}.$$

Given two words $u, v \in \mathbb{Z}_{+-}(n)^*$, u is a *subsequence* of v if $v = v_0 u_1 v_1 u_2 v_2 \cdots u_n v_n$, and $u = u_1 u_2 \cdots u_n$, where $u_i, v_i, v_0 \in \mathbb{Z}_{+-}(n)^*$, $1 \leq i \leq n$. Notice that in the definitions of shuffle and subsequence, the variables x_i, y_i, u_i refer to words of any length.

3   Data Preprocessing

The main purpose of this section is to preprocess the *Oxytricha trifallax* genome in order to obtain a sufficiently large data set for the analysis of parsimony. Although this does involve calculating some basic statistical properties of the genome, we refer to [3] for a more thorough investigation.

The data used was raw genome data from *Oxytricha trifallax* retrieved from NCBI on May 20, 2015 in the form of 22,363 MAC contigs and 25,720 MIC contigs (a contiguous sequence of DNA created by repeatedly assembling overlapping sequenced fragments of a chromosome). The procedure for determining the order of MDSs on the micronuclear chromosomes was chosen to be the same as Chen et al. [4] for the same purpose. The MAC contigs were aligned against the MIC contigs by using Nucleotide BLAST (parameters of [-ungapped -word_size 20 -outfmt 10]). For each MAC contig (almost all containing a single gene [4]), the MIC contig that matched with the lowest E-value (Expect value) was chosen and defined to be a *MAC/MIC sequence pair* (a MIC contig could then be matched with many MAC contigs). Of the 22,363 MAC contigs, only 9 of these sequences did not match with a MIC contig. Other MIC contigs that matched with lower scoring values were ignored as only the best matches were needed for the parsimony analysis.

Then, for each MAC contig, if n subwords matched a MIC contig, then a permutation of $1\ 2 \cdots n$ was determined giving the order of the matching segments on the matching MIC segment. The *MIC MDS sequence* of a MAC contig is the order of MDSs in the contig as determined by this procedure. Among the 22,354 matching sequences, the MIC MDS sequence of $18, 315$ MAC contigs were unscrambled of the form $1\ 2 \cdots n$ for some n, or equivalently, $-n\ -(n-1) \cdots -1$ (here the '$-$' sign represents that the MDS is oriented in the opposite direction). These are called the *unscrambled sequences*. There are 4039 other MAC contigs called the *scrambled sequences*.

Every scrambled sequence was divided into two categories: one with MDSs only in one direction, called the *unidirectional sequences* (2443 total) and those with MDSs in both direction, the *bidirectional sequences* (1596 total). Of the bidirectional sequences, each is divided into its two subsequences, one containing the non-inverted MDSs, and one containing the inverted subsequences. These were treated separately for the next part of the analysis and will be managed later. The set of unidirectional sequences produced is called the *extracted unidirectional sequences*. Then, the total number of scrambled sub-sequences for further analysis is 5635 (2443 scrambled unidirectional sequences, and 3192 scrambled extracted unidirectional sequences).

Next, the 5635 scrambled sequences were processed by collapsing all consecutive numbers, to one number (removing unused numbers). Henceforth, only these sequences will be used. This was done to investigate more about the scrambled patterns of the data. There is also some evidence that IESs between consecutive MDSs are removed first [15]. Of the 2443 unidirectional sequences after removing consecutive numbers from the unidirectional sequences, these are called *renumbered unidirectional sequences*, and of the 3192 extracted unidirectional sequences, after removing consecutive numbers, these are called *renumbered extracted unidirectional sequences*. Consecutive even-odd and odd-even patterns were common. Of the 2443 renumbered unidirectional sequences, there were 986 consecutive odd-even sequences, and, 985 consecutive even-odd sequences, and 472 others, called *complex scrambled sequences*. This is consistent with the analysis from [3]. From the 3192 renumbered extracted unidirectional sequences, there were 2443 unscrambled sequences, 280 consecutive odd-even sequences, 302 consecutive even-odd sequences, and 167 other complex scrambled sequences.

4   Parallel Descrambling Order Analysis

As discussed in Sect. 1, the patterns of the order of MDSs in micronuclear genes (Fig. 3) shows evidence of some parallel operations that can be computationally described with shuffle. The order of MDSs of a MIC chromosome corresponding to a MAC chromosome is represented by a permutation $\pi = \pi_1 \pi_2 \pi_3 \cdots \pi_n$ (as defined in Sect. 2). Informally, the descrambling order analysis problem is to determine the minimum number of "parallel steps" required to transform an input permutation π into the identity permutation. This attempts to predict the descrambling order at a higher level of abstraction suggested by the patterns occurring in ciliate MIC data, instead of changes at the molecular level. Thus, the operations do not represent any single molecular level biological operation (inversions, or loop deletion operations); instead, it represents a parallel operation. Because we do not know the exact mechanism by which descrambling takes place, we will study two similar systems involving shuffle to see how the minimum number of operations differs. If one system of moves gives significantly lower numbers of required moves, then there are advantages to this system in terms of parsimony.

As seen in Sect. 3, there are a number of sequences with consecutive odd-even (even-odd) patterns. When the odd and even numbers are in consecutive order, it only requires a single application of shuffle to transform the permutation into the identity permutation. For example, the permutation of alpha-telomere-binding protein genes of *Sterkiella histriomuscorum* is 1 3 5 7 2 4 6 (Fig. 3), which can be descrambled in one step by taking the shuffle of two subwords 2 4 6 with 1 3 5 7. In that case, there is a possibility that recombinations take place in parallel (or without significantly changing the structure between individual recombination) to descramble the MIC chromosome, and therefore a structural component is partially enforcing an alignment of appropriate MDSs so that the operation is applied correctly. Note that the this operation applies shuffle to segments of the same input string rather than on two separate strings. The two systems will be described next.

- **Contiguous Increasing System (CIS):** Given an input permutation $\pi = \pi_1 \cdots \pi_n, \pi_i \in \mathbb{Z}_{+-}(n)$, $1 \leq i \leq n$, a CIS partition of π is a set of subwords $\{u_1, \ldots, u_m\}$ of π, with each $u_i \in \mathbb{Z}_+(n)^+ \cup \mathbb{Z}_-(n)^+$, with u_i increasing for each i, $1 \leq i \leq m$, such that $\pi = u_1 u_2 \cdots u_m$.
- **Non-contiguous Increasing System (NIS):** For a given input permutation $\pi = \pi_1 \cdots \pi_n$, $\pi_i \in \mathbb{Z}_{+-}(n)$, $1 \leq i \leq n$, a NIS partition of π is a set of subsequences $\{u_1, \ldots, u_m\}$, with each $u_i \in \mathbb{Z}_+(n)^+ \cup \mathbb{Z}_-(n)^+$, and u_i is increasing for each i, $1 \leq i \leq m$, such that $\pi \in u_1 \ u_2 \ \cdots \ u_m$.

Notice that for every CIS partition $\{u_1, \ldots, u_m\}$, the identity permutation is in $\overline{u_1} \ \cdots \ \overline{u_m}$. This system allows the shuffle on increasing subwords (each either positive or negative). The smallest number of increasing subwords of the input permutation such that the input permutation is the concatenation of the subwords is desired. In such a case, the identity is in the shuffle of the subwords after taking the inversion of any negative subwords. For example, the permutation $5 \ 6 \ 2 \ - 8 \ - 7 \ - 4 \ - 3 \ - 1$ can be split into three increasing subwords, $u = 5 \ 6, v = 2, w = -8 \ -7 \ -4 \ -3 \ -1$, the input is indeed uvw, and the identity is in $\overline{u} \ \overline{v} \ \overline{w}$. For every NIS partition, the input permutation is in the shuffle of the segments, and the identity permutation is in $\overline{u_1} \cdots \overline{u_m}$. In this case, both the input permutation, and the identity permutation are strings of numbers derived from shuffle. For example, the permutation $5 \ 6 \ 2 \ 1 \ 3 \ 4 \ 7 \ 8$ can be split into three increasing subsequences, $u = 5 \ 6 \ 7 \ 8, v = 2$, and $w = 1 \ 3 \ 4$, with the input permutation in $u \ v \ w$, and the identity in $\overline{u} \ \overline{v} \ \overline{w}$. For both of the systems, we are interested in calculating the number of segments, which corresponds to the number of shuffle applications plus one. A CIS partition of π can be thought of as a parallel recombination of different subwords, where the inversion of a subword can occur before a parallel recombination. The NIS system is intended as an investigation as to whether the number of operations can be reduced by adding an addition layer of the shuffle operation.

Proposition 1. *Given an input permutation π of n elements. Let m be the smallest such that there exists $u_1, \ldots, u_m$ with $\pi = u_1 \cdots u_m$ and $id_n \in \overline{u_1} \cdots \overline{u_m}$. Then $m - 1$ is the size of a smallest CIS partition.*

Proof. Given any two positive increasing words u, v which use disjoint numbers, then there is a positive increasing word in $u \ v$. Similarly, if both are negative and increasing then there is a positive increasing word in $\overline{u} \ \overline{v}$. If u is positive and v is negative, then there is a positive increasing sequence in $\overline{u}$ shuffled with

$\bar{v}$. And in general, given $\pi = \pi_1 \cdots \pi_n$ and a CIS partition $u_1, \ldots, u_m$, then the identity must be in $\overline{u_1} \cdots \overline{u_m}$. That is, if there is a partition of size m, then the identity can be obtained with $m - 1$ shuffle operations.

Conversely, if $\pi = u_1 \cdots u_m$, and the identity is in $\overline{u_1} \cdots \overline{u_m}$, the each u_i, $1 \leq i \leq m$ is either positive increasing or negative increasing. Hence, counting the number of segments in a CIS partition is always exactly one more than counting the number of applications of shuffle.   □

4.1   Contiguous Increasing System

Next, an algorithm to determine the minimum sized CIS partition will be given. In an input permutation $\pi = \pi_1 \pi_2 \cdots \pi_n$, a pair of adjacent elements π_i and π_{i+1}, $1 \leq i \leq n - 1$, are called *neighbours* if $\pi_i < \pi_{i+1}$ and either π, π_{i+1} are both positive or both negative; otherwise the pair is called a *cut-off point*. Then $c(\pi)$ is the number of cut-off points in π. If π has an increasing positive or negative subword $\pi_i \cdots \pi_j$, i.e. $\pi_i < \cdots < \pi_j$ all the same sign, then each adjacent pair in $\pi_i, \pi_{i+1}, \ldots, \pi_j$ are neighbours. Thus, in an increasing positive or negative permutation $\pi = \pi_1 < \pi_2 < \pi_3 < \cdots < \pi_n$, $c(\pi) = 0$. In contrast, if π is a positive or negative decreasing permutation, then $c(\pi) = n - 1$, because $\pi = \pi_1 > \pi_2 > \pi_3 > \cdots > \pi_n$. The size of the smallest CIS partition depends on the number of cut-off points.

Proposition 2. *Let π be an input permutation. The size of the smallest CIS partition is $c(\pi) + 1$.*

Proof. Let $\pi = \pi_1 \pi_2 \pi_3 \cdots \pi_n$ have $c(\pi)$ cut-off points after positions (in order) $c_1, \ldots, c_m$ of π. Then, it is impossible to have an increasing segment that includes a number from both before and after a cut-off point, as the identity must be in the shuffle of the potentially inverted segments. Therefore, any CIS partition has at most $m + 1$ elements in it. Furthermore, there exists a CIS partition with $m + 1$ elements in it, because there is one increasing positive or negative subword that has the elements in between π_1 and the element at position c_1, and an increasing positive or negative subword between positions $c_i + 1$ and c_{i+1} for each i, $1 \leq i < m$, and one last increasing positive or negative subword that has the elements starting from $c_m + 1$ to π_n. As $m = c(\pi)$, the smallest number of increasing subwords in π will always be $c(\pi) - 1 + 2 = c(\pi) + 1$.   □

Therefore, we constructed an optimal algorithm called *IncreasingSubwords* (Algorithm 1) that determines the minimum size of a CIS partition of an input permutation π by simply counting the number of cut-off points $c(\pi)$ for each input permutation π which can be done in linear time (the algorithm is optimal in the sense that it finds the smallest segments). For example, 1 3 5 7 9 2 4 6 8 10 has one cut-off point between 9 and 2, and two increasing subwords: 1 3 5 7 9, and 2 4 6 8 10. The sequences having consecutive odd-even patterns (or even-odd patterns) will always have two increasing subwords — one with the consecutive odd numbers, and the other with the even numbers, as these sequences will always have a single cut-off point.

Algorithm 1. Minimum number of segments in CIS.

```
 1: procedure INCREASINGSUBWORDS(π = π₁ ⋯ πₙ)
 2:     segments ← 0;
 3:     cut_off_points ← 0;
 4:     for i ← 1 to n − 1 do
 5:         if πᵢ > πᵢ₊₁ or sgn(πᵢ) ≠ sgn(πᵢ₊₁) then
 6:             cut_off_points ← cut_off_points + 1;
 7:         end if
 8:     end for
 9:     segments ← cut_off_points + 1;
10:     return segments;
11: end procedure
```

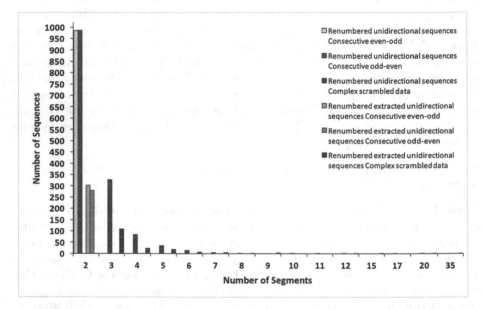

Fig. 4. Relationship between the number of segments (increasing subwords) and the number of sequences in the dataset achieving that for renumbered unidirectional sequences and renumbered extracted unidirectional sequences.

The graph in Fig. 4 shows the number of segments versus the number of sequences achieving that minimal number of segments from the preprocessed *Oxytricha* data. The sequences that have only 1 increasing subword are already unscrambled, and only the sequences having the consecutive odds and evens will have 2 increasing subwords. In the graph, the rest of the sequences have at least 3 increasing subwords. The following sequence 1 4 6 8 10 12 2 5 7 11 13 3 9 requires at least 3 increasing subwords, as the identity is in 1 4 6 8 10 12 2 5 7 11 13 3 9.

Table 1. Increasing subword statistics with Contiguous Increasing System for renumbered unidirectional sequences (and renumbered extracted unidirectional sequences in parentheses).

Sequence patterns	No. of sequences	Avg. number of increasing subwords	Max. number of increasing subwords	Avg. length of increasing subwords	Max. length of increasing subwords
Consecutive odd-even patterns	986 (280)	2 (2)	2 (2)	2.300 (2.323)	36 (20)
Consecutive even-odd patterns	985 (302)	2 (2)	2 (2)	2.305 (2.488)	37 (25)
Complex scrambled patterns	472 (167)	3.619 (4.126)	20 (25)	2.741 (3.452)	43 (86)

Table 1 shows the average number of increasing subwords determined by Algorithm 1, along with the maximum number of increasing subwords, the number of sequences in each sequence pattern, the average length of increasing subwords, and the maximum length of increasing subwords.

4.2   Non-contiguous Increasing System

This system allows shuffle on increasing subsequences (i.e. non-contiguous) instead of increasing subwords only. As discussed above, if $\pi = \pi_1 \cdots \pi_n$ is a given input permutation, then a NIS partition of π is a set of increasing subsequences $\{s_1, \ldots, s_m\}$, such that $\pi \in s_1 \ s_2 \ \cdots \ s_m$, and the identity is in $\overline{s_1} \cdots \overline{s_m}$. For example, consider $\pi = 6\ 1\ 7\ 2\ 8\ 3\ 4\ 9\ 10\ 11\ 5$. Then both the input permutation and the identity permutation is in $6\ 8\ 9\ 10\ 11 \quad 1\ 2\ 3\ 4\ 5$. Next, an optimal algorithm is described for determining the segments within this system. At first, it adds the first element of π to an increasing subsequence s. Then it finds the next larger element to the right, adds it to increasing subsequence s, and continues doing this until reaching the end of π. Then s becomes the first increasing subsequence. Next, the algorithm deletes the elements of s from π, and repeats until π becomes empty. The final number of increasing subsequences is the size of the smallest NIS partition.

We will prove that Algorithm 2 calculates an optimal NIS partition, but first, an intermediate lemma is needed.

Lemma 1. *Let π be a positive or negative input permutation. If π has a decreasing subsequence of length m, then every NIS partition of π has at least m elements.*

Algorithm 2

1: **procedure** NEXTINCREASINGELEMENT($\pi = \pi_1 \cdots \pi_n$)
2:     $segments \leftarrow 0$;
3:     **while** π *is not empty* **do**
4:         $element \leftarrow \pi_1$;
5:         *append element in subsequence* s;
6:         **for** $i \leftarrow 2$ to n **do**
7:             **if** *element* $< \pi_i$ **then**
8:                 $element \leftarrow \pi_i$;
9:                 *append element in subsequence* s;
10:             **end if**
11:         **end for**
12:         **if** s *is not empty* **then**
13:             $segments \leftarrow segments + 1$;
14:             *delete the elements of* s *from* π;
15:         **end if**
16:         *Clear* s;
17:     **end while**
18:     **return** $segments$;
19: **end procedure**

Proof. Let $\pi = \pi_1 \cdots \pi_n$ be an input permutation, and assume that there exists $i_1, \ldots, i_m$ such that $1 \leq i_1 < \cdots < i_m \leq n$, but $\pi_{i_1} > \pi_{i_2} > \cdots > \pi_{i_m}$. Assume, by contradiction that there exists some NIS partition X with $k < m$ elements. Then there has to be two of π_{i_α} and π_{i_β}, $\alpha < \beta$ such that π_{i_α} and π_{i_β} are in the same sequence s of X. But, then the identity cannot be in the shuffle of $\bar{s}$ with other elements. $\qquad\square$

Proposition 3. *Let* π *be a positive or negative input permutation. Then Algorithm 2 calculates the minimum size of an NIS partition.*

Proof. Let $\pi = \pi_1 \cdots \pi_n$ be an input permutation, and assume first that π is positive (similarly if π is negative). Let $X = \{s_1, \ldots, s_m\}$ be the output from Algorithm 2, such that $s_1, \ldots, s_m$ is the order as determined by the algorithm.

Let k be the size of the smallest NIS partition. It is clear then that $k \leq m$. Let i satisfy $1 \leq i \leq n$. Let $f(i)$ be the number at position i of π, and also for $1 \leq j \leq m$, let $g_i(j)$ be the largest position x of π such that $x < i$ and $\pi(x)$ is in s_j. By the algorithm, $s_2(1)$, at position i_2 say of π, must be smaller than the number at position $g_{i_1}(1)$ of π (a letter of s_1). More generally, let i_m be the position of $s_m(1)$ in π. Then notice that $f(g_{i_m}(1)) > f(g_{i_m}(2)) > \cdots > f(g_{i_m}(m-1)) > s_m(1)$, otherwise, the smallest α such that $f(g_{i_m}(\alpha)) < f(g_{i_m}(\alpha+1))$ would have caused Algorithm 2 to include $f(g_{i_m}(\alpha+1))$ in s_α. Thus, π has a decreasing subsequence of length m, and therefore by the lemma above, m is the smallest size of an NIS partition, and $k = m$. Hence, Algorithm 2 is optimal. $\qquad\square$

Also notice that even though Algorithm 2 is not linear time, there is a linear time variation whereby, whenever it is determined that the current sequence s_1

should not contain the next element, in line 7, it starts a new sequence s_2, and then preferably adds new elements to s_1, and if not s_2, and if not start s_3, etc. Therefore, an optimal linear time algorithm exists to solve this problem.

Table 2 shows the average number of increasing subsequences determined by Algorithm 2, along with other properties. The graph in Fig. 5 shows the number

Table 2. Increasing subsequence statistics with Non-contiguous Increasing System for renumbered unidirectional sequences (and renumbered extracted unidirectional sequences in parentheses).

Sequence patterns	No. of sequences	Avg. number of increasing subsequences	Max. number of increasing subsequences	Avg. length of increasing subsequences	Max. length of increasing subsequences
Consecutive odd-even patterns	986 (280)	2 (2)	2 (2)	2.301 (2.323)	36 (20)
Consecutive even-odd patterns	985 (302)	2 (2)	2 (2)	2.306 (2.488)	38 (26)
Complex scrambled patterns	472 (167)	2.915 (3.221)	6 (7)	3.403 (4.421)	43 (87)

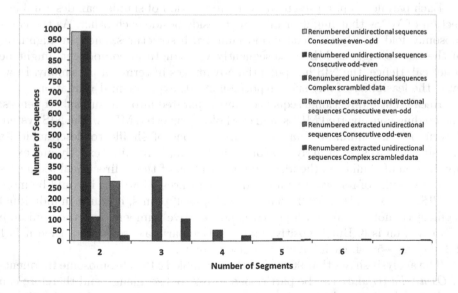

Fig. 5. Relationship between the number of segments (increasing subsequences) and the number of sequences in the dataset achieving that for renumbered unidirectional sequences and renumbered extracted unidirectional sequences.

of segments (minimum size of NIS partitioning) versus the number of sequences achieving that number of segments. Most of the complex scrambled sequences were partitioned into only 3 increasing subsequences by this algorithm, and the maximum number of increasing subsequences is only 7.

5 Result Analysis and Discussion

NIS often gives a much smaller number of applications of shuffle versus CIS. The largest of the minimum CIS partition sizes for CIS is 20 and 35, for renumbered unidirectional and extracted unidirectional sequences respectively, whereas for NIS, this number is 6 and 7, respectively (Tables 1 and 2).

There are 986 consecutive odd-even and 985 consecutive even-odd sequences in the renumbered unidirectional dataset, and 280 consecutive odd-even and 302 consecutive even-odd sequences in the renumbered extracted unidirectional dataset. Thus, there are a total of 1266 consecutive odd-even, and 1287 consecutive even-odd sequences among the 3192 scrambled input sequences. Algorithm 2 partitioned all of these 2553 consecutive odd/even sequences into 2 increasing segments, which is optimal. There are 472 categorized as complex scrambled sequences in the renumbered unidirectional dataset, and 167 complex scrambled sequences in the renumbered extracted unidirectional dataset. Thus, there are a total of 639 complex scrambled sequences among the 3192 scrambled input sequences. Algorithm 2 partitioned 136 sequences of these, into size 2, and 405 sequences into 3 segments. There are 98 sequences that have an NIS partition size between 4 and 7, and there is none higher than 7.

Each parallel step, represented by an application of shuffle, can descramble a section of MDSs that might or might not reside beside each other. As the chromosomes fold mostly in a coiled and lampbrush structures, such an alignment of the non-contiguous MDSs subsequently via structural component, might be practical. Hence, the NIS has potential advantages in terms of parsimony. However, the feasibility of any such hypothesis needs experimental validation.

Recall that bidirectional sequences were separated into two sub-subsequences: one holding non-inverted MDSs, and one holding inverted MDSs. The NIS system determines the minimum number of applications of shuffle to descramble its two subsequences, separately. To combine the two, it requires exactly one extra application of shuffle, as the identity permutation of the bidirectional sequences is in the shuffle of its two descrambled subsequences. However, it could be more for CIS. For example, $1 - 6\ 2 - 5\ 3 - 4$ has 5 cut-off points, because an individual segment cannot contain both positive and negative numbers, and the minimum CIS partition is 6. But if positive and negative parts are separated, then it is 1 2 3 and $-6 - 5 - 4$, each having no cut-off points.

The analysis shows that 96.63% of the scrambled MIC chromosome fragments of *Oxytricha trifallax* can be partitioned into 2 to 3 segments, and therefore can be descrambled by only 1 or 2 applications of shuffle, where each application of shuffle corresponds to a parallel recombination. This small number lends theoretical evidence that some structural component is enforcing the shuffle-like behaviour, by properly aligning segments in an interleaving fashion, and then parallel recombination is taking place for MDS rearrangement. The sheer number of MIC chromosome fragments that can be rearranged with very few applications of shuffle yields evidence that this type of behaviour could be occurring, using parsimony. Indeed, the number of applications of shuffle is far lower than the number of MDSs, and therefore the principle of parsimony dictates that there is significant computational advantages to such a system, as the arrangement of the large number of MDSs do not need a large number of parallel steps to descramble.

References

1. Angeleska, A., Jonoska, N., Saito, M.: DNA recombination through assembly graphs. Discret. Appl. Math. **157**(14), 3020–3037 (2009)
2. Angeleska, A., Jonoska, N., Saito, M.: Rewriting rule chains modeling DNA rearrangement pathways. Theoret. Comput. Sci. **454**, 5–22 (2012)
3. Burns, J., Kukushkin, D., Chen, X., Landweber, L.F., Saito, M., Jonoska, N.: Recurring patterns among scrambled genes in the encrypted genome of the ciliate *Oxytricha trifallax*. J. Theor. Biol. **410**, 171–180 (2016)
4. Chen, X., Bracht, J.R., Goldman, A.D., Dolzhenko, E., Clay, D.M., Swart, E.C., Perlman, D.H., Doak, T.G., Stuart, A., Amemiya, C.T., Sebra, R.P., Landweber, L.F.: The architecture of a scrambled genome reveals massive levels of genomic rearrangement during development. Cell **158**(5), 1187–1198 (2014)
5. Ehrenfeucht, A., Prescott, D.M., Rozenberg, G.: Computational aspects of gene (un)scrambling in ciliates. In: Landweber, L.F., Winfree, E. (eds.) Evolution as Computation. Natural Computing Series, pp. 216–256. Springer, Heidelberg (2002)
6. Herlin, J.L., Nelson, A., Scheepers, M.: Using ciliate operations to construct chromosome phylogenies. Involv. J. Math. **9**(1), 1–26 (2015)
7. Jones, N.C., Pevzner, P.: An Introduction to Bioinformatics Algorithms. MIT Press, Cambridge (2004)
8. Keil, J.M., Liu, J., McQuillan, I.: Algorithmic properties of ciliate sequence alignment. Theoret. Comput. Sci. **411**(6), 919–925 (2010)
9. Khan, N.A.: Chromosome descrambling order analysis in ciliates. Master's thesis, University of Saskatchewan, Saskatoon (2016)
10. Landweber, L.F., Kari, L.: The evolution of cellular computing: nature's solution to a computational problem. Biosystems **52**(1), 3–13 (1999)
11. Landweber, L.F., Kuo, T.C., Curtis, E.A.: Evolution and assembly of an extremely scrambled gene. PNAS **97**(7), 3298–3303 (2000)
12. Meyer, G., Lipps, H.: Chromatin elimination in the hypotrichous ciliate *Stylonychia mytilus*. Chromosoma **77**(3), 285–297 (1980)
13. Meyer, G., Lipps, H.: The formation of polytene chromosomes during macronuclear development of the hypotrichous ciliate *Stylonychia mytilus*. Chromosoma **82**(2), 309–314 (1981)
14. Meyer, G., Lipps, H.: Electron microscopy of surface spread polytene chromosomes of *Drosophila and Stylonychia*. Chromosoma **89**(2), 107–110 (1984)
15. Möllenbeck, M., Zhou, Y., Cavalcanti, A.R., Jönsson, F., Higgins, B.P., Chang, W.J., Juranek, S., Doak, T.G., Rozenberg, G., Lipps, H.J., et al.: The pathway to detangle a scrambled gene. PLoS One **3**(6), e2330 (2008)
16. Prescott, D.M., Ehrenfeucht, A., Rozenberg, G.: Molecular operations for DNA processing in hypotrichous ciliates. Eur. J. Protistol. **37**(3), 241–260 (2001)
17. Prescott, D.M., Rozenberg, G.: How ciliates manipulate their own DNA–a splendid example of natural computing. Nat. Comput. **1**(2–3), 165–183 (2002)

Author Index

Printed in the United States
By Bookmasters